John Hannah

The relation between the Divine and human elements in Holy Scripture

Eight lectures preached before the University of Oxford in the year MDCCCLXIII

John Hannah

The relation between the Divine and human elements in Holy Scripture
Eight lectures preached before the University of Oxford in the year MDCCCLXIII

ISBN/EAN: 9783337282950

Printed in Europe, USA, Canada, Australia, Japan

Cover: Foto ©Lupo / pixelio.de

More available books at **www.hansebooks.com**

THE
BAMPTON LECTURES

FOR MDCCCLXIII.

LONDON
PRINTED BY SPOTTISWOODE AND CO.
NEW-STREET SQUARE

BETWEEN THE

DIVINE AND HUMAN ELEMENTS IN HOLY SCRIPTURE.

EIGHT LECTURES

PREACHED BEFORE

THE UNIVERSITY OF OXFORD

IN THE YEAR MDCCCLXIII.

ON THE FOUNDATION OF

THE LATE REV. JOHN BAMPTON, M.A.

CANON OF SALISBURY.

BY

J. HANNAH, D.C.L.

WARDEN OF TRINITY COLLEGE, GLENALMOND, AND PANTONIAN PROFESSOR OF THEOLOGY;
LATE FELLOW OF LINCOLN COLLEGE, OXFORD.

LONDON:
JOHN MURRAY, ALBEMARLE STREET.
1863.

EXTRACT

FROM

THE LAST WILL AND TESTAMENT

OF THE LATE

REV. JOHN BAMPTON,

CANON OF SALISBURY.

———

——' I give and bequeath my Lands and Estates to the Chancellor,
' Masters, and Scholars of the University of Oxford for ever, to have
' and to hold all and singular the said Lands or Estates upon trust, and
' to the intents and purposes hereinafter mentioned; that is to say,
' I will and appoint that the Vice-Chancellor of the University of
' Oxford for the time being shall take and receive all the rents,
' issues, and profits thereof, and (after all taxes, reparations, and
' necessary deductions made) that he pay all the remainder to the
' endowment of eight Divinity Lecture Sermons, to be established
' for ever in the said University, and to be performed in the
' manner following :

' I direct and appoint, that, upon the first Tuesday in Easter Term,
' a Lecturer be yearly chosen by the Heads of Colleges only, and by
' no others, in the room adjoining to the Printing-House, between the
' hours of ten in the morning and two in the afternoon, to preach
' eight Divinity Lecture Sermons, the year following, at St. Mary's
' in Oxford, between the commencement of the last month in Lent
' Term, and the end of the third week in Act Term.

' Also I direct and appoint, that the eight Divinity Lecture
' Sermons shall be preached upon either of the following Subjects—
' to confirm and establish the Christian Faith, and to confute all

EXTRACT FROM CANON BAMPTON'S WILL.

'heretics and schismatics—upon the divine authority of the Holy
'Scriptures—upon the authority of the writings of the primitive
'Fathers, as to the faith and practice of the primitive Church—
'upon the Divinity of Our Lord and Saviour Jesus Christ—upon
'the Divinity of the Holy Ghost—upon the Articles of the Christian
'Faith, as comprehended in the Apostles' and Nicene Creeds.

'Also I direct, that thirty copies of the eight Divinity Lecture
'Sermons shall be always printed within two months after they are
'preached, and one copy shall be given to the Chancellor of the
'University, and one copy to the Head of every College, and one
'copy to the Mayor of the City of Oxford, and one copy to be put
'into the Bodleian Library; and the expense of printing them shall
'be paid out of the revenue of the Land or Estates given for
'establishing the Divinity Lecture Sermons; and the Preacher shall
'not be paid, nor be entitled to the revenue, before they are
'printed.

'Also I direct and appoint, that no person shall be qualified to
'preach the Divinity Lecture Sermons, unless he hath taken the
'degree of Master of Arts at least, in one of the two Universities of
'Oxford or Cambridge; and that the same person shall never preach
'the Divinity Lecture Sermons twice.'

CONTENTS.

LECTURE I.

INSPIRATION AND REVELATION; THEIR RESPECTIVE DEFINITIONS AND RANGE . . . . PAGE 1

[*Delivered March* 8.]

ROMANS viii. 16.

'*The Spirit itself beareth witness with our spirit, that we are the children of God.*'

INTRODUCTION.—The influence of the Holy Spirit, whether before or since the Fall, not such as to supersede the free agency of man. The unfettered action of our faculties within their own sphere compatible with our dependence on the grace of God for all good. The consequent combination of a divine and human element in all our holy thoughts and works.

Probability that in that purest form of spiritual influence to which we owe the Holy Scriptures the divine and human elements will both be complete.

Erroneous tendencies of opposite theories, which on the one hand cause the divine to exclude the human, and on the other hand cause the human to blot out the divine.

In suggesting that these may be corrected by admitting the completeness of both elements, we make no attempt to draw a frontier line between those elements, or to define the mode of the Divine influence; but we know the avenue through which the Holy Spirit reaches us—namely, through the spirit in ourselves.

The starting-point, then, must be sought for in the doctrine of Inspiration; to which the doctrine of Revelation supplies the counterpart: the distinction between these words corresponding, though not with perfect exactness, to that which we draw between the writers of Scripture and the subject-matter of their record. The two terms not coextensive, either with each other or with Scripture.

I. INSPIRATION implies the existence of a spirit in man, which is capable of holding communion with the Holy Spirit of God.

1. Uniform accuracy with which, from creation to resurrection, Scripture treats the human πνεῦμα as a separate principle, which must be carefully distinguished from the soul. St. Paul's trichotomy not to be confounded with the Aristotelian, which rests upon a different method. The proper place and province of the spirit, especially in regard to the differentia of man.

2. The Presence of the Holy Spirit not to be limited to any one particular form of Inspiration. Difference of degrees under which the Presence of all the Persons in the Trinity is revealed to us.

Presence of the Holy Spirit in the material universe; in the intellect, the will, the moral faculties of man; but in old times more especially as inspiring the series of the Old Testament writers. Great change traceable in the New Testament, where the Baptism of John and all other gifts previous to the day of Pentecost are counted as nothing in comparison with the gifts, themselves also widely diversified, which are bestowed under the conditions of the Christian covenant. Inspiration of the New Testament writers analogous to what was noted in the Old.

Illustrate by the distinction between comparative and absolute condemnation and exclusion, as applied to other aspects of the gifts of God.

The wide range of Inspiration no argument against our belief in the special intensity of its peculiar influence in the Bible.

Converging proofs of the canonical authority of Scripture.

II. REVELATION supplies the main feature in the differentia, by which that special inspiration is defined. But here again we can trace fainter kinds outside of Scripture, in manifestations of God through the works of nature and the conscience of man.

Revelations granted in Scripture, and there distinguishable from human materials, differ from both the above kinds of manifestation, as being direct communications to the human spirit of objective knowledge which it could not or did not otherwise command:—

1. Looking at Scripture externally, it contains two series of facts, which answer to each other in the Old and New Testaments, and which are combined into unity by a uniform and supernatural interpretation revealed to its writers.

2. Taking the chain of facts as one, it is all along accompanied by the revelation of a higher series, belonging to a supernatural order. Impossibility that this could have been supplied from human resources.

The Presence of the Spirit, which gave that revelation, to be again carefully distinguished from His Presence in the hearts of all Christians, as the sole source of a holy life. Answer remonstrances against the bondage of a historical religion, by pointing out that

1. Scripture not only embodies the results of the highest spiritual gifts; but

2. Records the only certified revelations from the unseen world.

These explanations intended to form the basis of an enquiry into the completeness of both the divine and human elements, to each of which subjects three of the succeeding Lectures are devoted.

LECTURE II.

THE DIVINE ELEMENT—REALITY OF THE REVELATION, AS ESTABLISHED BY A CONTRAST WITH HEATHEN RELIGIONS . PAGE 38

[*Delivered March 15.*]

ACTS xvii. 30, 31.

'*And the times of this ignorance God winked at; but now commandeth all men everywhere to repent: Because He hath appointed a day, in the which He will judge the world in righteousness, by that Man whom He hath ordained; whereof He hath given assurance unto all men, in that He hath raised Him from the dead.*'

The comparison between the divine element of Scripture and the substance of other religions to be worked out first as to truth, and secondly as to falsehood.

I. The five classes under which the whole subject may be arranged:—

   1. The religious knowledge of the heathen, as ascertained independently of Scripture. Different theories on its source, and on its relation to the contents of the sacred record. The two main aspects in which it has presented itself to the observation of the Church. Common point of departure for both streams of sacred knowledge to be sought for in the primeval promise.

   2. The same as traceable within the Scriptures themselves. Relation of the Church from the beginning to the outer world with which it came into immediate contact.

   3. The divine element of Scripture properly so called. Nature of its development; rather analytic than synthetic. That development traceable both through theology, in the gradual disclosures of the Name of God; and through morality, as it is deepened and organised in the writings of the prophets.

   4. The positive ordinances by which it was guarded; their nature and true relation to spiritual religion.

   5. The human element through which it was conveyed. The characters and other qualifications of the inspired writers.

II. Falsehoods and shortcomings of heathen religions:—

   1. The truths which can be traced in them never embraced any entire system; the religions were ever ready to go over to the side of evil; they degenerated till they represented a lower moral stage than that of their own worshippers; when the forms of religion broke away from their substance, and mythologies became the least religious portion of the national life.

   2. Their whole framework was manifestly human, not divine; as proved by an inspection of both theologies and philosophies of religion.

   3. The difference illustrated at length from St. Paul's Discourse at Athens. Nature of his appeal; and the partial support which each portion of it would secure from different sections of his hearers. His 'new doctrine:'

   α. As to God; the Creator, the Preserver, and the Governor of men.

   β. As to mankind; all men brethren of each other and equally sons of God.

γ. As to the new relation between God and man through the Redemption and Resurrection.

The contrast thus brought to its issue in the Incarnation of Christ, and the grand results which depend upon it. Mode in which the one fatal defect of all false religions was remedied, when a way was thus opened, through which man could again find access to God.

LECTURE III.

THE DIVINE ELEMENT—REALITY OF THE INSPIRATION, AS ILLUS-TRATED BY THE ANTINOMIES OF SCRIPTURE . . PAGE 74

[*Delivered April* 19.]

1 Cor. xiii. 12.

'*Now we see through a glass, darkly; but then face to face.*'

From the reality of Scripture Revelation, we pass to consider its Inspiration; and first, for the Antinomies of Scripture; or the mode in which great truths were brought within the range of the human intellect.

General character of Scripture accommodation; nature and limitations of the doctrine; the revelation as explicit and direct as the qualifications of its hearers would permit them to receive.

Two modes in which alleged contradictions in Scripture can be dealt with; indirect, or apologetic; and direct, or expository. The latter course to be now pursued; moral difficulties, however, being reserved for Lecture VI.

Distinction between contradiction in the *text* and contradiction in the *comment*. The latter on no account to be mistaken for the former.

The general characteristic of the highest principles, that they can only be set forth fully in contrasted statements, of which neither is exclusively true. Show this both in speculation and in revelation. Causes of this peculiarity twofold:—

1. Relative; in cases where a counter-truth is revealed by the same authority.

2. Absolute; in cases where the difficulty emerges of itself,

if we make the effort to fathom a principle which baffles the operation of our thought.

General list of illustrations from Scripture; and different degrees in which the apparent difficulty can be removed.

These instances supply the basis for the following remarks on the method of Scripture:—

    1. That each alternative is usually stated unreservedly, simply, and emphatically; with no attempt to weaken its force by any suggestions of a reconciliation. Such concentration a foremost sign of earnestness and truth.

    2. This fearlessness of enunciation seen most conspicuously, when the antithesis is brought out in one passage, in one chapter, in one book, or in one department of Scripture.

    3. Illustrated by the εἰρωνεία of the Jews; as shown, not only by their acceptance of the Book of Job, but by the language of Abraham and Moses, of David, of Asaph, of Solomon, of Jeremiah.

Detailed examination of two more prominent instances:—

    1. The apparent corrections supplied by later writings to the earlier teaching; the Second Commandment compared with Ezekiel xviii.; and passages examined which seem to impose limitations on the claims of the Law, and point to its approaching cessation at Christ's Advent.

    2. The apparent contrariety between St. Paul and St. James, on the respective provinces of faith and works.

Marvellous unity of Scripture, as traceable beneath the external diversity of its various writers, contrasted as they are with each other in position, character, and previous training.

LECTURE IV.

THE DIVINE ELEMENT—REALITY OF THE INSPIRATION, AS ILLUS-
TRATED BY THE DUPLEX SENSUS . . . . PAGE 107

[*Delivered April 26.*]

ROMANS xv. 4.

'*Whatsoever things were written aforetime were written for our learning, that we through patience and comfort of the Scriptures might have hope.*'

Two conditions of a revelation; that it shall be adjusted to its original hearers, yet capable of future expansion. The latter the basis of the *duplex sensus*; a doctrine which has been much misunderstood and suspected.

The necessity of admitting such a doctrine, under proper limitations, established both from the very conception of a revelation, and from the facts which are presented in Scripture; and that, whether we look at the language of the prophets, or at the interpretations furnished by Christ and His apostles.

The explanation to be found in what may be called the double authorship of Scripture; and in the peculiarity that the *res* beneath the *voces* are significant as well as they.

But we have here to note especially:

1. That the rights of the human writers are invariably respected and reserved. Each always had one primary and sufficient meaning, connected with his special mission. The secondary application, which is often repeated more than once before the end, is in addition to, and in no way subversive of, the original or primary meaning.

2. That the first sense does not lose its use and interest when the second is disclosed. Abiding value of the Mosaic Law.

The New Testament usage suggests three classes of interpretation:—

1. *Symbolical*; when objects and events, which in themselves were real and historical, are found to embody a spiritual lesson.

2. *Typical*; when that spiritual lesson is distinctly prophetic.

3. *Representative*; when rules are translated back into their principles.

Illustrations at length of all these, and especially of the first, by a detailed examination of St. Paul's mode of dealing with the history of SARAH AND HAGAR.

Extension of the same principle to explain the New Testament quotations from the Old Testament.

Enquiry whether we are to confine ourselves to the recognition of such secondary meanings as are authorised in Scripture.

Summary of the objections which the above course of argument proposes to remove.

LECTURE V.

THE HUMAN ELEMENT—HISTORY AND SCIENCE . PAGE 139

[*Delivered May* 3.]

2 COR. iv. 7.

'*We have this treasure in earthen vessels, that the excellency of the power may be of God, and not of us.*'

A well-instructed faith need not fear the complete recognition of the human element. Evil of deductive definitions and exaggerated language, with instances of both.

Real ground for uneasiness because of the attempt to argue across from alleged historical inaccuracy to general untruthfulness, and even moral and religious error. Restrictions under which the enquiry must be conducted.

I. HISTORICAL QUESTION.—Light thrown on the subject by
    1. Various readings in Scripture;
    2. Apparent method of its composition, and its relation to earlier materials;
    3. Traces in the older Scriptures of slight editorial glosses or corrections.

Examination under each of these heads of the precise significancy of the facts established; and contrast between the little which they really prove, and the exaggerated conclusions which have been rested on them.

II. SCIENTIFIC QUESTION.—Grand distinction between the *form* of Scripture and its *substance*; and danger of thrusting human interpretations into the exegesis of Scripture itself. Meaning of the warning, that we are not to tie down Scripture to theories of science, which may have coloured the contemporary language of its human authors. That language optical or phenomenal; and in other respects also adjusted to its earliest hearers.

Examination of the record of creation; which should be regarded rather as a theological revelation than as history or tradition, or as visions, parable, or psalm. The geological attack confined in general to the form, not the substance, of the record. Reasons for which we may conceive that this particular form was imposed; and its connection with the Fourth Commandment.

Evil of misunderstandings, on either side, in relation to the scientific question. True position of Scripture in its bearings on science.

LECTURE VI.

THE HUMAN ELEMENT—MORAL DIFFICULTIES . . PAGE 171

[*Delivered May* 10.]

MATT. xiii. 33.

' *The kingdom of heaven is like unto leaven, which a woman took, and hid in three measures of meal, till the whole was leavened.*'

The obstacles which retarded man's recovery of truth after the Fall. Light thrown on this subject by the figure of leaven, as suggesting the gradual introduction of a counter-principle of good, to thwart and exterminate the influence of evil. Illustrate by the gradual unfolding of intellectual and moral truth, and the establishment of purer national customs and laws.

Instances of moral difficulties raised on ancient Scriptural histories; as to the apparent neglect of truth, justice, and mercy.

Fragmentary character of the earliest morality; its want of organisation and discrimination.

Proof afforded by more detailed narratives in Scripture, that a mixture of sin in the motives of actions was followed by a mixture of evil with the reward.

Necessity of avoiding the error which would treat all parts of Scripture as standing on the same level, and would examine its lessons without reference to the circumstances under which they were conveyed.

Position of the older Jews; the worth and work of the old Jewish zeal; and the extent to which Scripture everywhere recognises the need of righteous anger as a guard against sin.

Detailed examination of the SONG OF DEBORAH; its date, its circumstances, and the explanations under which its words must be received.

Correction in form to which such a narrative must be subjected before we can see the exact bearing of its lessons for ourselves. The love for good incompatible with the tolerance of evil; as illustrated from the history of Moses, of St. John the Divine, and of our Lord.

Exact relation of lessons drawn respectively from the Old and New Testaments.

LECTURE VII.

THE HUMAN ELEMENT—SUPERIORITY OF SCRIPTURE TO ITS WRITERS . . . . PAGE 198

[*Delivered May* 17.]

ACTS xiv. 15.

'*We also are men of like passions with you.*'

The subject of the preceding Lecture to be completed by a more minute examination of two leading instances taken from the New Testament, where fuller materials for analysis are given.

Human interest of Scripture largely dependent on the fact, that its writers were 'men of like passions' with ourselves. Yet the divine message never tarnished by the errors of those through whom it was conveyed.

I. Exemplify by the records of St. Peter's life. Three great illustrations of the uneven balance between faith and knowledge in St. Peter's character :—

1. His declaration of the Divinity of Christ, followed by his denial;

2. His announcement of the approaching free admission of the Gentiles, followed by the doubts which it needed a heavenly vision to remove;

3. His speech at the council of Jerusalem in favour of releasing the Gentiles from the Law of Moses, followed by his vacillation at Antioch.

Evidence that both by the side of these events in his speeches, and subsequently in his Epistles, his Divine message stood completely free from any weakness which could thus be traced in his personal character.

II. Difference of character between St. Peter and St. Paul. The double aspect in which the earlier life of St. Paul can be regarded. Continuity of what was good, but sudden removal of the earlier evil. Three questions arise after his conversion :—

1. Do we find any traces of his Christian development after that period?

2. Supposing it to exist, does it imply that there were imperfections in his earliest message?

3. Can we trace the vibrations of uncertainty in his writings?

Admitting the first point, we do not find that the evidence is sufficient to give an affirmative answer to the second and third of these questions. Examination of the three subjects in detail. Proof of the unity which marked his message, gained by comparing his speeches with his Epistles. Characteristics of his method, as shown by his statements on the Law, and on the position of the Jews.

Great importance of the human element in Scripture.

LECTURE VIII.

GENERAL CONCLUSION . . . . . . PAGE 226

[*Delivered June 7.*]

2 TIM. ii. 15.

'*Rightly dividing the word of truth.*'

I. Purport of this closing Lecture to sum up the results which it has been endeavoured to establish.

Our question is the narrowest, though not the least important, of three great controversies; relating to the respective differentiæ of SCRIPTURE, of CHRISTIANITY, and of MAN.

Duty of dealing with all three calmly; and of recognising without fear the generic resemblances, so long as the specific distinctions are properly guarded.

For our immediate question; dwell on the importance of according a complete recognition to both the divine and human elements, as the only apparent mode of reconciling the perplexities of the great problem.

Analogy with the twofold nature of Christ; how far we may appeal to it; what it accounts for; and wherein it stops short.

The dread of acknowledging the human element in Scripture rests on a mistaken conception of the place and effect of sin. Parallel with the 'divine decorum' which is traceable throughout Christ's life, though He 'was in all points tempted like as we are.'

The principle maintained is to be regarded as 'he result of an enquiry, not the dictate of a theory. Our examination of the facts has traversed the documentary history of Scripture, as to various readings, editorial glosses, and enduring misconceptions; its relation to older materials, as well as to tradition and heathen history and literature; and the form in which it resembles other ancient histories, though arguments from chronology and numbers are to be used with caution. Application of the same to scientific language. The 'divine decorum' has been found to exist in all respects unsullied; the moral difficulties admitting of a similar explanation.

On the other hand, the reality of the divine element is manifest, as objective in its origin, perfect in its moral and religious teaching, broad in its grasp of fundamental principles, and embodying a deeper sense beneath the letter.

Verification of the induction by the application of some reasonable conditions:—

 1. The principles found to be such as man could not have discovered:

 2. The *duplex sensus* being real, and capable of a sufficient explanation;

 3. The work being in all respects above the compass of the human writers.

II. Lessons to be drawn on the subject of Scripture interpretation:—

 1. That interpretation must be spiritual; and must differ from that of any other book, so far as Scripture itself is distinguished from any other book by its possession of a divine as well as human authorship.

 2. It must also be comprehensive; not rested on isolated texts.

 3. It must be widened to embrace both sides of teaching, on any subject where a narrower view would be the mistake of half-truths for truths. Practical illustration, in the blindness of the Jews on the Divinity of Christ.

 4. It must cover all parts of Scripture, even those of which the present application is obscure. Fatal tendency of the opposite method.

CONCLUSION.—The deep practical importance of passing on from enquiries into the inspiration of Scripture, to seek the living inspiration of a holy life.

NOTES.

	PAGE		PAGE
ON LECTURE I.	255	ON LECTURE V.	330
ON LECTURE II.	278	ON LECTURE VI.	346
ON LECTURE III.	300	ON LECTURE VII.	352
ON LECTURE IV.	318	ON LECTURE VIII.	360

LECTURE I.

ROMANS viii. 16.

'The Spirit itself beareth witness with our spirit, that we are the children of God.'

THROUGHOUT the argument completed in the context of this passage, St. Paul unfolds the secret operation of the Holy Spirit, which rescues our spirits 'from the law of sin and death,'[a] to give them a living interest in the incarnation of Christ. But our dependence on that gracious presence is not to be confounded with the dumb expectation of inferior creatures; nor need we limit our exposition to that contrast with the legal system which gave shape to the immediate reasoning of the Apostle. In a broader sense we may accept his teaching, that the Divine Spirit addresses us as sons, not as servants; that it uses the language of adoption, not of bondage; that it bears its witness with a spirit in ourselves; that it never supersedes our own responsibility, nor subjugates our natural faculties. The ground of our salvation is wrought out *for* us by our Lord; the work of our renewal is wrought out *with* us by His Spirit. That deathless principle, which

[a] Rom. viii. 2.

was once so degraded, which now hears His voice and follows His guidance, and yields to the gentle influence of restoring grace—that principle was planted when man was created; and, however carnalised it may be by transgression, has never been completely silenced or destroyed (1). We still at our very worst estate retain it, like the lingering element of health, which the Good Physician uses as the groundwork for His healing process : it listens when the Spirit whispers of the love which moved the Father to send His Son, and moved the Son to die for man; it speaks in the feeble tones of prayer, while ' the Spirit itself maketh intercession for us, with groanings which cannot be uttered.' [a]

In this doctrine we trace a twofold truth, which admits of universal application through religious history and thought. The character of God's moral government would lead us to believe that when He made man in His own image,[b] He gave him all the faculties he needed for working out the end of his creation. But a just conception of the source of holiness would connect this belief with the corresponding conviction, that the grace of God was always indispensable, before any excellence in the creature could be achieved—that it was requisite before, and with, and after every movement, to prevent, cooperate with, and crown the work (2). It cannot be supposed that there was any exception in Paradise to that supremacy of the Divine sanctity, which claims every form and

[a] Rom. viii. 26. [b] Gen. i. 26, 27.

phase of good as the direct operation of the Spirit of the Lord. It cannot be doubted that the Holy Spirit bore witness with man's spirit in its original state of purity; inspired it with filial love for its Heavenly Father; and taught it the lessons of obedience which it required for the guidance of a holy life. When man's moral trial had issued in his sin, and when sin had grieved his Divine visitant, and had brought discord and weakness into his forsaken nature, we have no reason to think that his punishment involved the loss of any organic endowment which he had previously possessed. Through the gradual training of our restoration, we still trace everywhere the continued working of this double law, whether in Gentile experience, or in Jewish revelation, or in Christian light. That law combines a divine and human element in every holy deed or thought of man. Our recovery is the work of the Spirit of God; yet man, though so fallen, retains a moral right of will, which resists compulsion even in the act of salvation, and can be renewed and restored upon no other principle than by the leading and guiding persuasion of grace. On the one of these laws rests all morality, which assumes the free responsibility of man; on the other of these laws rests all theology, which teaches us the necessary dependence of the creature on the energy and help of God. If we deny that man was created as in some sort a law unto himself,[a] we break the very mainspring of the moral system. If we admit that man

[a] Rom. ii. 14.

possesses any independent virtue, by which he can perform good actions without assistance from the grace of God, we sanction the disposition to rebel against God's supremacy which tempted our first parents to their fall. The two principles, we doubt not, would have worked together in perfect harmony, had not the balance been disturbed by the intrusion of sin. The restoration of that balance does but readjust the relation which it was not the will of God to cancel. It is still through the witness of the Holy Spirit that we learn to know ourselves to be His children; but we could not understand that witness if we did not retain a spirit in ourselves, which can recognise and answer to the voice of God.

It will be my object, through the course of Lectures on which we are now entering, to call your attention to the completeness of the divine and human elements in the Holy Scriptures, which we receive as the result of the highest operation of God's Spirit on the spirit of man (3). In carrying out this design, it is my wish to base the suggestions which I shall venture to offer on the wider principle which I have endeavoured to explain. If God's dealings with us seem to rest in all cases on the assumption that the organisation of man is complete within its own province, and is only elevated and enlightened, but never superseded, by the help of God, then we may expect to find that in that purest form of spiritual influence to which we owe the Holy Scriptures, we shall be able to trace the presence of both elements; existing, indeed, in their highest known perfection, but not departing from the general relation which prevails throughout all lower spheres.

The doctrine which we are now concerned to establish must be guarded on both sides against two opposite, but not equally imperfect, theories; in the one of which the divine is made to exclude the human, while in the other, by a far worse error, the human is allowed to blot out the divine.

It is possible, on the one hand, to become so absorbed in the thought of the Divine Giver, that the writer ceases to be recognised as anything more than the mere lifeless instrument through which the Spirit makes itself heard, and is reduced to an agency so purely mechanical, that the human factor is really destroyed.

It is possible, on the other hand, to dwell so strongly and unduly on the proofs of human agency, that the work of the Inspiring Spirit is reduced to the vague influence, which might be said to preside over any great work of human genius. On this view, which can be subdivided into several separate opinions, the guarantee of a distinctly divine element is equally cancelled and withdrawn.

But it must not be supposed that, in maintaining, against these extremes, the completeness of both the divine and human elements in Scripture, we are bound to attempt the determination of a frontier line between them; any more than we are bound, by the Catholic faith, to draw a similar frontier through that union of the divine and human natures in the person of Christ, which there is a growing disposition to accept, as the model for our belief upon His written Word (4). Nor, again, can any attempt be made to explain the *mode* in which the mind of man has, in this or any other case, been moved and influenced by the Spirit of God. But, though the mode of operation must remain undefined, the avenue through which the Holy Spirit reaches us is explained beyond all doubt in Scripture. The witness of God's Spirit is addressed to the spirit in ourselves. All practical religion must assume the principle, that man is endowed with spiritual faculties, which enable him to enter into communion with God.

The starting-point of our enquiry, then, must be sought for in the doctrine of Inspiration; to which we shall find that the doctrine of Revelation supplies the proper counterpart and completion (5). These two terms correspond, though not with exact precision, to the distinction which we should draw between the sacred writers and the subject-matter of their record. The doctrine of Inspiration belongs mainly, though not exclusively, to the one head; the doctrine of Revelation belongs mainly, if not exclusively, to the other. The sacred writers were inspired to record what was revealed; and their works preserve the substance of the revelation, under the guarantee which their inspiration furnished. The revelation, then, implied a corresponding inspiration, to enable men to receive and transmit the Divine message; and it was necessary that this inspiration should first exist in the spirit of the writer, though we can detect its presence in the message also, because that message is often freighted with a deeper store of spiritual meaning, and exerts a living influence of greater spiritual power, than its original recipient could foresee.

But some confusion has arisen from overlooking that these two words are not co-extensive, either with each other or with the sacred record. Both may be applied, with more or less propriety, to phenomena which lie outside of Scripture: and while it is maintained that every part of Canonical Scripture is inspired, it is needless to claim Revelation for those portions of the narrative which could be derived from ordinary human sources. On these points, therefore, we may offer, in the outset, a more detailed explanation.

I. The doctrine of Inspiration, on its human side (6), implies that recognition of man's spiritual nature, which distinguishes the mental analysis of Scripture from divisions with which a hasty observation might confound it. On the other hand, the doctrine of the province and operations of the Spirit rests in turn upon certain positions on the source and nature of that higher element, which philosophy might reject as theological limitations,[a] but which Scripture assumes as the basis of its teaching, on the relation between man and his Maker. 'The Spirit itself beareth witness with our spirit.' This

[a] Sir W. Hamilton's *Lectures on Metaphysics*, i. 134.

is the simplest statement of the point of contact between our inspiration and its source in God. When the usage of Scripture goes on to distinguish between the spirit and the soul, it indicates the exact difference between the lines that can be traced by human science and the proper sphere of the religious element. This distinction is maintained, with an accuracy which bears witness to its importance, through the long series of Scripture writers —from the history of the Creation to the latest forecast of the future exaltation of the resurrection body. We learn, in the beginning, that from dust came the materials of which our body was composed; that from God came the inspiration, which breathed into our frame the spirit of a higher life; and that these were united in the 'living soul,'[a] to which mental analysis is more commonly confined. Pass to the other end of Scripture, and we find that the same distinction gives its deep significance to St. Paul's account of the glories which shall elevate the risen body, when the frame, which is now adjusted to the needs of the soul, shall be fitted for the higher functions of the emancipated spirit.[b] We trace it through the Old Testament, in the many passages which tell us of the glory of the spirit and its gifts. We trace it in such language as that of Isaiah, 'With my soul have I desired;' 'with my spirit within me will I seek Thee early:'[c] in such passages as that great prophecy in the 16th Psalm, 'Wherefore

---

[a] Gen. ii. 7. [b] 1 Cor. xv. 44.
[c] Isa. xxvi. 9. Cf. Gen. xlix. 6; Ps. vii. 5; Prov. xx. 27.

my heart was glad, and my glory rejoiced; my flesh also shall rest in hope:'[a] in such words as those which meet us at the beginning of the Magnificat, 'My soul doth magnify;' 'my spirit hath rejoiced.'[b] And the special teaching of the Gospel is everywhere coloured by the same discrimination, which causes the distinction between flesh and spirit to differ so widely in significance from the common distinction between soul and body; and which finds its highest expression in such contrasts as the words of Christ, 'That which is born of the flesh is flesh; and that which is born of the Spirit is spirit;'[c] or in the words of His Apostle, 'to be carnally minded is death; but to be spiritually minded is life and peace.'[d]

The Scripture trichotomy, then, of spirit, soul, and body[e] (7), is distinguished by its combination of the physical and theological aspects, which science deals with under different methods. We are familiar with the process by which the heathen philosopher advances[f] from one series of vital phenomena to another, arranging them as though it were in stages, like the concentric steps of some great pyramid: first, the signs of mere organised growth, like that of plants; then the signs of sensibility, like that of animals; then the moral feelings; then the intellectual faculties; in each of which progressions we trace the gradual perfecting of attributes which are faintly shadowed forth in

[a] Ps. xvi. 10; Acts ii. 26.　[b] Luke i. 46, 47.
[c] John iii. 6.　[d] Rom. viii. 6.
[e] 1 Thess. v. 23; Heb. iv. 12.　[f] Ar., *Eth. N. I.* xiii., &c.

creatures of a lower order. He thus constructs, I say, a pyramid of being, which reaches its culminating point in man. All this is perfectly clear and intelligible. But when all this has been set forth, in its neatest and most finished form, we have seen no more than τὰ τῆς ψυχῆς μέρη· the description of man still lacks its noblest element—the spirit which descends upon him from a higher sphere, to meet the ascending principle of vitality and fill it with celestial light (8). The labours of physiologists have suggested a scale by which we can measure, more or less exactly, each step in the series, and can span by an interval of fixed degrees the gulf which intervenes between the highest capacity of the most perfect brain in brutes, and the meanest capacity of the least perfect brain in man (9). But they can no more measure the difference which the presence of the spirit introduces, than they could complete the description of a material pyramid by gauging the sunlight which crowns its apex with a brightness streaming straight from heaven.

When ancient poets wished to point the contrast between the shame and glory of our compound nature, they borrowed from religion the ennobling thought, that our spirit is a portion of the breath of God.[a] Let us only be careful to exclude the Pantheistic conception—that God's gift was a part of His own essence; that man's spirit is itself divine—and we trace in such words the vivid recognition of that religious faculty, which flushes through the naked

[a] Hor., *Sat.* II. ii. 79, &c.

framework of our earthly organisation, and transfigures it with heavenly radiance. Our text alone would guard us from the error of confounding the created spirit of man with the uncreated and eternal Spirit of the Lord.

In the universality of this endowment we find the natural explanation for the prevalence of certain fixed religious ideas among mankind (10). But this capacity to receive an inspiring energy from higher sources exerts an influence which reaches far beyond the range of the religious emotions, and embraces within its quickening impulse far more than those who call themselves religious men.

The gifts of God are always found to overflow the narrow limits which are recognised by the faint gratitude of man. And it is scarcely too much to say, that the spiritual principle is the true crown of dominion which secures our superiority over the beasts that perish. At all events we cannot doubt that it exerts the chief influence in producing that general elevation of all rudimentary capacities which seems to constitute the true differentia of our race. We should touch with diffidence on scientific controversies which have absorbed the deep attention of so many highly qualified enquirers (11); but amidst views so diversified as those which have been urged, we may reasonably ask whether it is not possible that the true solution may be found in a sphere which lies beyond the range of science; namely, in the endowment of man with a spiritual element, which is identical with no one faculty, but which enters into each of our higher faculties, and raises them all to a loftier power. What else but some special gift of a diviner character could enable us to rise above the faint traces in animals of love for their offspring, and homage for their master, up to the wide range of the moral emotions, and the ennobling influences of the religious life? And may it not be the collateral operation of the same high principle which lifts our mental processes from observation to abstraction, which empowers us to express our thoughts in articulate language, and to pass upwards from fixed instincts to governable habits, from the stationary sensibility of brutes to the 'progressive and improvable' intelligence of man? It can scarcely be doubted, I repeat, that this capacity supplies the source and strength of man's loftiest endowments: the kindling eye, with its 'splendid purpose;' the tameless resolution of the steadfast will; the force of character which binds even worldly aims into a semblance of the unity which lies beyond this earthly sphere. Surely nothing less than such an element could exalt fancy into imagination, and understanding into reason, and conscience into faith. Nothing less could transform man from the noblest of animals into the image and likeness of God.

Such may we conceive to be the nature of that higher principle, which enables us to hold intercourse with Heaven. It would necessarily be the spiritual element, in which man would suffer the deepest injury from the Fall, when sin closed its direct communion with the Holy Spirit, and dropped a veil of ignorance and blindness over the abandoned heart. But though clouded and weakened, it was never obliterated. That darkness never wholly quenched its light, is proved by all the holier aspirations which heathen records bring to our knowledge; by every word and act of virtue which the heathen ever uttered or performed. Its loss would have reduced us to the level of mere animals, with a somewhat nobler organisation. Its complete perversion would have had the still more fatal effect of transforming us into the likeness of the fallen angels.

And now let us turn from man to God, and contemplate the various forms of influence which the Holy Spirit exerts throughout the universe, and to some of which the term 'inspiration' is with varying propriety applied. That these forms must, from the nature of the case, be manifold, a very short consideration will establish.

What is true of the Divine Presence must be true in particular of that peculiar presence of the Holy Spirit which we understand by the term 'inspiration.'

But the Divine Presence is at once universal and special (12). It is universal; for God is omnipresent. It is special; for the omnipresent God must everywhere be distinguished from His creatures; the denial of which is formal Pantheism. There have always been places, again, where He has been specially pleased to fix His name. There have always been persons in whose hearts He has been preeminently present. There have been repeated theophanies, wherein His peculiar presence has been revealed to mankind.

And though it follows, from the περιχώρησις of the Blessed Trinity, that where one Person is present, all in a sense are present—even as Christ said, 'He that hath seen Me hath seen the Father'^a—yet it is undoubted that the economy of revelation distinguishes in each case between the modes of their presence and the ways or degrees in which it is granted.

(1.) The Father is God, and therefore He is omnipresent; yet He dwells especially 'in the light which no man can approach unto; whom no man hath seen nor can see.'^b By another figure He is called a God that hideth Himself; dwelling 'in the thick darkness;' whose 'greatness is unsearchable;' whose 'footsteps are not known.'^c

(2.) The Son is God, and therefore He is omnipresent; yet He told His disciples that unless He went away, the Comforter would not come to them;^d and since His departure from earth at His ascension, His presence in His human nature has been confined to His session at the right hand of the Father. But still He continues to be present amongst us, in many special ways, in, and through, and with His Holy Spirit. He is present with His Church, according to His promise, 'alway, even unto the end of the world.'^e He is present in prayer; present in sacraments; present wherever 'two or three are gathered together in' His 'name.'^f

(3.) Now the same principle must be applied in the

---

^a John xiv. 9.   ^b 1 Tim. vi. 16.
^c Isa. xlv. 15; 1 Kings viii. 12; Ps. cxlv. 3 (Bible v.); Ps. lxxvii. 19.
^d John xvi. 7.   ^e Matt. xxviii. 20.   ^f Matt. xviii. 20.

case of the Holy Spirit; and it would be as unreasonable in this as in the former cases to insist upon confounding one form of the Divine Presence with another.

Thus the Holy Ghost is God, and therefore He is omnipresent; and yet there are countless different manifestations under which His special presence is made known. He is present in the works of nature, as when He 'moved upon the face of the waters,' and when He reneweth 'the face of the earth.'[a] He is present in the higher forms of the human intellect and will, giving skill to 'Bezaleel and Aholiab, and every wise-hearted man,'[b] teaching the poet to sing, and the ruler to govern, and the warrior in the cause of truth to conquer; putting the 'spirit of the holy gods' in such as Daniel, 'light and understanding and wisdom, like the wisdom of the gods.'[c] He is present in man's moral nature, originating everywhere all pure and holy thoughts that man can cherish;—for what can be pure and good and holy without Him? He fills, indeed, through all its functions, the entire range of that created spirit, in which we have been tracing the true honour of our race. And yet there is a more peculiar sense in which He is present in the spirits of all Christians, whose bodies are His temple,[d] abiding there under the conditions of so distinct a covenant, that we are taught to discriminate between the feeblest Christian and the purest heathen by the presence or absence of this grace alone.

Through all parts of the sacred history, we can

[a] Gen. i. 2; Ps. civ. 30. [b] Ex. xxxvi. 1.
[c] Dan. v. 11. [d] 1 Cor. iii. 16, &c.

read the unquestioned signs of His presence in degrees of intensity which plainly vary from the highest to the lowest. He dwelt in the hearts of the ancient patriarchs; or how could they have walked and talked with God?[a] He nerved the strength of that great army of confessors and martyrs, who died in the faith which the promise of a 'better country'[b] had inspired; whose eyes had never seen 'the King in His beauty,' yet who lived in the confident hope that they should become citizens of 'the land that is very far off.'[c] The Spirit of the Lord was ever near the people of the Jews, to guide, to warn, to elevate, to strengthen; imparting courage to their heroes, and wisdom to their rulers, and glory to their national life. Such are the signs of living inspiration which preceded the gifts of the Christian covenant. And by their side, and as their record, we find the productions of a lofty line of writers, who were qualified, by the highest and most specific inspiration, to transmit the Word of God to man. Lawgivers and psalmists, prophets and historians, alike found voice in words of most exalted import, springing from lips that had been touched as if with coals from God's altar.[d] Pass to the times of John the Baptist, and who can doubt that some gifts of the Holy Spirit must have waited on his summons to repentance—gifts higher than any which the heathen shared, and higher than any which had heretofore been granted to the Jew? But though greater than the greatest of all earlier sons of

[a] Gen. v. 24; vi. 9, &c.   [b] Heb. xi. 14, 16.
[c] Isa. xxxiii. 17.   [d] Isa. vi. 6.

men, the Baptist himself was less than the least who has participated in the outpouring of Pentecost. His baptism was only the baptism of water, in contrast with the gifts of Him who baptised 'with the Holy Ghost and with fire.'[a] And at this crisis comes a change so mighty, that all earlier gifts are swept into the shade by the surpassing brightness of the gifts which Christ had won for man. So great in themselves, so priceless to their recipients, yet, when contrasted with that better gift which was reserved for us, they are as nothing: they can be set aside in absolutely negative and exclusive language; as when we are told that 'the Holy Ghost was not yet (given), because that Jesus was not yet glorified;'[b] or that even John's disciples knew as good as nothing of the character and working of the Holy Spirit[c] (13).

But further. The Holy Spirit is present with a difference, even among Christians. Even yet 'there are diversities of gifts, but the same Spirit.'[d] For all alike there is the gift of Baptism, the gift of Confirmation, the gift of Holy Communion—each with its special presence of the Holy Spirit. And for some, again, there are such distinct and partial gifts as those conferred in holy orders, with their several degrees. And in the early Church, too, there were other gifts of a still loftier and rarer character;[e] gifts which enabled men to work miracles, and to speak with tongues, and to exercise many other wonderful

[a] Matt. iii. 11.   [b] John vii. 39.
[c] Acts xviii. 25; xix. 2.   [d] 1 Cor. xii. 4.
[e] Rom. xii. 6-8; 1 Cor. xii. 8-10, &c.

powers, which it was needless for their Giver to perpetuate, when His Church had been established in the world.

Now through all the classes which have been mentioned the word 'inspiration' *might* be used, and in some instances often *is* used, of each separate and distinct form of communication between the Holy Spirit and the spirit of man. Yet it is clear that no such special usage could limit any of the other meanings; still less could any such general use of the word be employed as an argument against the special character of that greatest and rarest gift of the Spirit, which we believe that He vouchsafed to all the writers of the Holy Scriptures. It is surely futile, then, to tell us, what no one could have doubted, that the early Christian fathers often claimed the presence of this Spirit in themselves. It is futile to remind us that our own Church, in its late and scanty use of the word, is chiefly set on teaching us to pray that God's holy inspiration may guide our own thoughts, and govern our own actions; that He will 'inspire continually the universal Church with the spirit of truth, unity, and concord;' that He will 'cleanse the thoughts of our hearts by the inspiration of' His 'Holy Spirit' (14). Nor is there any cause to fear that the claim of special inspiration for the writers of those Scriptures, which guarantee the permanence of such a blessing for ourselves, can 'teach us to quench the Spirit in true hearts for ever.' When we are dealing with the relations between man and God, it is perpetually necessary to distinguish between com-

LECTURE I. 19

parative and absolute condemnation and exclusion (it). 'Behold even to the moon, and it shineth not; yea, the stars are not pure in His sight. How much less man, that is a worm, and the son of man, which is a worm!'ª Thus words which seem to assert unqualified absence may be meant to describe only a lower and less perfect form of presence. If the language of Eliphaz or of Bildad seems to supply an insufficient instance, we may recollect that Christ taught us to call no man good, while Barnabas is called 'a good man' in the Acts of the Apostles; the reason, however, being immediately added, because he was 'full of the Holy Ghost and of faith.'ᵇ In like manner, the theological use of the word 'uncovenanted' can be best defended on the ground that it describes the position of those who live under a lower or less specific covenant. St. Paul's expression, 'having not the law,'ᶜ refers to those who were left to the guidance of a fainter law within themselves. The Evangelist's assertion that the Holy Ghost was not yet given, can only mean, under any possible rendering of the passage, that His most abundant gifts were still unknown. In the same way, the word 'uninspired' can be applied, with perfect propriety, not only to those, if there be any such, who are excluded from all share whatever in the Spirit's gifts, but also to those whose participation in its various blessings bears no resemblance to that supreme illuminating presence to which the Scripture writers can alone lay claim.

ª Job xxv. 5, 6; cf. iv. 18; xv. 15.   ᵇ Matt. xix. 17; Acts xi. 24.
ᶜ Rom. ii. 14.

The wide extent, then, of the influences through which the Holy Spirit operates, is no hindrance to our conviction that there is an innermost centre of inspiration, found only in the Word of God. There may be circle within circle of Divine communion; just as Christ Himself, the friend of all men, drew apart the disciples from among the multitude, and the twelve from among the disciples, and the three from among the twelve, and out of the three chose one to be preeminently distinguished as 'the disciple whom Jesus loved.'[a] Even in ordinary characters, it is depth which forms the only safeguard for expansiveness. Much more may we believe, that in a fallen world, where sin had to be arrested, and the leaven of a higher life diffused, the special and extraordinary inspiration of the few would form the natural centre and security for visitations extending to mankind at large.

Assuming, then, the possibility and probability of high special inspiration, we proceed to affirm that no other books can put in any kind of plea, which brings them even nearly towards the level of the books of the Canonical Scriptures. It is not well to ground the canon on any separate branch of the proofs, by the combination of which it is established (16). No narrow view of canonical authority can stand: not mere authorship, for the authors of some books are still uncertain, nor is it agreed that every work of every inspired writer is comprised within the canon: not internal evidence alone, for it would be a paradox to

---

[a] John xxi. 20, &c.

say that every list of names in Chronicles or Nehemiah ' shines by its own light,' and contains a higher spiritual witness than the loftiest composition which is rightly accounted in the strict sense uninspired: not mere testimony, lest, in days of gainsaying, we should be unable to give, as Hooker says we ought, an account of ' what *reason* there is, whereby the testimony of the Church concerning Scripture, and our own persuasion which Scripture itself hath confirmed, may be proved a truth infallible.'[a] We are not to rest on any of these singly, but on all in combination, each in its due proportion. The light of God in which we see God;[b] the eye that seeks us out; the Spirit which *finds* our inmost spirit: this is one class of evidence which no one who has felt its depth and strength can undervalue. But before this, and by its side, we need the evidence of testimony, to guard us from accidental errors, and ascertain the Divine original of many things which might be wrongly cast aside by a hasty superficial judgment : testimony to prove prophetic or apostolic authority, in cases where such authorship is known; to prove the witness of the Church herself, in cases where such authorship is unknown : and all these lines of evidence conspire together and corroborate each other, converging to form an arch of proof, which bears the Scriptures on its steady basis; and defining the sphere of what we mean when we maintain the special inspiration of the writers of the Books of Scripture.

[a] *E. P.* III. viii. § 14.   [b] Ps. xxxvi. 9.

It is of the canon of Scripture thus established that we claim to uphold a peculiar inspiration, which differs fundamentally from every other mode of the Divine Presence to which the same name can be given. Nor do we admit that we have placed any limitation on the general influence of the Spirit, by maintaining that the capacity of receiving and again imparting special spiritual knowledge, which Scripture itself enumerates amongst the highest spiritual gifts,[a] bore immediate fruit, through both dispensations, in the production of writings which were properly and preeminently inspired, and which were to form the foundation of all exact theology in every age.

II. But whither shall we turn for the *differentia* of Scripture, and for the characteristics of this special inspiration?

The chief element in that differentia will be found in the subject-matter which it deals with; that is to say, in the nature and character of Scripture Revelation (17). But here again we are dealing with a term which has received, though with less propriety, a wider application. There have been other manifestations of God to man besides those which are recorded in the volume of Scripture; and to these also the term 'revelation' has been sometimes less properly applied.

It has often been remarked, that the difference between adequate and inadequate conceptions of

---

[a] John xvi. 13; Rom. xii. 6; 1 Cor. xii. 8–10.

Scripture might be thus expressed: that the former accepts it, as containing revelations from God to man; while the latter regards it as the mere record of man's higher speculations about God. The former view is that which is maintained by every Christian. Yet, that we may not uphold it in an exclusive spirit, Scripture itself directs us to acknowledge that real, though vague, manifestations of the Deity have been granted beyond the pale of the guardianship to which His written oracles have been confined. A fuller examination of the passages will come before us at a future time. It is sufficient for my present purpose to remind you of such sources of what has been called God's unwritten revelation, as the voice of the heavens declaring His glory, and the seasons of the earth proclaiming His goodness; the heart of man, on which the rudiments of truth are traced, and the history of man, which tells of God's dealings with our fathers in the days of old.[a] To these may be added Christ's own appeal to the teaching of Nature, as it sets forth fundamental truths of religion: the sun rising equally on the evil and on the good; the lilies showing forth their Maker's care; the preservation of the feeblest creatures, as a witness to His watchful goodness; and the love which we claim from earthly parents, as a shadow of His deeper love.[b]

Scripture teaches us to recognise three different

[a] (1.) Ps. xix. 1; Isa. xl. 21; Rom. i. 19, 20. (2.) Ps. lxv. 8–13; Acts xiv. 17. (3.) Rom. ii. 14, 15; Acts xvii. 27. (4.) 1 Cor. x. 11, &c.; cf. Ps. xliv. 1, and lxxviii.
[b] Matt. v. 45; vi. 30; Luke xi. 13.

media for the Divine manifestations; the works of Nature, the conscience of man (18), and that special intercourse between the divine and human spirit, which reaches its height in the sacred writings themselves. St. Paul appeals to each of these three sources of Divine knowledge, according to the different characters of those whom he addressed. To the unlettered Lycaonians he speaks of the rain from heaven and fruitful seasons, which, even in the darkest days, bore witness to the bounty of God.[a] To the cultivated Athenians he speaks, not only of the Creator, the Governor, the Guardian of mankind —though such truths as these had the value of new revelations, when contrasted with their intellectual visions of impassive God—but still more closely of the nearer conception of a Heavenly Father, whose offspring were made by their birth in His image; a Father in whom we live and move and have our being; who had once winked at times of ignorance, but had now sent His Son to save men from their sins.[b] Such were the two branches of the Apostle's argument with Gentiles : they are developed from the two great sources of truth among the Gentiles — the world, as the workmanship of God without ; and man's conscience, as the representative of God within. Towards Jews he holds a different language. His appeal then lies to the law and to the testimony : the lively oracles, which it had been their privilege to guard ; those older Scriptures, which, through times

---

[a] Acts xiv. 17.   [b] Acts xvii. 24–31.

of unbelief and darkness, had kept alive the knowledge of God's love.[a] To the Romans, again, he addresses all three kinds of argument. They were Gentiles; therefore he appeals to both the manifestations which God had granted to the Gentiles: the law in their heart, which is conscience; the teaching of things visible, which is the voice of Nature.[b] But again, they were Gentiles who had already accepted the Old Testament, and would therefore answer to the words of Moses and the prophets. For this reason he appeals to the numberless passages in the Old Testament by which his conclusions were foreshown.

It is to the third of these classes that we have now to confine ourselves; and we have to deal with it only in the restricted sense to which it is limited by the subject-matter of Scripture, which we shall presently endeavour to describe. But this strictest kind of revelation, again, is not co-extensive with the whole sphere of Scripture, which embraces a wide range of earthly knowledge, in addition to direct disclosures from above. We must further distinguish, therefore, between the divine and human sources of the materials out of which the sacred record was constructed. When it is alleged that the holy writers were throughout inspired, there is no necessity to add that the materials of their record were the subjects of an equally pervading revelation. We see from St. Luke's preface, to go no farther, that the fullest use was everywhere made of historical materials and

[a] Acts xiii. 16, &c. [b] Rom. i. 20; ii. 14.

human testimony. We shall therefore find it necessary to discriminate in Scripture between what was revealed to inspired men for the purpose of being recorded, and what was simply recorded by them from their own knowledge, or from accessible human sources, under the safeguard and guidance of perpetual inspiration.

Scripture, as viewed externally, presents us with two series of facts, which answer to each other, and which are combined into unity by the continued presence of a uniform interpretation (19). The first series begins with the creation, and stops short four centuries before the incarnation of Christ. The keynote of this earlier portion is the voice of preparation. A church is set apart from the rest of the world; special commissions and special promises are given to individual members of it; complex arrangements are instituted, under Divine authority, to guard the rich treasure of the national expectation, which looked forward to the advent of One, who was to be at once the King of Israel and the means of extending Abraham's faith to all the world. Through captivity and restoration, through foreign wars and civil dissensions, amidst cowardice and heroism, amidst failure and success, the stream of fact flows broadening onward towards the fulfilment of that glorious hope. The curtain does not fall till all has been made ready. Every type is furnished; every symbol is assigned; a deeper moral element has been wrought in by the prophetic teaching; and certain conspicuous landmarks have been fixed, by which the proximate date of the great event might be foreknown. The second series of facts takes up the answer, and supplies the counterpart for which those distant centuries were waiting. Point by point, and detail by detail, it meets the expectation, fulfils the promise, and completes the work. 'The Word was made flesh, and dwelt among us.'[a] Old things were swept away; but the form only perished, while the spirit was preserved and quickened. The Christian Church was established, and Christ was preached through all the countries of the then known world. The historical record closes before the holy city of Jerusalem, which had been the stronghold of the earlier life, was overthrown. In that event the warnings of the prophets were fulfilled; and the most sacred ties were snapped asunder, to complete the removal of local restrictions which Christ had announced when He said, 'Believe me, the hour cometh, when ye shall neither in this mountain, nor yet at Jerusalem, worship the Father.'[b]

But now, so far as these are simple facts, bearing a plain historical character, and holding definite external relations to dates, to geography, to the histories of surrounding nations, it is clear that no special revelation was required for their record. We can imagine that even uninspired historians might have narrated the whole contemporary portion of the facts of Scripture, in histories of the common type and order. But such records would have differed widely from the existing Scriptures, because they

[a] John i. 14.   [b] John iv. 21.

could not have presented the facts under the aspect which a knowledge of their purpose and significance supplied. Revelation, properly so called, is the supernatural counterpart to this double series of facts, uniting them together under one religious explanation. Scripture consists, then, not of facts only, but of facts arranged with a view to one overruling purpose, and lighted up by a peculiar interpretation, which the unassisted mind of man could never have projected or supplied.

The case might be stated in another manner. The chain of events which forms the external history of both dispensations, is all along accompanied by the revelation of a higher series, belonging to a supernatural order. The various utterances of the words of God, His commands, His promises, His warnings, His expostulations, these are all facts of a superhuman character, and pass beyond the historical sphere. Such facts as these are connected with doctrines, and with the disclosures of mysterious truth, on the nature of God and the spiritual history of man. Everything of this kind is pure and simple revelation. Yet it is the very key-stone which holds together the whole fabric of Scripture; so that, if we allow ourselves to doubt its truth, our belief in the special character of Scripture falls. As all this is, in the ordinary sense of the word, miraculous, we make no further demand on faith, when we add that it was coupled with many other manifestations of miracle; prophecies which none but God could pronounce; direct interpositions of His sovereign will to alter or suspend His ordinary laws.

The preparation of the Old Testament extended to many points which passed beyond the knowledge of the Jews. The fulfilment of the anticipations which were expressed in its records, could not, in the nature of things, be furnished till long after the canon was closed. This whole mass of knowledge, then, was due to simple revelation; to disclosures so directly superhuman and divine, that even the inspired writers must, in many cases, have had but a dim conception of the ultimate bearing of the truths which they set down. The Divinity of Christ, for instance, is a doctrine rather than a fact of history. It is a Divine revelation, which gives new force and meaning to the history and destiny of the creatures whom He made and ransomed. But the Jewish nation, with few honoured exceptions, had gained so feeble a mastery over the true teaching of their own Scriptures, that they found an insuperable stumbling-block in the cardinal truth of what is most strictly termed theology—the truth that He whom they looked for as the Son of David was really David's King and God.

The presence of this series of Divine revelations is the chief element in the differentia of Scripture—the chief mark which distinguishes the inspiration of the Bible from the inspiration of a holy life. When David prayed, with a deep sense of sinfulness, ' O give me the comfort of Thy help again, and stablish me with Thy free Spirit,'[a] he sought, as each of us should

[a] Ps. li. 12.

daily seek, for the cleansing inspiration of the Holy Spirit's purifying presence; that 'ministration of the Spirit,'[a] to which we are admitted more freely than the ancient Psalmist, which first regenerates and then renews us; which first implants a better will, and then enlightens it with clearer knowledge; which assures us of forgiveness, and advances us in grace; and enables us to bring forth good works in this life, and to look forward with confidence to the life everlasting. It was a very different kind of influence to which he reverted in his dying declaration: 'The Spirit of the Lord spake by me, and His word was in my tongue.'[b] The word that God gave him was the thing that he must speak; the revelation which he was commissioned to disclose; the word which unfolded heavenly truths, and raised common facts to a higher significance, by disclosing their eternal import.

But as before of Inspiration, so now of Revelation: we find that it often reaches beyond its proper province to enrich mankind with wider blessings than those which belong strictly to the sphere of religion. Being a disclosure of the highest and most universal laws of God, its influence overflows into all parts of moral knowledge, supplying motives and explanations of the loftiest import. It cannot be doubted that Revelation has combined with Inspiration to impart that quickening power to Scripture which has made it the prolific source of kindling life, in the spiritual

[a] 2 Cor. iii. 8.   [b] 2 Sam. xxiii. 2.

histories of the nations of mankind. But we may account these gifts to be a portion of God's additional and superabundant bounty, and we need not embrace them within the rigour of the definition which secures the higher aspect of Scripture Revelation.

And here, again, let us pause to repeat, that when we thus claim for Scripture a peculiar and unapproached inspiration, and point to the revelations which it embodies, as explaining both the need and nature of that higher influence, we do not trench upon the fundamental principle, that no religion anywhere is worthy of the name, unless it looks to the abiding presence of God's Holy Spirit as its only source of sanctity and life. The duration of the Church itself rests on the promise that Christ should continue with it, through the presence of the Comforter, even unto the end of the world. The religious life of each separate spirit depends on the operation of that holy inmate who can alone give efficacy to sacraments and strength to faith; who can alone maintain within us holiness of conduct, purity of thought, and elevation of knowledge; who can alone assist the fallen to secure that glorious restoration which Christ's sacrifice has brought within our reach. A religion that is *not* spiritual stands condemned by the confession. We might as well speak of a religion that is earthly, but not heavenly; that is human, not divine: of a religion which finds its centre in ourselves, instead of leading us to fix the centre of all our motives and thoughts in God.

But surely this admission—I would rather say this

earnest declaration of our deepest convictions—surely this can form no reason for such questions as the following:—Why should you seek, then, to interpose the barriers of a book religion; to fetter man's spirit with the forms and obligations of an ancient creed; to intercept the free communion between God's Spirit and his own? Why should you erect, for instance, on the teaching of Scripture, a complex system of doctrine, and proclaim that 'this is the Catholic Faith; which except a man believe faithfully, he cannot be saved'? Why load man's conscience with the burthen of what is called an *historical* religion; instead of leaving him free to tell his griefs to the Great Spirit of the universe, with no bar from Bible or church, from priest or creed, from ritual or form?

We might answer, in the first place, that Holy Scripture surely has a priceless value, if it were no more than the record of God's spiritual disclosures to those human spirits whom He has vouchsafed, in long-past times, to visit with His personal grace. To doubt this would be to set aside the principle on which all human progress in all branches must depend—the principle that later days are heirs of all the previous ages, and may attain a higher eminence in every province, by their command of the accumulated treasures of the past. But what I have said would indicate the grounds on which this reply, though true as far as it goes, may be set aside as comparatively unimportant, when we bear in mind the real reasons for the unapproachable eminence which Scripture gains from its subject-matter, and its positive disclosures from a higher world. We believe that it records the acts and words of God incarnate; that its earlier pages are the preparation for that august advent, when the Son of God became the Son of Man; that it interprets the facts which lie beneath its doctrines, and which give them a firm standing-ground in the midst of human history. We believe that Scripture embodies countless disclosures from a higher world, which differ in kind, as well as in degree, of revelation, from any communication, however lofty, which His Spirit vouchsafes to ourselves. It records by inspiration; it explains by revelation. It contains the only distinct and certified messages from God to man; and it places in our hands the only clue of infallible guidance, by which man, in his exile, may feel the way home to his Heavenly Father.

And now I trust that these explanations will enable us to restate the doctrine of the inspiration claimed for Holy Scripture, in such a manner as to ward off some current misapprehensions, and to lay a safe foundation for further enquiry into the relation of the divine and human elements. The possibility of inspiration rests upon the fact, that God has endowed man with a capacity for Divine communion, which serves, more than even the broadest marks of physical or intellectual superiority, to stamp him as a citizen belonging to a higher world than this. 'The spirit of man is the candle of the Lord.'[a] It is the ground of all religion, the proof of our Divine

[a] Prov. xx. 27. Cf. Job xxxii. 8.

sonship, the faculty whereby we know the Father, the germ of that eternal life which will assume its full proportion in the spiritual body, and in the unveiled presence of the Lord. The voice of God's Spirit may be heard within that spirit, wherever the true and listening worshipper is found. But our belief that the Divine gift is shed forth so abundantly is not at variance with our belief in the special intensity of its peculiar presence, as manifested in the Books of Scripture, and confined within the limits of the Sacred Canon.

And next; when we study the characteristics of that special inspiration, we find that it lays a firm grasp on objective support, in the supernatural revelations which were entrusted to its keeping, and which anchor it on the eternal shore. Through these God makes Himself known to man, under such conditions as the spiritual capacities of finite creatures would allow. It is by a series of objective facts and supernatural disclosures that He reveals Himself to us as the Father of an infinite majesty; His honourable, true, and only Son; also the Holy Ghost, the Comforter.

When we have thus noted the manner in which the Holy Ghost has filled to overflowing selected representatives of the most religious human spirits, and has supplied them with supernatural material for their messages to men, we should go on to observe that it has performed that work without obliterating a single human peculiarity, or destroying the free rights of the human will, which yielded glad obedience to the heavenly impulse. We thankfully accept the inspired announcement, that God spake unto the fathers 'in divers manners,' as well as at 'sundry times.' We know that the same law is traceable even in the last days, after He had 'spoken by His Son.'[a] We are perfectly aware that the voice of James is not the voice of Paul; that we can distinguish in a moment between the utterance of Peter and the utterance of John. And with this reservation we accept and explain the various images which have been used to set forth the different phases of the truth of inspiration. The inspired writers are not pens only, but trusted penmen; not organs alone, but living instruments; not mere 'ministers' and 'stewards,' like slaves employed upon a servile duty, but 'ambassadors for Christ,' beseeching men, 'in Christ's stead,' to be 'reconciled to God.'[b] (20). The most mechanical illustrations, when intelligently used, need no more contradict the higher truth which they fail to express, than St. Paul's figure of clay in the hands of the potter is meant to negative the responsibility of the free will of man.[c]

When we enter more at large upon the details of the subject, I shall propose to consider first the nature and relations of the Divine element in Scripture; together with some of those difficulties which appear to rise from its presentation under the forms of the human intellect. To the different branches of that topic, our next three Lectures will, with God's

[a] Heb. i. 1, 2.   [b] 1 Cor. iv. 1; 2 Cor. v. 20.
[c] Rom. ix. 21.

permission, be directed. In the later part of our course we shall consider in its turn the human element, and devote our best attention to such questions as the following :—What has been the effect of the Divine message on the vehicle through which it has been given ? How far has Divine truth suffered, if at all, from the human form through which it was received ? Has that form imposed any drawback of imperfection on the matter ? Or is it possible that any grains of error may lie embedded in the form, without injury or disparagement to the spiritual revelations which it enshrines ?

It would be idle to attempt to conceal the consciousness that much of this subject brings us within the range of painful controversy, and deals with questions causing deep disquietude to many hearts. Under such circumstances, it may not be thought unbecoming to tender the assurance that I shall not venture to approach these topics, before such an audience, in any controversial spirit. It is precisely the fact that so much controversial heat has been evolved, which has caused, perhaps on both sides, so much general alarm. It is clear, at least, that on one side what men have dreaded has been the suspected animosity of a 'remorseless criticism.' There is no peril to be apprehended from the honest recognition of the human element. The vast majority would readily grant it. But they draw back in alarm when they imagine that books which they hold dear as life itself, and with which their holiest thoughts are blended, are assailed with a hostility from which Herodotus would be protected; and are rent in pieces with a ruthlessness which scholars now refuse to tolerate towards Homer. We need not ask whether these suspicions have ever been too vehement, or whether they have not been sometimes exasperated by the spirit in which they have been met. It is better to make the question practically useful, by drawing for ourselves the lesson, that we must be careful to shun, on either hand, the errors and exaggerations of unyielding tempers. With patience and courage, with candour and forbearance, let us endeavour to place ourselves so far aloof from the contest, that we may contemplate with perfect calmness the materials which it has served to bring into one focus; and may wait with humility to catch the lineaments of truth, as they rise above the mists of strife. Above all things, let us recollect that purity of thought is the only avenue to sacred knowledge; and that if we wish to enter on the mind of Christ, we must seek the constant help of that Divine Spirit, who will lead us to the pastures of heavenly wisdom through the portals of meekness and love.

LECTURE II.

Acts xvii. 30, 31.

'And the times of this ignorance God winked at; but now commandeth all men everywhere to repent: Because He hath appointed a day, in the which He will judge the world in righteousness, by that Man whom He hath ordained; whereof He hath given assurance unto all men, in that He hath raised Him from the dead.'

MY former Lecture was mainly devoted to the task of examining the two terms, 'Inspiration' and 'Revelation,' with the view of showing that though not co-extensive, either with each other or with the Bible, they are both distinguished in Scripture by such exalted characteristics, that the difference in degree is superseded by a difference in kind (1). Thus of Inspiration, we believe that the Holy Spirit speaks to man's spirit in many forms of diversified blessing, yet nowhere else in accents so distinct and certified as He uses through the medium of the sacred writers; and of Revelation, we believe that God has unveiled Himself in other ways to man, through the voice of conscience and through the works of Nature, yet nowhere else with the same kind of certainty and fulness as He did in the person of the Divine Saviour,

LECTURE II.

and as He did to the prophets who foretold His advent, or to the apostles and evangelists by whom it was proclaimed.

I now propose to enter on an examination of the Divine element in Scripture, as contrasted with those external systems of religion with which it seems natural to compare it. Believing as we do that Scripture alone conveys a revelation of unmingled truth, and that in all those other systems truth is grievously weighed down by falsehood, we may let this leading distinction suggest the division of our immediate subject. Let us take up the comparison of Christianity with Heathenism, first as to truth, and next as to falsehood; asking, in the first place, how the truth of Scripture stands related to the partial truths of independent systems; and dwelling afterwards on the light which Scripture throws, by the mere force of contrast, on the falsehoods by which all heathen systems are debased.

I. For the first head, it will be convenient to begin by classifying the whole subject of religious knowledge, so as to mark the exact sphere which the Divine element in Scripture occupies.

Five such classes will suffice, I think, to span the subject, and form, as we might speak, five zones of knowledge. In the first, we may arrange those glimpses of truth which were granted to the heathen, as we can ascertain them independently of the sacred records. In the second, we may place the Scripture proofs that similar but somewhat clearer knowledge was possessed by the heathen who came under the observation of the inspired historians. The third class would contain the Divine element of special revelation, as received and recorded by special inspiration, and holding a position incomparably higher and more distinct than either of the former classes. Fourthly, we may rank those positive ordinances by which the special revelation was accompanied; ordinances which sprang from a Divine origin, but received their particular mould or frame from conformity with the actual needs of man. Lastly, we place the purely human element which is contributed by the writers of Scripture themselves.

1. To begin with the subject of the religious knowledge of the heathen. It needs but a short survey of the higher classes of heathen writers to convince us that from the first there has existed a large body of moral and religious truth on the outside of the sphere to which God's special revelation is confined. This is a fact which cannot be overlooked, and which it is only reasonable to expect us to account for; but it is a fact which we cannot account for on the narrow view of making God's gift of sacred knowledge the exclusive possession of His chosen race. Are we to say, then, that these truths are relics of Paradise, which lingered in the memories of men; the dying embers of a primeval illumination, which had not yet been lost in the prevailing darkness (2); or shall we say that they were all borrowed from the fire which was kept alive upon the Jewish altar, though the means of such a general transfer are as inconceivable as they are

unknown (3)? Both of these views have received a certain support from research and argument. The facts disclosed by comparative mythology, and the similarity of traditions which are traceable through remote and scattered nations, have been believed to give some countenance to the favourite thought, that all men have retained, though unconsciously, a direct inheritance from that primeval period, when 'the whole earth was of one language and of one speech,'[a] and the families of man still owned a common centre. Men have loved to look upon these scattered treasures as the 'wreck of Paradise,' which still,

> 'Through many a dreary age,
> Upbore whate'er of good and wise
> Yet lived in bard or sage.'[b]

But the other opinion also has exercised considerable influence, especially among the earlier apologists, who pointed out the modes in which the light of revelation might have glanced aside into the darkness which it was not meant to dissipate, and actual glimpses of the laws, the miracles, the prophecies of Scripture, might have flashed upon the vision of the Gentile world.

These two hypotheses are of very different value; but it is needless to lay further stress on either for our present purpose, since we shall find a surer basis for our own enquiries in the authoritative declaration of St. Paul. The Apostle teaches, as we have already seen, that the heathen owed that knowledge partly

[a] Gen. xi. 1.   [b] *Christian Year*, Fourth Sunday after Trinity.

to the law of God, which was written on their hearts, and which speaks there through the voice of conscience; partly to the dim manifestation of Him who is invisible, as it reached them in their darkest days, through the veil of His visible creation.

A firm belief, then, in the special character of the Divine revelation in Scripture is quite compatible with the conviction, that God has always granted to mankind a universal, though vague, manifestation of Himself, by leaving in man's nature the traces of His own Divine image, and by enabling man to read the witness of His presence through the signs of the material universe. It has been a task of deep interest, in all the more enlightened ages of the Church, to gather and register these scattered truths; to verify them by comparison with God's special revelation; to group them round their earthly centre in man's conscience; to estimate precisely what their disclosures amount to; and to point out exactly where they fail. It is with this design that men have compiled histories of the Dispensation of Paganism, the Unconscious Prophecies of Heathendom, the Religions before Christ (4). And these enquiries have run the same course in earlier as in later days. A frank recognition of the Divine truths contained in heathen creeds has been pushed on to the untenable position, of claiming for them equality with Scripture revelation; and the heathen creeds, in turn, have been depressed below their proper level by the orthodox recoil (5).

The Church, indeed, has always held two different relations to heathen religions: on the one hand, sympathy with their partial truth; on the other hand, abhorrence for their pervading errors. The weight of her judgment would preponderate on this side or on that, according as the balance of truth or error varied in the separate cases. We may suppose that so long as it was their single mission to convert the heathen, Christian teachers would seek to attract the sympathy of their hearers by a recognition of the truth which they already held; as St. Paul did when he was 'made all things to all men,' that he 'might by all means save some.'[a] But when the influx of heathen converts made it needful to repel the aggressions of heresies, under cover of which the vanquished sought to lead their victors captive (6), they were compelled to denounce the evil of the pernicious leaven, by which false religions were degraded below the level of the purer characters among their worshippers. And when the evil became universally more conspicuous than the good, and the contagion of error began to exert a more baneful influence, then the opposing current of Christian condemnation set in with a steady and resistless tide, which tended to deprive the heathen of their just proportion in the common spiritual heritage of man. The researches of later times may perhaps have diminished the immediate pressure of the danger, but they certainly have not lessened our conviction of the evil which was infused into such systems by the corruption of the heart of man. They have widened our acquaintance with the details of the

---

[a] 1 Cor. ix. 22.

creeds, and deepened our insight into their fundamental affinities; but they have not removed the ancient landmarks which were fixed by the Apostle. The lines of demarcation still remain as he drew them, to distinguish between the true revelation and the vague manifestation; though we can confirm the distinction by a cloud of witnesses, who lay beyond the range of knowledge which the observation of that period could command.

The position of these exiled truths, which wandered homeless, yet not unwelcome, through the darkest ages of the heathen world, might be described by an application of the Platonic image;[a] they were like shadows thrown before the eyes of prisoners, who had no power to turn and view the substance, as contrasted with the realities presented to the Church of God, which flow from the revelation of the Deity in Christ. Throughout both the Old and New Testaments, we see, in the revealed object of our common adoration, a true and Divine Person, who gives coherency and reality to the blessed truths by which we live. To change the figure, we may say, that light reached the heathen through so thick a cloud, that the face of the sun was entirely hidden, and its very form remained unknown. In the revelation of the Old Testament, the clouds were broken, and the rays burst forth; but the sun himself remained concealed. The advent of Christ gave all the light that man could bear, when 'life and immortality' were brought 'to light through

[a] Plat. *Rep.* vii. *init.*

the Gospel'[a]—light which resembled that of noon, in contrast with the clouded daybreak; yet light which, in its turn, will seem pale hereafter, when contrasted with the brightness of heaven.

Now the point of departure between these two collateral but unequal manifestations of Divine knowledge must be sought in the earliest incident recorded of our fallen race—the promise which was given in Paradise, before the forfeited blessings of our first abode had been withdrawn. It follows, that to claim a Divine source for the religious knowledge of the heathen, is so far from being a denial that salvation comes only through the name of Christ, that it simply asserts our Lord's rightful position, as the sole Head of renewed humanity—of the race which would have perished in that hour of disobedience, but for the hope of salvation through the promise of Christ's advent.

2. But within the range of the authenticated Scriptures, we find many traces of a revelation of religious knowledge, which was granted through unusual channels to others besides those who were entrusted with the oracles of God (7). So far as the worship of primeval nations is referred to in Genesis, it seems not unlike the worship which was offered by the patriarchs; and the stranger was often favoured by Divine visitations, resembling those which were granted to the chosen nation. Thus 'God came to' the Philistine 'Abimelech in a dream by night,' and

---

[a] 2 Tim. i. 10.

admitted his appeal to the 'integrity of' his 'heart and innocency of' his 'hands,' while He withheld him from an unintended sin.[a] Another Abimelech was enlightened to see in Isaac 'the blessed of Jehovah,' and on that ground made a covenant with him.[b] Abraham and Ephron, or Joseph and Pharaoh, converse in precisely the same tone, and apparently under the influence of similar principles of belief and conduct.[c] God sent His messengers to visit Sodom, and hearkened to the pleadings which Abraham offered for that guilty city.[d] The same fact is traceable through the history of the idolatrous Laban, and the Midianite Jethro, and the Egyptian women who 'feared God, and did not as the king of Egypt commanded them.'[e] At a later date, God's blessings or warnings are sent through Elijah to the Sidonian widow, through Elisha to the Syrian Naaman, through Jonah to the Ninevites, through Daniel to Nebuchadnezzar, through other prophets to adjacent nations;[f] yet with no intimation, in any such cases, that the recipient of God's message incurred the obligation to accept the forms of the Jewish ritual. But there are many other instances more remarkable than these. Of four women whom St. Matthew mentions in the lineage of Christ, the purest was a daughter of the

---

[a] Gen. xx. 3-6.   [b] Gen. xxvi. 28, 29.
[c] Gen. xxiii. 8-17; xli. 38, 39.   [d] Gen. xviii.; xix. 1.
[e] Gen. xxiv. 31; xxx. 27, 30; xxxi. 24, 49; Ex. xviii. 1, 9, 10, 11, &c.; i. 17, 20, 21.
[f] 1 Kings xvii.; 2 Kings v. (Luke iv. 25-27); Jonah iii. 5 Dan. ii., &c.

Moabite.ª Another was the Canaanitish Rahab, who is commemorated by two different apostles as an eminent example both of faith and works.ᵇ God caused Melchizedek, whose race and ancestry we know not, to be a special and exalted type of Christ.ᶜ He overruled the spirit of Balaam the Aramæan, who 'loved the wages of unrighteousness,'ᵈ to be His instrument for blessing those whom He had blessed; for uttering precepts of as lofty import as any embodied in the older Scriptures;ᵉ for announcing from afar the 'Star out of Jacob,' and the 'Sceptre' that should 'rise out of Israel.'ᶠ He vouchsafed to reason with Job, 'a perfect and an upright man,' who, though no Israelite, is called His 'servant,'ᵍ and who steadfastly persisted, under all his temptations, in speaking the thing that was right of God. All along the frontiers of God's Church, we see the light of revelation resting on the faces of those who were attracted to approach its borders, even down to the time when a star brought the Magians to the cradle of Christ, and the woman of Samaria was looking for the decisions of the expected Messiah, and the Roman Cornelius was constantly offering up acceptable prayers unto God.ʰ But these, again, are only partially connected with that special revelation, which mainly constitutes the Divine element in Scripture, and which can be distinguished from the transient

ª Matt. i. 5. ᵇ Matt. i. 5; Heb. xi. 31; James ii. 25.
ᶜ Ps. cx. 4; Heb. vii. 3, &c.   ᵈ 2 Pet. ii. 15.
ᵉ Num. xxiii. 10; Mic. vi. 8.   ᶠ Num. xxiv. 17.
ᵍ Job ii. 3; xlii. 7.   ʰ Matt. ii.; John iv. 20; Acts x. 2.

gleams of light which occasionally flashed forth by its side.

3. From these, as well as from the outside heathen knowledge, the main stream of revelation is discriminated, by its depth, by its purity, by its far-reaching coherency, but, above all, by its close connection with the Person of our Lord. As I have before pointed out, Scripture presents us with a long chain of facts, bound together by a uniform Divine interpretation—facts which might have been narrated by an uninspired historian; with an interpretation which could never have existed amongst men, except by an explicit disclosure from God(s). And it is important to observe, that from the beginning its course was rather analytic than synthetic. Revelation advances, not so much by addition as by development. There is but little in the later portions which is not dimly foreshadowed in the earliest record. The promise of a future Redeemer dates from the very gates of Paradise; and from the first it gave the forecast of His double character — the tribulation through which He was to enter upon glory. 'I will put enmity between thee and the woman, and between thy seed and her seed: it shall bruise thy head, and thou shalt bruise his heel.'[a] The Unity unfolds into the Trinity; yet the thought of the Divine conference and counsel is suggested in the earliest page of Scripture, as we read, 'Let *Us* make man in *Our* image, after *Our* likeness:'[b] and Christian theologians can

[a] Gen. iii. 15. [b] Gen. i. 26.

find no fitter starting-point for the exposition of the doctrine, than the Mosaic declaration of the Divine Unity, expressed in the terms of a mysterious triune formula, 'Hear, O Israel; the Lord our God is one Lord.'[a]

But though the boundaries of the current might be fixed from the beginning, the constant onward flow of revelation was ever deepening its channel, and giving men profounder conceptions both of the nature of God and the moral obligations of mankind. This principle supplies an explanation of the statement in Exodus, on the introduction of the knowledge of the name Jehovah, which has recently given rise to some renewed discussion[b] (9). It is the usage of Scripture to ascribe a high and special significance to the knowledge of the name of God; just as in the New Testament the power of faith and miracles is so often connected with the name of Christ. The name of God stands for God as revealed to us. The fundamental principle of the Third Commandment enjoins proper reverence, not for God in the abstract, but for that revelation of the Deity which is contained in Scripture. And this doctrine pervades the whole narrative in Exodus. 'By my name Jehovah was I not known to them:' that is to say, they were never taught to fathom the full depth of significance which lay hidden beneath a well-known term. The question which Moses expected the Israelites to ask him was, What is the *name* of the God of our fathers, who sent

[a] Deut. vi. 1; Hooker, E. P. v. li. 1.   [b] Ex. vi. 3.

thee? The answer which he was told to give them was, 'I am that I am.' 'Thus shalt thou say unto the children of Israel, I am hath sent me unto you.'[a] And the proclamation of the meaning of this name Jehovah is a later act of preeminent significance and solemnity. 'The Lord descended in the cloud, and stood with him there, and proclaimed the name of the Lord. And the Lord passed by before him, and proclaimed, The Lord, the Lord God (Jehovah, Jehovah-El): merciful and gracious, longsuffering and abundant in goodness and truth, keeping mercy for thousands, forgiving iniquity and transgression and sin.'[b]

It is perfectly consistent with these declarations, that the mere letters of the name Jehovah, which can be traced, as it is correctly urged, through so many parts of Genesis, conveyed before this period none of the deep meaning which was thus brought out by special revelation, as the promises began to receive their first fulfilment; precisely as we cannot suppose that the patriarchal name of God, 'the God of Abraham, and the God of Isaac, and the God of Jacob,' conveyed to those who used it that profound teaching on the Resurrection which Christ disclosed beneath its outward form.[c]

While the theological side of revelation, then, was thus deepened in the providential course of sacred history, we can trace the same kind of progression through its moral aspect also (10). The righteousness of God was always manifested in His jealousy for holiness,

[a] Ex. iii. 13, 14.   [b] Ex. xxxiv. 5–7.
[c] Matt. xxii. 32.

in His anger against sin; yet Christ Himself seeks words no clearer or more forcible than those of Moses, when He tells us how God claims the utmost strength of human love: 'Thou shalt love the Lord thy God with all thine heart, and with all thy soul, and with all thy might.'[a] And so onward, through Deuteronomy, and still more plainly through the long series of the Prophets, the moral element, which had been thus broadly sketched from the beginning, and with which from the first had been blended the love of our neighbour, as the second law of man,[b] was ever receiving its more full development, as the counterpart to the theological; till the time when the last of the old prophets handed on his message to the evangelist—

'First filial duty, then divine,
That sons to parents, all to Thee may turn.' [c]

But before we pass on to a further exposition of this revelation, in contrast with the religions of heathenism, there remain two points for brief explanation; and first, the position of those ceremonial ordinances, which formed the casket for the preservation of that precious trust, the prophetic announcement of the Saviour of mankind.

4. It is probable that, from the outset, the service of religion was fenced in by positive ordinances, such as many have traced in the alleged primeval obligation of the seventh day's rest. But without entering on the obscure topic of the forms of worship in the

[a] Deut. vi. 5; Matt. xxii. 37. [b] Lev. xix. 18; Matt. xxii. 39.
[c] Mal. iv. 6; Luke i. 17; *Christian Year*, St. John Baptist's Day.

patriarchal Church, we naturally turn for the most conspicuous instance of this kind of revelation to the subsequent introduction of the Law of Sinai, with its special adaptations to the transgressions of men. The Mosaic precepts differed widely from the promise, which is the more exact anticipation of the Gospel. It is true that they embodied a lofty code of moral obligation; but their chief characteristic is, that they were positive and protective(11). We shall have occasion to return in the sequel to their typical character. For our present purpose, we need regard them only in that stern, external, and repressive aspect in which they were so framed as to fence in and isolate the Jewish nation, for the double purpose of impressing them with deep convictions of the character of sin, and compelling them to guard the treasure, of which they were the stewards in the universal interests of mankind. Now it is the tendency of all who have to administer a code of positive precepts to overrate their value on the ground of their obligation — a defect which is condemned in ordinary cases as legal pedantry, and which finds a ready correction in the common sense of society. In the case of the Jews, this error was more dangerous, because the ordinances which they obeyed claimed a superhuman authority; and it still misleads the historian who cannot reduce the Law to its proper level, and who urges us to cut ourselves adrift from the entire Old Testament system, for the sake of liberating Christianity from its alleged Jewish element. We must draw, then, a clear line of demarcation between the pure revelation of eternal truth, and the ordinances which were merely framed to guard it for an appointed season. We must bear in mind that faith was always taught as the sole principle of acceptable obedience; and that God's true servants always lived in a more spiritual atmosphere than that of the narrow Pharisaic Jew.

5. The Mosaic ordinances, however, and all others which resemble them in Scripture, were matters of God's own appointment: they were 'the example and shadow of heavenly things, as Moses was admonished of God when he was about to make the tabernacle; for, See, saith He, that thou make all things according to the pattern shewed to thee in the mount.'ᵃ They are only the positive side of an entire dispensation, which was in the strictest sense throughout divine. They must be distinguished, therefore, in the fifth place, from the personal style and characteristics of the inspired writers, and from the whole class of peculiarities which belong as distinctly to their separate provinces in the economy of Scripture, as the language or the imagery which they severally used belonged to the nations in which they had been brought up. It is this consideration which introduces us to the purely human element of Scripture; in the outer fringe of which, again, God has left room for varied contributions of ordinary knowledge: the 'wisdom' of Egyptians, the 'tongue' of Chaldæans,ᵇ the science of Greece and the laws of Rome; the stores of moral and

---

ᵃ Heb. viii. 5.   ᵇ Acts vii. 22; Dan. i. 4; v. 11.

political experience, which had been gathered through the histories of the tribes with which the chosen people came in contact; and even acknowledged quotations from heathen writers, such as we meet with in the teaching of St. Paul[a] (12). To this head, again, we must refer erroneous arguments, which are often reported in Scripture, sometimes at great length, as in the speeches of Job's friends; sometimes more briefly, as in the message of Amaziah, the priest of Bethel:[b] and much more that appears to be recorded on the principle that knowledge must cover both contraries, and that Scripture must not only tell us what is right for our guidance, but must also record what is *not* right for our warning.

II. Thus far we have sketched the five classes of religious knowledge which I named in the beginning; and sufficiently, I trust, to guide us in our further task of drawing, in the second place, a broad contrast between false and true religions—between the systems of Paganism and the revelation of the Scriptures. We see that, before we enter on its relation to error, Scripture revelation must be distinguished on the one side from the indistinct manifestations of truth, which God vouchsafed in different measures to the Gentile world, and which are traceable within the record of Scripture itself; and that it must be distinguished as carefully, on the other side, from the temporary ordinances which were framed for its protection, and from the human

---

[a] Acts xvii. 28; 1 Cor. xv. 33; Tit. i. 12.   [b] Amos vii. 10–13.

LECTURE II. 55

characteristics which were never obliterated by the inspiration of the sacred writers. Let us now confine ourselves to the intrinsic nature of that special revelation, as it is brought out by contrast with the various organisations of heathen religion.

1. While we admit and teach that those religions present occasional traces of undoubted truth, which should be recognised and welcomed as the gift of God, we must observe that these truths never embraced any entire system with which they were connected. This is the foremost difference between Paganism and revealed religion; that while the lessons of Scripture form portions of one perfectly true and holy system, the truths which we find in heathen religions are like grains of gold embedded in a base material: the religion, as a whole, is constantly liable to pass over altogether to the side of evil; the sins of men are rivalled and surpassed by sins ascribed to beings who are accounted as divine (13). Such systems were the final issue of that false worship, the downward course of which is indicated by St. Paul: when both the two lights of nature had been darkened; when conscience had lost the keenness of its insight, and the visible world had become the medium for changing 'the truth of God into a lie.'[a] Then worship degenerated into systematic idolatry, and idolatry was the prolific parent of immorality, and gods were made the patrons of human vices, and temples became the centres for the foulest sins. 'They did not like to retain God in

[a] Rom. i. 25.

their knowledge;' therefore 'God gave them over to a reprobate mind.'[a] Their 'understanding' was 'darkened, being alienated from the life of God, through the ignorance that' was ' in them, because of the blindness of their heart.'[b] Though it were true that man never lost the conviction of the existence of God, yet dark times came when he ceased to glorify Him as God, or be thankful. Though it were true that he never lost the fainter feeling of the real position of our own nature, in the Divine sonship but estrangement of man, yet corruption led him to judicial blindness, when God gave him up to vile affections, because he had 'worshipped and served the creature more than the Creator.'[c]

As soon as systems of this kind had been fully formed and established, the better thoughts of men were left to work in the presence of a veil of darkness which sin had drawn anew across the vision of their spirits; and they were overpowered by the strong rebellion of their sensual impulses, which made them the bondslaves of a corrupted worship. And whenever purer aspirations intervened, to save some among the worshippers from utmost degradation, the result was, that the forms of religion broke away from their substance, and mythologies became the least religious portion of the national life (14). We are all familiar with the lofty language in which the old Greek poets proclaim the eternal laws of purity and truth, or show how crime is ever tracked by the sure step of the

[a] Rom. i. 28.   [b] Eph. iv. 18.   [c] Rom. i. 21, 25.

avenger, and how the guilty father cannot shield off retribution from his race. But by the side of these very passages we trace the continued recognition of a mythology, in which truth and purity are overborne together, and the very throne among the gods is given to triumphant sin. Now this fact, that the worshippers of heathenism were often better than their gods—that on the side of man there had grown up a reasonable and orderly society, while the mythology in which they still acquiesced presents a mere tissue of repulsive vices—this fact seems to admit of no other explanation than that which we have traced in the words of Scripture; namely, that such mythologies had germinated at an earlier date in the corruption which had followed on the wilful loss of Divine knowledge, and had simply lived on unchallenged through the force of habit, till a time when the plastic power, to which they owed their birth, had passed away.

2. It is obvious that such systems contained no lingering element of religious life to keep them on a level with any national improvement, which God's Spirit might vouchsafe to quicken. But even if contemplated at a higher stage than that of ultimate corruption, they were exposed to a second objection, in addition to this mixture of gross error with their truth—in the fact, that the whole framework by which their particles of truth are rounded out into a system betrays the handiwork of man rather than the inspiration of God. We are here brought back to the great distinction, which I have before referred to, between God's words to man and man's thoughts of

God (15). Review in memory the various outlines which we trace amongst the religions of mankind; take the coarse conceptions of old Nature-worship; include the higher moral elements which find occasional admission to the complex mythologies of Egypt, Greece, or Rome; pass onward to a wider sphere, and scrutinise the mystic systems which the East has furnished; extend the examination from religions properly so called, to the speculative efforts of the philosophic faculty; and in all cases alike the conviction ever deepens more and more, that they present the very opposite character to that by which the whole course of revelation is distinguished; that in every detail below the few grand principles which God had really implanted in their hearts, these theologies or philosophies are man's thoughts of God, and not the words of God to man. We can trace the very tide-marks as the waves of speculation rise and fall; while the revelation of even the earliest Scriptures stands out clear before us like a rock. It was the enslaved imagination which led men through the mazes of mere Nature-worship; it was the self-absorbed intellect which entangled him in riddles on the infinite and finite; it was the debased fancy which enabled him to project his own vices on the mists which surrounded him, and to worship those vices as gods. His own thoughts thus bore their unconscious witness to the fatal loss of that Divine communion which had formed the true life of the spirit. Men felt after the lost clue in the midst of their darkness. They invented formulas of varying value, by which they hoped that they might reconnect the broken links of union, and join again the sundered human and divine. At one time Deity is figured under a spurious incarnation; the infinite masking in the visage of the finite. At another time man himself is deified; the finite is invested with imaginary attributes, which are borrowed from vague conceptions of the infinite God. At other times, again, dim intermediate phantoms are imagined, to fill, if they could but really fill, the vast and dreary void which interposes between earth and heaven. Such are three main classes of religious speculation. But mark well their essential characters, and you will find that the first destroys the human; the second destroys the divine; the third obscures both by its dim series of shadowy beings, who have no true semblance of *either* human or divine. Compare the best of them with the religion which the ancient Israelites were taught; and they seem like trembling mosses, which afford no footing, in contrast with a solid causeway, stretching strong and firm through the morass. Or we might change the figure, and say that they are but ghostlike apparitions of the heated brain; while Scripture revelation represents the living figure which reaches out its powerful arm to save us from the dim caverns of unaided thought.

3. But to bring this contrast to a more definite issue, let us turn to St. Paul's discourse at Athens, where the 'chief speaker'[a] among the apostles addressed himself to the most cultivated population in

[a] Acts xiv. 12.

the Gentile world. The Apostle's argument is strictly framed on his own principle, that it is well to become all things to all men, in the sense of appealing to each, if possible, upon the basis of some general and conceded truths[a] (16). To the Athenians he offers no reasonings from Moses or the Prophets. The common law of conscience, the words of their own poets, the creed of their own philosophers, the inscriptions on their own altars—these furnish the text of the argument by which he introduces the revelation of our Lord. Commencing with a recognition of their zeal for religion, he avails himself of the inscription, 'To an unknown God,' which seems to have been the natural expression of a desire to propitiate a local deity, whom man would not be always able to identify and name. By this reference he would command some attention from the more religious of the people, who had filled their city with its groves of shrines. Other parts of his discourse would secure agreement from a different class. His philosophic hearers would accept his repetition of St. Stephen's declaration, that 'the most High dwelleth not in temples made with hands.'[b] All schools and parties would agree to the position, that the divine nature is *nihil indiga nostri*,[c] exalted far above the need of such unworthy homage as the hearts and hands of man could furnish; and many would respond to the words of their own poets, who proclaimed that man is the offspring of God. For each of these principles St. Paul could claim a

[a] 1 Cor. ix. 20–22; 2 Cor. iv. 2.
[b] Acts vii. 48.   [c] Lucret. ii. 649.

separate assent from some around him: that, in some dim sense, man is the son of God; that the obligation of worship extends even beyond our knowledge as a fundamental duty of the human spirit; that the speculative mind, however, must regard the Deity as residing far back in the recesses of unseen infinity, beyond the reach of human perturbations, and, as some of his hearers might have wished to add, beyond the sound of human prayers. On these he constructs an argument, which corrects each one of the three partial errors, and raises the whole from contradictory guesswork to consistent truth. The creed of philosophers would fix the true value of that cluster of temples which crowned the summit of the Athenian rock. The poet's claim of man's Divine paternity might suggest nobler thoughts of Deity than the poor expedients of idolatry could furnish. And to these, if only these could have borne the addition, the common creed would have added the obligation of worship, and would have denied the necessary existence of the barrier which philosophy had established between man and God.

'Hitherto,' as Bentley remarks, 'the Apostle had never contradicted all his audience at once; .... every point was agreeable to the notions of the greater party,'[a] till he came to the doctrine of the resurrection of the dead. But in each case there would be less agreement amongst his several hearers than they found respectively with him. The vulgar was blind

[a] Bentley's *Works*, iii. 31; ed. Dyce.

to the spirituality of God. The philosopher either doubted the possibility, or denied the use, of human worship. The dreams of sages had not closed one temple, nor banished one idol from the altars of the city. The phrases of poets had taught no Athenian to acknowledge that his slave or his captive had the claim of brotherhood, because moulded like himself in the image of God (17). All this did but conceal a hollow unreality under disjointed fragments of superficial truth; and Athenian poets and philosophers themselves would teach us that high aspirations, and acuteness in theory, and even the outward semblance of zeal for religion, were not incompatible with the toleration of even the most degrading sin.

And now, what was the Divine revelation by which the Apostle breathed fresh life and reality into these old and outworn semblances of truth? His 'new doctrine,' though compressed into these few verses, covers all three topics which fill the Divine element in Scripture; namely, God and man, and the relation which exists between them.

(1.) Of God he declared that He is at once the Creator of the universe, and the Preserver and the constant Governor of men. As Creator, He 'made the world and all things therein.' This is at once an advance on the whole tenor of ancient belief, which found in the alleged eternity of matter its futile explanation of the origin of evil (18). As Preserver, 'He giveth to all life and breath and all things.' These words disclose with the full weight of revelation the active presence of a personal and all-loving

LECTURE II. 63

God. As Governor, He fixes by His own decrees the epochs of all history. He decides by His own supreme authority the bounds, the dates, the destinies of nations. 'He ruleth,' as He taught a heathen monarch, 'in the kingdom of men, and giveth it to whomsoever He will, and setteth up over it the basest of men.'[a] In these few clauses we have a firm, clear, and consistent account of a creating, preserving, governing Deity, such as the scattered lights of heathen antiquity could never be combined to supply. And the same remark holds good if we turn to trace the truths which St. Paul interweaves with this teaching, on the true position of our human nature.

(2.) Two main principles are laid down on this subject; the one, that God 'hath made of one blood all nations of man;' the other, that He has endowed them with so indelible a consciousness of His existence, that in some dim way or other they never cease to 'feel after Him,' in hopes that they may 'find Him.' The one of these principles supplies a basis for the brotherhood of man, because all are children of one common Father; the other supplies a basis for practical religion, because all are thus endowed with something of a religious sentiment, the testimony to God which is written in their hearts, and which marks them as His human offspring. This doctrine, with its clear view of the proper dignity of human nature, puts an end to all distinctions between Greek and barbarian, between bond and free. And this

[a] Dan. iv. 17, 25, 32.

new creed of universal brotherhood must have come with the more impressive force when uttered by a Jew, as the outgrowth of the most jealous religion which the world had ever witnessed; the creed that God is no respecter of persons, announced by one whom Tacitus would have branded as the enemy of all humanity,[a] and who would but recently have despised the claims of any Gentile to share the blessings of the sons of Abraham. Thus the old view of human nature is as much enlarged as the old conception of the Deity was corrected and exalted. The Apostle had preached God, not as a vague abstraction, still less as the mythical ruler of a crowd of deities, imagined in the forms of men; but as man's Creator, Guardian, ever-bounteous Lord. He now sets man before us, by a corresponding revelation, not as the mere masterpiece of Nature, the mere summit of the series of the animated world; but as the sole earthly representative, through all his scattered tribes and families, of the image and likeness of God.

(3.) But it was the union between these two conceptions which formed the most distinctive message which St. Paul had been commissioned to convey. What is the true relation between man and God? That was a question which heathen knowledge failed to answer (19). How could man reach the true thought of the mystery of redemption, when so thick a darkness was resting over the history of his creation and his fall? This is the point on which St. Paul

[a] Tac. *Ann.* xv. 41 ('odio humani generis'); *Hist.* v. 5 ('adversus omnes alios hostile odium').

speaks with an emphatic force, befitting the central revelation to which his other arguments converge. There had been 'times of ignorance' with which God in His wisdom had borne for a season: such is his brief allusion to that night of darkness which Christ's advent had brought to its close. Now had arrived the true Redeemer of mankind. Now came the call to repentance, as the foremost duty of all who would share in the redemption He had brought. Now came the Gospel of the risen Saviour, whose second advent was appointed for the judgment of the world. In this great truth the apostolic message finds its height and termination. God as our Redeemer is more than Creator, more than Guardian, more than King. All are authorised and urged to claim that redemption, on the sole condition that they fulfil the requisite of repentance, and render faithful obedience to the commandments of Christ. How far is he thus raised above the dark enquirer, who was feeling doubtfully, and often erroneously, after God! God is now found to be indeed 'not far from every one of us;' ready to make these bodies His temple. Where is the power of heathen worship, where is the worth of heathen speculation, beside the preaching of the glad and certain tidings of the resurrection of Christ Jesus, as the firstfruits and assurance of our own?

This is the Divine creed, then, which St. Paul announced to the Athenians, instead of their popular superstitions or their philosophic theology: — faith in a God who was not satisfied to rest in grand seclusion in the highest heavens; but who issued forth, in the depth of untold ages, to create a universe which it was His pleasure thenceforward to protect and rule. Not only so, but He peopled this world with intelligent beings, on whom His own image was impressed. Nor only so, again, but when that image had been defaced by the sin of His creature, He came from heaven to earth, and 'was delivered for our offences, and was raised again for our justification,'[a] and reopened the avenue of intercourse through which man might receive the grace of God. This is He in whom we too live and move and have our being; to whom we owe not only the full perfection of our human existence, but the lower blessings of vital organisation, and even the privilege of life itself, which rests as its sole basis upon Him. This is He to whom we further owe the certainty of future resurrection, which raises our anticipations above the diversified guesswork of a wider circle than was represented in the Athenian audience of St. Paul — above the annihilation which was expected by Samaritan and Sadducee, as well as Epicurean — above the absorption which was looked for by Oriental and Arabian Pantheists, in common with at least some teachers of the Stoics — above the purely intellectual individuality of the resurrection which the Gnostic believed to be past already[b] — above that highest faith in immortality, without a resurrection, which limited the loftiest term of hope to which man had ever reached independently of Christ (20). Truths like these we should not repeat,

[a] Rom. iv. 25. [b] 2 Tim. ii. 18.

even in this hasty general outline, without offering, as we pass, the earnest prayer that we may not make a hollow formalism of Christian doctrines which the Apostle preaches as an earnest life.

Trace back that line of light to the beginning, and the farthest point you reach still leaves you in the presence of the same truths; on the one hand, the high capacities and aspirations, yet the mean achievements of mankind; on the other hand, the unity, the immutability, the power, the righteousness, yet with all of these the love of God. Re-examine throughout history the systems of Paganism, and they offer precisely the same contrast to the truths of revelation which we have traced in the Athenian sermon of St. Paul. The highest heathen creeds of God were partial; representing Him now as a power, now as a law, now as a distant abstraction, and now as the capricious likeness of a human despot. But revelation combines the partial truths which each of these several creeds had covered, and excludes the falsehoods by which those truths had been neutralised. This it does by declaring that, though almighty, though unchangeable, though veiled in the light which no man can approach unto, God is described most faithfully and most completely when we address Him as the Father of mankind. God is our Father; Christ is our Brother; the bond of brotherhood is the indwelling Spirit. All men everywhere are sons of God, and all men everywhere are therefore brethren of each other. All are of one blood. All spring from the same first parents. All are bound together by the universal ties of common kindred. All may hope to find perfection in a common heaven. That image of God, through which we hold our Divine sonship, is stamped as certainly, if not as brightly, upon the rudest savage of the Eastern seas as upon the noblest representative of European culture. And the practical expression of this common sonship is the obligation of universal charity; 'for he that loveth not his brother whom he hath seen, how can he love God whom he hath not seen? And this commandment have we from Him, that he who loveth God love his brother also.'[a]

Such is the general character of the Divine element in Scripture, and such the contrast it presents to the false religions of the heathen world, even when the scanty grains of truth which they embody have been most carefully numbered and recognised. I have not wished to dwell at any length on the darker features of ancient superstition — its sensuality, its cruelty, the degradation of its more debasing rituals, the foul enormities of Nature-worship. We need not follow out our argument to those remoter consequences, when it can be sufficiently established by the contrast of revelation with the fairest forms of belief which the purest of man's own thoughts can unfold. If we confine our attention to our Saviour's incarnation, the contrast will assume its loftiest and most striking aspect. That incarnation re-established under new

[a] 1 John iv. 20, 21.

conditions the relations held by man to God. In seeking for its parallel, let us exclude the mere guesses of a so-called natural religion; let us exclude the few remnants of old tradition which were constantly escaping from men's feeble grasp; let us confine ourselves to the purest theology which the speculative thinker could maintain as credible and could attempt to support by argument; and we shall find that the Deity which we are told to accept is no more than an intellectual reflection of man's highest mind, the postulated perfection of all indications of goodness which are confessedly imperfect in man; and the chief proof of His existence is only the apparent convergence of our highest thoughts towards some centre of supreme intelligence far from the sphere of human action (21). To the general range of the more thoughtful minds among the heathen, no ray of the Divine brightness seemed to rest upon the business of our common life. To be finally absorbed and lost in His glory might be the ambitious vision of the sage; but there was no hope nor reward in such a Deity for the man condemned to active labours; as the whole field of action, like some dark and confused battlefield, where fallen good was wrestling with evil, was excluded from, because unworthy of, its light. If such a creed had any common ground at all with ours, it lay simply in this, that both alike believe that God 'only hath immortality, dwelling in the light which no man can approach unto, whom no man hath seen, nor can see.'[a]

[a] 1 Tim. vi. 16.

But this, which is the remotest point in our vision, was the nearest point in theirs. They had no knowledge of the glorious range of truths which lie between us and that distant heaven. They knew nothing of Him who once spoke 'unto the fathers by the prophets,' and who, 'in these last days,' hath 'spoken unto us by His Son;'[a] nothing of God as a distinct and personal Being, who is invested with certain declared attributes, who watches with the tenderest mercy over every creature of His hand, who hears and answers every fervent prayer, and who will receive His faithful servants when their work is done, to restore them completely to His Divine image, and to employ them in endless adoration round His throne.

The fatal defect, then, of false religions is the impassable chasm which, in spite of every effort to the contrary, seems to separate their worshippers from any God who is worthy of their adoration. The more thoughtful heathen have acknowledged this, and acquiesced in it, silent, if not satisfied. They have translated the feeling into philosophic language. They have hardened it down into the formal creed which pronounced that the Deity was inconceivably above all knowledge, and which scarcely needed to pronounce the implied yet far more bitter sentence, that He was therefore inconceivably above all love. In this temper they have striven to describe the deep serenity of that untroubled intelligence, that unfathomable sea of central light, on which no shadow

---

[a] Heb. i. 1, 2.

should be reflected from the tainted atmosphere of worlds which are overclouded by misery and sin (22). The recoil from this feeling doubtless had some influence in perpetuating the gods many and lords many of Polytheism. Idolatry, however strange and debasing in its forms, is but the unconscious testimony which is borne by ignorance and frailty to that craving of the human spirit for some nearer and more accessible representative of Deity than they could find in the remote abstractions of an intellectual God. It was an effort in each case to bridge over the abyss which reduced man to a hopeless exile from heaven. It has ever failed, and must ever fail, to yield the slightest breath of consolation, because the phantoms which it raises are no reflections of the Deity, but are mere shadows which men project on the dark clouds that surround them — shadows which exaggerate mere human attributes, the worship of which is pure self-worship, veiled beneath a thin disguise.

That gulf, which man had found impassable, was destroyed for ever at our Saviour's incarnation, when the Eternal Son of the Eternal Father vouchsafed to clothe Himself with the garments of Time. That doctrine lays hold at once of earth and heaven, and brings them into union through the Person of our Lord. Christ was Man; and He has left us the noblest example of all loving and tender sympathy for man: but He was also God; and it is the duty of His followers to lift their thoughts from earth to heaven, and seek to fit themselves for entrance there. The heathen might fear God; might marvel at each witness of His majesty and power; might catch their echoes in the spheres of heaven, and trace their reflections in the rushing river or the ancient mountain. But it was the incarnation alone, in promise or in fulfilment, which made it possible for man to entertain the thought of *loving* God. Christ is God's image, and He is love: therefore we know that God is love. In seeing Christ we see the Father: therefore we know that in loving Christ we love the Father. And thus the gulf is bridged over; the dark clouds are rent asunder; the prayers of earth are heard in heaven. We can pass on from that cheerless image of the far-off unfathomable sea of light; we can pass on to the touching Gospel picture of the father who fell on the neck of the returning prodigal. And thus, through the portals of the holiest manhood, we rise to the conception of the absolute Divine.

Let no shadow steal across the vision of our spirits, to separate our souls again from God. There have been many such to shed a baleful deadness over the darkening eye of man. There is the dreamy mistiness of a remote abstraction; there is the vulgar heathenism of a debased idolatry; there is the miserable formalism of a lifeless and uninfluential creed; there is the chilling falsehood of an unloving intellectual faith. What are these things when contrasted with the warm devotion of a Christian heart, which searches the Holy Scriptures daily for the living witness which they bear to Christ? We know whom we have

LECTURE II.

believed.^a We are redeemed; but it is by a personal Redeemer, whose words of love are left to guide us. We are called to be sanctified; but it is by the personal Spirit, whom that glorified Redeemer sends to testify of Him.^b The voice of our prayer and praise can reach the loftiest throne of Deity; but it is because Christ has enabled us to approach God as our Heavenly Father. 'The word was made flesh and dwelt among us;'^c and we, who never saw His glory, may now attain a still higher blessing, if we reach Him in faith through the Holy Scriptures, and realise throughout that sacred Presence which fills their earthly framework with the Spirit of the Lord.

[a] 2 Tim. i. 12.   [b] John xv. 26.   [c] John i. 14.

LECTURE III.

1 Cor. xiii. 12.

'Now we see through a glass, darkly; but then face to face.'

THE reality of Scripture revelation has been thus far dealt with as a question of simple fact, which could be established by the ordinary branches of evidence, and confirmed by the contrast with heathen religions. But when we advance from revelation to inspiration, and state the grounds for our belief, that Scripture not only contains a true Divine message, but is throughout the work of inspired writers, whose inspiration still addresses our own spirits through the language which they used, we must proceed from the proof of that external fact to trace the general character of the conditions under which the revelation was recorded. There are two of these especially which seem to call for consideration at the present time; namely, the Scriptural use of antinomies and of double senses:—the one subject determining the mode in which great truths were brought within the range of the human intellect; the other subject supplying a leading proof of the Divine authorship, in the existence of a depth of significance which the human authors could not have commanded. To these two topics I propose to invite attention in the present and the next succeeding Lecture.

We need not enter here upon the general question of the limitations which the laws of thought impose upon the forms in which we receive this revelation from God (1). It cannot be doubted, as the Church has always held, that Scripture employs a kind of economy, accommodation, or condescension, to adapt the eternal truths which it reveals for admission within the range of finite thought. But for my present purpose I may venture to assume, that though these restrictions cause such disclosures to be constantly expressed under the form of double and contrasted statements, yet the revelation which results is as absolutely true as the love of God could make it for the children of His hand ; that the adaptation of truth to inferior capacities involves no loss of any fraction of its living power; and that the seen may be accepted as an index to that mysterious unseen, which it is confessed that its symbols cannot adequately measure. If proof were needed, we should find in it such declarations as these:—that man was created in the image of the unseen God, and that he retains a true though broken impress of that image even since his fall [a] (2) ; that God's perfection is the standard at which our feeble efforts are encouraged to aim ; that God's mercy is the pattern which man

[a] Gen. ix. 6 ; Ps. viii. 5, 6 ; Acts xvii. 29 ; 1 Cor. xi. 7 ; James iii. 9.

ought to imitate, as He shows it by making His sun to rise on the evil and on the good, and by sending rain on the just and on the unjust.[a] It is plainly indispensable that man should know clearly what God is, before he can hope to restore to its original brightness the likeness of God, which was tarnished by sin. Or again, we find it in such truths as these:—that even through the veil of nature, 'the invisible things' of God 'are clearly seen, being understood by the things that are made;'[b] that even 'Gentiles which have not the law' 'shew the work of the law written in their hearts;'[c] and above all, that 'God, who commanded the light to shine out of darkness, hath shined in our hearts, to give the light of the knowledge of the glory of God in the face of Jesus Christ.'[d]

We have already seen that no doubt is left on the medium of communication, through which these eternal truths are granted to mankind. On our side, 'there is a spirit in man, and the inspiration of the Almighty giveth them understanding.'[e] On the side of God there is the gracious influence which 'the Father of spirits'[f] sends into our hearts, through the personal agency of His quickening and enlightening Spirit. The Divine intercourse, which sin had interrupted, was reopened on the advent of our Saviour, in whom 'dwelleth all the fulness of the Godhead bodily.'[g] The conditions under which we

[a] Matt. v. 45, 48.   [b] Rom. i. 20.
[c] Rom. ii. 14, 15.   [d] 2 Cor. iv. 6.
[e] Job xxxii. 8.   [f] Heb. xii. 9.
[g] Col. ii. 9.

enjoy that communion are prescribed by a specific revelation, which protects us from the uncertainty of human fancies ; and they are maintained by the continuance of an organised society, which exists through the promise and presence of the Spirit. Within these bounds it is, that what we apprehend by faith becomes the subject of our knowledge; and though that knowledge is still partial and imperfect, its portions are all absolutely true. We see, as St. Paul says, δι' ἐσόπτρου, ἐν αἰνίγματι· as though the rays were received on an imperfectly reflecting mirror, which gives an incomplete representation of the figure which is thrown upon it (3). Yet though the form of the revelation may be adjusted to the laws of human thought, we cannot hesitate to believe that in its substance and reality it is the most direct reflection of the truth of Heaven which could be cast upon the spirits of a fallen but regenerated race. The Giver of revelation was the Maker of man's nature; and we cannot doubt either His will or His power to adjust the conditions of the one to the other. Whatever impediments, then, may have existed, either through the general imperfections of our fallen race, or through special obstructions in particular cases, it may be safely assumed that Scripture never fails to reveal as much spiritual truth, in as explicit and direct a shape, as the qualifications of its hearers would permit them to receive. I proceed to apply this doctrine to the antinomies of Scripture, or those apparent contradictions which, from the earliest days of ancient heretics, the gainsayer has gathered from the sacred page (4).

The subject has indeed an apologetic value; though that point is secondary to my present purpose. Whatever freedom of interpretation may be claimed under the formularies of the English Church, it is allowed that one restriction at least is expressed in terms which cannot be mistaken. She has explicitly disclaimed the power of so expounding 'one place of Scripture that it be repugnant to another;' and she has been careful to guard against any revival of the Marcionite heresy, by asserting that 'the Old Testament is not contrary to the New.'[a] This rule is obviously of vital importance. Whatever may be the relation between Scripture and science, it is clear that on all such subjects as fall within its proper province, the voice of Scripture must be consistent and uniform; for a trumpet which gave 'an uncertain sound'[b] could never be the instrument of God. If Scripture, then, could be convicted of contradictory teaching on any moral or religious question, it would follow that some erroneous tendencies in the human element had been strong enough to modify the influence of inspiration. If it can be shown, on the other hand, that the alleged cases of contradiction are really conformable to the limitations of the human intellect, and consistent with our reasonable expectations on the character of a Divine revelation, we shall not only remove a difficulty, but establish an evidence, which will be all the stronger for the fact that it did not lie upon the surface, and was not unfolded without

---

[a] Art. xx. vii.   [b] 1 Cor. xiv. 8.

enquiry and thought. To this subject, therefore, let us now address ourselves, reserving for a future time one portion of it, namely, the moral difficulties connected with some events in the older Scriptures which might be treated as contradictions to the spirit of the Gospel. It will be more convenient to treat of these moral difficulties at a later stage of our argument, and to approach them rather from the human side.[a]

We must, in the first place, be careful to distinguish between contradiction in the *text* and contradiction in the *comment*. The mere fact that opposite theorists are equally ready to claim support from Scripture, is not always sufficient to raise even the presumption of contradiction in Scripture itself. There is no difficulty in understanding how truth in the text is consistent with error in the comment, even when the inference has been honestly drawn. For it is the common characteristic of mistaken views, that they rest more frequently upon an exclusive or exaggerated statement of a truth than upon the positive assertion of a falsehood (5). Persons who have strongly realised the importance of some principle which they believe to be the only key for unlocking the mysteries of either religious or philosophical difficulty, are unwilling to concede the rights of any complementary statements which may claim to take rank by its side. Limitations, abatements, compromises, and qualifications, seem to curtail the fair proportions of a cherished

[a] See Lecture VI.

doctrine. They reduce it to the lower dignity of only half a truth; and they are proportionably distasteful to those eager tempers which resent the suggestion that their cardinal dogmas may require a counterpoise, as an insult to the authority, whether of theory or revelation, on which those dogmas are believed to rest.

Yet it is the characteristic feature of the highest principles, that they cannot be reduced to the simplicity of one expression, but can only be set forth fully in contrasted statements, of which neither is exclusively true. It is one main duty of religious philosophy to guard the equipoise on such subjects as evil or freewill against theorists who would push either into the fancied solution of a single extreme. You cannot treat evil as a lower form of good, without destroying the reality of man's hatred for sin. You cannot merge in one conception the contrasted ideas of personality and law, without obliterating either the distinction between mind and matter, or the distinction between man and God. Absorb will in law, and you contradict man's universal witness to the nature of the will as the causal source of all free action. Resolve all laws into the present operation of the will of God, and you destroy the belief in man's responsibility, while you cannot avoid the moral anomaly of regarding sin itself as an issue of His holy will. A large portion of the predestinarian controversy has arisen out of a similar attempt to exclude, on speculative grounds, either one or other of the two fundamental conceptions—the freedom of man and the supremacy of God.

LECTURE III. 81

If we turn from theory to Scripture (6), we trace the same law in those revelations of the Deity which constitute the central topic of the sacred record. It is thus that we are taught to believe in three Persons, yet one God : a unity of substance, which must not be divided ; a trinity of Persons, who must not be confounded. It is thus that we maintain the perfect manhood, yet the perfect Godhead, of the one Saviour, Christ our Lord; the union of two natures, which cannot be intermingled, in one Person, who cannot be divided. And when we pass from God's own nature to mark the relations which He bears to His creatures, we find that Scripture is equally explicit in bidding us recognise at once the foreknowledge of God and the freewill of man ; the omnipotence and love of God, yet the misery in which rebellion has plunged His creatures; the grace of God, and the perfect freedom of our own responsibility; and the double position held by man himself, as at once 'a creature, yet a cause.'[a] But it is not pretended that Scripture always pauses to adjust the balance amongst the truths which it reveals or declares. Hence it follows that errors resting on detached parts of most of the statements which I have mentioned, might be defended by isolated extracts from Scripture : and it is the same system of partial quotation which has in every age been employed by one-sided reasoners, who have tried to 'set the word itself against the word;' Deuteronomy against Leviticus,

[a] *Lyr. Ap.* xlii.

G

and Ezekiel against Deuteronomy; Prophets against Moses; the New Testament against the Old; one Evangelist against another; the Epistles against the Gospels; St. James against St. Paul.

But if inferences and interpretations need abatement, it does not follow that we may extend that process to the truths on which they rest. There is very little promise in any attempt to effect a union between two such principles by paring them down till they can be adjusted together, and thus robbing each of some portion of its strength and meaning. Such compromises seldom fail to weaken both the truths which are thus forced into unnatural combination. It is better to acknowledge at once that passages of this kind bring us into the presence of one of those antinomies which can be traced as clearly in Scripture as in reason, and in which the appearance of contradiction is produced by the fact that two contrasted propositions contain an incommensurable element, which creates in our mind the impression of two opposite allegations (7).

The causes of this phenomenon are twofold. In some cases we should readily accept the one truth but for the presence of another which is equally authoritative. At other times we realise the difficulty for ourselves whenever we make the effort to fathom a principle which baffles the operation of our thought. Disclosures of pure revelation commonly belong to the former class. We should rest satisfied with the one half-truth, if the other were not given to counterbalance it. But whenever we approach those mysteries which are more closely analogous to the antinomies of reason, we could work out the obscurity on either side by simply unfolding the impossibility of resting satisfied with either extreme. It is just as with the familiar commonplaces; that we can conceive neither greatness which admits of nothing greater, nor littleness which admits of nothing less; that the mind fails equally when we try to understand either the beginning of time, or the eternal succession of past ages without a beginning. A similar difficulty emerges if we attempt to grasp such a thought as that of infinity. The notion that we comprehend it is a mere deception. We think of it as though it were some vast mountain confronting us, which stretches on all sides into limitless space; or some ocean reaching away before us, whose waves are bounded by no farther shore. But let us note the fallacy: as confronting ourselves, those conceptions are finite; the mountain has its limit toward us; the sea has its verge on which *we* stand. In claiming for ourselves an independent position, we do ourselves place a limit or condition on the infinite; and it seems as though we could not escape the difficulty without merging our own individual being in some self-destructive creed of Pantheism. We cannot wonder that this cause also should have given rise to many seeming contradictions in Scripture. We could expect nothing else on the assumption we began with, that Scripture conveys a revelation on points to us so incomprehensible as the relation between the infinite and the finite, or the relation between eternity and time (8).

We might easily draw up from Scripture a long list of such contrasts, presenting in each case the semblance but not the reality of contradiction. Besides the instances which have been mentioned, we might cite such illustrations as the following :—the changelessness of God's purpose, yet its adjustment to the ever-varying will of man ; the universality of His laws, yet the minute watchfulness of His special providence ; His perfect holiness, yet His longsuffering patience with a sinful race; the object of Christ's coming as compared with its results ; and the connection between God's superintending care and the sedulity which is demanded from ourselves. The texts referred to would be such as these :—'God is not a man, that He should lie, neither the son of man, that He should repent;' yet 'it repented the Lord that He had made man on the earth.'[a] He dwelleth 'in the light which no man can approach unto;' yet He is about *our* path, and about *our* bed, and spieth out all *our* ways.[b] With Him 'is no variableness, neither shadow of turning ;' yet He is emphatically a God that hears and answers prayer.[c] He 'tempteth' not 'any man;' yet 'God did tempt Abraham.'[d] 'The pure in heart' 'shall see God;' 'whom no man hath seen nor can see.'[e] 'Thou art of purer eyes than to behold evil, and canst not look on iniquity;' yet 'Thou hast set our misdeeds before Thee, and our secret sins in the light of Thy counte-

---

[a] Num. xxiii. 19 ; Gen. vi. 6.
[b] 1 Tim. vi. 16 ; Ps. cxxxix. 2.   [c] James i. 17 ; Ps. lxv. 2, &c.
[d] James i. 13 ; Gen. xxii. 1.   [e] Matt. v. 8 ; 1 Tim. vi. 16.

nance.'ᵃ 'On earth peace,' was the angelic message; 'not' 'peace, but a sword,' was our Lord's interpretation.ᵇ 'Man is born unto trouble as the sparks fly upward;' yet 'the Lord is loving unto every man, and His mercy is over all His works.'ᶜ 'Turn ye unto me, saith the Lord of Hosts, and I will turn unto you;' yet 'Turn Thou us unto Thee, O Lord.'ᵈ 'What I say unto you I say unto all, Watch;' yet 'except the Lord keep the city, the watchman waketh but in vain'ᵉ (9).

In some of these instances reconciliation is easy. There are others in which the apparent contrariety may be diminished by devout meditation, with the assistance of the Holy Spirit. There are others, again, which carry us up into the presence of the highest mysteries—the relation between the finite and the infinite; and the possibility of evil in a world which is governed by perfect power, wisdom, and love. In dealing with doctrines so vast and obscure, we can do no more than fix the limits of our ignorance, and take care that it shall not be mistaken for knowledge. Yet it is clear that on considering the analogies of reason, and the perplexities which confront us in all speculations on the same topics, a true interpretation would not admit that in any one of these examples either side has been overstated by the inspired writer, or needs the modification which a diluting exposition would supply. And from this

---

ᵃ Hab. i. 13; Ps. xc. 8.   ᵇ Luke ii. 14; Matt. x. 34.
ᶜ Job v. 7; Ps. cxlv. 9.   ᵈ Zech. i. 3; Lam. v. 21.
ᵉ Mark xiii. 37; Ps. cxxvii. 2.

negative conviction we may advance to the positive assurance, that nothing short of inspiration could have given so clear and full an utterance to both the great truths embraced in each of these and similar questions, without in any instance flinching from the needful breadth of statement, and without in any instance leaving either half of the truth unguarded, by the provision of a counterpart in some other passage.

Many other texts of the same kind crowd upon the memory, in connection with both the revelation of God and the discipline of man. God condescends to reveal Himself under the form of labour, yet His eternal life must be existence of unstirred repose. He 'fainteth not, neither is weary;' yet 'He rested and was refreshed.'[a] *Quamvis ea quietus feceris, requievisti*.[b] 'He rested on the seventh day,' though His rest was never broken. And while thus resting, yet He rests not, as our Lord declares: 'My Father worketh hitherto, and I work.'[c] With regard to man, again, the regenerate are called holy, yet are liable to fall, and still burdened by 'the body of this death.'[d] The Church is to be spotless; yet wheat and tares must grow together in its borders till the harvest.[e] The conception of moral probation might be unfolded in a series of contrasted assertions, combining the spheres of man's accountability and God's control. No evil temptation can originate in God; yet He

---

[a] Isa. xl. 28; Ez. xxxi. 17.
[b] S. August., *Conf.* xiii. 51.   (*Opp.* i. 244.)
[c] Gen. ii. 2; John v. 17.
[d] Rom. i. 7, &c.; vii. 24.   [e] Eph. v. 27; Matt. xiii. 30.

LECTURE III.   87

permits what He does not originate. The forbidden
tree of knowledge stood within man's reach. Satan
was not debarred from entering Paradise to tempt
him. The Holy Spirit *led* our Lord to His temptation.[a] Balaam was allowed to go, yet condemned
for going.[b] The king whom Israel wished for was
granted as a token of God's anger.[c] It is God's law
of discipline to grant men their desire, and, through
that very concession of an ill-judged prayer, to send
'leanness withal into their soul.'[d] This is the solution of the paradox, that while it is His will that
all men should be saved, yet 'whom He will He
hardeneth.'[e] The key is found in the universal principle, that self-induced blindness is penal blindness,
according to that message of God through Isaiah,
which is quoted at each crisis in the Gospel history:
applied by Christ in three evangelists to the teaching
by parables;[f] applied by the fourth evangelist to
Christ's ministry, as it drew near its close;[g] and
applied by St. Paul to the position of his fellow-
countrymen, both when he was writing to the Romans
and when he was arguing with the Jews at Rome:[h]
'Hear ye indeed, but understand not; and see ye
indeed, but perceive not. Make the heart of this
people fat, and make their ears heavy, and shut their
eyes; lest they see with their eyes, and hear with their

[a] Matt. iv. 1, &c.   [b] Num. xxii. 20, 22.
[c] Hosea xiii. 11.   [d] Ps. cvi. 15.
[e] 1 Tim. ii. 4; Rom. ix. 18.
[f] Matt. xiii. 14; Mark iv. 12; Luke viii. 10.
[g] John xii. 40.   [h] Rom. xi. 8; Acts xxviii. 25.

ears, and understand with their heart, and convert, and be healed.'[a] He who framed the moral law, by contravening which the heart is hardened, may be said to have hardened the heart of Pharaoh, though it was Pharaoh's selfwill that really hardened it.[b] He who warns us against the bad influence of Satan, yet will not win for us that victory which the conditions of our moral nature bind us to achieve for ourselves, may be described as having 'moved David' to number the people, though Satan is elsewhere said to have 'provoked' the work.[c] The sin, in fact, was David's own; for all sin finds its real commencement in the offender's own responsibility of will. But the phrases of Scripture become clear when we remember that Satan was the tempter, and was thus accountable for the temptation; while God had created the nature and the laws which were perverted in that act of distrust and rebellion (10).

1. It will be clear, from the proofs already cited, that the method of Scripture rests upon the principle that the most direct way of grappling with such difficulties is to state each alternative, in its own proper place and connection, unreservedly, simply, and emphatically; leaving the task of reconciliation, which surpasses the powers of human intellect, to be either attempted by the higher faculties of the enlightened spirit, or postponed in all the confidence of faith, till the time when we shall cease to know in part. Con-

---

[a] Isa. vi. 10, 11.   [b] Ex. iv. 21, &c.; viii. 15, &c.
[c] 2 Sam. xxiv. 1; 1 Chron. xxi. 1.

LECTURE III. 89

centration is a foremost sign of earnestness; just as we say of the concentrated love of God,

'Thou art as much His care, as if beside
Nor man nor angel lived in heaven or earth.'[a]

It is the same with God's truths when proclaimed by His servants. Each fills the eye, and exhausts the attention, and strains the expressive power of human language. But why should we speak of God's servants only? Christ Himself did not pause to ward off misconstruction when He told us of the 'joy' that 'shall be in heaven over one sinner that repenteth, more than over ninety and nine just persons, which need no repentance.'[b] The elder brother in the parable asked a not unnatural question, when he remonstrated against the welcome granted to the prodigal, which seemed to make it more acceptable to sin and repent again, than simply to abstain from sin. Yet even then Christ would not qualify the revelation of the gladness of God's pardoning love. His answer does not remove the difficulty, though it is framed to calm down the jealous temper which the language of the elder brother had displayed: 'Son, thou art ever with me, and all that I have is thine. It was meet that we should make merry and be glad; for this thy brother was dead, and is alive again, and was lost, and is found.'[c]

2. This fearless recognition of the seeming contradiction which hangs over the expression of the highest

[a] *Christian Year*, Monday before Easter.
[b] Luke xv. 7.   [c] Luke xv. 31, 32.

truths, is still more forcibly illustrated when the two sides of the antithesis are brought close together in Scripture, without the slightest attempt to weaken either, by explanation or abatement. To this cause we might trace the common Scripture use of paradox; as in our Lord's own words, 'He that findeth his life shall lose it;' 'Let the dead bury their dead;' 'Whosoever hath, to him shall be given.'[a] St. Paul employs the same figure in such passages as these:— 'What I would, that do I not; but what I hate, that do I;' 'The foolishness of God is wiser than men, and the weakness of God is stronger than men;' 'She that liveth in pleasure is dead while she liveth;' and even in such single phrases as θυσίαν ζῶσαν, λογικὴν λατρείαν.[b] We trace it at an earlier date in such texts as that in Proverbs, which bids us answer, yet *not* answer, 'a fool according to his folly;'[c] and in the close reflection of the style of Scripture which we observe in some parts of the Apocrypha; for instance, in that striking passage: 'Weep for the dead, for he hath lost the light; and weep for the fool, for he wanteth understanding: make little weeping for the dead, for he is at rest; but the life of the fool is worse than death.'[d] From passages of this kind we may proceed to texts which compress the deepest problems in a single sentence. St. Paul condenses in one phrase the whole controversy on the limitation of the mind of man, when he prays that we may 'know the love

---

[a] Matt. x. 39; viii. 22; xiii. 12.
[b] Rom. vii. 15; 1 Cor. i. 25; 1 Tim. v. 6; Rom. xii. 1.
[c] Prov. xxvi. 4, 5.   [d] Ecclus. xxii. 11.

LECTURE III. 91

of Christ, which passeth knowledge.'ᵃ He brings within two words, κρίναντες ἐπλήρωσαν, the entire debate upon predestination and freewill; which is summed up again with almost equal brevity in that earliest of the apostolic Church's hymns: 'for to do —whatsoever Thy hand and Thy counsel determined before to be done.'ᵇ St. John presents in one view the double aspect of the Mosaic dispensation, when he says that the law of love is at once a new, yet not a new, commandment.ᶜ And the broadest antinomies are often found within the compass of a single paragraph; just as the same chapter in Samuel contains one assertion that God cannot repent, and two assertions that 'the Lord repented that He had made Saul king over Israel.'ᵈ Thus, again, in one chapter of Exodus we read, 'The Lord spake unto Moses face to face, as a man speaketh unto his friend;' and 'Thou canst not see My face, for there shall no man see Me and live.'ᵉ In two adjacent verses of St. John, Christ teaches that 'God sent not His Son into the world to condemn the world;' yet that 'he that believeth not is condemned already.'ᶠ In the same chapter of Romans, faith is described as both intellectual and moral; for 'faith cometh by hearing;' yet 'with the heart man believeth unto righteousness.'ᵍ One chapter of Galatians brings before us the contrasted spheres

---

ᵃ Eph. iii. 19.   ᵇ Acts xiii. 27; iv. 28.
ᶜ 1 John ii. 7, 8.   ᵈ 1 Sam. xv. 11, 29, 35.
ᵉ Ex. xxxiii. 11, 20.
ᶠ John iii. 17, 18. Cf. ix. 39; εἰς κρίμα ... ἦλθον· and xvi. 11.
ᵍ Rom. x. 17, 10.

of social sympathy and individual responsibility; 'Bear ye one another's burthens' (βάρη); yet 'every man shall bear his own burthen' (φορτίον).[a] Or to pass on to books from single chapters. In the 5th of St. John, Christ says, 'If I bear witness of myself, my witness is not true;' in the 8th He tells us, 'Though I bear record of myself, yet my record *is* true.'[b] In the 12th of St. Luke, He describes how the lord, on his return, makes his servants 'sit down to meat,' and serves them; in the 17th He asks, Who would say to his servant, when returning from the field, 'Go and sit down to meat'?[c] In the 9th of St. Luke He says, 'He that is not against us is for us;' in the 11th, 'He that is not with me is against me.'[d] In one place of the Gospels we are told to call ourselves 'unprofitable servants;' in another the same word forms part of the sentence of eternal death.[e] On this instance it has been remarked: 'Miser est quem Dominus *servum inutilem* appellat; beatus, qui se ipse'[f]—a solution which is capable of wider application, in so far as it suggests the mighty difference between the claim of merit and the bounteousness of grace (11).

3. The firmness of the faith which could record these sayings without an attempt to weaken their force by reconciliations, is further exemplified by the perfect freedom with which the sacred writers treat the apparent contradictions of our present life. A

[a] Gal. vi. 2, 5.   [b] John v. 31; viii. 14.   [c] Luke xii. 37; xvii. 7.
[d] Luke ix. 50; xi. 23.   [e] Luke xvii. 10; Matt. xxv. 30.
[f] Bengelius on Luke xvii. 10.

weak faith would tempt us to avoid the subject, or would try to gloze over its obvious difficulties. It would frame vain speculations, in which it would either shut its eyes on the reality of human misery, or would fall into the pantheistic error of treating evil as only a lower form of good. A strong faith acknowledges the pressure of the difficulty, and proclaims it in the frank and fearless confidence, that the obstacle will be hereafter found to lie in us, not in our Maker; in the weakness and uncertainty of our present vision, not in any limitation of either the power or love of God. We may observe a sort of sacred εἰρωνεία in the way in which the Jews used to deal with the darker problems of our present existence (12). They believed so firmly in God's immutability, that, as we have seen, they were not afraid to speak of His repentance, even in the very chapter in which it is recorded that He cannot repent like a man. They reposed such implicit trust in His righteousness, that they did not hesitate to complain of their afflictions in the language of strong expostulation. They relied with such confidence on His unfailing goodness, that they did not fear to deprecate actions which would rather have sprung from a hard taskmaster, in the very tone which a child might use towards a most loving parent at the moment when most completely assured of his love. Some have thought that, in this respect, the book of Job was a protest against Judaism. But what is there in the words of Job which is not urged by Jews themselves in other parts of Scripture? How can we distinguish the remonstrances of Job from those of Abraham and Moses, or the reproaches of Job from those of David, of Asaph, of Solomon, of Jeremiah?[a] And could anything show more clearly the real position of the double element in Scripture than the perfect submission with which, in the issue, these dark thoughts are put aside, yet the perfectly natural character of the human emotions, which are thus associated with the reception of the knowledge of God?

But it may be well to test these positions by a more detailed examination of two prominent instances, which have formed the favourite fields of controversy; namely, the apparent corrections supplied by later writings to the earlier teaching, and the seeming diversity on faith and works between the writings of St. James and St. Paul.

1. The commonest argument advanced by those who regard Scripture antinomies as real contradictions, is based on an attempt to prove that the later parts of Scripture are rather corrections than developments. The success of this attempt would justify the inference, that the Divine element must have been penetrated by an admixture of purely human imperfection, which it was afterwards found needful to withdraw.

The second commandment, it is urged, declares that the Lord God is 'a jealous God, visiting the

---

[a] Gen. xviii. 23–33; Ex. xxxii. 32; Num. xvi. 22; 2 Sam. xxiv. 17; Ps. lxxiii.; xciv. 3; Eccles. i. 3, 13, &c.; Jer. xii. 1; Lam. ii. 1, &c.; Hab. i. 2–4; Mal. iii. 15.

iniquity of the fathers upon the children unto the third and fourth generation of them that hate' Him, 'and showing mercy unto thousands of them that love' Him, 'and keep' His 'commandments.'[a] In explicit contrast, it is said, with both the warning and the promise, Ezekiel proclaims, with earnest reiteration, the distinct responsibility of each separate soul, alike for its good works and its sins: 'Behold, all souls are mine: as the soul of the father, so also the soul of the son is mine: the soul that sinneth, it shall die.' The just man 'shall surely live, saith the Lord God.' If the just man's son is evil, 'he shall surely die: his blood shall be upon him.' And if he, in turn, begets a son who abandons the evil courses of his father, the father shall perish, but the son shall be saved: 'he shall not die for the iniquity of his father; he shall surely live.'[b] The same principle is further applied to changes of character, so as to establish in every detail the rigid justice of the Lord (13).

Now in truth there is no real opposition between these contrasted statements. To call them contradictions is mere *ignoratio elenchi*; they cannot contravene each other, because their movement lies in different planes. The commandment is part of the law of the theocracy which fixed the external disparagement of sin among God's people; while the prophets were commissioned rather to enforce those deep truths of personal religion which a formal system,

[a] Ex. xx. 5, 6; Deut. v. 9, 10. Cf. 2 Kings v. 27, &c.
[b] Ezek. xviii. 4, 9, 13, 17.

even of Divine appointment, has always some tendency to obscure.ᵃ But the answer can be rested on a still wider basis. It is the universal law of God's providential government, that, in many external respects, the innocent *must* suffer for the guilty; and especially the innocent descendants for the crimes of a father. All experience abounds in proofs that those who indulge in vicious courses possess the fatal power of involving their descendants also in the outward penalties which vice entails: such penalties, I mean, as weakened constitutions and enfeebled bodies, in addition to the heavy heritage of a dishonoured name. This is the necessary consequence of our common membership one of another, and especially of that social unity which the theocracy exhibited in its most striking form. But social unity is not more certainly a law of God than that individual responsibility for which each will have to answer in the presence of his Judge. Not in any detail are these two at variance. They may act and react, like many other conditions in our state as men. Parental influence has a mighty force for good or evil, and the honour of the old is in their sons.ᵇ But in the crisis of our doom, all these things pass away like other adjuncts of our spiritual life. Each stands alone in the last appeal. Each heart knows its own bitterness.ᶜ Each conscience has to bear its own burthen. The words of the prophet might have stood side by side on the tables of the lawgiver with the words

---

ᵃ See above, p. 52.   ᵇ Prov. x. 1, &c.   ᶜ Prov. xiv. 10.

which were written by the finger of God.ᵃ It is equally true that God visits the iniquity of the wicked on their children, and that the soul that sinneth, it *alone* shall die.

But it is urged that there are many other passages in the Prophets which impose limitations on the claims of the Law, or point with increasing clearness to a time when those claims shall cease to be binding. That the Law itself asserted a paramount and durable obligation, seems to stand clear upon the surface of the record: 'Cursed be he that confirmeth not all the words of this law to do them.'ᵇ Thus Moses taught the people to regard it as permanent. He hedged it round with the most solemn exhortations. He pronounced a wide range of earthly blessings on obedience; and he strove to deter the disobedient by a fearful picture of national disaster, which far surpasses, in its anxious vehemence, the thought of any merely temporary warning, and which could not have been fulfilled by any calamity of lighter import than that which was inflicted at the fall of Jerusalemᶜ (14). Yet the inspired guardians of the Law have themselves deepened its teaching within the limits of the older Scriptures; and, as they gradually learnt to look forward to a brighter era in the future, have implied that the Law would cease to be obligatory when its types were fulfilled at the coming of the Christ.ᵈ But how is it,

---

ᵃ Cf. Ex. xxxii. 32; Deut. xxiv. 16; 2 Kings xiv. 6.
ᵇ Deut. xxvii. 26; Gal. iii. 10.   ᶜ Deut. xxviii. 15–68.
ᵈ Ps. cx. 4; Isa. lxvi. 21; Jer. xxxi. 31; Dan. ix. 26; Zech. vi.

we are asked, that they could thus be taught to lessen the pressure of a public obligation, which had been imposed under such solemn sanctions? Or what other sense can be put on such compositions as the 51st Psalm, or the 1st of Isaiah, or the 7th of Jeremiah, than that they really abate the force of the older statements on the value of atonements under the Law?

To the first point we should answer, that even human lawgivers are accustomed to speak with similar, if not equal, emphasis of laws which may nevertheless be repealed, should it be needful, by the power which imposed them; and it is right and natural that a still stronger impression should be given, in the case of laws which had a deeper significance than any human legislation could command, and when the power which had imposed them was Divine. It was enough that the same God who had spoken by Moses was known to speak as surely and as clearly by the prophets, whom He commissioned to explain His earlier ordinances. It was enough, too, that Moses had himself prepared the way for the change, by warning the people to expect a Prophet, who was to teach them with authority at least equal to his own.[a] Rights which are inherent in all earthly governments must be conceded to the Divine source of every government, by whose wisdom alone 'kings reign, and princes decree justice.'[b] But again, it is erroneous to suppose that the interpretations which were thus afforded brought any premature abrogation

---

13; Mal. i. ii., &c. Cf. Luke xxiv. 27; John i. 45; v. 16; Acts xxvi. 22.

[a] Deut. xviii. 15–22.   [b] Prov. viii. 15.

LECTURE III.

of the Law. They only recalled men from the vain practice of a formal obedience to the spirit which gives its sole value to obedience; in the temper of the lesson which Saul had long ago received from Samuel: 'Hath the Lord as great delight in burnt offerings and sacrifices, as in obeying the voice of the Lord? Behold, to obey is better than sacrifice, and to hearken than the fat of rams.'[a] Again, the precise position of the Mosaic dispensation is taught in the New Testament with a clearness which leaves nothing to be desired, and which is in perfect harmony with the deeper interpretation of the original record. When the life and death of Christ brought out in strong relief the fact that the Mosaic ordinances had been deeply marked by a typical character, it followed that, in the same extent and proportion, the temporary nature of their obligation would be recognised. At the same time it became clearer that the oldest Scriptures had established limitations of their force, and explanations of their meaning, which the later Jews had simply overlooked or forgotten. Thus Christ Himself reminded them that God had vouchsafed an earlier stream of revelation, which overruled the stipulations of the Law of Moses; and that a degree of knowledge had been granted to the patriarchal Church which the special objects of the Law had caused it in some measure to obscure. Of the Jewish marriage-law, for instance, He said that 'from the beginning it was not

---

[a] 1 Sam. xv. 22. Cf. Ps. xl. 6; l. 8, 14; li. 17; Prov. xxi. 3; Isa. i. 13; Jer. vii. 22; Hos. vi. 6; Mic. vi. 5, &c., and see Matt. ix. 13; xii. 7, &c.

so;' but that its Mosaic form must be attributed to the hardness of their hearts.[a] Circumcision, He also said, was not 'of Moses, but of the fathers;'[b] therefore it took precedence of the Mosaic Sabbath; and much more did mercy, as the obligation of a still earlier law (15). We have here the very outline of the argument, which St. Paul afterwards enlarged when he showed, by appealing to the revelation made to Abraham, that the Law possessed only a secondary and temporary character;[c] and that its narrow scope bore no proportion to the worldwide promise of a Saviour, who was to spring from among the sons of Abraham, and in whom all nations of the earth were to be blessed. Comparing the Law with the earlier and later revelations between which it stands, we see that, like both, it balances the gift of grace by the duty of obedience; the election of the Israelites to special privileges by their obligation to love the Lord their God with all their heart and soul and might.[d] But in all revelations alike, the greater stress is laid on that side of these twofold principles which most needed enforcing in each succeeding age. It is not true, however, that any age was ever left so completely to the undivided operation of the one principle, as to be pardonable for forgetting the other. The Jews had no defence for the spiritual blindness which had learnt to look for salvation to the thing that they saw, rather than to Him who is 'the Saviour of all.'[e] They had no excuse

[a] Matt. xix. 8. Cf. Matt. xii. 8; Mark ii. 27, 28, &c.
[b] John vii. 22.   [c] Gal. iii. 17.
[d] Deut. vi. 5.   [e] Wisd. xvi. 7.

for the confusion which had substituted the works of the Law for faith in the Promise; and which relied on that scrupulous legal obedience, which is at best the mere fruit and evidence of faith, as the meritorious ground for the acceptance which they owed solely to the favour of God. And the fact that Scripture, from time to time, counteracts similar errors by reiterating similar language, is a witness to its unity, the absence of which would cause a greater difficulty.

2. Let us pass now from the consideration of historical development to the leading example of alleged contradiction between contemporary writers; namely, the doctrine of faith and works, as respectively taught by St. Paul and St. James (16). But this familiar controversy really carries us back to the same antithesis which we have just been examining. It is traced by both inspired writers alike to the history of Abraham. It can be followed up to the earliest period in which we possess the terms of any covenant between man and God. Both elements were found in Paradise itself, where grace was given to make obedience possible; and then obedience was exacted, as the sole condition of continued grace. When that covenant was cancelled by the sin of man, the foundation of a new covenant was immediately laid, through which all mankind became sharers in certain promised blessings.[a] In the days of Abraham this covenant passed from general terms into the form of a definite assurance,

[a] Gen. iii. 15.

which constituted the election of a peculiar race. The conditions of that promise were, first, faith; and secondly, obedience. Abraham 'believed in the Lord, and He counted it to him for righteousness.'[a] Faith, then, which resigned all vain hopes of self-recovery from the low estate of fallen man—faith, which rested on a promised blessing, and which restored the heart of man to the Divine communion which sin had interrupted—faith came first, before the rite of circumcision was ordained. But after faith came obedience, of which circumcision was the sign, and of which that wonderful act of faith, the offered sacrifice of Isaac, was the most remarkable proof. There is no real difference in this point between the fundamental conceptions of St. Stephen, St. Paul, and St. James. All alike would place faith first, as the groundwork which made obedience possible. All alike would have allowed, though they might have expressed their meaning under different forms, that 'faith' afterwards 'wrought with' Abraham's 'works, and by works was faith made perfect.'[b] All alike would have agreed, that these works would have been worse than useless if they had been done in opposition to the spirit of faith; because that would have amounted to an assertion of independent ability, and would therefore have been equivalent to a declaration of rebellion.

If, then, it is certain that each branch of teaching is unquestionably true, and that each can be traced

[a] Gen. xv. 6; Rom. iv. 3.   [b] James ii. 22.

LECTURE III.

with equal clearness in the inspired records to which both make their appeal, it is surely unreasonable to allege that the apostolic upholders of these two positions could really contradict each other. What St. Paul urges is true: that the best works of man are worthless, if they are done without reliance on the help of God. But what St. James urges is equally true: that professed trust in God is spurious if it does not lead to active effort on the part of man. Works without faith would be the watchword of a self-asserting reliance on man's strength, and a denial of his need of grace. Faith without works is the symbol of that antinomian self-deceit, which substitutes a dreamy reliance on religious sentiments for a practical attention to religious duties. The contrast is the same which always emerges, when we compare the respective provinces of the labour of man and the grace of God: and the emphatic language used by each apostle is explained on the principle which I have endeavoured to lay down. Each states, strongly and forcibly, the truth which he was commissioned to deliver in opposition to prevailing error. St. Paul was confronting a system of formalism, which pleaded privileged position and ceremonial obedience as sufficient grounds for acceptance in the sight of God. St. James saw room to fear, that a belief in spiritual acceptance, independently of obedience, might sap the foundations of practical holiness. Each, therefore, supplies the half-truth which he saw to be deficient, yet without any real contradiction of the other; and the Holy Spirit has provided that, as both alike stand together in the canon, so the whole truth shall emerge from the union between them.

And now, without dwelling longer on diversities which are thus found to rest on a most intelligible principle, let me close this Lecture by calling attention to the opposite phenomenon, which is surely worthy of deep consideration. Much has been said of contrariety: what shall be said of that marvellous unity which reaches from end to end of Scripture, though veiled under a not less wonderful diversity in source, and character, and outward form? (17) The grand truths of Christian theology are revealed or confirmed by the voices of a long range of utterly dissimilar writers, speaking without the slightest possibility of concert; doing each his own duty, seeking each his appointed end; busied consciously with objects of comparatively small importance, while unconsciously furthering the far mightier purpose of delineating, stroke by stroke, and feature by feature, the great image of the revelation of God. No other book contains such unity of result; no other book has ever sprung from such diversified variety of source. It is the work of many men, in many lands, through many ages: the work of lawgivers and heroes, side by side with shepherds and herdsmen; the work of accomplished intellects and untrained peasants; embodying history and poetry, records of the past and predictions of the future, all degrees of legislation, all forms of enquiry, together with confessions of sin, and prayers for mercy, and hymns of triumph; leading up to the life of Christ set forth in the New Testament, and the letters by which the early Church was governed, guided, rebuked, and cheered. God, who called Elijah from the desert and Elisha from the plough, summoned others of His witnesses from flocks and cattle, as well as from the race of priests or lineage of kings. Moses spent the best forty years of his life as a keeper of sheep amongst the mountains of Arabia, nerving his spirit to high purpose in the solitude of the lonely desert. David was taken from the sheep-folds[a] to become an active warrior, a prudent ruler, a governor beset by the lifelong perplexities of complicated trials. Solomon was his 'father's son, tender and only beloved in the sight of' his 'mother,'[b] and became the wise king of a prosperous and settled kingdom, till he fell in old age under the temptations of luxurious opportunity. Isaiah and Daniel came from royal courts; Jeremiah, Ezekiel, Ezra, from the priesthood; while Amos was 'no prophet' nor 'a prophet's son,' but 'an herdman and a gatherer of sycomore fruit,' whom God chose to be a teacher as he was following his flock.[c] But why pursue a list which would simply repeat the name and circumstances of every known writer of Scripture, and complete the contrast between their vocation and their work? If we pass to the writings of Christ's first disciples, we find that they

[a] Ps. lxxviii. 70. [b] Prov. iv. 3.
[c] Amos vii. 14, 15.

too differed nearly as widely from each other and from all. The teachers of Christ's Church were chosen from the boat of the fisherman and from the seat of custom, as well as, like Paul, from the schools of learning, or, like Luke, as it seems, from the practice of science. Problems of disputed authorship only serve to increase the marvel. If the writers had less authority than the Church has ascribed to them, the unity which pervades their common message is a still more unanswerable testimony to the Divinity of its source. The alleged contrariety is the strongest proof of the unity. The argument from design receives in this case its most direct and conclusive application; and the sheer impossibility that such a result should have sprung from any human agency supplies us with the surest ground for our belief that it was throughout inspired and overruled by God.

This position forms the proper basis for the next enquiry on which I shall propose to enter; viz., the precise conditions of the *duplex sensus* — the real position of the literal meaning of Scripture in relation to the secondary senses which it is believed to have subserved.

LECTURE IV.

—✦—

Romans xv. 4.

'Whatsoever things were written aforetime were written for our learning, that we through patience and comfort of the Scriptures might have hope.'

IF we believe that Holy Scripture contains a revelation, which was made by God, 'at sundry times and in divers manners,'[a] through a varied series of human agents, we must expect to find that its language would be adjusted, in the first instance, to the level of the original hearers, and would yet be endowed with a power of rising far above that level, in proportion to the needs of more advanced humanity. The first of these conditions is obvious in itself, though it seems to be forgotten when men find stumblingblocks in such necessary results of it as the adaptation of Scripture language to the early state of scientific knowledge. The second is the basis for the doctrine of secondary senses—a doctrine which can be represented in so invidious an aspect as to make its defence a task of considerable difficulty (1). Let a writer be only suspected of maintaining that Scripture meant

---

[a] Heb. i. 1.

something different from what it seems to say; that its expositors are free from the laws by which all other classes of interpreters are bound; and that, in defiance of the canons of criticism, they may claim the right of relying solely on their private conceptions of 'that which is good to the use of edifying;'[a] and the reader is disposed to protest, without further hearing, against so insecure a method, and to maintain that it throws doubts upon the literal value of the written word.

Yet this doctrine seems inseparable from the conception of a revelation, which implies that the suggestions of a Divine Author lie behind the expressions of the human writer. If revelation be a condescension from the higher to the lower, if it be the transfusion of knowledge from a wider to a narrower sphere, the truths thus entrusted to the expressive power of an inferior language must embody a life and expansiveness which only need the fit occasion to burst forth. The spirit is tenanting an earthly framework, and can issue, when need is, from its narrow mansion, to shine in broader and distincter light. And so, in point of fact, through every portion of the inner mind of Scripture, we trace a clear capacity for future elevation, above the level of the writer through whom it was made known. This, I repeat, is precisely what we ought to have expected. Granting that the inspired writers were employed, not as mere mechanical instruments, but as God's chosen and enlightened

[a] Eph. iv. 29.

servants, speaking only under the guidance of the Holy Spirit; granting that the revelation would be moulded by the human element, and would bear broad traces of the individual characters of those through whom it was conveyed; we should still expect to find that the Divine meaning would rise far above the level of the human writer, and that his message would show signs of deeper truth and more comprehensive purpose than his words could compass or his mind could understand. I am not now dealing with that larger proof of inspiration, which is furnished by the intrinsic dignity of its teaching and its essential superiority to any truth which unaided reason seems to grasp. I am speaking solely of this formal characteristic, the capacity of spiritual development, as one of the chief internal credentials which we might expect to find, and which in fact we *do* find, in the book of revelation.

It is scarcely possible, for instance, to read the writings of the prophets, and compare them with their contemporary history, without the perpetual conviction that more was meant—not perhaps by the human speaker, but by the inspiring Spirit—than met the earliest listener's ear. Just as in complex harmonies of music we may detect the undercurrent of some simple and familiar strain, so we hear tones through the prophetic volumes which sound like parts of a wider and more commanding system—notes in a more extended chorus, responding across broad intervals of varied measures, and arresting attention by a depth of unity which no superficial diversity can hide.

Thoughts rise, as we read, which haunt us like the hidden signs of the Platonic ἀνάμνησις. We pass beyond the sacred writer with his obvious meaning, and see him to be the willing instrument of One whose purposes and mysteries he has not fathomed. He is a servant, not a master, of the truths which he declares, though his service is a glad and ready service. He is no more than a private in a mighty army, and knows little of the great designs which his obedient movements are directed to subserve. His tongue is controlled to utter words of larger import than is exhausted by the object on which the earnest attention of his present purpose is expended. Free from the sin of Balaam, he yet reminds us of the overruling influence which forced Balaam to pour forth blessings beyond his wish and prophecies beyond his thought. Free also from the blinded worldliness of Caiaphas, yet, like him, he speaks words which plainly come 'not of himself,'[a] but from the immediate suggestion of the Spirit(2). The peculiarity extends to the symbolical as well as the typical. The strain may begin with personal anger against an individual offender; but pursue it a moment, and you will find it purged from all the bitterness of earthly passion, and rising into righteous condemnation of sin. Or it commences with the glory of God's earthly temple, and then swells, as if the seer could not control his language, to describe the far-off vision of the eternal temple in its everlasting grandeur in the heavens.

[a] John xi. 51.

It is this capacity which St. Paul recognises in the words of our text : ' Whatsoever things were written aforetime were written *for our learning*;' or, as he elsewhere expresses it, '*for our admonition*;' or again, in other passages, '*for our sakes*,'[a] as well as for the sake of the original hearers. Taken in connection with the context, and illustrated by the method of his own quotations, the Apostle's meaning must amount to this, that the earlier Scriptures were intended to serve a wider purpose than the immediate occasion of their utterance furnished, or than the immediate agents of their disclosure comprehended. This is precisely what was meant by the double condition which I named at the outset. If the necessity that a revelation should first of all things be *intelligible* caused God's earlier disclosures to be modified in form by temporary considerations, the loftier use to which they were destined in the future prevented their full meaning from being exhausted by the applications to which they were confined for a season. A spiritual sense, then, must always have lain hid beneath the letter, and must have been gradually unfolded, in proportion to the elevation of the human faculties, in their deepest relation to God. We must admit the existence of that spiritual sense before we can trace the successive disclosures of the ever-brightening light which penetrates the letter of God's earlier word. Throughout the entire range of the Old Testament Scriptures, there exists a deeper signification than

---

[a] 1 Cor. x. 11; ix. 10; Rom. iv. 24.

the literal—a signification which is veiled alike under command and precept, type and symbol, history and prophecy, stern denunciation and triumphal psalm. On this basis rests the process of development which Christ and His apostles have unfolded. Throughout the New Testament, facts, prophecies, and simple precepts—disclosures of God's own nature, and records of the wanderings of men—the prayer of the penitent, the thanksgiving of the humble—the lamentations of the captive, and the triumphs of the conqueror—are all treated alike, as richly fraught with that double sense which Christ's advent brought to open light. Sometimes the proof of this is direct and simple. Such is the interpretation of the broader types and prophecies, which bore their distant witness to the person or the work of Christ. Such is that remarkable instance in which Christ Himself gave the explanation of God's patriarchal title—the God of Abraham, and of Isaac, and of Jacob; the God of the living, not the dead.[a] Such is St. Paul's mode of dealing with both primitive and Jewish history, in the facts of which he descries deep allegories, containing the germs of Christian doctrine. A complete account of this characteristic of Scripture would trace the gradual growth of prophecy, from its first faint lines to its most detailed disclosures; from the victory promised to the woman's seed up to the minute indication of so many particulars in Christ's personal history. It would teach us to recognise His image in

---

[a] Matt. xxii. 32.

LECTURE IV. 113

the heroes, who were raised as successive saviours for His people; in the Prophet, who was to be like unto Moses; the Priest, who was to hold an imperishable priesthood; the King, who was to claim the title of the royal David's Lord.[a] It would teach us to read Him alone in such types as the Star of Jacob, the Sceptre of Israel, the Root of Jesse, the Sun of Righteousness who was to 'arise with healing in His wings;'[b] to find Him alone in such historical shadows as the bread from heaven, and the uplifted serpent, and the water springing from the smitten rock;[c] to see in the sacrificial lamb the figure of 'the Lamb slain from the foundation of the world;' and to trace the minutest details of His passion in the victim who was led 'as a lamb to the slaughter;' in Him whose hands and feet were pierced; whose garments they parted; who was buried 'with the rich in His death'[d] (3).

The doctrine of the spiritual sense, then, rests on the belief that, in the composition of Scripture, it was God Himself who furnished or suggested the materials which His chosen servants, under His continued guidance, clothed in such language as their own intelligence and position prompted. The reality of the Divine element in Scripture is the truth on which the possibility of such senses must depend; for it implies that the *res* beneath the *voces*

[a] Deut. xviii. 15; Ps. cx. 1, 4. Cf. Acts iii. 22; Matt. xxii. 45; Heb. v. 6.
[b] Num. xxiv. 17; Isa. xi. 1, 10; Mal. iv. 2; Rev. v. 5, &c.
[c] Ex. xvi. 15; Num. xxi. 9; John vi. 31; iii. 14; 1 Cor. x. 4.
[d] Rev. xiii. 8; Isa. liii. 7; Acts viii. 32; Ps. xxii. 16, 18; Isa. liii. 9.

I

shall be significant as well as they^a (4). But before we proceed to further proofs and instances of that significance, we must premise one important principle, which has been too often overlooked in these discussions, namely, that such rights as might fairly be claimed for the human authors of the Scriptures, are in every case respected and reserved.

It cannot reasonably be doubted, that every inspired writer, even when unable to fathom the full import of his message, would still affix to every word he uttered some one primary and sufficient meaning, which would be directly connected with his special mission. In cases of prophecy, this is often plain and unquestioned. Amos must have thoroughly understood that God would transport His people beyond Damascus, even though he did not know, what the light of the fulfilment told St. Stephen, that they would be carried beyond Babylon also.^b Isaiah must have perfectly comprehended the sense in which he described the ruin of the King of Babylon as the fall of 'Lucifer, son of the morning,' though he might not be able to regard it as the type of that overthrow of the power of iniquity to which Christ referred when He said, 'I beheld Satan as lightning fall from heaven.'^c God's wrath against old guilty nations is expressed with as much clearness and precision, as if it had no further bearing on more spiritual forms of evil. The chastisements of Israel, and God's forgiveness on their repentance, are all as closely adjusted to the original circumstances as if

---

^a S. Thom. Aquin., *S. Th.*, I^{ma} Qu. i. Art. x. 3.
^b Amos v. 27; Acts vii. 43.   ^c Isa. xiv. 12; Luke x. 18.

they had never been meant to be extended to the whole Church of God. Precisely in the same way, to take an earlier instance, Abraham must have attached a definite significance to the Divine title when he called a place Jehovah-jireh, though we are told that God was not revealed to him by the full signification of His name Jehovah.[a] And to take a later instance, the words of Christ Himself, which were uttered by direct omniscience, bear as sharply and precisely on the fall of Jerusalem as if they were not coupled with other expressions of a broader range and deeper meaning, which can receive no earlier fulfilment than in the solemn events of His second advent. Or to turn to cases where prophets look back to the facts of history ; we may rest assured that Hosea was thinking of the Exodus as he wrote, ' When Israel was a child, then I loved him, and called my son out of Egypt;' and it is a mere misapprehension of the question to suppose that the believers in his inspiration are bound to maintain that he used these words with any primary reference to Christ[b] (5). The same remark applies to Jeremiah's allusion to the mourning of Rachel, which St. Matthew quotes in the same connection.[c] The prophets referred to well-known facts, and God had caused those facts to be typical. But the record of a typical fact becomes a prophecy, though it might not in all cases be known to be such at the time when it was written down. *Dum narrat gestum,*

---

[a] Gen. xxii. 14 ; Ex. vi. 3 (above, p. 50).
[b] Hos. xi. 1 ; Matt. ii. 15.   [c] Jer. xxxi. 15 ; Matt. ii. 18.

prodit mysterium.[a] Events in the Old Testament reappear as truths in the New Testament; but the prophets who cite them in their earlier character must on no account be put on the same level with the evangelist who was inspired to see their prophetic import, and to record the circumstances in which they were fulfilled. To recur to my former illustrations. The private understands the step that he is taking, though he knows but little of its ulterior objects; and the subordinate member of a numerous chorus sees clearly the note which he himself is striking, though he might be unable to tell you its exact position in the complex harmony of the great master. And this firm belief, that each writer thoroughly understood the primary meaning of his own language, is quite compatible with the conviction, that the true fulfilment, when it came, drew out a meaning far closer, deeper, and worthier, than the contemporary or intermediate application could supply.

There might, indeed, be repetitions of such provisional applications, as once and again the law took effect, the principle found expression in an historical event, and the prediction was strengthened by the addition of a type, which each such fact of history yielded (6). It was as though the reflection of the coming future rested brightly and yet more brightly on the crest of each advancing wave. But while each of these applications might be real in its own place, and might form a solid element in the onward movement

---

[a] S. Greg. Magn. *ap.* S. Thom. Aquin., *S. Th.*, I. i. Art. x. (*Opp.*, i. 635: 'Dum narrat *textum*,' &c.).

of events, still the sign of imperfection would be found to linger over all such partial shadows of the end. We could not mistake them for that exhaustive fulfilment which came at last to light up every line and feature in the mysterious forecast, when the advent of the grand reality brought the series of types and anticipations to its close.

Here, then, is the first caution which we must observe when applying the doctrine of secondary and spiritual interpretations of Scripture. We are by no means to suppose that any inspired writer was so mere a mouthpiece of the Holy Spirit, that he used words to which he did not himself attach a definite meaning; and that, too, a higher meaning than his own thoughts could have furnished. We are on no account to imagine that any sower of the seed of the Spirit could have been ignorant of the spiritual nature of his work. What we allege is, that over and above that one clear meaning in which the original writer used the words of Scripture, they are often found to cover a secondary and deeper sense, sometimes more than one such sense, which it was a function of the later revelation to disclose.

On the other hand, it is just as little to be thought that, after this second sense had been extracted, the first wholly lost its use and interest. The Mosaic laws, for instance, still retain their distinct value as the forms impressed by God Himself, for a most important purpose, on universal principles of right and wrong—a value which is entirely independent of such well-meant but questionable explanations as have been offered by Kabbalistic, Hutchinsonian, or Swedenborgian schools. Increased study only enables us to extend the remark with greater confidence to every portion of the older Scriptures; and to suspect that the Church was meant by her Master to apply, with careful sobriety of judgment, a similar interpretation for large portions of the New Testament. The earlier moral lessons, for instance, will no longer be thought to be the mere vehicles of an unrelenting sternness, fitted for the world's childhood, but unworthy of its maturity. We shall no longer look on that old Jewish zeal, which bore fruit in hatred for evil as well as love for good, as though it could yield no precedent for Christian conduct, no pattern meet for Christian men. The same is true of every portion of that ancient record. To the devout and enlightened Christian intelligence, the words of those elder Scriptures can never become like the narrow cottage which is abandoned to decay and desolation when its inmates have left it for an ampler home. Still less are they like the dead husk which may be cast away when the fruit has been secured, or like the dead body which may be buried when the spirit has departed. Rather they are still and for ever alive with the abiding presence of the indwelling Spirit; they rise in themselves to a nobler elevation, in proportion as their loftier meaning is unfolded: just as the image of the Saviour glorifies that long line of ancient worthies in which it was foreshown; just as what man might have mistaken for the petty laws and narrow policies of one small tribe in a secluded district swell out into the

LECTURE IV. 119

reflection of the everlasting country, when the Gospel discloses their eternal model, abiding in its glory in the heavens.

But our safest guidance on this subject must be sought from the recorded examples of the mode in which Christ and His apostles were accustomed to deal with the Old Testament Scriptures. Two main principles appear to be suggested by that enquiry: the one, which is again divisible into two parts, that facts in the history of God's ancient Church are regarded as sometimes symbolical, and sometimes typical—in other words, as indicative at one time of truths and at other times of events, which meet us in the history of the Christian dispensation; the other, that the enactments of the Mosaic system were frequently invested with so representative a character, that we can still derive the greatest advantage from translating them back into the more universal laws on which they rest.

We have here three different modes of explanation, under one or other of which most secondary meanings can be arranged (7). In the first place, objects and events which were in themselves perfectly real and historical, are found to possess a symbolical force when they are seen to embody a deep spiritual or moral principle, which clothes itself in different ages under varying outward forms. The case of types is rather more complex, as they add to the symbol the element of prophecy. And under this division may be included two heads of interpretation which were anciently marked by different names, the allegorical and anagogic; the one containing those types in the Law which anticipate the Gospel; the other comprising those characteristics of the Church militant which prefigure the eternal glory of the Church triumphant. To the symbolical and typical I have proposed to add a third class, containing cases where the secondary sense merely resolves a rule into the deeper law, which gives it an abiding interest.

1. Of the symbolical kind of secondary senses, the leading instance is furnished by St. Paul's interpretation of the history of Sarah and Hagar[a] (8). The word ἀλληγορούμενα which he employs plainly means, as St. Chrysostom interprets it, that the history referred to οὐ μόνον παραδηλοῖ ὅπερ φαίνεται· (mark the care with which the literal meaning is secured;) ἀλλὰ καὶ ἄλλα τινὰ ἀναγορεύει·[b] it gives a symbolical representation of principles, while it retains the character of a plain historical record. The Apostle tells us, then, that what is written about the members of Abraham's household may be viewed in the more general light of an allegory; for that 'these are the two covenants; the one from the Mount Sinai, which gendereth to bondage,' the other from that heavenly Jerusalem, which 'is free,' and 'is the mother of us all.' This is plainly a very remarkable claim to find a double sense in a simple narrative, and to read the spiritual relations of Jew and Christian in the representative records of the house of Abraham. As such it calls for a closer examination when we are enquiring

[a] Gal. iv. 21-31. [b] Cramer, *Caten. G. P.*, vi. 69.

into the Scriptural usage as to secondary senses. My reason for assuming that in this case the purely symbolical element is more conspicuous than the typical will be made clear in the course of exposition.

The analogy, let us observe, is drawn from the entire history, as well as from the persons. Viewed in themselves, Hagar and Sarah are both mixed characters. There was plainly much that was excellent in Hagar, who twice received angelic visits, in each case with the promise of a special blessing, and who had realised a deeper truth than others of her age and condition, when she said, 'Thou, God, seest me.'[a] There had been passing traces of unbelief in Sarah, though her doubts had been conquered by the noble influence of Abraham's faith.[b] But even in their merely personal aspect, the parallel would thus far hold good, though it forms no part of the Apostle's argument. For on the one hand, the law is 'good, if a man use it lawfully,' and the 'commandment holy and just and good;'[c] and on the other hand there have always been multitudes of unworthy Christians who have been gathered within the outer fold of the Gospel. When both these women were alike members of Abraham's household, each had her own position and duty. Sarah was the mistress, and Hagar was the handmaid. It was the place of Sarah to rule, and it was the place of Hagar to obey. Precisely analogous, within God's household of the Jewish Church,

[a] Gen. xvi. 7; xxi. 17; xvi. 13.
[b] Gen. xviii. 12–15. [c] 1 Tim. i. 8; Rom. vii. 12.

was the relation between the Promise which was the basis of the Gospel, and the Law, which was the ruling instance of ceremonial precepts and forms. The Promise represented the free gift of God's Spirit. The Law represented the more fleshly and servile element of ritual obligation, which was 'added because of transgressions.'[a] When Hagar despised Sarah, and when the son of Hagar turned against the son of Sarah and mocked him,[b] the true domestic order was subverted. The mistress was taunted by her handmaid; the heir of the freewoman became the sport of the son of the slave. The same thing happened when the Law received the faith and reverence which properly belonged to the Promise only; when men looked for salvation to the works of the Law, rather than the faith which had led to the justification of their fathers; when the hard details of their legal duties, which were the mere bond-slaves of their nobler privileges, were allowed to absorb their entire devotion, and the flame of spiritual worship died out within their hearts.

And now observe the manner in which this interpretation is applied by the Apostle. The Galatians had fallen back from the spirit to the letter. To counteract this evil tendency, he appeals to that very reverence for the letter which they had selected as their field of vantage. The history of Abraham stood in the very forefront of those Scriptures which would be especially described as the Law. What are the

---

[a] Gal. iii. 19. [b] Gen. xvi. 4; xxi. 9.

lessons of the life of Abraham? Do they exalt Law against Promise, flesh against Spirit, forms against grace, works against faith? The very contrary is true. You may see it, he elsewhere argues, from the history of the justification and circumcision of Abraham.[a] You may learn it here, he says, from the records of his household history. You may learn it if you will duly study what you are told about Sarah and Hagar, and will draw forth the lessons which that history should convey.

The son of Sarah was by special covenant to be the ancestor of Christ; for 'in Isaac shall thy seed be called.'[b] But though no such glory rested on the son of Hagar, God had listened with favour when Abraham had prayed that his son Ishmael also should be blessed.[c] His very name was a pledge that God should hear.[d] He was ordained to be a great nation. He did not die till this blessing had been abundantly fulfilled; till the twelve promised princes of his race could be gathered together from their towns and castles, that he might die 'in the presence of all his brethren.'[e] But the promise which proved God's goodness towards Ishmael was darkened from the outset by the prophetic shadow of his wild and lawless career.[f] His proper province was to yield to Isaac loyal service. This was the highest household dignity that belonged to him. So far as his domestic rights went, he was not even so much as Esau was to Jacob,

[a] Rom. iv. 10.   [b] Gen. xxi. 12.
[c] Gen. xvii. 20.   [d] Gen. xvi. 11.
[e] Gen. xxv. 16, 18.   [f] Gen. xvi. 12.

or as Eliab was to David (9). When he mocked the son of Sarah, he fell into domestic rebellion, and was cast out into the desert, as the complaint of Sarah was ratified by the sentence of God.[a] After this he held his greatness as an alien and a stranger. He had for ever forfeited his highest blessing. Henceforward he was, as God presignified, 'a wild man; his hand against every man, and every man's hand against him.'[b] Henceforth he represented the resistance of the flesh against the Spirit; the developed rebellion of our fallen nature when it rises up against the grace of God. Now it is this secondary, corrupted, and unnatural relation which furnishes the Apostle with his parallel for the not less forced, corrupted, and unnatural position which the Galatians were claiming for the Law of Moses. Ishmael might have kept God's blessing if he had rendered due respect to Isaac. And in the same manner, the Law of Moses never gendered to bondage, except when approached in a spirit at once servile and rebellious. We may be sure that it was no bondage to Moses and Joshua, to Gideon and Barak, to Samson and Jephthah, to David, and to Samuel, and to the prophets.[c] But to the Scribes and Pharisees it had become the sternest, though unconscious, bondage; that of the fleshly, formal, and self-righteous heart. Against these, and such as these, the Apostle, like his Master, urges, that other heirs had now been born to Abraham.[d] Again the barren had been blessed with

[a] Gen. xxi. 12. [b] Gen. xvi. 12. [c] Heb. xi. 23, 30, 32.
[d] John viii. 39. Cf. St. John Baptist in Matt. iii. 9.

offspring, and a new seed had been gathered from the deadness of the Gentile world. Again had the ancient prophecies received a further and more noble fulfilment: for many were now the children of the desolate, in comparison with her who had the husband; in comparison, that is, with the debased and downcast earthly Jerusalem, which was 'in bondage with her children' of the older covenant.[a]

Now the whole of this exposition plainly rests upon the principle that events of this kind happened under God's special control, and may be regarded as symbolical expressions of fundamental truths, which appear and reappear, though less conspicuously, in the leading incidents of every age. But we cannot admit that there is the slightest disposition to interfere with the literal sense of the original record. That sense stands out as firm and unshaken as in the record of any other history. Nor does the Apostle mean to teach us that the facts to which he appeals had happened or been narrated for no other purpose than to furnish the lessons which he shows that they subserve. Those chapters in Genesis are the literal account of real occurrences which happened under the guidance of the providence of God. They are recorded with perfect simplicity and singlemindedness, the writer being guided, but not trammelled, by the supervision of the Holy Spirit. But they occurred in a household, by which God's Church was then represented, at a time when there was a peculiar energy in the operation of

[a] Isa. liv. 1; Gal. iv. 27.

God's spiritual laws. The events, then, are conspicuously symbolical of fundamental truths, which perpetually rise to the surface in the course of history, though it is seldom that they can receive so vivid an illustration as we find in that antagonism between Judaism and Christianity, which lay open to the observation of St. Paul.

2. It will not be necessary, in the second place, to dwell at any length on the types of Scripture, many of which I have already enumerated, while their main characteristics must be familiar to our thoughts. The whole history of the Jewish nation may be described as one long type of Christianity; of its privileges, its obligations, the rewards which it offers to obedient faith, the calamities which disobedience and distrust involve. The chastisements which God inflicted on the Jews for their lust, idolatry, and other sins, are expressly called 'types,' which happened for our guidance, and were recorded for our admonition.[a] The whole Mosaic ritual, as we may learn from the Epistle to the Hebrews, was thickly sown with typical references, which were fulfilled in the office and the sacrifice of Christ. Of other Scriptural expositions which belong to this head, the leading examples are the following:—Christ Himself teaches us that the serpent which was lifted up by Moses in the wilderness was a sign of the Son of Man, who must be lifted up;[b] that the history of the prophet Jonas was

[a] 1 Cor. x. 6 (τύποι ἡμῶν ἐγενήθησαν), 11 (τύποι, al. τυπικῶς, συνέβαινον ἐκείνοις).
[b] John iii. 14.

a type of His resurrection;[a] and that the bread from heaven which was given through Moses prefigured Himself as the true bread from heaven.[b] St. Paul, in like manner, unfolds the hidden meaning of the cloud and sea, the spiritual meat and the spiritual drink, the spiritual rock which was Christ.[c] He draws out the position of the first Adam in his typical contrast to the second.[d] He treats the primeval law of marriage as a mystery which foreshadowed the relation between Christ and His Church.[e] He dwells on the veil which covered the face of Moses, and finds in that history a series of typical images, to illustrate the greater fulness, freedom, and perpetuity of Christian light.[f] All teaching of this kind must be carefully distinguished from such modes of instruction as the use of parables, or the employment, throughout the Apocalypse, of earthly representations to shadow forth the kingdom of heaven. It is the fundamental character of what may be strictly called a typical system, that it rests on the basis of real objects, or events of history. And confining ourselves to this signification, we shall trace the unvarying presence of the same principle which I have pointed out in the former cases. Histories may, indeed, be typical, but that circumstance never causes them to be any the less real; and that reality was quite sufficient to fill the thoughts of the original actors, and occupy the attention of the original narrators, even if they enter-

[a] Matt. xii. 40.   [b] John vi. 32.   [c] 1 Cor. x. 1–4.
[d] Rom. v. 14 (τύπος τοῦ μέλλοντος); 1 Cor. xv. 45.
[e] Eph. v. 32.   [f] 2 Cor. iii. 13–18.

tained in any case the dim suspicion that their works or words bore divine traces of the reflection of some distant future. Taking the fullest and most complex portion of that system, the types embodied in the Law of Moses, Christians are now enabled to perceive their manifold significance, because they read them by the light of their fulfilment in Christ. But the Jew could only see them by the eye of faith, which would tell him that God's temporal ordinances must embody a spiritual import beyond the depth to which his present insight reached. And if he was ever roused to profounder meditation, by the flash of an unearthly splendour which was seen for a moment to gild with strange glory some details of his ritual forms, his dim forecast could but resemble the vision of that stranger seer, whose tongue was overruled to proclaim the God of Israel among the fires of Balak: seen, but not now; beheld, but not nigh; the distant promise of the star of Jacob, as descried from the mountains of Moab.[a]

3. Of the third class of secondary meanings which I mentioned, namely, the cases where specific enactments are translated back into the universal principles on which they rest, we have a marked instance in St. Paul's repeated application of the Mosaic rule, 'Thou shalt not muzzle the mouth of the ox that treadeth out the corn.'[b] 'Doth God take care for oxen?' he asks us; 'or saith He it altogether for our sakes? For

[a] Num. xxiv. 17. Cf. Gen. xlix. 18; 2 Sam. xxiii. 5; Luke x. 23-4; John viii. 56; Heb. xi.

[b] Deut. xxv. 4; 1 Cor. ix. 9, 10; 1 Tim. v. 18.

our sakes, no doubt, this is written.' The expression is here so strong and conclusive, that some have represented the Apostle as entirely depreciating the literal meaning, however worthy the precept, in its original connection, of the mercy of God. The words of the Apostle show, they urge, that 'the mystical meaning *was* intended by the Holy Ghost, and the literal meaning was *not.*'[a] Without pushing the argument to that extreme, we must admit that in this instance St. Paul resolved a rule of labour, which was laid down for oxen, into the broader principle which covers the case of the Christian ministry; namely, that all earthly service has the right to receive its adequate reward. But perhaps a still more important illustration can be drawn from the manner in which our Lord Himself subjects the Jewish Sabbath to a loftier explanation, and thus unfolds a deeper sense beneath its literal precept.[b] I need not now revert to the discussion on the exact relation existing between the Sabbath of the Jew and the Lord's Day of the Christian (10). But members of our Church must bear in mind the fact, that each Sunday and holiday she teaches us to pray that God in His mercy will incline our hearts to keep *that* Law. And further reflection may dispose us to believe, that the Fourth Commandment gives the foremost instance of a positive ordinance, which had been meant at the outset for all humanity, which was reduced to stricter rules under the Jewish system, and which has resumed its

[a] Dr. Neale, *Commentary on the Psalms,* i. 383.
[b] Matt. xii. 8; Mark ii. 27.

ancient and more noble authority now that the Jewish ceremonial has been fulfilled and superseded. In its fundamental import, it embodies the broadest law of religious dedication. In its commemorative aspect, it has ever been associated with such acts of God's mercy as the completion of creation, the deliverance from Egypt, the dealings of God with His chosen people, and, finally, that great and crowning act of blessing, the resurrection of our Lord. In its prophetic character, it reminds men of the rest that remaineth: a partial rest within God's Church on earth; a rest of untroubled happiness hereafter, in the Sabbath of eternal life. This great representative ordinance, then, may be explained on the same principle with other laws of wider obligation which were embodied in the Jewish code; and if it is not so usual to quote it under our present subject of secondary meanings, it may now be seen that the language in which our Lord describes it really furnishes a prerogative instance of the principle on which many obviously secondary meanings rest—that of resolving special rules into universal laws, and thus falling back from the temporal to the eternal.

And now let us ask, whether this doctrine of the relation between the divine and human element, which is found to explain all classes of secondary meanings, will not go far to solve the apparent difficulty of the seeming discrepancy between the quotations found in the New Testament and their original context? (11) We are frequently reminded that such quotations do not always correspond to the exact words or connection of the original writer; and that you cannot carry back into the Old Testament the meaning which they receive in the later Scriptures. Sometimes, it is urged, there is only a verbal resemblance. Sometimes the new meaning sounds only like a play on words. Sometimes passages are combined from the most distant quarters, sentences that were uttered at intervals of centuries being compounded in a single text. In one instance, at least, an argument is rested on the use of a singular instead of a plural word.[a] But in answer we may fairly plead the operation of that Divine intention (12) which overruled a seemingly independent writer to provide for the possibility of the future interpretation, by employing one word rather than another. And inspired authors may reasonably claim the privilege of interpreting the books to which they appeal, under the guidance of the same Holy Spirit who presided over their earlier utterance; the right of developing the more spiritual relations which lay beneath the ancient forms. When *facts* are referred to, we may of course expect that they shall be repeated correctly; though the adoption of traditions not elsewhere recorded in Scripture may sometimes cause a passing difficulty. But as to *words*, there was no reason for such rigorous exactness as we are bound to use in our own quotations. The inspired writers of the New Testament were not jurists, dealing with the exact shade of

[a] Gal. iii. 16.

meaning embodied in a written code; nor were they philologists, whose observations would have rested on the precise and literal reproduction of the language. They were God's interpreters, commissioned to reveal the predetermined counsels of His will. As such they were charged with the duty, not so much of simply repeating, as of unfolding and applying His earlier commands. It follows that, in all cases, and at all times, they were likely to fix on the relative rather than on the absolute meaning of a passage, and to read it by the light of their own immediate purpose, rather than by that of the purpose of the original writer. Being themselves also inspired, their function was not so much to quote as to interpret; to snatch from their dark places the scattered lights of earlier teaching, and rearrange them to disclose the convergent witness which they bear to the central revelation of our Lord.

In all that has now been said, I have confined myself to such exhibitions of secondary senses as rest on the explicit authority of Scripture. But we shall here be met by the obvious question, whether the principle is to be rigidly limited to those instances which the later portions of Scripture furnish. So some have thought; believing that in such a limitation they found their only possible protection against the baseless dreams of mystic unreality. Yet I cannot but think that this limitation is unreasonable, and not borne out by the indications of Scripture. If it were put in this form, that we must never go beyond the authority or *analogy* of the sacred writings, the rule would probably include all that is requisite. But it includes much less than is requisite when the appeal to that analogy is excluded (13). Consider that in such a case we should be debarred from any extension of that symbolical interpretation which enabled St. John to describe the powers of evil under the names of Sodom, of Egypt, or of Babylon.[a] For typical instances, we have no direct Scriptural authority for regarding Isaac, or Joseph, or Samson, or David, or Elijah, as each in his turn contributing such special and conspicuous types of Christ as the offered sacrifice; the release from the Egyptian dungeon; the victory won, by the very act of dying, over those Philistine enemies, whom we must no longer regard as symbolical of evil; the overthrow of Goliath, to whom the same restriction will apply; and the forty days' fast and translation of the prophet: to which we might add many similar instances, in which the Church has ever loved to read conspicuous illustrations of the office and work of her Lord (14). And under our third class we should be forbidden to extend to any other portion of the Mosaic system the same interpretation which St. Paul affixed to the rule about oxen; or which enables us to recognise the fundamental law of the Jewish Sabbath in the loftier uses to which the Christian's Lord's Day is devoted. To the example of Scripture, then, let us add its analogy; according to St. Paul's own rule for

[a] Rev. xi. 8; xvi. 19, &c.

prophecy or preaching, that it shall be κατὰ τὴν ἀναλογίαν τῆς πίστεως·[a] that is to say, shall conform to the ripened judgment of those who can look most deeply into the mind of Christ, and can trace most clearly the relations existing between one truth and another, and the respective proportions of the different principles of faith. There is one important rule, however, which may not have bound the inspired writers, but which should always be obeyed implicitly by uninspired interpreters—the rule that *ex literali solo potest trahi argumentum*: the spiritual sense supplies us with no secure ground for argument, unless we find that what is spiritual in one place is literal in another (15). We must not, then, be over-hasty to draw a spiritual interpretation, for which we cannot elsewhere find a literal basis. The secondary senses furnish no new and independent teaching, but only deepen, illustrate, and confirm the teaching which the literal sense of other texts affords. To this restriction we may add, if we please, such further rules as formal expositors of the doctrine have endeavoured to establish (16). But after all, I think that we shall find that, as contrasted with times when the search for spiritual senses drew men away from a sober and critical study of the text of Scripture, what we now need is, not so much more perfect rules, as a sounder tact in using them. We could scarcely expect or wish to recall men to the temper which saw Jesus and the Cross in the number of Abraham's

[a] Rom. xii. 6.

servants^a (17); but we never fail to find a wide and sympathising answer to every sober endeavour to deepen our spiritual insight into less prominent portions of the Word of God.

That the Church was to retain the enjoyment of such a privilege is indicated by the fulness with which the method is pursued up to the very close of the canon, in teaching which was to serve as our abiding model, and on materials which were furnished by the New Testament itself (18). Our Lord set the example when He spoke in dark sayings of the temple of His body;^b when He dwelt in one continuous passage on our spiritual awakening from the death of sin, and the future resurrection of all men for the final judgment;^c and when, in His repeated warning, 'He that findeth his life shall lose it,' He drew the analogy between temporal and eternal death.^d St. Paul employs the same method when dealing with events so recent in occurrence, and so eminently important in their literal signification, as the death, burial, and resurrection of our Lord. In the literal sense, it was a heresy to say that 'the resurrection is past already;'^e in the spiritual sense, it is a fundamental truth to declare, that each Christian rose again in baptism from the death of sin. Throughout all Christ's life He traces out these double meanings. We are 'buried with Him by baptism into death,' yet we are 'risen with Him through the faith of the operation of God, who hath

^a Gen. xiv. 14.   ^b John ii. 19.   ^c John v. 24–9.
^d Matt x. 39, &c.   ^e 2 Tim. ii. 18.

raised Him from the dead.' 'Our old man is crucified with Him.' We must therefore reckon ourselves to be 'dead unto sin,' and must prove that we belong to Christ by crucifying 'the flesh, with the affections and lusts.'[a] Now we must bear in mind that these applications impose a spiritual sense on the letter of the most important truths in Scripture. It cannot be said that they are an attempt to discover depth of spiritual significance, in cases where we do not find it in the literal meaning. The simple facts of Christ's crucifixion, death, burial, and resurrection, do themselves supply the vital power which gives all energy and reality to our own recovery from the deadness of a fallen nature. Yet, beneath that letter, the overwhelming importance of which no thoughts of man could overestimate, the Apostle habitually draws out these secondary senses, as types of that great spiritual conversion, to which their literal meaning gives the power. What inference can we draw, but that the Church has always been justified in seeing parables of heavenly truth in every word and act of Christ? The history of the good Samaritan affords us one out of a thousand instances. Who can doubt that Christ Himself is the true example, who lies concealed under that model of neighbourly love? In that narrative He gave a hidden picture of His own great work of mercy, when the guilty wanderer, who had left the heavenly

---

[a] Rom. vi. 4; Col. ii. 12; Rom. vi. 6, 11; Gal. v. 24.

for the accursed city, lay dying of the wounds which Law and prophet could not cure.

And now let it be considered whether the current objections to this doctrine of secondary meanings do not rest, to a great extent, on misapprehensions, which a little calm and patient explanation would remove. Is it alleged that the supporters of that doctrine shake the credit of the literal narrative? On the contrary, we uphold it in the very strongest language, and we accept every inference which that acknowledgement involves. Is it asserted that we claim for the inspired writers a direct participation in the Divine omniscience? On the contrary, we claim for them no more than this, that besides their high endowments in the way of human faculties, they were made the vehicles for communicating to mankind divine messages, which often reached far beyond their present thought. In a much stricter sense than it was true of Christ, they only spoke what they knew, and testified what they had seen, of the truths which were disclosed from above.[a] Is it averred that we propose to sanction a lax system of interpretation, by which almost any doctrine could be made to emerge from almost every text? On the contrary, we recognise and uphold the principle, that, to us at least, the literal meaning only can supply a sufficient foundation for argument. Is it asserted that the method employed claims a licentious freedom from the critical laws of exegesis?

---

[a] John iii. 11.

We answer, that a rule of sufficient stringency is obeyed by those who decline to pass beyond the precedent or the analogy of Scripture. Such are the rejoinders by which these objections could be met. But let us not forget that they form the mere outworks for defending that great positive principle, the belief in the real Divine authorship of Scripture, on which the theory of secondary senses rests. There is no other faith but this which can enable us to grasp the full conception of that spiritual presence which interpenetrates the whole of Scripture; arranging the facts, and suggesting the record, and controlling at times the very form in which the inspired writers shaped their language; planting the early seed-plots of primeval and patriarchal history with the germs that should burst forth into a glorious harvest at the coming of the Son of Man; and resting the entire mass of the sacred writings on a firm substratum of Divine significance, which proves them to be, through all their portions, not more the genuine words of men than the real and undoubted Word of God.

LECTURE V.

2 Cor. iv. 7.

'We have this treasure in earthen vessels, that the excellency of the power may be of God, and not of us.'

IF we have formed a just conception of that special revelation which supplies a supernatural counterpart to every portion of the facts of Scripture, and if we have realised the influence of that special inspiration which distinguishes the sacred writers from every other class of human agents, the strength of our own faith should be enough to save us from sharing in the fears which have been aroused, by the assertion that the human element, through which those divine gifts were communicated, was not only moulded by the individual characteristics of the writers, but was adjusted to the scientific opinions and literary habits of the times in which they severally lived. And this is the subject to which our attention must be now directed. We have dwelt on some few of the leading features which prove the reality and influence of that Divine presence which shines through every part of Scripture; reconciling the seeming contrarieties of human formulas, and spreading out a broad range of divine significance, as the basis on which the human language rests. We know that the record begins in mystery, and ends in miracle; the mystery of the Divine nature, the crowning miracle of Christ's resurrection from the dead. We discover that the narrative is raised at every step above the level of man's unaided intellect, by affording further glimpses which deepen our sense of the mysterious, and by recording continuous agencies, with which the miraculous is intimately blended. When we are now asked to gaze, with reverence but with firmness, on the nature of the earthly apparel in which these shapes of heavenly truth are robed, we may surely enter on the task in a spirit of frank confidence, and with entire freedom from any unworthy alarm. We risk but a small venture on the separate value of the 'earthen vessels,' when the possession of the heavenly 'treasure' is secured. It is not that we may treat such questions with indifference. If Scripture be only the hem of Christ's garment, it is well to imitate the faith of her who said, 'If I may but touch His garment, I shall be whole.'[a] But it has been well observed, that 'it makes a wonderful difference in the apparent magnitude and importance of a difficulty, whether it be regarded as the possible entrance to an entire unbelief, or an acknowledged perplexity on the fringe or edge of a strong and impregnable faith.'[b] Setting forth from the firm foundation of such faith,

[a] Matt. ix. 21.
[b] Dr. Moberly, Preface to *Sermons on the Beatitudes*, p. xxiii. (=p. xxvii. 2nd. ed.).

we shall find that disputes on details have a growing tendency to settle themselves and disappear. It is a dangerous and mistaken policy to raise these disputes to adventitious importance, by treating them as though they necessarily involved the issue of our highest interests. We can understand a writer saying that he holds 'the sixty-six books of the Old and New Testaments to be verbally the Word of God, as absolutely as were the ten commandments written by the finger of God on the two tables of stone' (1). Whether we adopt the phrase or not, we can certainly comprehend the creed which it expresses, and we cannot deny that it is a legitimate form of Christian conviction. But should a person think to move us by telling us, If you deny that every jot and tittle was thus given, you will make me an infidel, we can only answer, that such is not the language of a healthy faith. In a case of this kind, the real strength of the faith is in an inverse ratio to the violence of its language; and the suspicion cannot be repressed, that the bare mechanical theory has been adopted, like the theory of an infallible Church at other times, for its ease, its simplicity, and the relief it gives from further trouble (2).

On the other hand, a real reason for uneasiness may be found in the pertinacity with which the argument has been urged on, in opposite quarters, from exaggerated scruples on subjects of science or history, to moral and religious doubts, of deeper and more certain danger. We might be willing to attend to Paley, when he warns us against making 'Christianity answerable with its life'ᵃ for difficult questions connected with the Old Testament (3). We might see the risk of arguments which urge that if one assertion is doubted, all is in peril; if one link is allowed to be unsound, the chain is broken; if one stone is removed, the whole structure 'collapses into a shapeless and unmeaning ruin' (4). We might readily admit that these illustrations rest on wrong presumptions as to the kind and degree of scientific accuracy which we are authorised to expect in Scripture language; and that no fair reasoner has a right to stake the credibility of Christianity itself on the obscure adjustment of an isolated text, or the doubtful interpretation of a subordinate passage. But it is a different matter when such points as these are made the stepping-stones for inroads on the substance of the Christian faith. We cannot listen to the exhortation to refrain from bringing 'the Sacred Ark itself into the battle-field,' if we have reason to fear that the advice is meant to induce us to resign a solid bulwark, by which the citadel of faith is guarded. We have learnt from experience that it is only a narrow frontier which divides the alleged proof of scientific or historical mistakes from the imputation of moral or religious unsoundness. We know that the assault is soon extended from the supposed discovery of unimportant discrepancies to charges of fabrication and general untruthfulness; and that we may very soon be called upon to hear,

---

ᵃ *Evidences of Christianity*, III. § 3.

LECTURE V.   143

not of 'error' alone, but of 'infirmity, passion, and ignorance;' of 'the dark patches of human passion and error, which form a partial crust upon' the surface, in contrast with 'the bright centre of spiritual truth within' (5). It is surely not unreasonable to ask that these two subjects may be kept entirely distinct, and that no attempt may be made to construct an illegitimate inference extending from the one to the other. The topic of alleged moral defects in the earlier teaching will come before us in the succeeding Lecture. Let us now confine ourselves to the allegations of inaccuracies in history and science, and content ourselves for the present by protesting against the confusion which hurries us on from such subjects to those deeper questions which cannot be stirred without exciting reasonable alarm.

I. We must acknowledge, in the outset, that there are some definitions of inspiration which make it a very serious matter to detect the slightest variation between collateral accounts of the same transaction, and which subject their supporter to a constant restlessness of doubt, so long as he finds it difficult to adjust each link in every pedigree, or to harmonise each detail in contemporary records (6). But it is open to question whether these definitions are supported by the facts; whether they leave sufficient room for the free play of those laws of narrative by which all human histories are governed; and whether they make sufficient allowance for habits of composition which were necessarily very different from our own.

1. There was a time when men feared a similar danger to the faith from the discovery of the countless various readings in the MSS. of Scripture, and from the attempt to use that discovery as the basis for an attack on deeper interests (7). That danger has passed away and is forgotten. But we may draw a useful lesson from the well-worn topic, through the proof which it affords that God has not been pleased to exercise any miraculous superintendence over the text of the Scriptures, to protect them from the incidents of other ancient writings. This is a definite and undoubted fact, which throws more light upon the question than we could expect to derive from our own precarious anticipations of the probable conditions of a Divine revelation, a subject on which we are not competent to judge. That God has allowed the usual dust of age to gather over these sacred records is a simple historical fact which lies beyond the reach of controversy. The common text of the Bible does demonstrably contain letters and words, and even sentences, which were certainly never written by the finger of God. And this simple fact, that without obscuring a single truth, the critical study of MSS. has considerably modified the older text, is pregnant with significant instruction, when we are enquiring into the real nature of that human element which is traceable throughout the Word of God.

2. And if this remark is suggested by the docu-

mentary history of the text of Scripture, a similar lesson may be drawn from the apparent method of its composition, and its relation to the older materials which its writers may have used. For that the inspired writers did make free use of existing materials, is a fact which rests on the explicit witness of the Scriptures themselves. Revelation, as I have before pointed out,[a] is not conterminous with inspiration. Granting that throughout every part of Scripture, as well as 'in old time,' 'holy men of God spake as they were moved by the Holy Ghost,'[b] we have every reason, from their own expressions, to believe that they did not rely on any supernatural revelation for that vast mass of general knowledge which was collected into the canon of the Holy Scriptures, under the guidance of the Spirit of the Lord.

The very Gospels rest on testimony (s). St. Luke puts his authorities in the forefront of his work. St. John, alike in Gospel and in Epistle, pleads his special nearness to Christ as his title for claiming our attention to his teaching. 'This is the disciple which testifieth of these things, and wrote these things; and we know that his testimony is true.' 'That which was from the beginning, which we have heard, which we have seen with our eyes, which we have looked upon, and our hands have handled, of the Word of life, that which we have seen and heard declare we unto you.'[c] A new apostle was elected in the room of Judas, from among the limited number of those who

---

[a] Above, p. 25.   [b] 2 Pet. i. 21.   [c] John xxi. 24; 1 John i. 1, 3.

had companied with the rest from the beginning, for the express purpose that he might be a witness with them of Christ's resurrection.[a] The name of witness soon became the noblest title by which the *martyrum candidatus exercitus*, the suffering saints of God, were known. Human powers, then, both of observation and testimony, were used, not superseded, by the Holy Spirit. In the same way, we may rest satisfied that the genealogies of Christ were copied from authentic Jewish tables, and that this circumstance explains some peculiarities in their form (9). Turn to the Old Testament, and the language of quotation is varied and frequent:—' Is not this written in the Book of Jasher?' 'Behold, it is written in the Book of Jasher.' 'It is said in the Book of the Wars of the Lord.'[b] In this and several similar instances, the reference may point to collections of hymns or songs by which the histories were preceded (10). But the historical books, again, rely in all fit cases on such public and authentic documents as the census of the people, the registers of lands and tribes, the genealogies of families, or the records of the gratitude and deeds of kings. Pass to the oldest history of the Pentateuch, and we cannot doubt that its inspired author was abundantly supplied with all available tradition, and with every kind of existing record (11). Many institutions are referred to, which must have been handed down by use from earlier ages; and the dim mythologies of other lands establish the existence of a

---

[a] Acts i. 22. [b] Josh. x. 13; 2 Sam. i. 18; Num. xxi. 14.

LECTURE V. 147

primitive stock of historical and sacred information, some streamlets of which had overflowed into the less pure channels of Gentile recollection, from points which lie farther up the current than the date when they were brought together by the agency of the Spirit, through a human writer, into the Word of God.

These facts supply definite answers to two important questions:—Is it true that the text of Scripture has been so highly honoured, above that of every other ancient history, that it has been preserved intact in every detail, so that without raising any needless scruples about translation, we may place implicit reliance on the copy of the originals which we hold in our hands, as a literal reproduction of the sacred autograph? And is it true that the contents of Scripture stand out in self-sustained independence, so as to own no obligations to any anterior records of literature? Both these questions must be answered in the negative: and in these two positions we find a basis of fact for further argument, which bears directly on a large class of Scripture difficulties, and indirectly on the whole subject with which we are concerned.

Both facts, I repeat, are pregnant with significant instruction. But we must be careful not to overestimate the amount of that significance. With regard to various readings, in the first place: though criticism has frequently turned on texts of great doctrinal importance,[a] it is allowed that the removal of some of these texts has not exerted the smallest influence

---

[a] Acts xx. 28; 1 Tim. iii. 16; 1 John v. 7.

over the certainty of the doctrines which they teach (12). The only effect has been, to throw back the proof from the precarious support of salient passages, upon the surer foundation of continuous arguments. In the case of the text of the Three Heavenly Witnesses,[a] we need not doubt the venerable antiquity of at least its Latin form; and it seems not impossible to conjecture its origin (13). The several clauses of the Creed were the most authoritative attempts to put the coping-stone on converging lines of doctrine, which were less systematically revealed in Scripture; and the text in question might be an early symptom of that formulating tendency to which the creeds themselves are due. If, however, it cannot be proved to have been generally known in the fourth century, 'then Arianism, in its height,' as Bentley said, 'was beaten down without the help of that verse; and let the *fact* prove as it will, the *doctrine* is unshaken.'[b] We may resign it, then, without the slightest fear that its loss will weaken the fundamental proofs of faith. The same remark might be extended to the declaration of the eunuch, 'I believe that Jesus Christ is the Son of God.'[c] Such texts as these have, under any circumstances, a distinct value, because they bring to the surface, like the creeds themselves, great truths which form the basis of the circumjacent arguments. But if it can be proved that they are no portion of the Scripture record, they lie beyond that special reverence which we owe to the inspired Word of God.

[a] 1 John v. 7.   [b] *Works*, ed. Dyce, iii. 185.   [c] Acts viii. 37.

While it is not pretended, however, that any Christian doctrine has been really modified by the results of criticism, it must be thankfully acknowledged, on the other hand, that there are many cases in which the truth has been a gainer by them; and it may be expected that the amount of this good service may be considerably enlarged hereafter. We might instance the transposition of three words in St. Paul's speech at the Pisidian Antioch, which destroys a supposed contradiction to a date in the Old Testament.[a] The omission of a few words in the last chapter of St. Matthew removes an obstacle to the arrangement of our Lord's appearances after the resurrection.[b] The excision of two words in St. Matthew's record of our Lord's rebuke to Jerusalem would cancel another historical difficulty; but seems still to rest on somewhat slighter authority.[c] And though conjecture, as a general rule, has been rightly excluded from any interference with the sacred text, it is possible that room may yet be found for the cautious use of this highest instrument of criticism, in adjusting such purely formal matters as numerals, or lists of obscure names, which are scantily corroborated by collateral narratives, and have therefore been especially exposed to error (14).

And next, to turn to the lessons suggested by the

---

[a] 1 Kings vi. 1; Acts xiii. 20 (*transp.* A, B, C, &c., Lachmann, Wordsworth).

[b] Matt. xxviii. 9 (*om.* B, D, ℵ, Lachmann, Tischendorf, Tregelles).

[c] Matt. xxiii. 35 (υἱοῦ Βαραχίου, *om.* ℵ, *primâ manu*).

use of earlier materials in Scripture. The chief of these is the conviction, that so far as Scripture is simply historical, it was meant to obey the laws of other histories; and even to accept occasional modifications of familiar facts, like the omission of generations for the sake of symmetry, which were found in the records it employed. In like manner when it is objected, that while St. Matthew and St. Luke draw the lineage of Joseph through a different father, it is impossible that both should be historically true, we answer that it is sufficient if we can establish, that while the one is historically true, the other is legally correct and formal; and that legal correctness was precisely the aspect in which the object of one of the two Evangelists would have led him to regard it. It is needless to detail the service which this principle would render, in defining the real character of large portions of the earlier Scriptures. But I may add, that in the Gospels themselves, the frank recognition of that common mass of materials which St. Luke's opening language would suggest, relieves us from the difficulties which have been raised on the similarity of large portions of the three earlier Gospels; and supplies a fair answer to cavils based on small discrepancies, by reminding us of the universal law of human testimony, that two or more separate reporters of any scene which they have witnessed can seldom succeed, without collusion, in laying hold so exactly on the same circumstances, or adopting so precisely the same point of view, as to produce a narrative from which such variations are absolutely excluded (15).

This explicit recognition of earlier materials supplies an answer to another class of historical difficulties, which is due to the partial nature of our knowledge. It is well known that the later writers of Scripture frequently bear witness to the existence of a considerable amount of external tradition, by filling up the outlines of their references to facts with details not recorded in the earlier narrative (16). The acknowledgement of such traditions enables us to remove the chief stumblingblock in the speech of St. Stephen, who has been hastily accused of contradicting the history, while it is found that he was simply adding to our knowledge [a] (17). Again, the census of Cyrenius [b] supplies a very striking instance, and by no means the only one which we owe to recent enquiries, where an accusation of ignorance seems likely to recoil on those who made it, by a recovery of the genuine facts of the history (18).

But it is important to point out, that the principle which has been thus asserted stands in the strongest possible contrast to the theories which would disintegrate the books of Scripture, and distribute them among the earlier documents of which they are alleged to be compounded. That view is destructive of all real authorship, as claimed for the several writings in their existing form; an authorship which in many instances is sufficiently ascertained; though in others, where it has not been decided by testimony, it forms a legitimate subject for critical enquiry. That authorship, be it known or unknown, rests in each case with the inspired writer, who produced the book acknowledged in the canon; and the belief that he availed himself of earlier materials would no more entitle us to rend his work in pieces, and reassign its fragments to imaginary claimants, than the same argument would destroy the rights of an uninspired historian to the work which he had moulded into unity, and impressed with the full stamp of his own intellectual character, from such materials as he was able to command. No community of matter, for instance, could ever obliterate the clear features by which each of the four Evangelists is distinguished, and which the Church has recognised by corresponding symbols, through the sacred literature of every age.

3. There is yet another question which recent controversy has brought into more prominent notice—the question whether the books of the Old Testament have not passed through a process of ancient editorial revision, which places a limit on the powers of criticism to deal confidently with the evidence of its separate portions (19). An affirmative answer to this question may be counted to the credit of two opposite theories, according to the degree of alteration recognised. If the revision was so complete as to affect the genuineness of the entire document, the argument would add some weight to the opinion, that the inner unity which can be traced in Scripture is due in a great measure to the influence of changes and supplements, which may have been introduced by the studious labours of

successive generations in the Schools of the Prophets. If, on the other hand, the revision amounted to nothing more than the occasional insertion of explanatory glosses, the rights of the original author are secured; and we are simply furnished with a solution of the difficulties which have been caused by phrases of a later age. Now it is surely most consistent with the facts, to accept this latter answer rather than the former. No revision has in any sense obliterated those original diversities between one book and another, which have formed, since the very dawn of recent criticism, a leading topic in the arguments of the opposing theorist (20). No revision has cancelled the bare simplicity of those early representations, which have supplied another class of objections, resting on the hypothesis that later writers were compelled to modify their form, and deepen their meaning, in supplemental compositions of their own. Above all, no revision could have supplied those secret signs, those veiled or hidden symbols, by which the unity of Scripture is wonderfully established, and the meaning of which was not revealed till long after the last of the great prophetic schools was closed (21). But to admit that such notices as the later names of Laish or Kirjath-arba, and the references to the disappearance of the Canaanite, and the reign of kings in Israel,[a] may have been introduced at a later date by the inspired expounders of the sacred text, is only a natural consequence of the belief, that the Holy

---

[a] Gen. xiv. 14 (cf. Josh. xix. 47; Judges xviii. 29); Gen. xxiii. 2; xxxv. 27; xii. 6; xiii. 7; xxxvi. 31.

LECTURE V.

Spirit continued present through the entire series of the sacred writers, up to the completion of the older canon (22). If Ezra was inspired as well as Moses, there was no reason why Ezra should not change the mere form of the words of Moses, so as to make them more intelligible to those whose instruction was his primary personal object.[a] With this view he might insert glosses, comments, and various minor memoranda, which have supplied the basis of arguments for bringing down the whole composition to a later age. It cannot be necessary to maintain that Moses wrote out the entire Pentateuch, without erasure or correction, by a single impulse, on a single occasion; and that the sacred autograph was thenceforward protected from the slightest alteration, at the hand of either the author himself, or those who succeeded to his position in Israel. It is surely more reasonable to suppose, that Moses, whose youth was rich in all Egyptian learning,[b] began at an early age to collect, under God's guidance, all the knowledge which still lingered in the memories of the sons of Abraham; that he added to his stores as time went on, interweaving with these materials the direct revelations which were vouchsafed to him by God; that the great events which he subsequently witnessed and recorded, and the diversified occupations of his advancing years, might reflect a varying colour on the mere outward form of the expressions which he used; and that, just as the account of his own death

---

[a] Ezra vii. 10, 25.   [b] Acts vii. 22.

LECTURE V. 155

must have been appended by a later hand,[a] so other notices of a subsequent date might be inserted from time to time by those inspired authorities on whose charge the sacred writings afterward devolved. Such a view throws no suspicion on the Mosaic authorship, nor yet imputes imperfection to the earlier record, which it was the work of the revisers to remove. An archaic term is not an imperfection. The explanation of such a term by a competent authority conveys no slight on the original author. Just as in the parallel case of the quotations, in which the New Testament writers depart from the mere letter of the texts which they interpret,[b] so in this case too we must not confound the freedom with which the later agents of the Spirit might modify the human aspects of its earlier work, with any breach of the rigid accuracy and scrupulous respect which one human author justly claims from another.

It is the general result of these various considerations, that we have no right to begin by imposing on revelation a deductive theory, independent of the actual facts, and then to feel overwhelmed with faithless fear when we discover that a rigorous examination of the facts does not confirm the theory. We are also led to expect, that the text of Scripture, composed as it was under such different circumstances, and at so remote an antiquity, may possibly continue to present some few historical difficulties, which the most

[a] Deut. xxxiv. 5.   [b] Above, p. 130.

careful enquiry must relinquish as insoluble. It is the duty of a firm and steadfast faith to throw off all such embarrassments to the distant outskirts of its horizon, and to feel no hesitation in confessing that there are still many topics in Scripture, on which we must rest content to know in part. But we have met with no consideration which could justify men in exaggerating either the difficulties themselves, or their bearing on the inspiration of the Bible. It is not a worthy occupation to build up scattered fragments of difficulty into a coherent edifice of doubt. Such a work is unfortunately within the reach of any one who will devote time and powers to the undertaking, without the restraint of misgivings on the use of a method, which is so full of uncertainty and danger. By restricting to one sense a word which may be taken equally well in another; by excluding every suggestion, however reasonable, through which the pressure of a difficulty might be lightened; by ignoring the possibility of those practical arrangements which would naturally suggest themselves to an orderly and administrative people; by confounding generations viewed at their longest, as a measure of duration, with generations viewed at their shortest, as an instrument of increase; by insisting that a pedigree which is arranged on one principle shall be tested on another; and above all, by reducing all the details of a time of miraculous guidance to the standard of God's ordinary providential rule; it is possible to construct a network of improbability, which shall prove perplexing and distressing to readers of imperfect information and of timid faith (23). The cure for this evil must be twofold, like its cause. The information must be completed, and the faith must be strengthened; and we may rest satisfied with the assurance, that whatever obstacles may be allowed to linger, as a further test of our reliance on God's goodness, yet a resolute grasp on those central principles, which were wrought out so marvellously through the Exodus of Israel, will lead to a still further diminution of the perplexities by which the record of that 'wondrous march' has been surrounded.

II. And now, from the laws of literature and history, let us pass to those of scientific language, and trace their bearing on the human element of Holy Scripture.

Few of what are commonly called scientific questions, which are connected with the literal words of Scripture, are inseparably combined with the essentials of the faith. Rejecting all that would corrode the substance, we can avoid all over-anxiety as to anything which merely touches the form. Yet it is precisely the mere form of Scripture which has been constantly pressed into the service of human theories, and has then been unwarrantably risked in defending them. Hence the wisest teachers in all ages have warned us not to confound our own interpretations with God's word, and then pay homage to our own self-complacency by insisting that they must stand or fall together (24). There cannot be a greater error than to thrust our own expositions under the sacred shelter of the reverence which is due to the message of God. And this is what is meant when we are told that any old interpretation must be abandoned if scientific investigation shows it to be wrong (25). It is not that the laws of Scripture criticism may vary with the varying theories of science; nor has anything of that kind been meant by the warning. But whenever investigation has led us to believe that a phrase of Scripture was accommodated to a scientific creed which has now been abandoned, we simply translate that phrase into the deeper meaning, which no scientific theory can reach or alter. We refuse to lend the weight of Scripture authority to decisions on topics with which it was not dealing, and which did not lie within its proper sphere. We obey no laws, in interpreting the Scripture, except those which sound criticism and God's Spirit would prescribe; but we may find it a duty to divest ourselves of errors which have been forced into the exegesis by imperfect knowledge.

The principle that scientific language used in Scripture would necessarily be optical or phenomenal (26), has long been recognised, and is now seldom challenged. Few would now raise a difficulty on such expressions as the rising and setting of the sun, the pillars, doors, and windows of heaven, the foundations and four corners of the earth.[a] It is felt at once that these terms were either simply figurative, or adjusted to mere outward appearances; that they do no more than express the facts in current lan-

---

[a] Job xxvi. 11; Ps. lxxviii. 24; Gen. vii. 11; Ps. civ. 5; Isa. xi. 12; Rev. vii. 1, &c.

guage, and commit the writer to no theory on natural antecedents or sequences with which he was not called upon to deal. On this point it cannot now be necessary to dwell. But it is alleged, afresh, that scientific error has eaten, in some cases, into the very substance of the narrative; and that we cannot accept the conclusions of modern science without acknowledging that the inspired writers have fallen into such mistakes as must modify the older creed of inspiration. Let us meet this difficulty on the ground which is most frequently chosen by objectors—the crucial instance of the Mosaic record of creation.

In examining that record, we must be careful to distinguish between the facts and their framework: I mean, between the material assertions, which convey the theological doctrines of God's agency and purpose in creation, and the mere form or arrangement into which they have been cast. Setting aside, for the present, the reference to the Fourth Commandment, which will claim our further consideration in the sequel, we can find no reason, either in the passage itself, or in the numerous allusions to it which are scattered over the rest of Scripture, for laying equal stress in this case on the matter and on the form. But I think it will be found that the substantial facts embodied in this passage have been almost universally accepted as unassailable. No reasonable geology has ever claimed to contradict such positions as these: that God was the Creator of all things in the beginning; that the ordering of primeval chaos was the work of His Most Holy Spirit; that He framed earth and heaven and all their hosts with a distinct personal energy and unceasing care, of which the terms of human labour yield but a very imperfect symbol; that the crown of His creation was man himself, who was made in the image of God (27). Before controversy assails these fundamental principles, it must have reached a stage at which the disputants, on one side, have lost all interest in the literal worth of any Scripture statement. The geological attack, I think, has mainly been directed, not against these truths, with their details or consequences, but against the mere order of succession, under which creation is described, and against the terms 'evening,' 'morning,' and 'day,' by which its successive epochs are distinguished. Now in a case which lies so far outside of anything which can properly be called history, it is not easy to see any reason for placing the mere framework of the narrative on a level with the facts which it conveys. We are accustomed to draw this distinction in cases where there was less antecedent reason to expect it; and even in the Gospels themselves, which are surely the most vitally important narratives in Scripture. No diatessaron is possible, unless occasional trajections are admitted; i.e., unless it is allowed that the facts may have been arranged in accordance with some other law than that of simple succession in time. The order of our Lord's temptations, for instance, is different in the two statements which record them in detail.[a] It is well known that all these matters can

---

[a] Matt. iv. 1–11; Luke iv. 1–13.

be adjusted and reduced to rule without throwing doubts on such successions as are obviously historical, like the reigns and order of a line of kings. But there is a special reason why we should apply this principle to set free the present chapter from the restrictions of time like our own. So far as it unfolds God's purpose in creation, it belongs to the eternal rather than the temporal; and it is only by the help of economy or condescension that the eternal can be brought within our grasp. We are justified, therefore, in regarding the word 'days,' when applied to creation, as an expression of the same class with those which no one now would be likely to misinterpret, the eye, or hand, or finger of God. It is the nearest expression of the eternal truth which could be conveyed through human language for the purpose of its original revelation; but to take it in the strictest and most literal sense, is simply to bind the eternal by the forms of time. It may fairly be compared with the numbers in the Apocalypse, the figures which fix the square proportions of the city of the heavenly Jerusalem [a] (28).

The distinction which I have now suggested rests upon the twofold ground, that the revelation of causes which we gain from Scripture was not meant to interfere with the proper function of the human intellect in the discovery of scientific laws; and that the secrets of God's counsels could only be revealed to man under the veil of language which fails to fathom their full

---

[a] Rev. xxi. 16, 17.

depth of meaning. It is completely borne out, however, by examining the internal structure of the passage; in which, as it has been repeatedly pointed out, we trace as close a resemblance to the Hebrew parallels as could be expected in a narrative which presents no other signs of poetry. If we read the passage carefully, we can scarcely fail to see that there is a break at the end of the third day, and that the work of the fourth lies parallel to that of the first (29). The order is, that God created light, and firmament, and land: these three great acts are detailed as the work of the first three days. Then again, as if by a fresh beginning, we are told that He created orbs in heaven to hold that light; birds and fishes, to people the divisions which the firmament had sundered; beasts and man to occupy the land, which had been clothed with vegetation for their use and support. Such are the six days, each answering in pairs to each, and crowned on the seventh day by that rest of God, that great Sabbath rest, which is the fittest type for divine meditation, 'the haven and Sabbath'[a] of man's loftiest thought.

This explanation seems to meet the double requirements of reasonable expectation and the exegesis of the passage. We may further observe that it stands free from two objections which might be raised against many attempts at a more direct reconciliation; namely, that in some cases, they throw doubts on the substantial truth of the revelation, while trying to remove

---

[a] Bacon, *Works*, ed. Ellis and Spedding, iii. 351, 477.

objections which tell only against the form under which it is presented; and that in other cases, they are open to the retort, that if God had meant them, He would certainly have expressed them: they are as easy to understand as that which they are proposed to supersede. If it had been *meant* that these were visions, it would have been *said* that they were visions (30). It was no harder to write down 'the vision of Moses,' than to write down 'the vision of Isaiah, the son of Amoz.' If it had been meant that this was only an exposition of God's plan, it could surely have been made plain to us that the plan had been altered in the course of execution (31). The only tenable doctrine of accommodation rests upon this principle, that the words which are used are the closest and clearest that man could understand. Explanations which treat the narrative as parable or poem are more exposed to the first objection (32). They throw doubts, as I have said, on the reality and substantial truth of the revelation, to avoid scruples which rest solely on too literal an interpretation of the form in which that revelation is conveyed.

It is by no means admitted, however, that the form was indifferent, or without a meaning, though it is urged that the attempt to impose an historical meaning is in this case misapplied. On the contrary, it seems possible to see very clear and sufficient reasons for it. It pleased God to throw the record of His own workings into such a form, as would most clearly exhibit their archetypal character, in relation to the work of man. Just as man bears God's image, though unspeakably inferior, so man's work, with all its poverty and imperfection, may be modelled after the glorious image of the work of God. Are we commanded to labour for six days, and rest on the seventh? The creation of the world can be presented under a precisely similar formula. Our Creator also wrought for six days, and rested on the seventh, though His days are as much higher than our days as His image than our image, or His thoughts than our thoughts. The Fourth Commandment thus becomes the key to the record of creation. Accepting that record as what it manifestly is—rather a revelation than a tradition—it carries on our thoughts to the contemporary marvel, when God's finger wrote the Ten Commandments on the rock. And they answer on this point, each to each; and the work of God's creatures is ennobled and dignified when it is represented as a shadow of the great creating work of God.

If we are asked, then, whether we resign the historical reality of the beginning of Genesis, we answer, that we resign nothing but a deeply seated misapprehension, which has confounded records of a different order, and obliterated the distinction between theology and history, by transferring the conditions of the one to the other. The first step in what may be technically called the narrative of history, is taken at the beginning of the fifth chapter of the book of Genesis, in the words, 'This is the book of the generations of Adam;' words which are followed by the briefest possible summary of the previous account of creation, and then by the order of a lineage, and the regular chronicle of dates and ages. To this historical commencement, part of the fourth chapter has been guiding our thoughts:[a] but, with that and some other minor exceptions, the first four chapters are rather theological than historical; they belong to the head of pure revelation, rather than to that of ordinary narrative. They embody matter which no conjecture could have reached, which no tradition could have furnished. They unfold, in such order as God judged to be the fittest, the fundamental truths about God's purpose and God's workings in creation; and about the innocence, the sin, and fall of man. This, then, after all, is the sole residuum of that 'confident rhetoric' to which the Mosaic record has been exposed: the assailant has only succeeded in carrying a position, which a deeper interpretation makes it needless to defend.

But it cannot be denied that an examination of the literature which has gathered round this subject produces a discouraging impression of the effects of these misapprehensions on the minds of both theological and scientific disputants. Keep each enquirer to his own province, and he advances with a firm step and cheerful spirit in the track which God lays open to his knowledge : the one to read the marvellous lessons of the book of Nature ; the other to draw water from the inexhaustible wells of salvation for the refreshment of the souls of men. Give geology free course, and it prepares to render signal service by removing mistakes which used to obscure our earlier

[a] Gen. iv. 17–22, 25, 26.

conceptions of God's working. It has already corroborated our belief in special acts of creative energy, by disclosing the indisputable records of creation, in countless remains which prove beyond a question that God has again and again been pleased to introduce the beginnings of new races on the earth. It appears now to supply a safeguard against theories which substitute creation by the law of development for creation by the word of God. This end it answers by its witness, that though species may die, they are not found to be transmuted; that each spans independently its arc of life; some longer and some shorter; some to run a course which has long ago been ended, and which we know only from the uncovering of the graveyards of the past; others stretching forth into the living world around us, and connecting the relics of immemorial antiquity with forms which meet us in our daily path. If I do not venture to enumerate other services which have been sometimes claimed at the hand of the geologist, it is simply because 'he that believeth shall not make haste;'[a] and it does not become us to grasp at seeming gains from those who may yet alter their decisions and reclaim them (33). But for the gifts which science has already bestowed on us — gifts which we owe to God alone, though it has pleased Him to enhance their value by making them the prizes of the human intellect — for these, I say, let us be heartily grateful, and let us frankly acknowledge their importance. Let us above all

---

[a] Isa. xxviii. 16.

things shun that faithless and suspicious temper which watches askance the work of science, as if convinced that it is merely looking out for an opportunity to rob us of some treasure in the heritage of faith. But we may be allowed, in turn, to remind the scientific enquirer, that it is quite as great a fault of reasoning to overstrain a fact in science that it may be made to contradict a text of Scripture, as to stand stubbornly upon some old interpretation of a doubtful text, and insist that it condemns some new discovery in science. As a moral fault it is of course far worse, because the interests involved are incomparably more important on the one side than on the other.

A dread of enquiry, then, must be calmed by the reflection, that the same God who made the earth and all its marvels created and bestowed the intellect of man, by whose well-guided activity those ancient wonders have been gathered and revealed. On the other hand, a jealousy of inspiration must be checked by the assurance, that as certainly as God built the rocks, and peopled sea and land through untold ages with countless forms of life, so surely did He give to man the higher blessing of those Holy Scriptures, which disclose the birth, the fall, the restoration of our race. Why this strife among the servants of a common Master, the children of a common Father, who owe their varied gifts to Him? And why, again, this contest among the different members of the body which He made?[a] Each one of these members

---

[a] 1 Cor. xii. 12.

hath He planted as it pleased Him in the body of mankind. Let not the ear of faith declare its independence of the eye of science, which reads God's writing on the hidden tablets of the everlasting hills. And let not the eye of science declare its independence of the ear of faith, which has caught and understood the heavenly message of the reconciliation of man through the Son to the Father. The contest has not long to live when it is brought to the issue of a strong but reasonable faith. God's works, we know, cannot contradict God's Word. This is not even an open question. To think it so betrays the secret doubt that either the one or the other came from God. *We* are as certain that we hold God's Word, as *you* can be certain that you are dealing with God's work. If they seem for a moment to present a passing shade of contradiction, there is abundant room for explanation in the mingled ignorance and impatience of man: his impatience, which guesses before he knows; his ignorance, which makes his guesses wrong — an ignorance which assumes too hastily that we have already mastered all the mind of Scripture, and an impatience which snatches weapons for the contest which God intended for a very different purpose.

To sum up briefly, then, the view which has been urged. The records of Scripture range through a long series of ages, and were committed to writing by men of very different characters, who possessed very different attainments, and who spoke, in short, a very different language: under which head of language I include the forms of speech by which the phenomena of heaven and earth would be described. When the voice of God was heard in thunder from the rocks of Sinai, by that band of fugitives which was now being moulded, through stern discipline, amidst the sands of the desert into national life, what could they have comprehended of a revelation which anticipated the far-off conclusions of science, the results of the observations of laborious ages? It is surely mere misapprehension to suppose, that the revelation with which Moses was really entrusted could traverse the path of the modern geologist, or contain anything that would either confirm or contradict his readings of those buried rocks. From whichever side the error comes, we are bound to shake ourselves free from it; not by saying, with some, that God cared not though His instruments should make mistakes on scientific subjects, but by pointing out that there can be no error where there is no assertion; and that a purely theological revelation contains no assertion which falls within the proper sphere of science.

It is thus that we may find room for researches of the reason, without treachery to truths whose province they do not really invade. It is thus that we may give fair play to the enquiries of science, without surrendering to desecration a single corner of the heritage of faith.

Let us welcome all free enquiries so long as they are pursued with reverence and candour. The believer is not justified in trying to intimidate free thought by the accusation of atheism: still less is the freethinker justified in striking at faith under the shield of science. Each commits the same fault; that of coupling truth with his own private opinions, and insisting that they must stand or fall together. Each must be met by the same answer; that what God never joined, man is bound to put asunder — the speculations of man and the revelations of God.

LECTURE VI.

◆—

Matt. xiii. 33.

'The kingdom of heaven is like unto leaven, which a woman took, and hid in three measures of meal, till the whole was leavened.'

IN passing from the historical and scientific language of Scripture, to consider the moral difficulties presented by some parts of its earliest record, we must begin by endeavouring to form a clear conception of the obstacles which retarded man's recovery of truth after the Fall. To whatever quarter we turn for the early history of our race, we shall find its moral character all but unintelligible, unless we recognise the full influence of that mass of energetic evil which obstructed all its aspirations after good. The existence of this great hindrance, which man had thrown in his own path by abusing the gift of freewill, is a primary fact, which no human theory can account for, but which every theory must accept as its inevitable starting-point. It is one of those elementary considerations which stand above the sphere of discussion, and fix the conditions on which all discussion must depend. When we study the history of God's first revelation, we find that we are not dealing with the unembarrassed development of heavenly truth, unfolded for the guidance of a pure, obedient, sympathising race. We are dealing with the introduction of truth into the hearts of fallen creatures, whose conduct and tendencies it thwarted and condemned; with its promulgation in the face of unruly animosity, of resolute rebellion, of that 'carnal mind' which 'is enmity against God,' of a 'whole world' lying 'in wickedness.'[a] To judge of the revelation without taking account of the resistance which it had to overcome, is as unreasonable as to apply the principles of peace to a scene of warfare, and to complain of the cruel sternness which the soldier has to practise in the presence of a turbulent and active foe.

We may gain much aid towards forming this conception from the short parable contained in the words of our text (1). The image of leaven sets before us the secret history of God's kingdom as a counterpart to the picture of its outward growth, which the parable of the mustard-seed had furnished. Some qualities of leaven are so antagonistic and corrupting, that the usage of Scripture applies it more frequently to evil than to good.[b] But it is not the less fitted to illustrate that anti-leaven of righteousness by which the influence of evil is to be counteracted and subdued. It is a cause of change, which is external in its origin, but internal in its operation; which produces

[a] Rom. viii. 7; 1 John v. 19.   [b] Luke xii. 1; 1 Cor. v. 7, &c.

its effects by slow degrees, as it penetrates the substance in which it is hidden—attracting one part after another to itself—communicating its own virtue to every particle with which it comes in contact, and fitting it to leaven what it touches in its turn; a hidden power, as though it were working from the centre outwards; mixing with all parts, while scarcely traceable in any; but gradually and surely accomplishing its office, by transmuting the entire mass into that state of assimilation, when we can say that the whole is leavened.

Under this figure we trace the law of God's election, by which religion was brought back into a fallen and corrupted world. The sacred history establishes that it is the law of God's government to bring in good by slow degrees for the expulsion of evil. A few of God's chosen servants are planted in the midst of multitudes who have forgotten God. Blessed themselves, they enjoy the high prerogative of dealing out blessings to others in their turn. The beginning is small, and seems but feeble when compared with the resisting mass which it has to penetrate and influence. But the principle itself, like the existence of evil, is one which must be received as primary. We cannot tell why it is that God chooses to bless some only, for the future benefit of all; why He left the world to lie so long in darkness; on what grounds He gave such advantage to the Jew; for what reason He now bestows so many undeserved privileges on ourselves. The fact is all that we have to deal with; and that fact is clearly brought before us by this image of the leaven, to which Christ gives a place in the series of His earliest parables. It was *not* God's plan to convert the world by a sudden manifestation of His supreme power and glory. It *was* God's plan to bring back into the world that good which it had forfeited, by a providential arrangement which may be fitly compared to the natural process of hiding leaven in the midst of meal.

The principle applies with equal clearness to what is intellectual in theology, as well as what is moral; and illustrates with the same distinctness the reintroduction of religious knowledge, to enlighten the darkened spirit of mankind. It is the current objection to the earliest revelation, that it is less perfect than the fuller light of later times; so much less perfect that some have tried to prove it to be unworthy of God, and therefore no more than a purely human composition, embodying no true message from above. All are ready to confess that God's disclosures of His own name and nature were progressive.[a] The first signs of the Holy Trinity are veiled and obscure. The Pentateuch supplies us with but a faint shadow of Father, Son, and Holy Spirit, as compared with the broad light afforded on such occasions as the baptism of Christ, or in such forms of Christian language as the institution of baptism or the apostolic benediction. The doctrine of a future life, again, was taught so obscurely, that Christ is said to have 'brought life and immortality to light through the gospel.'[b] Pass

[a] Above, p. 49. [b] 2 Tim. i. 10.

from the doctrines of theology to the laws of civil organisation, and Christ teaches that these were modified in the Mosaic code for temporary reasons. The obligation of the original marriage law was lightened, because of the hardness of the hearts of the people.[a] The slave law, we may add, was permitted to be harsher than it might have been under a different social system, or in different relations toward surrounding races.[b] Parental authority, though cautiously qualified, was entrusted with larger power than it can claim in days which pay more scrupulous regard to all classes of social and individual rights[c] (2).

But supposing it granted that an explanation can be given for the gradual development of divine knowledge and the temporary defects of positive enactments, yet what answer can be made when we are pressed with such moral difficulties as meet us in the first seven books of Scripture? Did the God of truth approve and bless the falsehoods of the 'Hebrew midwives,' or the falsehood of Rahab at Jericho? Did the God of righteousness tell His people to spoil the Egyptians? Did the God of mercy inspire the blessing which is uttered by the fiery-souled prophetess over the treacherous murder of a trusting foe?[d] These, as you know, are only specimens of the questions by which this difficulty is brought under our notice: questions which are sometimes urged with a superfluity of rhetoric; yet certainly not without the clearest right to a fair consideration and a candid answer (3).

---

[a] Matt. xix. 8.   [b] Ex. xxi. 4, 20, 21.   [c] Deut. xxi. 18–21.
[d] Ex. i. 20; Josh. ii. 4; vi. 25; Ex. xi. 2; xii. 36; Judges v. 24.

I need scarcely remark, that whatever answer we do give, it must be one which shall approve itself to the enlightened Christian conscience, and not endanger the first principles of right and wrong, by suggesting that the Divine command could be employed for the purpose of turning evil into good. Whenever apologists attempt to force back the difficulty into the very sanctuary of the Godhead, we can only rejoin that they are seeking for soundings in very dangerous waters, where it is wisest to decline to follow them (4). It is a more hopeful course to ask, whether the conditions under which the recovery of mankind was brought round would not lead us to expect that the training of God's people in those early days would exhibit a mixture between good and evil, which our clearer light will enable us to analyse, by a discrimination in which we can apportion the good, as is most due, to God, while we ascribe to man himself the evil intermixture which debases it. Let us examine some of the alleged difficulties by the light of this suggestion; and let us enquire whether the leaven of truth may not have been sometimes intermingled for a time with the mass of error which it was ultimately designed to purify.

The answer is often expressed by saying, that the earliest morality, even in Scripture, was imperfect (5). Perhaps it would convey a clearer meaning if we affirmed that, to a certain extent, it is—not so much imperfect as—fragmentary. In other words, its several portions were for a time detached and unorganised. God's earlier people grasped moral truths strongly; but the pressure of surrounding evil sometimes prevented them from giving sufficient weight to those needful counter-truths, which claim an equal recognition at their side. Sin was to be crushed; therefore they slew the sinner, without weighing in all cases whether the blow could be struck justly by unauthorised hands. God's work was to be done at all costs; therefore they were not careful to observe whether their hasty obedience might not sometimes trample on other laws which were equally divine—the laws of truth, of brotherhood, of scrupulous tenderness for common rights and duties. Their conduct thus presents a blended texture of good and evil. On the side of good we rank the strong faith in God, the strong resolve that righteousness should conquer, the steady determination to root out wickedness. The evil was, that righteousness was not always tempered by mercy, nor faith by truth, nor retaliation by justice. But so far as any of these acts received the expression of God's approbation, we may rest satisfied that His blessing lighted simply on the virtue, while His patient forbearance with His creatures' ignorance forgave them the accompanying sin.

Is this, then, a fair parallel to the other difficulties which I mentioned, and which seemed to admit of an easier solution; namely, that theology was unfolded only by degrees, and that the Law obscured the sanctity of marriage, and the manhood which is the inalienable right of the slave? It might be objected, that the analogy cannot be stretched to defend an inferior morality; that there can be neither more nor less in right and wrong. The one of these illustrations, it might be said, is mainly intellectual; the other deals with arrangements, which national customs regard as in some degree conventional. How can they be used to palliate what will after all be represented by many as the Divine toleration of a lower moral standard, in those who were honoured by God's special approbation? We reply, that even if the moral truths were severally perfect, the separate excellence of detached precepts is no guarantee for the presence of a complete and coherent morality; that there can be no difficulty in comprehending how the gift of discrimination might be wanting in those darker days; and that men need not be supposed to have put faith in falsehood, because they could only command disjointed truths. A solitary truth may indeed become most injurious, if it is used as the instrument of a selfish purpose; but when coupled with the one great central virtue of faithful obedience, it may be the germ of the most hopeful promise, and may raise an entire nation, as such truths raised the nation of the Jews, far above the standard of less favoured peoples, who possess no such talisman of spiritual power. Yet all the while, such principles, though severally cogent, might lack the completeness which can only be attained by their combination in an ordered system.

If we further consider the brevity with which some of these complex actions are recorded, we cannot allege that, in cases where ignorance did amount to actual sin, the sinful element failed to bring that certain train of punishment and grief which is annexed to it by the just judgment of God. If the narrative extends to further detail, and enables us to see remoter consequences, the application of the law, that sin works sorrow, is emphatically proved. There are several of the more mixed characters in Scripture, in whose cases a general uprightness of purpose and strength of faith was occasionally crossed and discoloured by sin or weakness, where the course of the history seems to have been governed by the very intention of introducing the discrimination which was needed, and showing with how sure a step the sin found out the sinner in the shape of fitting retribution. It has thus been often pointed out,[a] that the early deceit of Jacob was avenged through all his later years by the withering influence of the fear of man; and that the one great crime of David caused the evening of his glorious day to be darkened by the clouds of lust and blood. Such was the discipline by which God at once chastised the offender, and warned others against being polluted by the example of his sin. Now there may have been, in other cases also, a similar adjustment, which the brevity of the narrative has concealed from us; cases in which a mixture of sin with the motives was followed by a mixture of evil with the reward.

In proceeding to examine one or two of the more

[a] Especially in Blunt's *Undesigned Coincidences*, pp. 46, 145.

perplexing instances in fuller detail, I must repeat the warning which I have already ventured to suggest, against the error of treating all parts of Scripture as though they stood on one and the same level, forgetting that its composition spans the whole range of utmost antiquity, and stretches onward, from the rudest ages, to days when the ancient culture which succeeded was already beginning to decline. We cannot understand it as a whole till we have learnt the relations of the several portions, and can discriminate between the lessons which they were respectively commissioned to convey. The Gospels are filled with the living brightness of our Saviour's teaching; as when He tells us how the Samaritan forgot his deep national animosity, and proved himself to be true neighbour to the suffering Jew. The Mosaic history relates to days when the love which comprehends our enemy would have been rather despised as a weakness than fostered as a grace. And yet, between these two strongly contrasted periods, there lies, we may rest satisfied, the deep harmony of Scripture, which enriches those old times, that looked so unloving and relentless, with a treasure of instruction to be blended with the lessons of the Gospel.

We may learn from St. Paul's argument to both the Romans and Galatians, that man's first step back toward the Paradise which he has forfeited must be taken in the conviction of sin. Now this is precisely the feeling which the earliest books of revelation are most fitted to arouse. The Law itself,

LECTURE VI. 181

with all its elaborate ceremonial and rich typical significance, was 'added because of transgressions.'[a] It was a bridle to curb that wayward race, to which the guardianship of the promise had been given. It moulded their religious knowledge by the element of restraint and severity, which is a feature of law within the moral sphere. And that training produced the Jewish zeal, which finds so glowing an expression in many a fervid hymn and psalm: in language which may render us the deepest service, if it strikes through the hard crust of polished unreality, which too often supervenes on the placid decorum of our civilised life; and if it warns us how we ought to treat the deadly principles of wrong which lurk in our own fallen hearts. The tone of severity is not peculiar to the Pentateuch. While it is gradually divested of its earlier harshness, it pervades all Scripture in the character of zeal against evil. We trace it onward from Moses to David, from David to Ezra, from Ezra to the greater authority of the Divine Teacher, on whose lips it was purged from the last lingering resemblance to human infirmity [b] (6). And it fails to effect its proper purpose with ourselves, if it ever leaves us exposed to the influence of that spurious charity toward offenders, which is equivalent to an indifference for the mischief which they cause.

The most striking instance of the difficulty which I have been describing is to be found in the song

---

[a] Gal. iii. 19.   [b] Ps. cxxxix. 21, &c.; Ezra x. 17; Matt. xxiii., &c.

of Deborah, and in the blessing which she pronounced upon an action which seems to us a piece of signal treachery (7). Let us devote to this instance, then, a more detailed examination; as it will be acknowledged that the views which it suggests may be applied to a number of less remarkable cases.

The common chronology places the date of Deborah at a full century earlier than the subject of the oldest uninspired heroic poem. We have no secular poetry which can be proved to go back to so remote a period (8). And this date is especially important. It is above all things necessary, as I have said, that when we wish to form a judgment of its character, we do not forget with what part of history we are dealing. While no literature of any age has given birth to a grander effort of lyrical poetry, we yet know that it belongs to a period when the fair fabric of classical civilisation was utterly unthought of and unknown—a period when Greece had not yet spoken any word that time has spared, and some centuries before the earliest ancestors of the Latin race had built their first huts among the hills of Rome. Now this fact, which on mere literary grounds would be remarkable, on moral grounds becomes particularly noteable. When we are looking at the points of difficulty which the history involves, it is indispensable to recollect that those servants of God were fighting His battles in an age when the world was still lying in the profoundest darkness—in an age still earlier than those heroic days, in which the utter recklessness for human life, which is shown even by their noblest characters, supplies so serious a drawback to our admiration for their various manly virtues.

I need scarcely say that the whole period of the Judges contains much to perplex us (9). It is indeed the chief arena for those moral difficulties with which we are now dealing, and which emerge through all parts of that record in their strongest and most striking forms. Evils had risen to a height so appalling, that God used instruments of rudest temper for their overthrow, such as confound the calculations of the calmer judgment, which is trained in the pure light of happier days. Such preeminently was Samson, the fit type of times when mere strength had its direct and special use in smiting down the powers of darkness. But indeed throughout those ages there was a closer connection than there now is between the internal and the external; while principles of everlasting obligation were veiled under the ruder forms of time. It was not so much that men could not see more than half the truth, but that they saw truths, as I have said, in fragments, rather than as connected portions of an ordered system. They saw them, too, confusedly, and without discrimination—saw them, as we might say, with their colours blended; just as in pure theology the doctrine of the Trinity was taught less clearly than the doctrine of the Unity of God. We may note this in the very framework of the Jewish polity. The nation and the Church were one. The foes of Israel were the foes of God. There was no distinction, therefore, between public policy and religious duty; and the soldiers of the state were at once ministers of justice and public guardians of the sacred laws. We may note it, again, in the connection which existed between obedience and prosperity. It would be too much, perhaps, to say with some, that the rewards and penalties, by which alone the Jews were actuated, were only such as this world could furnish. Such a limitation would be inconsistent with the paramount appeal to God's approbation, as the chief motive which was perpetually put before them. And yet it is certainly true that prosperity and adversity were the great badges and representatives of the favour of God (10). It is certainly true that the spiritual eyesight was not yet quickened to appreciate the rewards and penalties of an eternal life. In like manner the law of duty was enforced with a sternness and simplicity which left scarcely room to discriminate between the sinner and his sin. It was as though the ancient Jew had to hew down the rude primeval forest, that he might lay the deep foundations for the future temple of the Lord. Such a labour would call for unwearied vigour, for unconquerable zeal, for unhesitating obedience : but it would leave little room for the nicer and more accurate discrimination, which we are at once privileged and bound in duty to employ. In this, as in so many other aspects of the older history, we are reminded of our Saviour's words: 'Blessed are the eyes which see the things that ye see: For I tell you, that many prophets and kings have desired to see those things which ye see, and have not seen them; and to hear those things which ye hear, and have not heard them.'ᵃ

We find the most conspicuous proof of this in the invariable sequence which then connected the exercise of courage with external freedom, and the indulgence of cowardice with external bondage; and that, not only, as it might still happen, in the regular issue of national policy, spun out through a course of complicated action, but ready, instantaneous, and constant, as though in the unquestionable relation of effort and its reward. The Israelites had entered on the promised land (11). In some instances, they carried out at once their mission; and in such cases we read how the Lord was with Judah, and how the Lord was with Joseph.ᵇ But in many other instances they made peace with the enemies whom they had been commissioned to destroy. Benjamin did not drive out the Jebusites; Manasseh did not drive out the inhabitants of Bethshean or Taanach; Ephraim did not drive out the Canaanites of Gezer; nor Zebulon the people of Kitron and Nahalol; nor Asher the coastmen of what was afterwards Phœnicia; nor Naphtali the inhabitants of Bethshemesh and Bethanath; but they 'dwelt among the Canaanites, the inhabitants of the land.'ᶜ Toleration soon changed into an unhallowed alliance, when they took the daughters of the Canaanites to be their wives, and gave their own daughters to their sons, and served their gods.ᵈ Therefore came that stern message of the Lord at Bochim,

---

ᵃ Luke x. 23, 24.   ᵇ Judges i. 19, 22.
ᶜ Judges i. 21, 27, 29, 30, 31, 33.   ᵈ Judges iii. 6.

that these nations should be as thorns in their sides, and their gods a snare.^a Soon followed the actual proofs of God's anger, when His hand was against them for evil, and they were sorely distressed. In quick succession came the tyranny of various oppressors: first, eight years of slavery to the King of Mesopotamia, from which they were freed by the bravery of Othniel, which gave the land rest for forty years. Next, from the south-east, sprang the tyranny of Moab, which was ended, after eighteen years, by the vengeance of Ehud; and the land had rest fourscore years. Next, as it would seem, there was persecution from Philistia.^b And then came that despotism from the powers on the north-east, which is unfolded in completer detail, and which it was the boast of Deborah and Barak to destroy. A king of Canaan, under the old name of Jabin, still reigned from the site of that same Hazor which 'beforetime was the head of all those kingdoms,' when it was seized and burnt by Joshua.^c Jabin had nine hundred chariots of iron; and for twenty years, through his captain, Sisera, he mightily oppressed the children of Israel. His fastness lay above the waters near the sources of the Jordan, whence Sisera poured down his chariots into that great plain, which was traversed by the torrent of the storied Kishon before it issues into the sea beneath the heights of Carmel. The hymn of Deborah supplies many minute details, which prove the oppressive sternness of his rule.

---

^a Judges ii. 3.   ^b Judges iii. 8-11, 12-30, 31.   ^c Josh. xi. 1, 10.

The highways were forsaken, and travellers pursued their stolen journeys through the byways. The inhabitants of the villages had ceased. War was in the gates. No shield nor spear was seen among forty thousand in Israel. The very draw-wells, as the old interpretation seems to run (12), were disturbed by the noise of the archers of Canaan.[a] Such was the state of God's people under the oppressors, until Deborah arose as a mother in Israel. The prophetess and Barak gathered against Sisera the tribes which filled the centre of the promised land. There were Ephraim and Benjamin, and chiefs sprung from the son of Manasseh, Machir.[b] 'The princes of Issachar were with Deborah.' 'Zebulun and Naphtali were a people that jeoparded their lives unto the death in the high places of the field.' What wonder is it that she classifies the sons of Israel as good or evil, according to the zeal which they showed in coming to the help of the Lord against the mighty? What wonder that she records for their shame the councils which detained the distant Reuben, the indolence of Gilead who abode beyond Jordan, of Dan who remained in ships, of Asher who clung to his rich possessions by the sea? What wonder that she calls down a special curse on Meroz, if the position of that place caused its neutrality and indifference to be a peculiar disgrace to the national cause? And what wonder, we now ask—to come to the point which has for us the deepest interest—what wonder

---

[a] Judges v. 6, 7, 8, 11.   [b] Gen. l. 23; Num. xxxii. 39, 40.

that she gives high praise and benediction to that daughter of the Kenite, whose act seems to us so merciless and treacherous, for dealing death on the flying oppressor of the race which she had taught to conquer? All other questions were absorbed and lost in this grand issue:—Who had been on the Lord's side? Who had been against Him? For the former she had blessings; for the latter she had the sternest condemnation. In the glowing exultation of her triumph over the despot, she could no more see sin in any action by which his ministers were exterminated, than she could see cruelty in the stars which fought in their courses against Sisera; or in that ancient river, the river Kishon, which swept in its swollen flood their dead bodies to the sea.[a]

Now can we doubt that this high spirit of heroic zeal, of devotion to God's service, of relentless hatred to His foe, was a divine element of true inspiration, which God sent to strengthen the good and crush the evil, at a time when there was great danger lest the evil should triumph and obliterate the good ? Can we doubt that God was leavening His people with that nobler temper, which was indispensable to secure the very existence of their national life, as the witness to God's truth in the midst of darkness ? We must keep prominently before our thoughts the real wickedness of the Canaanitish people, and the undoubted necessity that they should be crushed before Israel, lest the truth itself should perish in the over-

[a] Judges v. 14–31.

whelming flood of sin (13). To represent the matter, therefore, in such an aspect as our own position would suggest, we must alter the terms of the comparison, and state them in a different form. We live under the law, 'I say unto you, Love your enemies.'[a] In its direct sense, then, we are not concerned with the benediction of Deborah, as she hailed the blow that smote the tyrant. But let us state the matter in this way:—Our oppressor is Satan. Those bad passions which he seeks to rouse within us are the iron chariots by which he would crush out the fair work of God within our hearts. His evil emissaries are like archers of the Canaanites, who keep watch and ward to slay our souls, beside the very wells of living water. The war which Israel had to wage against Canaan must not be regarded as a mere struggle between nation and nation, but as the resistance, in the cause of universal humanity, of God's law against the rebellion of the wicked; of God's work against the work of Satan. It is in this sense that these things were our ensamples, and have been written for our admonition by the Holy Spirit.[b] We are not to look merely at man as against man, but at the upholders of righteousness, who were bound subjects to a loftier cause than they could comprehend, as against the upholders of idolatry and rebellion from God, whose destruction was rather an act of the Divine vengeance than the operation of a human policy. Or, again, we might express it in this

---

[a] Matt. v. 44. [b] 1 Cor. x. 11.

manner: that the struggle is not between man and man, but between principle and principle. We shall fail to understand its nature if our thoughts rest only on the human agents. These were, as we might say, mere accidents in that great battle, in which Israel was fighting the wars of the Lord. It matters not, then, that there were sins on the side of the earthly armies of Jehovah, or that the infant children of their enemies did not deserve, as man would speak, the cruel doom to which they were consigned. It is the sad characteristic of this fallen world, that so far as mere external sufferings are concerned, the innocent must often be involved in common sorrow with the guilty; and the march of righteousness must often be retarded by the frailties of the instruments through which God vouchsafes to execute His work.

Apply these considerations to the present subject, and they will at least lighten the perplexity which we might feel in accepting such a composition as the song of Deborah under the character of inspired Scripture. Not for one moment may we dream that its burning words may overcloud to *us* the law of mercy; that they would palliate in *us* the exercise of cruelty; that they would justify *us* in being fierce and ruthless, even in cases where we might fancy that we were doing the work of the Lord. Such inferences would indeed set the letter against the spirit, and find the savour of death in Scripture. But there is no danger of any such misconception, if we make the right allowance for the historical position of the human element, through which that sacred lesson was conveyed. We must adjust the precedent to our altered sphere, so as to teach us the zeal with which we are bound to fight against our vices; to exemplify the earnest and unwearied battle which we must wage against the Canaanites of sin within our hearts. For most of us this is a sufficient lesson. The duty of punishing the sins of others has been delegated to comparatively few. Yet those few may safely infer from the history, that not by man's decision but by the eternal laws of God, there is a point at which the wicked will be swept from the earth: and if not by God's directer judgments, as when He brought in 'the flood upon the world of the ungodly,'[a] or when He poured forth rain of fire from heaven, or when He charged His ancient people to exterminate the Canaanites, then by the calm exercise of judicial punishment, on the part of those who are commissioned, as His representatives, to bear 'not the sword in vain.'[b]

Those who take an opposite view of such passages in ancient Scripture make it their ground for urging that the old has been, not merely unfolded, but cancelled; that Judaism was not so much transfused into Christianity as utterly destroyed; that it resembled not the seed of the tree, but the scaffold of the building, and has therefore become all but useless to ourselves. We should thus be recommended to contrast the two dispensations in the same manner in which we should contrast seen and unseen, temporal

[a] 2 Pet. ii. 5.   [b] Rom. xiii. 4.

and eternal, letter and spirit, bondage and freedom, fear and love. But this was never the meaning of these antitheses as they were employed in the reasoning of St. Paul. The fact really is, that both sides of the truth are deepened when both are discriminated and explained. The tie of free and loyal service is a more stringent obligation than the fetter of the slave. The perfect love which casts out a blind and cowardly fear,[a] fosters in our hearts that deeper reverence, in which St. Peter tells us that the time of our sojourning here must be passed.[b] The day of judgment, as disclosed in the New Testament, is an incomparably more awful revelation than any terrors which were threatened to the Jew (14). And precisely so it stands with reference to our present subject. Evil is ever seen to be most hateful when the aspect of goodness is most clearly unveiled; and the hatred for iniquity is only another phase of that love for righteousness, with which both Psalmist and Apostle unite it in their proclamation of the Prince of Peace.[c]

There is something especially dangerous, because especially deceptive, in that cold propriety of conduct, which feels in religion no strong consciousness of either love or hate. But by the examples of its characters, as well as by its precepts, Scripture always teaches that the love for good must be combined with an abhorrence for evil which forbids any tolerance of sin.

[a] 1 John iv. 18.   [b] 1 Pet. i. 17.
[c] Ps. xlv. 8; Heb. i. 9.

Such a character as that of Moses would illustrate at once the existence of the feeling, and the limitations by which it ought to be controlled (15). His history shows us how enduringly the union lasted, even under the veil of his proverbial meekness. To speak in round numbers, we may say, that the special instances of his warmth of temper are recorded at his fortieth, his eightieth, and close upon his hundred and twentieth year. The mention of his meekness is connected with the central period, near the time when he cast down and broke the tables on descending from the mountain. It was about forty years *before* this that he slew the Egyptian and hid him in the sand; but it was nearly forty years *after* this that he was provoked in his spirit, and spoke unadvisedly with his lips at the waters of strife, and 'was wroth with the officers of the host,' for saving alive the women of the Midianites.[a] Or look at the instance of St. John the Divine (16). Let us call to mind the zeal which caused that pair of brothers to be surnamed sons of thunder by their Master; the hasty temper in which they wished to call down fire from heaven on the Samaritans, when Christ told them that they knew not what spirit they were of; and the ambition which made them covet to sit on His right hand and on His left in His glory.[b] Now St. John's latest years present a picture of the calmest evening with which a long and stormy day can close.

[a] (1.) Ex. ii. 12 (Acts vii. 23). (2.) Ex. xvii. 6; xxxii. 19; Num. xii. 3 (Acts vii. 30). (3.) Num. xx. 10, 12; xxvii. 14; Deut. i. 37; Ps. cvi. 32; Num. xxxi. 14 (Deut. xxxi. 2).
[b] Mark iii. 17; Luke ix. 54-5; Mark x. 37.

The whole of his teaching was at last condensed into that single sermon, 'Little children, love one another.' Yet if there be any truth in the story which describes him as fleeing in horror from the bath which was polluted by the presence of a heretic, we may infer that to the very last his love was incompatible with even the mildest concession towards acknowledged and resisting evil. Or may we not turn for illustration to the double tone, which marks the language of Christ Himself, the God of love? He began and closed His public ministry with an act of strange severity, when the zeal of God's house led Him to cleanse with His own sacred hands the House of Prayer, which men were changing to a den of thieves.[a] And by the side of all His acts of love and words of mercy, we read the woes which He uttered on Scribes and Pharisees and lawyers who were hypocrites; on all who caused offences, and cast stumblingblocks in the way of their brethren, and substituted outward forms for the spirit of devotion, and passed over judgment and the love of God.[b] Such as these found no mercy from the Friend of sinners, who taught us how the contrite publican was justified when the self-righteous Pharisee found no justification.[c]

Even the sternest of the ancient lessons, then, finds its proper place and work in teaching us that they who 'love the Lord' must see that they 'hate the thing which is evil.'[d] Charity which is not guarded by the feeling of resentment lacks its needful protection

[a] John ii. 15 ; Matt. xxi. 12.
[b] Matt. xxiii. ; Luke xi.
[c] Luke xviii. 14.
[d] Ps. xcvii. 10.

against sin; while a seeming hatred of sin may itself be sinful, if it lacks the indispensable counterpart of love. The one error is like the false mercy of Saul, when he spared the king whom God had sent him to destroy—mercy which was condemned as rebellion and stubbornness, and which forfeited the promises of God.[a] The other error may resemble the false zeal of Jehu, when he inflicted stern and bloody vengeance on idolaters, and then became himself an idolater, in defiance of the law which he had professed to execute.[b]

The Old Testament examples, then, should teach us zeal. But the New Testament does not teach us that zeal may grow cold, though it shows us how to temper it with discrimination. The line is there drawn clearly between vengeance and compassion; between hatred of evil, and charity for man; between the anger that is righteous, and the personal animosity that is everywhere condemned. The blessing which Deborah pronounced on Jael is supplanted by the blessing which angelic lips pronounced on the highly favoured mother of our Lord.[c] The fierce shout of national animosity gives way to the calm voice of the Divine Instructor, who sent the haughty Jew to the despised Samaritan for an example of neighbourly love. The new law rises into greater distinctness, but the true purport of the old remains uncancelled. New life springs forth at the bidding of Christ, but nothing that was heaven-sent in the old has departed. The lesson of old times

[a] 1 Sam. xv. 22–3.　[b] 2 Kings x. 16, &c.　[c] Luke i. 28.

remains to teach us that evil must be rooted out before there is room for good to flourish; that the war against sin in our own hearts must be relentless, before they are chastened to receive the lesson of true charity which led the Samaritan to see a neighbour in the Jew.

Thus may we learn that God was bringing His new leaven of truth into the world, under the cover of those impetuous onslaughts upon evil of which we have so conspicuous a record in the song of Deborah. Let such narratives arouse us, not (which God forbid) to be relentless toward our fellow-creatures, but to be as ruthless in dealing with the corruption of our own hearts as she was in destroying the enemies of the Lord. Let it incite us to take, in every contest, the Lord's side against the side of wickedness, and to oppose ourselves to every kind of weakness, which would tamper with and apologise for sin. No archer of the Canaanites could harass with such fiery darts as Satan. No chariots of Sisera could spread such devastation as the inroads of sin upon the heart of man. The battle has passed to a different sphere; the weapons of our warfare are no longer carnal. But we need the same temper of energetic zeal, in assailing the strongholds of the evil spirit; we require the same firm unwearied resolution, to wield the weapons of our spiritual armour, against the resistance or the onslaughts of our inveterate foe. Cowardice in that great strife will lay us prostrate before the aggressor, and will desolate the fields in which the word of God is planted. But courage will raise us to a reward as noble; to a welcome more glorious than Deborah could offer to Zebulun or Naphtali, to Jael or to Barak; the welcome with which our Heavenly Master will receive His good and faithful servants, and bid them enter into the joy of their Lord.

LECTURE VII.

Acts xiv. 15.

'We also are men of like passions with you.'

IN the last two Lectures I have endeavoured to point out the effect of the human element in fixing the outward shape of the Scripture record on matters of history and science, and in accounting for the fragmentary character under which morality was brought back after the Fall. I now propose to approach the subject more directly, through the medium of two leading examples of the human writers, with the view of showing, in detail, that the acknowledged presence of individual characteristics was guarded against the influence of individual imperfections.

The examination of two such instances from the New Testament may serve to complete the argument which was pursued last Sunday, in explanation of a moral difficulty which meets us in the older parts of Scripture. If it is found that, in cases which admit of a more exact analysis, the human error is never allowed to vitiate the inspired teaching, we gain a strong confirmation of the view which I then ventured to suggest; namely, that the mere record of sins must on no account be regarded as their sanction; and that even words of commendation, when pronounced on actions of a mixed moral character, must be interpreted as a simple recognition of the virtue, which was confused, but not cancelled, by the intermixture of the sin.

A large portion of the human interest of Scripture depends upon the fact, that it brings us into close contact with the personal history of the several writers; that it faithfully records their gradual progression, their growth in grace, and, it may be, even their frailties, which proved how completely they were 'men of like passions' with ourselves.[a] But, while recognising this great advantage, we shall derive an instructive lesson from the proof, that the written documents were not tarnished by the evil influence which might have been expected to arise from their errors. The remark may be extended to instances where temporary imperfection has passed on into actual transgression of some law of God. Great saints are recorded to have fallen for a season; but the teaching which they deliver is not found to falter. We may trace out the sin and its issue in their lives; we may see the very blow which descends in chastisement; the Scriptures, of which they count among the human authors, may commemorate in fullest details the agonies of their repentance, the loud cryings of remorse for their sins. But those Scriptures are never discoloured by the evil temper, or other

[a] Cf. James v. 17.

infirmity, which exposed the writers to temptation; still less are they perverted to the utterance of erroneous doctrines which may have been connected with their temporary fall. We can observe this in the Old Testament in the cases of Moses and of David. We can observe it in the case of Solomon, displayed under still more striking circumstances. We can observe it in the New Testament, in the writings of both St. Peter and St. Paul.

It is, indeed, one lesson which we gather from the traces of discord in the earliest Church history, that the voice of divine instruction rises calmly and clearly above the tumults of the disputants; so that it is only by careful analysis and collateral information that we learn how far the most honoured names amongst Christ's servants were entangled in the bitterness of strife (1). Let us draw out in detail the two cases which most naturally suggest themselves: the apparent want of steady purpose in St. Peter; the alleged imperfection of the earliest teaching of St. Paul.

I. It is needless to dwell long, in the outset, on the prominent features of St. Peter's character (2): his impetuous, venturesome, and earnest faith; and that frequent intermixture of human weakness which might seem so strange an imperfection in the leader of the apostolic company, yet which comes home with so strong a sense of deep reality to all who have ever studied the frailty of their hearts. You will recollect how frequently it happens, that even the smaller details of the narrative bear traces of the uneven

LECTURE VII.

balance between faith and knowledge, by which his progress towards Christian maturity was retarded. At one moment he cries, 'Thou shalt never wash my feet;' at the next moment, 'Lord, not my feet only, but also my hands and my head.'[a] At one hour, he is striking with the sword; at the next, he is denying and abandoning his Master. And the rapid change is often signalised in words which were addressed to him by Christ, 'Blessed art thou, Simon Bar-jona: for flesh and blood hath not revealed it unto thee, but my Father which is in heaven;' and then, within a few verses, 'Get thee behind me, Satan: thou art an offence unto me: for thou savourest not the things that be of God.'[b]

The Gospels and Acts supply us with three great illustrations of this internal struggle, which divide into as many portions the whole Christian life of the Apostle. I refer to the three occasions on which St. Peter was put forward, to give, as it were, a formal and official expression to principles which marked three distinct and special advances in Christian knowledge; on every one of which occasions the Apostle's subsequent conduct proved that the truths which his lips had been so eager to utter had failed, when he pronounced them, to exert their proper practical influence within his heart.

1. First comes that earnest declaration of faith in his Master, which forms the foundation of the Christian creed, the first stone of that great edifice of

[a] John xiii. 8, 9.   [b] Matt. xvi. 17, 23.

doctrine in which the treasures of all Christian knowledge are enshrined: 'Then said Jesus unto the twelve, Will ye also go away? Then Simon Peter answered Him, Lord, to whom shall we go? Thou hast the words of eternal life. And we believe and are sure that Thou art that Christ, the Son of the living God.'[a] This is the first apostolic proclamation of the foremost tenet of the Catholic faith; that primary doctrine of the Divinity of Christ, which formed so great a stumblingblock to the whole nation of the Jews.

2. The second of the great principles with which St. Peter was entrusted, was the extension to the Gentiles of the benefits of Abraham's promise. The new Church had sprung from the very heart of Judaism, to which Christ and His apostles all belonged. The further change was foreshadowed, indeed, but not effected, throughout the acts of the earthly sojourn of our Lord (3). It was foreshadowed when He healed the centurion's servant, and the daughter of the Canaanitish woman, and the ten lepers of whom one was a Samaritan. It was foreshadowed when He Himself, on more than one occasion, approached towns and villages of the Samaritans, into which He had forbidden His apostles to enter. It was foreshadowed when He acknowledged Gentile faith as higher than any which He had found in Israel; when He announced that many should come from East and West, to take the places of the children; and that

---

[a] John vi. 67–9.

thus the first should become last and the last should become first.[a] It was foreshadowed when He excited the anger of the Jews, by reminding them that Elijah was sent only to the widow who dwelt in the Sidonian Sarepta, and that Elisha's healing power was exercised only upon the leprous Syrian.[b] But it was not yet effected. There is no positive proof, for instance, beyond the witness of a doubtful reading,[c] that though He withdrew into the borders of Tyre and Sidon, His own feet ever passed beyond the limits of the sacred soil which was the special heritage of Abraham's sons; and through the whole history of His life we find that He acted Himself on the law which He laid down, that He was 'not sent but unto the lost sheep of the house of Israel.'[d]

His ascension leads us to a different sphere. And it is St. Peter who proclaims the first stage of this great revolution when he says, 'The promise is unto you, and to your children, and to all that are afar off, even as many as the Lord our God shall call.'[e] But we receive an instant illustration of the spiritual difficulty of passing from the mere proclamation of a principle to the acceptance and acknowledgement of its whole practical significance. The intellect may be enlightened long before the current of the feelings has

[a] Luke vii. 2–10 ; Matt. xv. 21–8 ; Luke xvii. 12–19 ; ix. 52 ; John iv. 5 ; x. 16 ; Matt. viii. 10, &c.
[b] Luke iv. 25–7.
[c] Mark vii. 31 ($ἦλθεν$ $διὰ$ $Σιδῶνος$ $εἰς$ · $\aleph$, B, D, &c., Lachmann, Tischendorf, Tregelles).
[d] Matt. x. 5, 6 ; xv. 24.   [e] Acts ii. 39.

been changed. The Jewish prerogative, '*unto you first*,'[a] represented a truth which was more vividly apprehended in St. Peter's thoughts (4). He needed the instruction of the heavenly vision before he had completely mastered the wide range of the principle, that 'God is no respecter of persons;' that God's ministers must call no man 'common or unclean.'[b] The proclamation of the principle might be the first step; but it required for its completion the second step which was taken at the baptism of Cornelius, when the admission of the Gentiles was placed on the same level of privilege which was enjoyed by Jewish Christians. And the further declaration of the ground of this admission, through their equal participation in the outpouring of the Holy Spirit, was again entrusted to St. Peter, who brought the work to a completion, as the readiest leader in the apostolic band.[c]

3. But again we find the traces of a new and unexpected difficulty. The truth had been announced and acted on; but its full bearings and relations had not yet been made clear. It had been settled, indeed, that the Gentiles should be admitted freely to the Christian Church; and St. Peter never really forgot the lesson which was taught him by the heavenly vision, and on which he had acted in baptising the household of Cornelius. But on this there arose the further question, whether they should be admitted without passing through the gate of circumcision—

[a] Acts iii. 26.   [b] Acts x. 34, 28.   [c] Acts x. 47; xi. 15.

whether, in short, the new converts should be circumcised or no. On this great question, also, a formal decision was announced; and again it was St. Peter who was commissioned to declare it at the council of Jerusalem, when his words were forthwith ratified, in the name of the Church, by the most venerated leader of the Jewish Christians. It was the declaration of St. Peter which was translated into the formal sentence pronounced by the lips of St. James.[a] And thus far we can clearly see the slow steps by which these new truths were gradually sinking into men's thoughts and conduct, and above all into their hearts. And then came the time when the agency of St. Peter was mainly superseded, and the narrative passes on to the acts of St. Paul. Let us pause, before we follow it, to note the connection between these observations on St. Peter's history and his teaching as an inspired apostle.

Look back again to mark anew the wonderful significancy of those three sayings of St. Peter, round which our rapid summary has centered: the Divinity of Christ; the free admission of the Gentiles to the Christian Church, and their deliverance from the conditions of the Law of Moses. These positions cannot fail to be regarded as steps of almost unparalleled importance in the gradual unfolding of the Christian faith and system. And in every one of them it is the voice of St. Peter by which they were uttered; in every one of them it is the faith of St. Peter which reminds us

[a] Acts xv. 14, &c.

of the Rock, on which the Church was to be builded by the promise of her Lord.ᵃ Such is the one side of the picture. Let us turn to the other and more remarkable aspect. In every one of these cases we discover, that in the mind of the highly favoured Apostle himself, the advance movement was succeeded by a speedy, though temporary, ebbing of the tide. The first of these declarations was followed, after an interval, by that denial of our Saviour which stands out in Scripture as one of the most striking examples of the fearful possibility of faithlessness in Christians; the most emphatic warning, that he 'that thinketh he standeth' should 'take heed lest he fall.'ᵇ The second was followed by that relapse into the old Jewish feeling, which required the correction afforded through the heavenly vision; the very fact that the lesson was thus called for, being a proof that St. Peter's knowledge of the approaching admission of the Gentiles had not yet completely modified his personal belief in the prior claims and higher privileges of the Jew. A new question seems to have arisen, after the council of Jerusalem had passed its decree for the remission of Gentile circumcision. It may have been the case, that the question had already arrived at that new phase on which it must have shortly entered. The Gentiles, it was ruled, were no longer to be circumcised: but what was to be the usage for the Jewish Christians? Were they bound to keep up the old rite of circumcision, now that its ancient significance had

---

ᵃ Matt. xvi. 18.   ᵇ 1 Cor. x. 12.

passed away (5)? It would appear that this question was postponed by St. Paul, at the time when he circumcised Timothy, in whose case the doubt might have arisen; while he refused to circumcise Titus, who fell under the exemption, which had been explicitly established at the council.[a] But it would doubtless be in connection with this point, or some other question of a similar character, on which the controversy had assumed a new phase at Antioch, that St. Peter fell again under an injurious influence, which made it needful for St. Paul to withstand him 'to the face, because he was to be blamed.'[b] It is not to be supposed, that after the deep solemnity of the events which accompanied the baptism of Cornelius, and again after the careful deliberations and weighty conclusions of the council, St. Peter could have fallen back, as some have thought, from either the decision on the free admission of the Gentiles, or the resolution to admit them without compelling them to pass through the gate of circumcision. It is more probable that the dispute had arisen on some further complication in this deeply important controversy, when St. Peter had again failed to master some additional modification, the need of which was clear to the keen insight of St. Paul.

Such is the chequered history of the inner life of the Apostle, up to and even beyond the time when he disappears from the regular apostolic narrative. But we must now remark, that all along its course

---

[a] Acts xvi. 3; Gal. ii. 3.   [b] Gal. ii. 11.

throughout the Acts, we have a series of addresses which were delivered by St. Peter, and which cover a much wider field of teaching than the points to which we have referred. It is material to our present argument to note, that those formal discourses are free throughout from every trace of uncertainty or error, by which his conduct was occasionally biassed for a season (6). Historians have not failed to mark the signal change which was wrought by the descent of the Holy Ghost at Pentecost; the sudden conversion of the apostles from doubt, timidity, and lingering ignorance, to a confidence, a boldness, and a spiritual authority, which perplexed and overawed the rulers of the Jews. Of these great characteristics the sermons of St. Peter are the leading proofs; and from point to point they uphold and develope the foremost doctrines of revelation with a clearness of tone, and firmness of purpose, from which human imperfections are totally excluded. And recurring to the history, we observe that the notices which we have collected do not really close the page, nor leave us with the impression that the struggles of the Apostle brought him to no earthly haven of rest. The Holy Spirit has graciously afforded us that later record of a more comprehensive nature, the contents of which establish that all his failures had been finally surmounted, and that all his misunderstandings had been reconciled at last. It is here that the evidence of his Epistles may be brought in: and we may use them both without disturbance from any critical questions bearing on the genuineness of the second, because the character of both is in this respect one and the same. And if it were suggested that the argument which we have been pursuing might warn us against reasoning from the words of the inspired writer to the spiritual position of the man, the thought is overborne at once by the witness of their solemn tone, of conscious, unwavering, steadfast faith. In this light we may read the special notices, which prove how completely every earlier sore was finally healed: the touching allusions in the one epistle to the 'wisdom given unto' his 'beloved brother Paul;' in the other to the services of that 'faithful brother,' the well-known companion of St. Paul, Silvanus.[a] The personal nature of the details shows that a holy calm had settled down at last, after the casual storms of that eager, earnest, active life. Resting on the past, with full assurance for the present, and with high anticipations for the future — speaking as himself 'an elder and a witness' at once of Christ's transfiguration and His sufferings, and already 'a partaker of the glory that shall be revealed'— he writes that he may 'stir up' their 'pure minds by way of remembrance;' in the spirit of a man who knows how sorely he has himself been tempted, and can therefore encourage others to bear up against the fiery trial of temptation, and to resist the utmost malice of the devil.[b] It is his own experience which teaches him to place such absolute reliance on the

[a] 2 Pet. iii. 15; 1 Pet. v. 12.
[b] 1 Pet. v. 1 ; 2 Pet. i. 18 ; iii. 1; i. 12, 13 ; 1 Pet. i. 7 ; iv. 12 ; 2 Pet. ii. 9; 1 Pet. v. 9.

word of God, in opposition to false prophets, and in contrast to the perishable objects of this transitory world.ª It is the recollection of his own failure which urges him to bid them not to be ashamed if they are called upon to suffer as Christians; and which leads him to connect the Christian life with the courageous discharge of all earthly obligations, as the counterpart to those graces of the Spirit which are summed up in the injunction, to sanctify the Lord God in their hearts.ᵇ Well may we say, in Hooker's language, that his strength had been his ruin, and his fall had proved his stay.ᶜ Well may our thoughts pass quickly on, from the memory of his early vacillation to the solemn stillness of his closing doxology; when, as his thoughts revert to Him who had been 'thrice denied, yet thrice beloved,' he exclaims, ' to Him be glory, καὶ νῦν καὶ εἰς ἡμέραν αἰῶνος·' even throughout that eternity which is *dies sine nocte, merus ac perpetuus*.ᵈ Does not the record hold out to ourselves the promise, that a ready faith will never lose its reward; that a zealous struggle will never fail, through God's help, to lead to victory; that as, in some cases, His ' strength is made perfect in weakness,'ᵉ so in other cases His firmness is created beneath the unsteady efforts of uncertain strength; and that the doubts and disappointments of this world are not seldom closed even before the grave, and will unfailingly vanish, when we pass to the deep rest of heaven?

ª 1 Pet. i. 25; 2 Pet. i. 21; ii. 1. ᵇ 1 Pet. iv. 16; iii. 15.
ᶜ Sermon III., *Works*, ed. Keble, iii. 610.
ᵈ Bengel. *in loc.*   ᵉ 2 Cor. xii. 9.

All this it teaches; but it surely teaches no less clearly this lesson on the character of Holy Scripture: that its voice was always raised above the sphere within which earthly controversies are heard to wrangle; that the Holy Spirit uses the human character, but excludes the intermixture of human infirmity; uses the instrument, but forbids the discords which sometimes spoil its natural tones; speaks in the voice of sinful men, whose sins are set forth in its own records for our warning, but never permits those voices in its service to be swayed for one moment by the influence of the sin.

II. We pass to a very different character, when we turn our attention from St. Peter to St. Paul. In St. Peter we have noted the gradual advancement from the dominion of hasty impulses to the calm self-control of settled unity and strength. We can observe and mark the very crisis of the changes, when the whole man seemed to be bowed under the influence of the mighty agencies which lifted him on from one point to another, to take the lead in every movement of unfolding Christianity, with an impetuosity of purpose which left his tardier thoughts behind. In the case of St. Paul, we trace the operation of a firm consistent zeal, informed and governed by a resolute conscience; but by its side we find that the religious knowledge breaks asunder, at the great change of the conversion, into two distinct portions, which might be regarded as respectively typical of Jewish and of Christian faith. The language in which the Apostle speaks of his own former life is constantly coloured by two contrasted lines of reflection. On the one side he is undaunted in asserting the unbroken continuity of what was good; on the other side, he sorrows over the recollection of its earlier counterpart of evil. Whenever the question turns on zeal, he claims it for his younger years, in its highest fervour and its worthiest forms. 'Taught according to the perfect manner of the law of the fathers,' he 'was zealous toward God,' up to the very highest standard of those whom he addressed. 'After the most straitest sect' of their religion, he had 'lived a Pharisee.' In that religion he had profited above many his equals in his own nation, 'being more exceedingly zealous of the traditions of' his 'fathers.' 'Touching the righteousness which is in the law,' in short, he was 'blameless.'[a] Yet, on the other hand, he is as explicit and energetic in deploring the sin of that spiritual blindness, which had darkened his own vision, as it darkened the vision of the whole nation of the Jews. He says that he 'was before a blasphemer, and a persecutor, and injurious,' though he had 'obtained mercy, because' he 'did it ignorantly in unbelief;' and he had learnt to regard himself as in that aspect 'the least of the apostles,' not worthy, indeed, 'to be called an apostle,' because he had 'persecuted the church of God.'[b]

Now this is a very clear account of the spiritual

---

[a] Acts xxii. 3; xxvi. 5; Gal. i. 14; Phil. iii. 6. Cf. Acts xxiii. 1; xxiv. 14, 16; 2 Tim. i. 3.
[b] 1 Tim. i. 13; 1 Cor. xv. 9.

history of a most intelligible character. We see that the current of his religious zeal had always run strongly, and had filled to overflowing the channels through which it was directed. But its earlier course had been misguided into evil; and he never tried to palliate that evil, even while insisting on the honesty of purpose with which the mistaken course had been pursued. His conversion brought about the instantaneous change of guiding the whole strength of his will into a better channel, and removing the Jewish barriers which had enslaved its energies within the limits of a worn-out system.

Here, then, arise the questions on development, which become important for our present argument. First, what was the nature of that religious progress after his conversion, which is acknowledged in some expressions of St. Paul (7)? In the next place, does it appear to have exerted such a control over his inspiration, that we can detect its influence in his writings, in their gradual deliverance from earlier imperfections? In the third place, is it possible to trace in any passages the very process of development, the vibrations of a mind which is still balancing in doubt between two opposite judgments, unable to decide, yet unwilling to continue undecided? If we are compelled to answer these later questions in the affirmative, we shall have found an instance in which the human element has intruded its imperfections into the sacred record. If we can establish a reasonable right to answer them in the negative, we shall have gained a further example of the manner in which all human weaknesses are overruled and strengthened by the mighty presence of the enlightening Spirit.

1. It is beyond all question, in the first place, that St. Paul acknowledges a progress in religious light after his conversion. His companion, St. Luke, tells us at the outset, that 'Saul increased the more in strength;' and we cannot doubt that his spiritual insight was quickened, and his knowledge deepened, by the 'visions and revelations of the Lord.'[a] Nor does it seem difficult to illustrate from the history that former knowledge of 'Christ after the flesh' (8), which he tells the Corinthians he has finally abandoned.[b] We must not forget, as I have already remarked, that the early Church was reared under the shade of Judaism; that its earliest teachers, as well as hearers, were all 'children of the stock of Abraham;'[c] that its public ministrations were long connected with the central bond of the temple services at Jerusalem;[d] that Christ's own commission had originally limited the province of the twelve: 'Go not into the way of the Gentiles, and into any city of the Samaritans enter ye not; but go rather to the lost sheep of the house of Israel.'[e] 'Unto you first,' as we have seen, was the message of St. Peter: 'to you is the word of this salvation sent;' and 'it was necessary that the word of God should first have been spoken to you,' is the echo

---

[a] Acts ix. 22; 2 Cor. xii. 1.
[b] 2 Cor. v. 16.   [c] Acts xiii. 26.
[d] Acts ii. 46; iii. 1, &c.   [e] Matt. x. 5, 6.

of that language from St. Paul.[a] Three times throughout the Acts, as if by three different impulses of sorrowing indignation, at the obduracy by which his fellow-countrymen were hardened, the Apostle announces his intention of turning to the Gentiles, at Antioch, at Corinth, and at Rome.[b] There is no reason to doubt that St. Paul, like the others, had once sympathised completely with the Jewish anticipations of a national Messiah, whose earthly lineage should fix the main features of His character and purpose. There was a time when the apostles themselves imagined that Christ died chiefly for the Jewish nation; now they all knew that He had 'died for all,' and that 'He should gather together in one the children of God that were scattered abroad.'[c] At one time they had dwelt on the prior claims of Judaism; now they knew that in Christ Jesus 'there is neither Greek nor Jew, circumcision nor uncircumcision, Barbarian, Scythian, bond nor free; but Christ is all and in all.'[d] At one time those original witnesses had doubtless prided themselves on their acquaintance with the human person of the Saviour, and on being His brethren after the flesh, through their common descent from Abraham. Now they had learnt that faith had the promise of a higher privilege than sight, and that the very 'mother and brethren' of their Master 'are these which hear the word of God and do it.'[e] That the

---

[a] Acts iii. 26; xiii. 26, 46.   [b] Acts xiii. 46; xviii. 6; xxviii. 28.
[c] 2 Cor. v. 15; John xi. 50-2.   Cf. 1 John ii. 2; Luke xxiv. 21.
[d] Col. iii. 11.   [e] John xx. 29; Luke viii. 21.

'Apostle of the Gentiles'[a] would in like manner at one time feel a deeper conviction of the claims of those, 'of whom as concerning the flesh Christ came,'[b] is thus found to be both likely in itself, and borne out by the analogy of the gradual development of the other apostles, and entirely consistent with the course of the history.

2. But that we can detect any corresponding progression in his inspired teaching, seems to be a groundless suspicion, which a careful examination of the order of his speeches and epistles will remove.

The steadiness with which, in his epistle to the Galatians, the Apostle asserts the identity between his earliest and his latest message,[c] has been justly urged as a strong argument against the supposed enlargement or correction of the Gospel which he had originally taught. But it is a still stronger argument if we can find an antecedent witness of St. Paul's own teaching, by which that identity is explicitly established. Now it will not be denied that the discourse at the Pisidian Antioch dates earlier than the two Thessalonian Epistles, and that we can place implicit reliance on the accuracy with which St. Luke has reported it in the Acts of the Apostles. But as if to meet by anticipation the suspicion of a change, that Antiochene discourse contains the germs of all the later doctrine, even in points on which it has been most definitely challenged; and amongst them it embodies St. Paul's most emphatic assertion of the

---

[a] Rom. xi. 13 ; Gal. ii. 7.   [b] Rom. ix. 5.   [c] Gal. i. 8, 9.

impossibility of obtaining justification through the Law (9). It stands between the speech of St. Stephen and the elaborate arguments of the Epistles to the Galatians and the Romans. It resembles the former (10) in its rapid sketch of Jewish history, tracing the steps of the election from Abraham to David, and leading it up to the great Heir of David, whose advent was heralded by John the Baptist.[a] It resembles the latter in its doctrine of the fulfilment of the promise which had been made unto the fathers; of the revelation through Jesus Christ of the Divine righteousness, in relation to the sin of man; and the utter failure of the Law of Moses to yield the justification which the sinner sought.[b] But this question can be reduced to a single issue. The Thessalonian Epistles, it is alleged, 'say nothing of justification by faith, and not by the works of the Law.' The inference is, that this great doctrine had not at that time been unfolded in the mind of the Apostle. It is enough, by way of answer, to quote the explicit declaration which he made at an earlier date to the Jews of Antioch: 'Be it known unto you, therefore, men and brethren, that through this Man is preached unto you the forgiveness of sins; and ἐν τούτῳ πᾶς ὁ πιστεύων δικαιοῦται· by Him all that believe are justified from all things, from which ye could not be justified by the law of Moses.'[c] As to the contrast, too, between the Jew and Gentile, I have had a previous occasion to point out that the speech at Lystra sets forth the very same

[a] Acts xiii. 17-25. [b] Acts xiii. 32, 38, 39. [c] Acts xiii. 38, 39.

conception of Gentile knowledge, which the Epistle to the Romans afterwards unfolds. God had left them in times past 'to walk in their own ways,' yet had sent them His witness in the rains and seasons.[a] Precisely so at Athens, on the very same journey to which the Thessalonian Epistles must belong, the Apostle repeats this doctrine, with the variation needed for more cultivated hearers, when he shows how God had winked at times of ignorance, yet had made men to bear such traces of His image, that they never ceased to feel after their Heavenly Father out of the midst of their thick darkness.[b]

3. But again it is alleged, that we can discover the human workings of the mind of the Apostle, as it wavers between the opposite sides of a question, and as he loses the logical control over his argument, and is tossed from side to side, in the tentative progress from hesitation to faith (11). The proof of this position is commonly made out by limiting the Apostle's words, on each aspect of the question, to a narrower meaning than we can conceive them to possess; and by applying the stigma of wavering or contradiction to a method which is simply meant to bring out great truths in all their breadth and fulness, by an emphatic assertion of the contrasted alternatives, which are respectively necessary to give expression to the whole revelation. On this subject I must refer to some remarks which I have previously offered.[c] A fair solution of the difficulty may be found, I think, in every instance,

[a] Acts xiv. 16, 17.   [b] Acts xvii. 27, 30.   [c] Lecture III.

by prefixing to the argument the broad conception which is meant to be divided; and then marking the steps through which the Apostle unfolds it, as he presents us with first one view of truth, and then the other, urging with strenuous zeal the claims of each on our acceptance, and leaving to obedient faith, or the enlightened spirit, the duty of grasping the connection between them.

For a brief illustration of the Apostle's method, we might turn to his statements in the Epistle to the Romans on the presence, the nature, and the operation of a law (12). We may speak of the laws of God in three main senses, according as we wish to describe, now a fact of mere uniformity in nature; now the supreme authority, which imposed that uniformity by the action of His will; and now those principles of moral obligation, which fix the eternal landmarks between right and wrong. In this third sense, with which alone we are now concerned, law denotes revealed knowledge, connected with the conception of authority, obligation, or constraint. The term includes the teaching both of conscience and of special revelation; and the law of revelation is subdivided again, according to the two leading dispensations, into the Law of Moses and the Law of Christ.

Beginning from this outline, we may classify the usage of St. Paul. The constituent elements, I say, of moral law are knowledge and constraint. At one time, then, he applies the word in its vaguest sense to the law which was written on the hearts of the Gentiles, where both light and obligation existed only with their feeblest power. In a second and far more copious class of instances, he uses the word for the Mosaic dispensation, where the Law was as clear as God's hand could write it, and as inflexible as the granite (13) on which it was inscribed. Against both of these laws mankind had offended, with a uniformity which established a tyranny of wickedness, and so constituted, under a third usage, the law of sin and death, a law of evil, which mocks God's uniformities, while it displaces His obligation by the bondage of a more bitter service. Fourthly, the Gospel brought in a clearer light and easier yoke: yet both the elements continued present; and the Apostle therefore represents it as the Law of the Gospel, 'the law of the Spirit of life in Christ Jesus,' or what St. James calls 'the perfect law of liberty.'[a] Through these four meanings, we find, on examination, that the Apostle's argument moves clearly and distinctly; the context in every case fixing the application, and giving no ground for the charge of obscurity, unless we choose to bind him by a narrower usage, and refuse to give scope for the broader utterance of his thought.

We may add, that some of the stronger and more perplexing expressions in his argument are mere applications of the words of Christ. In explaining them we must remember a Scripture peculiarity which has been previously indicated,[b] namely, that lower degrees of either grace or knowledge are

[a] Rom. viii. 2; James i. 25.   [b] Above, p. 19.

often described as negations rather than deficiencies. To be without law means, then, in the case of the Gentiles, to be left to the guidance of that fainter law, which was only written on the fleshly tables of the heart.ᵃ When St. Paul says, 'I had not known sin, but by the law,' he no more means to deny that the Gentiles could sin without the Law of Moses, than our Lord meant us to draw a similar inference when He said, 'If I had not come and spoken unto them, they had not had sin.'ᵇ The reference of Christ is to the Law of the Gospel; the reference of the Apostle is to the Law of Moses. But behind both these there lay the Law of the Gentiles, which in their case also was the strength of sin, and which gave them such a knowledge of God's will, as invested their disobedience with the same character of guilt, which marks the deeper transgressions of the Jew and Christian. In all cases alike, God's law is 'holy, and the commandment holy and just and good.'ᶜ But when it rouses the opposition of our fallen nature, it evokes the latent mischief which it does not cause, displays it in its own evil tendency, and increases the condemnation of those who sin against the light of God. So far as St. Paul's argument is specially limited to the Law of Moses, the key to the entire difficulty must be found in the relation of that Law to the Promise, and in the uselessness of knowledge unaccompanied by grace.

From his conception of law the step is easy, to

ᵃ Rom. ii. 14.   ᵇ Rom. vii. 7; John xv. 22.
ᶜ Rom. vii. 12.

draw out a similar peculiarity which marks his explanation of the position and prospects of the Jews.[a] The germ of the argument by which this problem is answered can be detected before the date of St. Paul's conversion, in that speech of St. Stephen, to which he was a listener, and which draws so clear a distinction between such outward privileges as the Law and Temple, and the spiritual blessing of the approbation of God. It is a mere extension of that argument to show, that the election of the Jews was conditioned by its object, which was the ultimate salvation of the Gentiles also. The Jews were the people whom God had chosen to keep alive His truth among mankind, and to prevent the torch of inspired knowledge from utter extinction in the darkness. They were subjects of God's law, guardians of His oracles, kinsmen of His prophets, the fleshly brethren of the incarnate Son of God. To them pertained 'the adoption, and the glory, and the covenants, and the giving of the Law, and the service of God, and the promises; whose' were 'the fathers, and of whom, as concerning the flesh, Christ came, who is over all, God blessed for ever.'[b] But as individuals, they failed to attain 'to the law of righteousness,' by 'going about to establish their own righteousness,' and not submitting 'themselves unto the righteousness of God;'[c] and as a nation, they forfeited the privilege of their election when they abused their stewardship, and asserted an

---

[a] Rom. iii., iv., ix., x., xi.
[b] Rom. ix. 4, 5. [c] Rom. ix. 31; x. 3.

exclusive right to blessings which they held only in the common interests of man. A tenure of this kind could of course be described in varying language, as the thought dwelt more on the greatness of the blessing, or the danger of its loss. It could not be otherwise than that the argument should move through a series of contrasted phrases, as the Apostle passes on from the much advantage of the Jew to the rightful claims of the Gentile; as he weighs the ancient glories of the sons of Abraham against the sins which had caused their election to be annulled; as he balances God's promises against man's frustrations of His merciful designs; and as he qualifies the darkness of their present rejection by the dawning brightness of their future hope. But we have only to let the interpretation follow out the full breadth of the Apostle's meaning, and the apparent wavering is found to be the mere method of exposition, and not in any case the sign of any doubt about the truth.

The nature of our present purpose forbids us to go into any further details of criticism for establishing the position which has now been upheld. It is enough to have pointed out the grounds on which we are justified in rejecting the view of his spiritual development, which casts his earlier message into an imperfect form, and charges his later teaching with vacillation between the sides of incompatible alternatives. Let us turn, in the last place, to remind you again of the importance of the principle, which is the counterpart to what we have been studying; the inestimable advantage of that real human presence, which moulds all the details of Scripture instruction, yet without subjecting the record to any tarnish from man's sin.

If Scripture speaks to all hearts alike—if it meets every perplexity, strengthens every fainting spirit, comforts every mourner, and spans the whole compass of every intellect, from the highest to the lowest—one main reason of this many-sided influence may be found in the fact with which we have been dealing: the fact that the Holy Spirit speaks to us through men who were in all respects exposed to all the same emotions with ourselves; through men who represented every mode of thought, every shade of feeling, every social class, as well as every phase of the religious character. Throughout all its countless details we may see that Scripture is as certainly the book of man as we believe it to be the book of God. Its voice is the voice of those who were our fellows, however highly exalted they might be above ourselves. They were the chosen lights of human nature, which shone around the Sun of Righteousness. They formed the royal court of attendant ministers, who interpreted the will of Him that sits upon the throne as Son of Man; of Him who can still be 'touched with the feeling of our infirmities,' because He 'was in all points tempted like as we are, yet without sin.'[a] There

---

[a] Heb. iv. 15.

is no real difficulty in combining these two principles, that the human nature of the sacred writers might act in its completest development and freedom, yet might be guarded from communicating its own imperfections to the revelation which was sent from God to man through man.

The human characters of Scripture are all gathered round a common centre, to which they bear a widely different relation in proportion to their distance from its light. On their outskirts are crowds of undistinguished agents, who play the subordinate parts in the great drama it unfolds. The innermost circle of the sacred writers retains the perfect impress of man's threefold nature, while it rises towards a higher form of being, as it shares in a nearer spiritual intercourse with God. But God's light loses nothing of its heavenly purity because it is reflected back from human faces; while man gains all the advantage of the pervading presence of a sympathy which answers to the most varied emotions of his heart.

LECTURE VIII.

—✦—

2 Tim. ii. 15.

'Rightly dividing the word of truth.'

WE are now drawing near to the conclusion of the argument, through which I have endeavoured to unfold the completeness of both the divine and human elements in Holy Scripture. It remains that I should occupy this closing Lecture with a brief summary of the results which I have sought to establish, and the lessons which they are intended to convey.

The question with which our enquiries have been connected forms the narrowest, though not altogether the least important, of three leading controversies, which have recently aroused unusual interest: those which relate to the respective differentiæ of Scripture, of Christianity, and of mankind. The series widens outward, from doubts on the specific characteristics of Scripture, to doubts on the specific claims of Christianity, and to doubts on the specific distinctness of man. What is the peculiarity which justifies us in marking off Scripture from all other books, as being, not only the word of man, but the Word of God?

In what respects does Christianity rise so wondrously above all other religions as to justify the position which is assumed by its supporters? And what is the difference between man and the highest of those lower races which exhibit so strange a mockery of our reason? While dealing more particularly with the first of these questions, we have found it necessary to touch on both the others at different points in our argument.

But it would be an unwise course to trust our cause to any formal definition, which should be framed so dogmatically as to proclaim itself the end of controversy on any of these important topics. No reasonable person can hope to do more than offer such suggestions as may serve to establish the profound reality of the boundary line by which the specific difference is in each case guarded, and to relieve the alarm with which any recognition of the generic resemblance is commonly received. We believe that man is distinguished from all other tenants of this world which we inhabit, not only by a finer organisation and a keener intelligence, and the preeminence which is represented and secured through the gift of language; but above all, and perhaps as the cause of all, by that spiritual element which bears its living witness to our creation in God's image, and which enables us to enter into communion with God. We believe that Christianity differs from all other religions because it centres in the Divine Person of our Saviour, conveys the special earnest of the witness of God's Spirit, operates through sacraments and ordinances of covenanted efficacy, and is perpetuated by the establishment of a sacred society which preserves the deposit of religious knowledge, and enjoys the promised presence of the Spirit of the Lord. That deposit, we believe, was originally embodied in the Holy Scriptures, which differ from every other book, because they alone contain a guaranteed revelation, which lifts the veil, so far as needed, from both the earliest past and the remotest future, to disclose the motive, the sanction, and the law of man's labours; and because the Holy Spirit, which watched over the delivery of that revelation, filled the spirits of the writers with a more complete and pervading presence than ever presided over the execution of a merely human work. And so long as we hold these points with confidence, we may be ready to trace out with perfect calmness the signs of larger unity, which extend the analogy to other spheres; and we may admire, with reverent adoration, the widening witness which they bear to the uniformities of the Divine counsels. But 'it becometh well the just to be thankful;'[a] and it is not for the rich to be jealous of the poor, for those fragments of God's blessing which they share. Such jealousy would, indeed, betray dissatisfaction with our riches, or a doubt whether they are really our own. We cannot grudge God's lower gifts, when we know that He has endowed ourselves in more abundant measure. Rather should our own experience of His bounty lead us

[a] Ps. xxxiii. 1.

to expect, that it would often be poured forth in wider and less usual channels than those through which its ordinary blessings reach us. We may welcome the labours of scientific enquirers, who draw out man's affinities with lower races, if we have realised the independent character of those higher gifts, which make men alone the sons of God. We may be thankful to acknowledge the fatherly goodness with which God lent some jewels of His truth to the darkened heathen, if we feel sure of our own position within reach of that storehouse of His Church, from which 'every scribe which is instructed unto the kingdom of heaven' can bring 'forth out of his treasure things new and old.'[a] And we may rejoice to recognise the Spirit's presence in every lofty work of man, if we have learnt to appreciate the fiery force of that more certain inspiration, which fills God's Word with power and light.

In dealing with the question which has formed our own immediate subject, I have been guided throughout by the strong conviction, that very scanty success has rewarded any attempt to treat the Scriptures either as purely human, or as purely divine, or as compounded of those two elements in such a manner that man's reason or conscience can discriminate unfailingly between them. It has appeared to me that an escape from these perplexities might be found in the complete and fearless recognition of both elements, with all their natural results of

[a] Matt. xiii. 52.

characteristic influence, through every portion of the sacred record ; a union which is strictly conformable to the analogy of God's ordinary dealings with the human spirit, which He guides, and moulds, and strengthens, and perfects, but which He never deprives of its original endowment, of free and responsible action. It is not to be denied, indeed, that the subject-matter may cause now the one element and now the other to be specially prominent in particular passages; but it is maintained that this never happens so exclusively, that the one which is less prominent is utterly withdrawn.

The theologian can be at no loss for parallel cases, where two distinct agencies are found to cooperate throughout one sphere with so complete a presence that they cannot be distinguished, though they must not be confounded. Without seeking illustrations from the more mysterious regions of the interaction of the Persons in the ever-blessed Trinity, or from the less definite topic of the Sacramental Presence, we may venture to recur to the current illustration which is afforded to the Scriptures by the twofold nature of our Lord. We must not, indeed, use it without being careful to mark that there are limits to the resemblance, which can be traced between a Book and a Person : a Book in which two elements are combined together in one result; a Person in whom two natures are united together in one individuality. The analogy extends no farther than this; that in Christ, the Godhead and the Manhood are both perfect, yet are inseparably united without loss or limitation: in Scripture, the divine and human elements are both complete, yet, as contributed respectively by God and man, they meet in one common production, each without limitation, and each without loss. The necessary restriction of this analogy is no objection to our using it so far as it holds true. When the Athanasian creed compares the union of God and man in Christ to the union of soul and body in man, we know that we are dealing with an imperfect parallel, which cannot be treated as complete without falling into the Apollinarian heresy. Under the same reserve for an imperfect figure, we may illustrate the cooperation of the divine and human agencies in producing God's Word Written by the coexistence of the divine and human natures in God's Word Incarnate.

Now the doubts which make men fear to admit the full influence of the human element rest on a mistaken conception of the place and effect of sin; as though it were an essential portion of that human nature, which it does but derange and confound. Such a suspicion might be averted by the recollection that Christ took our nature with all its infirmities, yet without the slightest shadow of taint from our sin. Nothing could be stronger than the assertion of the inspired writer, that though absolutely sinless, yet He 'was in all points tempted like as we are.'[a] Nothing could be clearer than the testimony of the Gospels, that He 'increased in wisdom and

[a] Heb. iv. 15.

stature,' and hungered and thirsted, and was tempted by Satan and buffeted by man, and was 'sorrowful and very heavy,' and suffered even to the utmost agony by which our feeble nature can be torn and distressed.ᵃ But while He thus felt all, that He might pity all,ᵇ and through all His words and acts of mercy exhibited the most perfect sympathy for our infirmities, yet the dark cloud of personal guilt never cast the faintest reflection on His stainless spirit. Nay, more than this, there was a divine decorum (1) watching round His path, to ward off those sinless indignities from material agencies which it was not seemly that the Son of God should suffer. Though He ate and drank, and slept and rose, and fasted and was wearied, and had not 'where to lay His head;' though He was the mark for the blind assaults of evil men, and of spirits still more evil; though 'being in an agony He prayed more earnestly,' and His 'soul' was 'exceeding sorrowful, even unto death;'ᶜ though 'His pale weak form' was 'worn with many a watch of sorrow and unrest;'ᵇ yet we never read that actual sickness was allowed to fasten on His sacred Person. Though He laid down that life, which none could take from Him,ᵈ and conquered Death by the mere act of dying, yet He never permitted disease or mortality to tarry in His presence; but drove them

ᵃ Luke ii. 52; Matt. iv. 2; John iv. 7; xix. 28; Matt. xxvi. 67, 37; Luke xxii. 44.
ᵇ *Christian Year*, Tuesday before Easter.
ᶜ Matt. xi. 19; viii. 24; John iv. 6; Matt. viii. 20; Luke xxii. 44; Matt. xxvi. 38.   ᵈ John x. 18.

LECTURE VIII.

from their victims by an instant assertion of His divine supremacy, as baffled and impotent foes.[a]

And here we may gain a clue of guidance to tell us what we may expect to find in that element of Holy Scripture which was to come from the agency of man. It would be human to the very utmost, in the broadest acceptation, short of sin, in which the word can be properly employed; human in its sympathy with suffering, resignation, and rejoicing; human in its recognition of the obligations of the present; human in its keen longings for a brighter future. All this it might be; all this, and more than this, we actually find it; yet all the while it may be guarded from the slightest lapse into such errors as would be unseemly companions for a message from above (2).

But now it must be borne in mind, that I state this principle as the result of an enquiry, not the dictate of a theory. The proper way to learn the true character of revelation is not to conjecture what it ought to be, but to examine what it is. We cannot pay too much regard to Butler's warning, that 'we are not in any sort competent judges, what supernatural instruction were to have been expected,' and therefore, that we must not 'pretend to judge of the Scripture by preconceived expectations.'[b] When such an examination has carried us on, from a general acknowledgement of the deep human sympathies of Scripture, to compare the nature and history of its

---
[a] Matt. viii. 16; John xi. 21, &c.
[b] *Analogy*, II. 3 (pp. 211, 212, ed. 1836).

records with those of any other ancient writings, we find that it obeys implicitly the main conditions under which all other early literature was formed and handed down. Its text may be modified by various readings; its inspired guardians appear to have introduced the same kind of minor changes and explanations which persons of similar authority might introduce in parallel cases; its sense has often been obscured for centuries by mistranslations and misinterpretations; it stands in close contact with large masses of external material; it touches at a thousand points on heathen literature and history; its later writers do not hesitate at times to avail themselves of facts derived from outer sources, which tradition, and not Scripture, must have furnished. And while the strenuous labours of unfriendly critics have not succeeded in convicting it of any such departure from the present historical standard as we cannot account for without imputing error to the original writer, it is yet clear that the form in which the narrative is shaped and propounded is analogous to that in which other authentic histories of similar antiquity are moulded. The argument has indeed been confused by an over-estimate of the importance of various chronological details, many of which rest on mere hypothesis, and which are so far not an integral part of the record (3); as well as by laying undue stress on names or numerals, which may have been corrupted through the lapse of ages (4). Nor must we forget to claim a reasonable allowance on account of the brevity of the narrative, and our ignorance of details which would at once explain a seeming difficulty. But all these corrections and qualifications are in precise conformity with our general position, that the form of the narrative, and the mode of its transmission, belong, as a general rule, to the human framework; and yet that the human framework has been preserved by God's providence from any such imperfections as would offend against the decorum of His revelation to mankind. The facts which I have mentioned must be frankly acknowledged, but they must not be exaggerated. We believe that they have failed to exercise an evil influence over the sacred record. They do not prove that it is in any sense untruthful, unreliable, or unhistorical. They only establish this fundamental principle, that it shared in the external characteristics of analogous literature, as clearly as it shared in the human thoughts and emotions of those by whom its several portions were composed.

A further extension of this position, that Scripture was written in the language of mankind, and was meant from the first to be 'understanded of the people,' enables us to account for the use of terms adjusted to the scientific knowledge, or common modes of speaking, which prevailed in the ages when the books were written (5). We are ourselves in the daily habit of using words in their superficial significance, without appealing to the theories in which they originated, and from which they have descended into common use, through pedigrees which have frequently been lost. Great interest has been often thrown over philological studies, by the disclosure of such facts in the history of words, and by the ingenious analysis which has forced words themselves to reveal the original causes of their employment. But we should be ready to resist the tyranny which should try to rule our present usage by an antiquarian etymology, or make us answerable for views on which we have no particular call to form a judgment, and which scientific men have perhaps long since resigned as erroneous. Now, it is as unreasonable to argue that Scripture writers are responsible for the opinions under which their customary expressions were imposed, as to accuse men of ignorance when they continue to use the imperfect terms of an unfinished science; or to accuse them of superstition when they call months and days by their old heathen names; or to accuse them of pertinacious adherence to antiquated error, when they describe the changes and aspects of earth and heaven, of day and night, in phrases that have survived abandoned systems.

These remarks may serve to recall the train of thought by which we have endeavoured to establish the completeness of that human element which proves its presence so conclusively, even to the most careless reader, through the characteristics of the several sacred writers. And I have sought to show that this completeness may be maintained and taught, without the slightest disparagement towards that great truth which is its counterpart and consummation—the truth that the whole of Scripture is not less certainly penetrated by an influence which is absolutely divine. Objective in its origin, and thus broadly contrasted with the speculations of mankind; perfect in its moral and religious teaching, and thus strongly opposed to those false creeds, which have filled the earth with cruelty and sin; profound in its grasp of those eternal principles, which can only be brought within the reach of the human intellect by presentation in a series of balanced and contrasted statements; all-pervading in its presence, so that it lies everywhere beneath the human words of Scripture, and constantly suggests a deeper sense than the knowledge or designs of the original writer could command: the inspiration of the Bible combines with its revelations to form an element so conclusively divine, that we cannot mistake it for the dream of man; we cannot hesitate to recognise its heavenly source and spiritual power. Nor can we underestimate the fulness of its influence, without closing our eyes on the entire higher range of the phenomena of Scripture, and thus falling into the grave mistake of constructing a theory from which the more important series of the facts is excluded. Considerations of this kind enable us to complete our statement, by showing that Scripture is as divine as it is human; the voice of Him who dwells in eternity, though reaching us through the organs and minds of His earthly servants ; the work of the Holy Spirit Himself, filling all that He communicates with light to enlighten and with grace to save.

If these conclusions have been correctly drawn, we may expect to find that they will verify themselves by their fitness to meet some fair conditions, which we should not have been justified in demanding at the outset, but which will serve as a valid test of the results of our enquiry. From this point of view, for instance, we might reasonably ask whether the truths alleged to be revealed are really such as man's unaided mind was incompetent to furnish; whether the revelation possesses a depth of meaning which admits of progressive development in the spiritual sense, and is caused by the presence of a divine significance, lying hidden beneath the words of man; and whether the inspired record stands clear from any taint of human infirmity, while the characteristics of the separate writers are never obliterated. The importance of these positions has always been seen so clearly, that the attempt to disprove the affirmative answers has furnished three favourite topics to those who have wished to modify or weaken the common faith on inspiration. At one time such reasoners have tried to destroy the distinctive claims of revelation, by arguments which involve the further destruction of the distinctive claims of Christianity itself; alleging —what in a different sense indeed is true—that Christianity is as old as the Creation; and gleaning scattered passages from heathen authorities, to prove the wide diffusion of some fragmentary light, which they propose as a rival for the full illumination of the sacred record. At other times they have raised formidable difficulties against the doctrine of a double sense, in which work they have been too often assisted by the exaggerations of its upholders; affirming that the theory, as commonly explained, is inconsistent with the facts, or destroys the true position of the human writer, or is an unfair attempt to get rid of supposed contradictions, by representing them as mere developments. At other times, again, they have striven to prove that the human element exerts an influence of absolute error—an argument which they work out by overestimating the significance of alleged inaccuracies; by treating as mistakes what were mere accommodations; by thrusting scientific doctrines into the sphere of Scripture—an error, again, in which their opponents have been only too ready to keep them in countenance; and above all, by urging that the Old Testament is marred by the harsh dictates of an imperfect morality, and that defects less striking, but not less certain, can be discovered in the blessed teaching of the New. The answer to these cavils will be found, as we believe, in the careful discrimination which separates in all cases between the matter and the form; which distinguishes, in moral principles, between the record of a sin and its express approbation; which analyses mixed actions into their component elements, and confines the praise which is accorded to the element of good; which recognises the Jewish nation as an authorised instrument of God's vegeance against evil, and therefore invests its public acts with something like the judicial character, though careful to stop short of the extension of the principle, which would make God's command turn evil into good; and which points out that errors recorded in the lives of Scripture writers were not permitted to throw a shade of imperfection over the message which they delivered as ambassadors from God. To these subjects I have endeavoured to direct attention in such detail as the nature of my task permitted: with a deep sense of the responsibility which rests on any one who ventures, however diffidently, to suggest terms of peace, while men's thoughts are still agitated by the recollection of the strife, and while the atmosphere is still charged with tendencies to further controversy; yet in the earnest hope, and with the fervent prayer, that there may be some minds, at all events, which will be thankful to escape from the contest, and find refuge in a solution which aims at preserving alike the absolute divinity of the message, and the unimpaired humanity of those through whose lips and pens it was conveyed.

Let us pass on now to consider, briefly, the bearing of this argument on the great question of Scripture interpretation, to which all such enquiries lead our thoughts. It is the foremost duty of the Christian teacher rightly to divide the word of truth (6). The metaphor of this passage may be uncertain, but the precept is distinct and clear. The figure may either mean that, like a good steward, he is to apportion to each member of God's household his meat in due season; or perhaps, that he is 'to distribute the word rightly,'[a] by arranging it under different heads of belief, according to the just 'proportion of faith;'[b] or

[a] Hooker, *E. P.*, V. lxxxi. 2.   [b] Rom. xii. 6.

that he is to lay straightly out the road or the furrow, by drawing a direct line through the intricacies of error, without yielding to any bias from his onward course. Whichever sense we adopt, the duty of the interpreter is taught clearly and distinctly. It is far less pardonable in the case of Scripture than in the case of any other writing, to have recourse to the devices of a forced, unnatural, or, worst of all, an uncandid interpretation.

1. 'The principle,' says Warburton, 'which Grotius went upon, in commenting the Bible, was, that it should be interpreted on the same rules of criticism that men use in the study of all other ancient writings.'[a] Now what is the reason why the restatement of a precept, which has so much to recommend it, should have given rise in our own day to special opposition and remonstrance (7)? Perhaps Warburton's remarks may suggest the explanation: 'Nothing,' he says, 'could be more reasonable than his principle; but unluckily he deceived himself in the application of it.... He went on this reasonable ground, that the prophecies should be interpreted like all other ancient writings; and on examining their authority he found them to be truly divine. When he had gone thus far, he then preposterously went back again, and commented as if they were confessed to be merely human.' It is obvious that those who apply the principle in the same manner can only escape from the same inconsistency, by denying that the Books

[a] *Divine Legation of Moses*, VI. vi. 2; vol. iii. p. 230.

contain that special divine element which distinguishes them from every other composition of man.

The canon, then, which the last generation learnt under the form that the expounder of Scripture must follow 'the same mode of interpretation which is applied to classic authors,'[a] binds us precisely so far as Scripture resembles classic authors: but beyond that point it is necessary that Scripture interpretation should follow a course of its own. No fair interpreter could complain of the injunction to obey the conditions of truth and candour, to be biassed by nothing, to pervert nothing; to let no considerations of possible consequences deter him from accepting the primary meaning which the literal and grammatical interpretation would convey. But at that precise point where Scripture ceases to resemble any other book, the common rules of criticism fail. No one attempts to treat all other books as equal. Rhetoric and logic; history and speculation; poetry and prose; the suggestion of probable inference, and the rigorous deductions of scientific conclusions; all are dealt with alike, up to a certain point, and not beyond it. And when we allege that there is a line, at which Scripture passes beyond the analogy of other compositions, we thereby claim that beyond that line it shall receive an appropriate criticism.

It is important that this position should be distinctly comprehended; and that it should be known precisely what we mean when we allege, that Scrip-

[a] Bp. Marsh, *Lectures on the Criticism and Interpretation of the Bible*, p. 510, ed. 1828.

ture throughout contains a divine element, which is in itself as complete as the human element, and which is incomparably more important. We acknowledge that there is one sense in which Scripture must be treated like any other book, in so far as it is the work of those who had πάθη like unto other men.[a] We are thankful to every one who will give us sound advice on the grammatical, historical, contextual, and minute interpretation.[b] We ask for no difference in criticism as criticism. We merely stipulate that criticism shall be adjusted to the subject-matter, as it would be in every other instance. If Scripture were no more than any other book, the canon referred to would be irrefragable. So far as Scripture corresponds to other books, we use it, and claim it as our own, and welcome all suggestions by which it seems likely that the exposition will be served. But if Scripture is all this and more; if there is a point at which it outstrips the analogy of other writings; at that point it enters on a separate province, which must be marked by a variation in the laws of criticism. Within proper restrictions, and under proper explanations, the rule may be useful in reminding men that God's Scripture revelation is expressed in human language, and submits to the conditions of human thought. But if ever it is proposed as a sufficient canon of Scripture interpretation, we are compelled to rejoin that in that view it is either a truism or a petitio principii. If it merely means that the interpreter of Scripture

---

[a] Acts xiv. 15; James v. 17. [b] *Aids to Faith*, p. 439.

should be fair, should be truthful, should be accurate, should be just, should be candid—then it is a truism; for who can doubt it? If it is meant to involve the denial that God has imparted to the books which form the Bible any special quality of spiritual eminence, which distinguishes it from every other human work— then it is a petitio principii; for the existence of that higher element is the very ground on which the special principles of Scripture exposition rest. The distinction may be compared with that which must be drawn to limit the domain of positive science in its relation to religion. We accept the laws which science teaches, without permitting it to trench on that faith in God's providence which a blind regard to its submissive sequences has often tended to obscure. And we accept with gratitude the labours of the scholar, without resigning our faith in that diviner and more spiritual light, to which the deeper meaning of the Scripture text bears witness.

2. But Scripture interpretation should be comprehensive as well as spiritual. Its expounder should be ready to weigh one part with another, to give to each phrase its broader rather than its narrower meaning, to shun private opinion, to dread partial exposition, and to take the whole tenor of the faith for his guidance, when he seeks to enter on the mind of Christ. It is an error against this fundamental principle when men fall into the habit of relying too exclusively on isolated texts, without much regard to the context, and with still less respect for the analogy of Scripture (8). Controversialists are naturally dis-

posed to place an undue value on passages which seem to command the foremost place in argument, by the conciseness which condenses whole trains of reasoning into single phrases, and by the ease with which they are transferred to the memory of the hearer. But it often happens that the main principles of an argument lie rather beneath than on the surface, and are more characterised by the wideness of their influence than by the point and conciseness of their occasional expression; just as a mountain spring may prove its presence rather by the verdure that surrounds it than by the flashing of its unveiled waters in the sunlight; or as a tract of rock may rarely break the surface, yet may uphold wide districts on its basis, as a portion of the solid fabric of the earth. In that case single texts only serve to guide us to the neighbourhood in which the traces of that deeper influence may be found. If, on the other hand, we assume that a text is the sole vehicle of a doctrine, we suggest the suspicion that it could be detached without injury from the great framework of principles on which the revelation rests; just as a boulder could be removed from the surface of the ground, while no power of man could have upheaved it had it been a peak emerging from the living rock. And this suspicion has been fostered by the unwise alarm with which the orthodox have looked on the labours of criticism whenever it seemed likely to rob them of some favourite texts. We are bound, indeed, to defend the text in possession till reason has been shown for the change. But if criticism has proved in any case that the marginal notes of early Christians have found admission to the record, we may rest assured that such glosses can be removed without injury to the revelation, which, even were they genuine, they would not so much embody as epitomise.

3. Closely allied with this error, is the habit fostered by the controversial spirit, of taking a stand on one line of texts to the neglect of such modifications or corrections as other passages would furnish. This is the mistake, on which we have previously dealt in detail, of taking half-truths for truths, and yielding them an undivided instead of qualified obedience. A practical illustration may prove the most weighty; and I know not where we could find one of such surpassing magnitude, as the course of reasoning which seems to have led the Jews to the rejection of our Lord (9). At first thought, indeed, we never look after their reasoning. We only ask, in perplexed surprise, was ever guilt or penalty like theirs! To reject that Saviour, whose promise had been the sole day-star of humanity, ever brightening from the darkness of the Fall; to repudiate the long-sought descendant of Abraham, who had been foreshadowed for nearly two thousand years, as the culminating glory of their ancient line; to refuse allegiance to that Son of David, who was to found a nobler power than David's kingdom, and was to bear the rank of David's Lord: can we conceive of a more fatal national infatuation than that which thus cast away the single object of their own election, the one flower and perfection of their race and name? Our

LECTURE VIII. 247

very reason seems silenced by the greatness of their crime. We shrink from its analysis. We hesitate to account for it by ordinary motives. We take refuge in some theory of inexplicable frenzy, or demoniacal influence, which removes it beyond the rank of the common laws of human nature. And yet that solution is inconsistent with the clearness of the inspired narrative, and incompatible with any keen perception of the warning it embodies for ourselves. If we examine carefully the Gospel records, we shall discover, I think, that the Jews were simply acting upon their own narrowed interpretation of one portion of the Divine injunctions, in defiance of the obligations which countless other passages conveyed. Disappointed by the low estate to which our gracious Lord had condescended; vexed by the downfal of the carnal expectations which had looked forward to Messiah's promised kingdom, as a more splendid dominion than had hitherto been gathered under a Jewish sceptre; they simply sought for weapons to avenge their disappointment from misapplications of the word of God. And then they fell into the too common error of letting one text blot out a thousand; of dwelling on favourite dogmas, and misinterpreted passages, till the wide fields of Scripture truth were narrowed to the limits of their prejudiced and partial zeal. There can be little doubt that the Jewish leaders believed themselves to be acting under the authority of that command in Deuteronomy, which enjoins that they should slay the prophet who came to them with signs and wonders, in case he tempted them to 'go after other gods.'[a] They wilfully overlooked the promise of that other prophet, whom the Lord their God was to raise up from amongst them:[b] a promise which lies near to the other passage in the Mosaic record, and which is supported, explained, and unfolded in the great stream of prophecy which runs from one end to the other of the ancient Scriptures. It was a biassed zeal for a literal, isolated, and faithless interpretation, which made them set the special against the general revelation; and persuade themselves that Christ was teaching a new Divinity, 'because He made Himself the Son of God.'[c]

4. And from this lesson we may draw another inference; namely, the importance of paying due regard to every part of Scripture, alike for its place in the past, and its possible use in the future. This principle should lead us to retain a firm hold on those portions of the sacred record in which we can see no present utility, or which may seem to create some passing difficulty. Christianity does not come before us merely as a present life, which would continue to exist if dissevered from the past. It would be felt that an open attempt to set aside the Bible which records its history would be a definite attack on Christianity itself. Attempts of that kind, therefore, possess at all events that measure of security which accompanies an open and acknowledged danger. Much greater is the need of watchfulness against the more covert and perilous proposals, which would

---

[a] Deut. xiii. 1, &c.   [b] Deut. xviii. 15.   [c] John xix. 7.

break at least some of the many links of connection between our living Christianity and the Book of God. We have to resist the temptation which presents itself under the specious suggestion, that we might resign the letter with all its difficulties, yet retain the full blessings of its spiritual teaching. Thus some have tried to assail a book here and a chapter there; in one place a few sentences, in others a mere phrase; and they would persuade us that these may be allowed to fall away and perish, as withered leaves might drop from a tree which continues to flourish. It is a more true figure to say that the result would rather resemble the slow degrees by which life passes from the dying body: first, the extremities are chilled under the grasp of death; then the fatal numbness steals gradually onward, till it fastens on life's stronghold in the heart. Or we might liken it to the dying out of an illumination in a royal mansion: first, there is darkness in some distant chamber; then it steals along the corridors and halls; one room after another vanishes from sight; one light after another is extinguished; till the whole building rests in unbroken obscurity, when the last lamp of all has been withdrawn.

But the waning time reminds me that this is not the opportunity for entering more minutely into the details of Scripture interpretation, and that it is necessary to bring these observations to a close. How can I find a better conclusion than by reminding you of the lesson which the Church suggests, when the prayers for inspiration which she puts into our mouths recall us from theories on the inspiration of Scripture to seek the inspiration of a holy life? If the end is greater than the means, that living gift of the Spirit is greater than even those lofty endowments which raised men to become its authorised witnesses, and to guide us to the ordinances through which it is bestowed. Greater, indeed, yet very different; greater in its universality, its duration, its practical connection with our own personal experience; yet inferior in those high attributes of supernatural illumination, in which the writers of Scripture stand alone. When St. Paul has enumerated the most precious gifts that man can long for, he assigns the highest rank to charity, which sums up all the purest graces of the Christian life.[a] Prophecies and tongues and knowledge—the gifts of the teacher, the preacher, the expounder of God's will—these are but parts of the earthly organisation which God has established for the recovery of man. They fail, they cease, they vanish away. Our highest knowledge here is partial. Our spiritual vision does but resemble the wavering outline reflected from a clouded mirror. But the life of true love grows ever upward, with an uninterrupted progression, toward 'the measure of the stature of the fulness of Christ.'[b] And while the river of life is flowing past us, and each of us may drink and live for ever, no folly could be greater than to neglect the privilege, and waste time and pains in endless contests on the nature of its earthly source.

[a] 1 Cor. xiii. 13.   [b] Eph. iv. 13.

And let me close with an earnest exhortation to our younger brethren, that they will not perplex themselves with curious questions on the inspiration of Scripture till they forget to claim that present inspiration, 'the spirit of truth, unity, and concord,' which they are bound to pray for and to make their own. There may perhaps be others here, who need as earnest a word of warning against falling into such bondage to the pleasures of their age, that the voice of God's Spirit is scarcely heard within their hearts. It is well that they should rejoice in the gifts of their youth, if they do but remember to rejoice with trembling, and to pray that the Holy Spirit will continue to dwell with them, filling their bodies with purity and their spirits with devotion. The evil days will come before they are expected; and then where will be the pleasures which deceived them for a season? The sun and the light and the stars will be darkened, and 'the clouds' will 'return after the rain.' 'The daughters of music shall be brought low,' 'and the grasshopper shall be a burthen, and desire shall fail; because man goeth to his long home, and the mourners go about the streets.'[a] We have often had to look on faces that were younger than yours, and not less bright and hopeful, over which the cloud of death had gathered, when the child of God was summoned early to the blessed shelter of its Father's house. And now they draw nearer to God's hidden mysteries than the wisest student of God's Word can reach before the grave.

[a] Eccles. xii. 1–5.

The knowledge of God which we gather from the Scriptures is the earthly foretaste of that beatific vision, which is the crown and consummation of created bliss. The condition which admits us to all gradations of that knowledge is the childlike purity of heart to which its highest gifts are promised—the 'holiness without which no man shall see the Lord.'[a]

It is no light blessing, be assured, that your secular studies are in this place hallowed by the daily circle of religious duties; that your youth is trained to emulate the temper of great saints, because it is passed amidst the forms and memorials of ancient devotion. But the greater is the sorrow if the richness of God's gifts is wasted; the sorer will be the burthen of the grievous punishment, if you pass from the light of God's altar to the outer darkness of sin. Be it rather your lasting study and your earnest prayer that you may see God's Spirit present in His Word, and that you may feel God's Spirit present in your spirits; that the letter of Scripture, which is deadly to the sinner, may be found full of divine life by the humble faith which receives it gladly; and that the endowments which would turn to corruption in the service of sin, may be purified and elevated till you reach that heavenly kingdom, where there is no more sorrow, no more doubt, no more perplexity; but where we shall see Christ as He is, and know as we are known.[b]

[a] Matt. v. 8; Heb. xii. 14. [b] 1 John iii. 2; 1 Cor. xiii. 12.

NOTES.

NOTES.

LECTURE I.

Note 1, *page* 2. Expressions are often found in theological writers, which imply that the heathen entirely lost the human πνεῦμα, as well as the presence of the Holy Spirit. Compare Mr. J. B. Morris's *Essay towards the Conversion of the Hindus*, p. 320, &c. : 'The spirit here spoken of (1 Thess. v. 23) is that supernatural gift whereby Adam was what he was in Paradise.' 'Body is almost essential to the idea, man : it may be logically divided into body and soul; but man and this gift (i. e. spirit) together make up the idea, Christian.' 'The Christian man is this natural man with that supernatural gift which Adam had, restored to him.' Cf. p. 324. So Grotius on 1 Thess. v. 23 : 'Græci omnes *spiritum* hoc loco exponunt χάρισμα=*donum*.' On the opinion of Irenæus, see Mosheim's Note on Cudworth, *Intellectual System of the Universe*, iii. 329, ed. Harrison.

But the *donum supernaturale*, which man had thus possessed and lost, was not the human πνεῦμα, which must be regarded as an integral portion of his nature. It was rather the presence and operation of the Holy Spirit, which purified the created spirit and conformed man to the image of our Lord. See Mr. Scudamore's *Essay on the Office of the Intellect in Religion*, pp. 133, 139, &c. ; and, for the general tenor of English teaching, compare Hooker, *E. P.*, I. xi. 5, and Appendix to Book V., *Works*, ii. 539 ; Bull, *Life*, p. 440; *Works*, ii. 52, 82; iv. 211, 213 ; Waterland, *Works*, iv. 176 ; Mill, *On our Lord's Temptation*, pp. 38–42, 156 ; Wilberforce, *On the Incarnation*, pp. 62–3 ; Mozley, *On Predestination*, pp. 10, 111. Man *exspoliatur gratuitis*; but only *vulneratur in naturalibus* (Bede in S. Thom. Aquin., I^{ma} II^{dae} lxxxv. 1), and the human πνεῦμα is *naturale.* On another aspect of the subject, compare Olshausen's Dissertation, in which *Antiquiss. Eccles. Græcæ Patrum de Immortalitate Animæ Sententiæ recensentur; Opuscula,* No. vii. ' Patres Græci—de spiritu libentissimè concedunt, quod nostri animæ tribuunt, imo plus etiam spiritui dant, dicentes spiritum esse æternum, ἄφθαρτον, imo ζωοποιοῦν: at longè aliam volunt esse ψυχῆς conditionem. Hæc post hominis lapsum a spiritu sejuncta Θνητή est, atque tum demum immortalitatis particeps erit, si cum spiritu denuo fuerit conjuncta.' P. 171; cf. p. 174. On the position of the heathen, see also Lecture II., p. 40, sqq.

Note 2, page 2. See the positions laid down in 529 at Concil. Araus. II., Labbe, viii. 711. Compare S. Thom. Aquin., I^{ma} II^{dae} cix. 2; Hooker, *Works,* ii. 549; Bull, *Works,* ii. 134; Möhler, *Symbolism,* i. 36, &c.; Mozley, *Predestination,* pp. 163, 345, &c.; Bright, *Notes on XVIII. Sermons of St. Leo,* p. 144. The two lines of opinion are drawn out at length in an article on the relation of Calvinism to Modern Doubt, in the *Christian Remembrancer* for Jan. 1863.

Note 3, page 4. Following the more general expressions of Scripture, τοῦ Κυρίου συνεργοῦντος, Mark xvi. 20; Θεοῦ γάρ ἐσμεν συνεργοί, 1 Cor. iii. 9; συνεργοῦντες δέ, 2 Cor. vi. 1; the early Christian writers applied such terms to the composition of the Bible as συνεργοῦντος καὶ τοῦ ἁγίου Πνεύματος· Origen, *On Matt.* iii. 732, B.; cf. τῇ τοῦ Θείου Πνεύματος τοῦ συνεργοῦντος αὐτοῖς ἀποδείξει· Euseb., *H. E.,* iii. 24, p. 84, ed. Burton. Even so early an authority as Irenæus accounts for *hyperbata* in the style of St. Paul: 'propter velocitatem sermonum suorum, et propter impetum qui in ipso est spiritûs.'—*Contr. Har.,* iii. 7, p. 182. With this we may compare St. Augustine's 'inspiratus a Deo, sed tamen homo.' (*In Joh. Evang.* I. i., *Opp.* III. ii. 289.) But the complete recognition of the human element, in correction of the stricter definitions of the seventeenth century, was reserved for writers nearer to our own time, who are now accustomed, on all hands, to accept the distinction, which was once regarded with deep suspicion, as the very basis of their reasoning. See, for instance, among works expressly on the subject of inspiration, Gaussen's *Théopneustie,* p. 54: 'Tant s'en faut que nous méconnaissions cette individualité humaine, partout empreinte dans nos livres sacrés, qu'au contraire c'est avec une gratitude profonde, avec une admiration toujours croissante, que nous considérons ce caractère vivant,' &c. Dr. Lee, *Inspiration of*

Holy Scripture, 2nd ed., p. 18, &c.: 'The Bible presents to us, in whatever light we regard it, two distinct elements, the divine and the human. This is a matter of fact. On the one hand, God has granted a revelation; on the other, human language has been made the channel to convey, and men have been chosen as the agents to record it. From this point all theories on the subject of Inspiration take their rise.' Cf. pp. 369, 505, 507, 510, &c. Mr. Westcott's *Introduction to the Study of the Gospels*, Pref., init.: 'A message of God *through* men and *to* men.' P. 5: the wrong view, when 'men considered the Divine agency of Inspiration as acting externally, and not internally, as acting *on* man, and not *through* man.' P. 7: 'it is authoritative, for it is the voice of God; it is intelligible, for it is in the language of men.' P. 10: ' the divine element is already in combination with the human when we are first able to observe its presence.' P. 12: 'the combination of the Divine influence with the human utterance.' P. 14: ' the human element becomes part of the message from heaven,' &c. &c. Mr. T. R. Birks, *The Bible and Modern Thought*, p. 339: 'The two elements (doctrine and science) are blended throughout no less intimately than body and soul are united in man himself.' Pp. 475–85, an Appendix on ' the importance of recognising fully the human element in Scripture, as one integral part of the true doctrine of Inspiration.' (Cf. pp. 212, 216, 259, 261, 263, 283, 284, and *Christian Observer*, January 1863, pp. 65–7.) Dr. Davidson, *Introduction to Old Testament*, ii. 438: 'the Old Testament prophecies . . . bear the irresistible impress of their people and time, as well as the personality of the speaker; in other words, the coöperation of his own spirit.'

The list of these names indicates that the position may be made the starting-point for the most opposite opinions. But it will be worth while to collect a few more scattered quotations from writers equally distinct in view, to show the hold which the formula has gained upon contemporary language. Monod, *Les Adieux d'Adolphe Monod à ses Amis et à l'Église*, p. 170: 'Il a été clairement dans les vues de Dieu qu'à chaque page de ce livre que nous appelons la Parole de Dieu, on reconnût en même temps une parole d'homme.' Dr. Arnold, Appendix to *Sermons*, i. 427: ' Every prophecy has, according to the very definition of the word, a double source; it has, if I may venture so to speak, two authors, the one human, the other Divine.' Schaff, *Germany, its Universities*, &c., p. 298: 'The Holy Scriptures are strictly Divine and strictly human

S

from beginning to end. The two natures are here united in one organic whole. The Holy Spirit lived, thought, moved in, and spoke through, the prophets and apostles, but as conscious, intelligent, free agents, not as blind and passive machines.' Professor H. Browne, in *Aids to Faith*, p. 287 : ' When we come to consider it, there can be no doubt but that we must admit a human and a divine element.' P. 290: 'Such observations (of Chrysostom and Jerome) led to a greater appreciation of the human element in the composition of Scripture.' Cf. pp. 289, 293, 302, 308, 309, 313, 318. Dr. Vaughan, *The Book and the Life*, p. 108 : ' Impossible as it is accurately to define in such compositions the limits of the Divine and the human, yet unquestionably both elements enter largely, and must do so, into the result.' Mr. J. Grote, *Examination of Dr. Lushington's Judgment*, p. 23: 'I do not see why, so far as penalty is concerned, Dr. Williams may not as well say unqualifiedly that the Bible is an expression of human reason, as Dr. Lushington may say unqualifiedly that it is the result of Divine interposition. Each proposition is incomplete: the Bible is from God as well as from man; from man as well as from God.' Mr. Chretien, *Letter and Spirit*, p. 59: ' We look at the instrument; we see that one mind has adapted its parts to a single purpose: but we also see, that to form each of these parts, subordinate agents wrote with hand and mind. God in His providence has joined the several books together in a volume ; the several books were written by individual men.' Bishop of St. David's, *Letter to Rev. Rowland Williams, D.D.*, p. 62 : ' In common, I believe, with all on whose opinion I set any value, I not only recognise, but claim for Scripture a human as well as a divine element. That would be the fundamental condition of any "theory of inspiration" that I should lay down.' Bishop of Gloucester, in *Aids to Faith*, p. 411 : ' If asked to define what we mean by the inspiration of Scripture, let us be bold and make answer, that fully convinced as we are that the Scripture is the revelation, through human media, of the infinite mind of God to the finite mind of man, and recognising as we do both a human and a divine element in the written Word, we verily believe that the Holy Ghost was so breathed into the mind of the writer, so illumined his spirit and pervaded his thoughts, that while nothing that individualised him as man was taken away, everything that was necessary to enable him to declare Divine truth in all its fulness was bestowed and superadded.' Bishop of Brechin, *Sermons on the*

NOTES TO LECTURE I. 259

Grace of God, p. 108 : 'Looking at the human element in this Divine song.' Bishop of Oxford, *Fellowship in Joy and Sorrow*, *init.*: 'By no other token does Holy Scripture more manifest itself to the conscience to be the Book of God, than by that profound knowledge of humanity which makes it the book of man.' Bishop of London, *The Word of God and the Ground of Faith*, p. 31 : 'I do not wish to enter here on any intricate or subtle questions as to all that inspiration implies, or how far it is either possible or expedient to discern those fine limits which mark the convergence and separation of the divine and human elements in the aggregate written word.'

For recent remarks on the varying measure of the human element, compare *Christian Remembrancer*, ubi suprà, pp. 56, 57, with Dr. Stanley's *Lectures on the Jewish Church*, pp. 284, 427. Throughout the series quoted in this and the next note, both of which, as I need scarcely add, could be almost indefinitely lengthened, we may accept the recognition of both elements, without yielding to the disposition, in any quarter, to let the one element predominate to the exclusion or extinction of the other.

Note 4, *page* 6. The following extracts, which form a continuation to those cited in the preceding note, will justify the assertion that there is a ' growing disposition ' to accept this parallel, which is examined more closely in Lecture VIII., p. 230.

The 20th number of *Les Adieux d'Adolphe Monod*, p. 175, &c., draws out the thought in detail: 'L'une de ces paroles, Jésus-Christ, est la Parole vivante de Dieu, la manifestation personnelle de ses perfections invisibles au sein de l'humanité; l'autre, l'Écriture, est la Parole écrite de Dieu, manifestation verbale donnée par le langage de ces mêmes perfections invisibles,' &c. This is copied at length by Mr. Swainson, *Authority of N. T.*, p. 145, who adds: 'The analogy may be carried onward. The early heresies relating to our Lord's Person, and the efforts made by the Church to meet those heresies, have almost their parallels in the later controversies as to the inspiration of Scripture.' Also cited by the Bishop of St. David's, *l. l.*, p. 63, who remarks, that the 'idea has since been more fully carried out in very beautiful analogies by others.' Gaussen, *Théopneustie*, p. 71 : 'Oui, nous l'avons dit, c'est Dieu qui nous y parle, mais aussi c'est l'homme; c'est l'homme, mais aussi c'est Dieu. Admirable parole de Dieu ! elle a été faite homme à sa manière, comme le Verbe éternel !' Wordsworth, *Introd. to N. T.*, p. xix.: 'May we not even say, that the mystery of Inspiration bears some likeness to the highest of all mysteries, in which the human is joined with the Divine, the mystery of the Incarnation itself?' (So also in *The Inspiration of the Bible*, p. 6.) Williams, *Beginning of the Book of Genesis*, p. 35 : 'And thus the written Word of God in the world in some respects serves the same purpose as His Presence beheld in the flesh.' P. 39 : 'And here again, although the analogy must not be pressed too far, we may say that in some respects it is like the Incarnate Word, in that it is Divine and yet human,' &c. Bishop of Gloucester, in *Aids to Faith*, p. 413 : 'Theories of inspiration are what scepticism is ever craving for: it is the voice of hapless unbelief, that is ever loudest in its call for explanation of the manner of the assumed union of the Divine with the human, or of the proportions in which each element is to be admitted and recognised. Such explanations have not been vouchsafed, and it is as vain and unbecoming to demand them as it is to require a theory of the union of the Divinity and humanity in the Person of Christ, or an estimate of the proportions in which the two perfect natures are to be conceived to co-exist.' Burgon, *Inspiration and Interpretation*, p. 2 : 'Of the written Gospel, many of the self-same things are said in Scripture which are said of Him by whom that Gospel was preached.' P. 3 : 'But even more remarkable are the analogies which subsist between the written record of our Lord's life and teaching and the actual Person of our Lord.' P. 4 : 'Most surprising of all is the analogy observable between the union of the divine and the human element in the Gospels, and the strictly parallel union, as it seems, of the two natures, the Divine and the human, in the Person of our Lord.' (Cf. p. 107, and quotation from Eden, p. 267.) Birks, *The Bible and Modern Thought*, p. 476 : 'A simple reference to the analogy between the personal and the written Word ought to remove this hasty impression.' (Cf. p. 264, and *Christian Observer*, Jan. 1863, p. 66.) Westcott, *Introduction to the Study of the Gospels*, p. 15 : 'it may well seem that the image of the Incarnation is reflected in the Christian Scriptures, which, as I believe, exhibit the human and Divine in the highest form and in the most perfect union.' Cazenove, *On certain Characteristics of Holy Scripture*, p. 59 : 'The written Word embodies, we maintain, a divine and a human element; herein preserving, in some faint measure, that resemblance to the Eternal Son made man, of which we have just been speaking.' Magee, Oxford Lenten

Sermon, *Growth in Grace*, p. 4 : 'as with the idea of the Incarnate Word, so with the idea of the written Word: here, too, we have a union of the Divine and of the human, a Word that is God's word, and yet that is also the word of man.' Woodford, *ib.*, *The Spirit interceding*, p. 9 : 'And is it not precisely the same difficulty which besets us in regard to the question of inspiration ? The work of the Spirit and the work of man in the compilation of Scripture ; where the influence of the Divine agent ends and that of the human begins ; the way in which the one operated upon the other : all these are but the transfer to the subject of inspiration of the self-same inexplicable questions which exercised the mind of the Church in earlier times with reference to the Incarnation of Christ and Sacramental Grace.' Thorold, in *Radley Sermons*, 1861, p. 89 : ' Surely there is a real and close analogy between the human and Divine natures in the Person of Christ and the human and divine elements in the inspired Word.' See also Schaff, *Germany, &c.*, p. 298 ; Tait, *Inspiration and Justification*, 1861 ; Heard, *New Wine in Old Bottles*, p. 137 ; *Quarterly Review*, Jan. 1861, p. 304 ; *Journal of Sacred Literature*, July 1862, p. 470, &c.

Note 5, page 6. The history of this distinction is traced by Dr. Lee with his usual admirable fulness : *Inspiration of Holy Scripture*, 2nd ed., pp. 27, 462, &c. On the theological side of his theory, compare Coleridge, *Confessions of an Enquiring Spirit*, p. 20 : 'the revealing Word and the inspiring Spirit.' P. 77 : ' the inspiration, the imbreathment, of the predisposing and assisting Spirit — the revelation of the informing Word.' P. 88 : 'revelation by the Eternal Word, and actuation of the Holy Spirit.' For what may be said against this theological determination, that ' Revelation is the peculiar function of the Eternal Word, Inspiration the result of the agency of the Holy Spirit ' (Lee, p. 29) — a point which does not come under consideration in these Lectures — see *Christian Remembrancer*, Jan. 1856, p. 23, and Donaldson's *Christian Orthodoxy*, p. 309, with Dr. Lee's rejoinder in the Preface to his second edition, to which all references in these notes are adjusted.

More generally, compare Morell, *Philosophy of Religion*, p. 150 : ' all revelation, as we showed, implies two conditions : it implies, namely, an intelligible *object* presented, and a given power of recipiency in the *subject* ; and in popular language, when speaking of the manifestation of Christianity to the world, we confine the term *revelation* to the former of these conditions, and appropriate the word *inspiration* to designate the latter.' See on this, *Aids to Faith*, p. 299; and on the other side, Davidson's *Introduction to the Old Testament*, i. 445.

Whatever may be said of the alleged connection between this distinction and the objective truths of theology, and whatever difficulties may be raised against the subjective analysis, there can be no question that it is absolutely necessary, for the sake of clearness, to draw a broad difference between the materials, which may or may not have been supernaturally communicated, and the faculties which were in all cases enabled to receive them. The distinction, for instance, would tend to clear up the controversy on Tillotson's meaning, as discussed by Mr. Fitzjames Stephen, *Defence of Dr. Williams*, p. 135, and Dr. M'Caul, *Testimonies to the Inspiration of Holy Scripture*, p. 133. The assertion that 'all the penmen of the Old Testament were *inspired*,' is entirely consistent with the belief, that 'Moses might write' what things he had done or seen 'without an immediate *revelation* of them.' Cf. other similar cases in Stephen, pp. 146, 156, &c., and *E. and R.*, p. 345. Similarly in an argument of Mr. Burgon's, *l. l.*, pp. 94, 102, the difficulty arises from a confusion between these two conceptions. There is plainly truth on both sides; inspiration was not likely to come and go, as the subjects of successive chapters varied; yet we need not suppose that the list of the Dukes of Edom was dictated to Moses by a voice from heaven. The inspiration may be held to be all-pervading by those who acknowledge that the revelation was but partial. Compare Bull's Sermon, *Works*, i. 240, on *Human Means useful to Inspired Persons*: 'even persons Divinely inspired, and ministers of God, did not so wholly depend upon Divine inspiration, but that they made use also of the ordinary help and means, such as reading of books, with study and meditation on them, for their assistance in the discharge of their office.' And see below, Lecture II., *Note* 12.

Note 6, *page* 7. For definitions of inspiration, and criticisms upon them, besides the great magazine of materials in Dr. Lee, and other writers on the special subject, see Mr. Morell's *Philosophy of Religion*, pp. 149-92, and the remarks of Professor H. Browne, *Aids to Faith*, p. 316, and Mr. Farrar, *B. L.*, p. 40. Add Stanley, *Epistles to the Corinthians*, i. 253, 268, 1st ed.; Ellicott, *Aids to Faith*, p. 411; Westcott, *Introd. to Study of Gospels*, p. 8; Williams, *Christianity and Hinduism*, p. 471, sqq.; an article by

Tholuck, translated in *Journal of Sacred Literature*, July 1863, p. 353; J. M. Campbell, *Thoughts on Revelation*, p. 73, sqq.; Mr. Jenkins's pamphlets, *Scriptural Interpretation*, and *A Word on Inspiration*, &c. See also below, Lecture V., Note 6. But the main question of recent times has related to the conditions under which we must accept that wider view of inspiration which the formularies of our own Church embody. To give references on this subject would be to present a list of a large portion of recent controversial writings.

Note 7, *page* 9. The sense of the cardinal text, 1 Thess. v. 23, has been obscured by three imperfect interpretations, which respectively fail to exhaust it.

1. That it is only the same trichotomy with which we are familiar in the classical writers. See Whitby, *in loc.*; Donaldson, *Vindication of Protestant Principles*, p. 162 (cf. *Christian Orthodoxy*, p. 382); Mill, *Analysis of Pearson*, p. 87. Against this, see Bull, *Works*, ii. 95 : 'many learned interpreters tell us here, that St. Paul alludes to the threefold distinction of the soul, into the vegetative, the sensitive, and the rational, and so that the *Spirit* in St. Paul signifies no more than the τὸ ἡγεμονικὸν, or mind. But it seems plain to me, that the Apostle meddles not with the threefold faculty of man's soul (for what hath the body to do in that distinction?), but rather describes the threefold principle of the *compositum*, if I may so speak, of a Christian (which St. Paul calls the ὁλόκληρον), who, besides his body and soul, which make him a perfect natural man, hath also the Πνεῦμα, the Spirit (that Philo speaks on), to render him a perfect man in order to a supernatural life.' Compare Mr. Jowett, *Comment. on* Rom. vii. 14 : 'the language of the New Testament does not conform to any received views of psychology.'

2. That the πνεῦμα in this passage is the Holy Spirit. This is the meaning of Bishop Bull, in the argument just cited. But his statements on the subject vary. See *Works*, i. 32 : 'The same our blessed Saviour assures our belief of this truth by His own example, when, being at the point of death, He said, *Father, into Thy hands I commend my spirit*, Luke xxiii. 46. He believed that He had a spirit, a superior soul, that after the death of His body, and the extinction of His animal soul, should still remain ; and this He recommends to the gracious and safe custody of His Father. And lest we should think that this was a peculiar privilege of the soul of the Messias, St. Stephen, when dying, after the same manner

commits his spirit to Christ Himself, then exalted at the right hand of the Father, saying, *Lord Jesus, receive my spirit*, Acts vii. 59.' See also Grotius, *in loc.*, and Scudamore, *Office of the Intellect*, p. 141. But compare the extract from Tatian, *ib.*, p. 135; and Kaye, *Justin Martyr*, p. 183. Also Olshausen, *in loc.*: 'That πνεῦμα cannot here be understood of the Holy Spirit, but denotes the human spirit, is acknowledged by the latest interpreters,' &c. Bp. Ellicott remarks, that 'Bull's theory is, in fact, really a tetractomy — body, soul, spirit, and Holy Spirit.' *Destiny of the Creature*, p. 172.

3. That it is a gift peculiar to Christians. See above, *Note* 1.

A series of patristic quotations on the subject is collected by Mr. J. B. Morris, in a note already referred to, *Essay towards the Conversion of the Hindus*, pp. 319–29; and the doctrine, which has been elaborately worked out by Delitzsch, Olshausen, and others, is unfolded with great care in the Bishop of Gloucester's *Destiny of the Creature*, &c. Compare his *Commentaries* on 1 Thess., *in loc.*; Gal. v. 16; *Pastoral Epistles*, pp. v. vi., and 1 Tim. iii. 16, &c.; and *Historical Lectures on the Life of our Lord*, p. 112. The subject has also received much attention in recent periodical writings.

Note 8, *page* 10. A mere arrangement of the passages will show the different point of view from which Aristotle teaches the existence of a Divine principle in man: —

All things have something Divine in them (πάντα γάρ φύσει ἔχει τι θεῖον· *Eth. N.*, VII. xiii. § 6; and κινεῖ γάρ πως πάντα τὸ ἐν ἡμῖν θεῖον· *Eth. Eud.*, vii. 14, p. 1248, a. 26). The Final Cause, especially, in all things is Divine (τὴν ἀρχὴν δὲ καὶ τὸ αἴτιον τῶν ἀγαθῶν τίμιόν τι καὶ θεῖον τίθεμεν· *Eth. N.*, I. xii. *fin.*). In man, therefore, happiness is Divine (τῶν θειοτάτων—εἰ μὴ θεόπεμπτός ἐστιν, *Ib.*, I. ix. § 3, xii. § 4). The character of Divinity becomes more marked, in proportion as each thing advances nearer to that central light of God. Thus, as the πόλις is nobler than any individual man, so the end of the πόλις is more Divine than that of the individual (*Ib.*, I. ii. § 8). And the same rule exalts the universe itself, in proportion as it is thought loftier than man (*Ib.*, VI. vii. § 4). As the Deity is pure intelligence (ἔστιν ἡ νόησις νοήσεως νόησις· *Metaph.* Λ. 9, 1074, b. 34), it follows that νοῦς is the most pure and heavenly element in man (νοῦς—εἴτε θεῖον ὂν καὶ αὐτὸ, εἴτε τῶν ἐν ἡμῖν τὸ θειότατον· *Eth. N.*, X. vii. § 1, § 8; cf. *Metaph.*, p. 1074, b. 16). But this is especially the active intellect (*De An.*, III. 5). Νοῦς alone is entirely separable from the rest of man's nature (ἡ δὲ τοῦ νοῦ κεχωρισμένη· *Eth. N.*, X.

viii. § 3; cf. *De An.*, III. 5). It came to him from without, as something nobler than the rest of his organisation; a visitant from a higher sphere (ὁ δὲ νοῦς ἔοικεν ἐγγίνεσθαι· *De An.*, I. 4, 408, b. 18: λείπεται τὸν νοῦν μόνον θύραθεν ἐπεισιέναι, καὶ θεῖον εἶναι μόνον· *De Gen. An.*, II. 3, p. 736, b. 27). It survives alone when this mortal body perishes (*De An.*, I. 4, p. 408, b. 29; *Metaph.*, Λ. 3, p. 1070, a. 26). Therefore a life in which νοῦς receives the most undivided culture is the happiest life (*Eth. N.*, X. vii. *fin.*). By living it, man passes beyond his compound nature, into a state of being superior to his own; and through such a life we may conceive that the best man draws nearest to the state and happiness of God (*Eth. N.*, I. xii. § 4; VII. i. § 2; X. viii. § 13).

On looking back over these passages, we may say, with Sir W. Hamilton, that in the view of Aristotle, 'intellect, which he elsewhere (than in *Eth. Eud.*, vii. 14) allows to be pre-existent and immortal, is a spark of the Divinity' (*On Reid*, p. 773); but we must add, with Bishop Hampden, that 'he mistakes the nature of the Divine principle in man, not including in it a capacity of moral improvement, since he limits it to νοῦς, or intellect' (*On the Philosophical Evidence of Christianity*, p. 53, *note*); and with De Pressensé, that 'his God, as he himself says, is above virtue; it is pure thought, rather than moral perfection; indifferent and alone, He takes no cognisance of man; morality has no Divine basis, no eternal type, no aid to look for from above' (*Religions before Christ*, p. 134).

We may suppose him to maintain that there are gradations of Deity in all things that fall short of God; as though it were flashes of His light, particles of His essence, dispersed throughout the universe; springing from Him as their source, tending to Him as their centre; the final cause of all things being, in a less proper sense, and, as though it were unconsciously, the efficient cause of all things also, by virtue of an attractive or magnetic power. But it is rather in his commentators than in himself that we find the more explicit view, that all mind everywhere is but a portion of the Divine essence, and will be reabsorbed after death in the fountain of light from which it has been parted. Compare Mr. Farrar, *B. L.*, p. 140. Also Sir A. Grant, *Essays on the Ethics*, p. 238 : 'As long as the soul is described as bearing the relation to the body of sight to the eye, of a flower to the seed, of the impression to the wax, we may be content to consider this a piece of ancient physical philosophy. Our interest is different when the soul is said to be related to the body "as a sailor to his boat" [*De An.*, II. i. p. 413, a. 9]. But here is the point also where Aristotle becomes less explicit. Having once mooted this comparison, he does not follow it up.' A creed which is thus implicitly, if not explicitly, pantheistic, supplies no parallel for the Scripture doctrine, that God bestowed on man a created and separate spirit, which, from the moment of creation, would remain distinct from its Creator; the organ of Divine communion, the vehicle through which the Holy Spirit visits us with power and light.

Note 9, *page* 10. I refer to the discussions raised by Mr. Darwin, *On the Origin of Species*, Sir C. Lyell, *On the Antiquity of Man*, and Professor Huxley's *Evidence as to Man's Place in Nature*; to which I may add Professor Rolleston's Lecture *On the Affinities and Differences between the Brain of Man and the Brains of certain Animals*, in the *Medical Times and Gazette*, Feb. and March, 1862.

The following scale is given in Sir C. Lyell's work:—The largest gorilla brain, $34\frac{1}{2}$ cubic inches; smallest human, 62; largest human, 114 (p. 491; cf. Huxley, *l. l.*, p. 77, who there supplies the reason why, in an earlier part of Sir C. Lyell's book, p. 84, the smallest human brain is brought down to 46). Dr. Rolleston says: 'the maximum ape's weight is 14 ounces, the minimum human is, speaking roughly, 2 lb., i.e. 32 ounces avoirdupois;' *l. l.*, p. 262. Dr. Rorison had stated the difference in the following terms: 'On a centigrade scale of cerebral development, all values of the human organ shade into each other from one hundred downwards to seventy-five; while all values of the brute brain, from the fish to the ape, range upwards, in close sequence from zero to about thirty.' (*Replies to E. and R.*, p. 325; cf. *The Three Barriers*, pp. 92, 97, 161, 164, 175.) 'But,' he adds, 'there is no bridging brain between.' So also Huxley, p. 104. Compare *Anthropological Review*, i. 57.

Note 10, *page* 11. 'Alterum argumentum, quo probamus Numen esse aliquod, sumitur a manifestissimo consensu omnium gentium, apud quos ratio et boni mores non planè extincta sunt inductâ feritate' (Grotius, *De Ver. Rel. C.*, i. 2). I take this statement from an elementary work, to show that the limitation under which all reasonable men would propound it, excludes the appeal to the few doubtful and degraded instances which have been urged against the universality of the main proposition. Cf. the E. T. of Saisset, *Modern Pantheism*, i. 34, *note*; and Max Müller, *Ancient Sanskrit Literature*, p. 538.

Note 11, *page* 11. The following are among the chief recent opinions on the differentia of man:—LANGUAGE: Professor Max Müller, *Lectures on the Science of Language*, 1861, p. 13: 'However much the frontiers of the animal kingdom have been pushed forward, so that at one time the line of demarcation between animal and man seemed to depend on a mere fold in the brain, there is *one* barrier which no one has yet ventured to touch—the barrier of language.' Cf. Locke, on p. 14 : 'the power of abstracting is not at all in brutes,' &c. ; and p. 340 : 'Where, then, is the difference between brute and man ?. . . I answer, without hesitation, the one great barrier between the brute and man is *Language.*' Huxley, *Man's Place in Nature*, p. 103, *note*: 'believing, as I do, with Cuvier, that the possession of articulate speech is the grand distinctive character of man,' &c. P. 112: 'he alone possesses the marvellous endowment of intelligible and rational speech, whereby, in the secular period of his existence, he has slowly accumulated and organised the experience which is almost wholly lost with the cessation of every individual life in other animals; so that now he stands raised upon it as on a mountain top, far above the level of his humble fellows, and transfigured from his grosser nature by reflecting, here and there, a ray from the infinite source of truth.' SELF-CONSCIOUSNESS:—Bischoff, in *Anthropological Review*, No. I. p. 56. MIND, TONGUE, HAND:—Dr. Rorison, *The Three Barriers*, p. 128; cf. pp. 92, 96, 97, 127. IMPROVABLE REASON:— Archbishop Sumner, *Records of Creation*, p. 179, ed. 1850; cf. Lyell, *On the Antiquity of Man*, p. 496. MORALITY AND RELIGION:— M. de Quatrefages; see Lyell, *l. l.*, 496; translator of M. Saisset, *Modern Pantheism*, i. 34, *note*; also ii. 237. Compare Mr. Maurice, *Claims of the Bible and of Science*, p. 49: 'Let the physical enquirer make out the affinity of each of us to the ape—such humiliation is seasonable and profitable; but he shall not hinder us from bearing witness to him, that *he* has a glorious parentage; that *he* has the nature which was redeemed by the Son of God.' I need not point out in detail the completeness with which this view exhausts the imagery, in which the superiority of man over brute has been so repeatedly described; Huxley, *l. l.*, p. 111; Hallam, *Literature of Europe*, iii. 286 ; &c. We must only bear in mind the warning of Pascal : 'It is a dangerous thing to demonstrate to man how he resembles the brutes, without at the same time showing him his superiority over them.' *Thoughts*, iv. 15 ; p. 85, ed. Pearce. See further, Lecture VIII., p. 227.

Note 12, *page* 13. 'Among other things which revelation makes known to us concerning the Divine Nature, is this, that it is capable of divers kinds or manners of Presence, according to its own Will. . . . . First of all, while existing everywhere, He yet dwells by a purer and subtler influence, and, as we may say, by a more intimate Presence, in some creatures than in others, in angels than in men, in men than in the lower animals, and in these last, it should seem probable, than in inanimate matter. . . . Again, it has pleased Him on occasion to dwell, by intenser localisation, so to speak, in particular places: as in the cherubic forms (probably) at the gates of Eden after the Fall; in the burning bush; in the cloud at the Exodus, and on Mount Sinai; in the Tabernacle ere the ark of the covenant was made; on the outstretched wings of the cherubim above the ark, both in the Tabernacle and first Temple; and behind the veil, though there was no ark, in the second Temple.'—Freeman, *Principles of Divine Service*, ii. 157–8. I am not concerned with the inferences which Mr. Freeman draws. Cf. *ib.*, iii. 15. 'Undoubtedly there are many different degrees of the Divine Presence. God is in some real sense more present in heaven than upon earth, and in heaven itself most present on His heavenly throne; and so upon earth also, though He pervade the whole of it, yet is He chiefly in His sanctuaries, and in them (it may be) most present at the holy altar.'—Rawlinson, *Christianity and Heathenism*, p. 16. Compare Moberly, *Sayings of the Great Forty Days*, pp. 47, 84, &c.; Hessey, *B. L.*, p. 183.

Note 13, *page* 17. The δοθέν supplied in the E. V. of John vii. 39 is the old interpretation. See Suicer, *Thes. Eccles.*, ii. 777–8. Lachmann admits δεδομένον into his text. 'Quod dicit Evangelista, *Spiritus nondum erat datus, quia Jesus nondum erat glorificatus,* quomodo intelligitur, nisi quia certa illa Spiritus Sancti datio vel missio post clarificationem Christi futura erat, qualis nunquam antea fuerat? Neque enim antea nulla erat, sed talis non fuerat. Si enim antea Spiritus Sanctus non dabatur, quo impleti Prophetæ locuti sunt? cùm apertè Scriptura dicat, et multis locis ostendat, Spiritu Sancto eos locutos fuisse; cùm et de Joanne Baptistâ dictum sit, *Spiritu Sancto replebitur jam inde ab utero matris suæ*; et Spiritu Sancto repletus Zacharias invenitur pater ejus, ut de illo talia diceret; et Spiritu Sancto Maria ut talia de Domino quem gestabat utero prædicaret; Spiritu Sancto Simeon et Anna, ut magnitudinem Christi parvuli agnoscerent: quomodo ergo

Spiritus nondum erat datus, quia Jesus nondum erat clarificatus, nisi quia illa datio, vel donatio, vel missio Spiritus Sancti habitura erat quandam proprietatem suam in ipso adventu, qualis antea nunquam fuit?'—S. August., *De Trinit.*, iv. 20; *Opp.*, viii. 829. But see the ample collection of passages and criticisms in Archdeacon Hare's *Mission of the Comforter*, note H., pp. 231–97. The highest form of the Presence of the Spirit in the spirit of man must be distinguished from His Presence 'not by measure' in our Lord; John iii. 34. 'Habere Spiritum *non per se*, sed *per participationem*, ut Theologi loquuntur, id est ad mensuram habere; et eo modo dare, est ad mensuram dare.'—Maldonat. *in loc.* 'Dixit R. Acha: Etiam Spiritus S. non habitavit super Prophetas, nisi mensurâ quâdam. Quidam enim librum unum, quidam duos vaticiniorum ediderunt.'—Schoettgen., *Hor. Hebr. in loc.* Cf. Origen, *Hom. in Luc.*, xxix.; *Opp.*, iii. 966.

Note 14, *page* 18. See Mr. Fitzjames Stephen's *Defence of Dr. Williams*, p. 207, &c.; *E. and R.*, p. 78; Dr. Stanley's *Lectures on the Jewish Church*, p. 442, &c. Mr. Chretien says: 'It has often been remarked, that the word "inspiration" is employed in the Prayer Book only to express the action of the Holy Spirit on the mind and heart of the believer. It has not been so often observed that even in these instances the word is of comparatively recent introduction.' —*Letter and Spirit*, p. 179. The passages are as follows:— (1.) Collect for Fifth Sunday after Easter, Gelasian, *te inspirante*; Muratori, i. 585. (2.) Prayer for the Church militant. (3.) Collect for purity before Communion, *per infusionem*, Muratori, ii. 383; Sarum Missal, p. 579, ed. Forbes. (4.) The *Veni Creator Spiritus*; 'Thy heavenly grace *inspire*,' 1552; 'Our souls *inspire*,' 1662. (5.) Article XIII.: 'Works done before the grace of Christ, and the *inspiration* of His Spirit;' *spiritus ejus afflatum*, 1552–62. Cf. Concil. Trid., *Sess.* vi. *Can.* 3: 'si quis dixerit, sine præveniente Spiritus Sancti *inspiratione*,' &c.

Note 15, *page* 19. Compare a similar distinction drawn by Hooker on another subject, *E. P.*, III. viii. § 5: 'The cause why such declamations prevail so greatly, is, for that men suffer themselves in two respects to be deluded: one is, that the wisdom of man being debased either *in comparison* with that of God, or *in regard of some special thing* exceeding the reach and compass thereof, it seemeth to them (not marking so much) as if *simply* it were condemned.' 'As there is a sense in which the grant of glory was made even under the Law, as in its miracles, . . . so in another point of view it belongs exclusively to the promised blessedness hereafter. Still there is a real and sufficient sense in which it is ascribed to the Christian Church.'—Newman, *Parochial Sermons*, iii. 281. 'Now what were all these but pledges and earnests of a bliss which is to come hereafter? Real and high as was this fellowship with God, it was but the first manifestation of that glory which shall be revealed. It was the foretaste of this Beatitude; the inheritance of the pure in heart; a faint anticipation of that vision in bliss, which makes blessed all who behold it. Let us then go on to consider, so far as we may, what is the nature of the beatific vision. It is plainly something that is yet to come. "The pure in heart *shall* see God." This was not finally fulfilled in the visions of seers, nor in the presence of Christ in the flesh, nor in any manifestation that has yet been made of God to His servants. Such beginnings and first intuitions as they may have had here in this life did but lead on to the perfect sight of the Divine Presence. They were of old both *fulfilments and prophecies, earnests and actual gifts*, in part realities, and in part adumbrations, of that vision of God which shall be hereafter.'— Manning, *University Sermons*, p. 123. 'The gift, then, of written revelation in the Law, the Prophets, and the Psalms, is distinctly and expressly referred to the Spirit of God. But the Gospel is eminently the dispensation of the Spirit. His Presence after our Lord's ascension was to be *so much more fully* manifested, that *by comparison* it is said to be vouchsafed for the first time.'—Birks, *The Bible and Modern Thought*, p. 238. Cf. Maldonat. on Matt. ix. 13.

Note 16, *page* 20. 'When the Church is asked for her proofs of the Divine authority of the Scriptures, her first word is—Testimony; and her second is—Testimony; and her third is—Testimony. It is true there are countless subsidiary confirmations of their claim to be what she says they are; just as there were many subsidiary things which went, in Demosthenes' view, to make an orator. But in the last resort, when pressed with the enquiry as to what her mind rests on as ultimate and beyond appeal and gainsaying, the proof which the Church alleges is one and one only. The whole thing has been a matter of testimony from the beginning.'—*Christian Remembrancer*, Jan. 1856, p. 6. 'We receive the books of Holy Scripture on the testimony of Christ, speaking in His Church.'— Wordsworth, *Inspiration*, p. 82. We must distinguish, however, between the testimony of the Church and the personal authority of the individual writer. Thus, when Mr. Swainson says: 'By an amount of evidence which seems to be overwhelming, it is proved that when a book claimed to be admitted on the Canon of the Church, only one enquiry was made, and that was, *Who was the Author?* and if the document or letter could be proved satisfactorily to have proceeded from an Apostle of our Lord, the enquiry was closed' (*Authority of N. T.*, p. 9), we feel that the account leaves some difficult questions altogether without an answer. E.g., on p. 18 he says: 'The question which so long agitated the Church as to the authority of the Epistle to the Hebrews, was really a question as to its author, and not until it was believed that the Epistle was written by St. Paul, does it seem that men's minds were satisfied, and the work allowed to take its place among the acknowledged documents of the Christian covenant.' It seems to follow, that whenever they *doubt* whether it was written by St. Paul, they are justified in being dissatisfied again. We must be cautious not to lay down unguardedly a principle of only partial application, which would needlessly increase the responsibility of all critical enquiries. Mr. Chretien, *Letter and Spirit*, p. 49, dwells on the difficulties in point of fact; and Dr. Wordsworth says: 'We *cannot* say, with some persons, that we receive the Scriptures as Divine because *we* know *who* their writers were, and that they were good men, full of the Holy Ghost, and that *therefore* whatever they wrote must be inspired of God. The truth is, we do *not* know by *whom* some of the books of Scripture were written.'—*Inspiration*, p. 81.

On the other hand, 'a true revelation of God must be its own witness.'—Campbell, *Thoughts on Revelation*, pp. 13, 26, 71, &c. 'The question of the Canon of Scripture, and the question of the Inspiration of Scripture, are in no way to be confounded. The O. T. Canon we receive now, as it was recognised by the O. T. Church. The N. T. Canon, the N. T. Church, after a time, felt called to fix, and proceeded to ascertain and fix accordingly. . . . . But the question of Inspiration is altogether prior to, and independent of, this matter. The existence of inspired writings having Divine authority was a fact known and familiar to the Church from the beginning. The N. T. Scriptures, successively as they were written, added themselves to the Old in the Canon of men's faith, as new stars appearing in the firmament would take their place among the stars of heaven.'—*Ib.*, p. 103. This conception of 'proving itself by its own light' has been the subject of much recent criticism. See of Calvin, *E. and R.*, 328; Stephen, *Defence of Williams*, p. 88; M'Caul, *Testimonies*, p. 83: of Jackson, Stephen, p. 97; M'Caul, pp. 84, 115: of Chillingworth, M'Caul, p. 84, &c. Compare Mr. Goldwin Smith, *Rational Religion*, p. 16: 'The histories which contradict the Article as to the matter of fact require elaborate confutation. If we can *know God, and know His voice*, these difficulties are as nothing; if we cannot know God, they are death.' ' In short, whatever *finds* me bears witness for itself that it has proceeded from a Holy Spirit.'—Coleridge, *Confessions*, &c., pp. 10, 13, 72. Cf. Browne, *Aids to Faith*, pp. 297, 314; Stanley, *Jewish Church*, p. 454; Ellicott, *Aids to Faith*, p. 409; 'The Book has found him,' &c. '*Eye* of God's Word!'—*Christian Year*, St. Bartholomew; with the quotation from Miller's *B.L.*, p. 135: ' this eye, like that of a portrait, uniformly fixed upon us, turn where we will.'

' But how do we know the Bible to be the Word of God? *Both* by testimony and by the answer of its Spirit to our spirit—by external authority, and by its own.'—Chretien, *Letter and Spirit*, p. 17. ' A healthy eye is required for perfect vision. But it is not needful, happily, to know whether our sight depends on the cornea or the crystalline lens, on the aqueous or the vitreous humour, or " on a combination of the four, or of some of them, and in what order and proportion," before we can discern and rejoice in the presence of a beloved friend. A humble heart and a healthy conscience will lead the most unlettered Christian to a firm belief in the Gospel, and in the truth of the sacred Scriptures, though he may never have cared to settle what share each kind of evidence may have had in this result.'—Birks, *Bible and Modern Thought*, p. 201.

The Scripture testimonies have been collected by Gaussen, Dr. Wordsworth, the Bishop of Gloucester, and others; the patristic proofs are arranged in Routh, *Rell. Sacr.*, v. 335-53; Lee, *Appendix G.*, pp. 484-527; Westcott, *Introd. to Study of Gospels, Appendix B.*, pp. 383-423: and the witness of the English Church is discussed in the speeches of Mr. Fitzjames Stephen and Sir R. Phillimore, and the work of Dr. M'Caul. On the *consilience* of reasonings, compare Lyall, *Propædia Proph.*, pp. 138, 351; Birks, *Bible and Modern Thought*, p. 202; Westcott, *l. l.*, p. 18.

Note 17, page 29. Mr. Morell has collected several definitions of Revelation; *Philosophy of Religion*, p. 148. Many others will be found in treatises to which reference has been already made in

Note 6, and elsewhere. A definition proposed by Dr. Rowland Williams gave rise to a controversy, which ran through several pamphlets:—' Revelation is an unveiling of the true God, especially as Love and as a Spirit, to the eyes of our mind;'—*Lampeter Theology*, p. 35, criticised by the Bishop of St. David's, *Charge*, 1857, p. 73. The reply of Dr. Williams is in his *Earnestly respectful Letter*, p. 23; the Bishop's rejoinder, on p. 24 of his *Letter to the Rev. Dr. Williams*; and Dr. Williams's further answer on p. 2 of his *Appendix*, and p. 18 of his *Persecution for the Word*. Compare *Christianity and Hinduism*, p. 26. I annex one definition from the interest attached to the name of its author: ' Revelation is a voluntary approximation of the Infinite Being to the ways and thoughts of finite humanity.'—*Remains of A. H. Hallam*, p. 176. In the first edition of Mr. Jowett's *Commentary* on Galatians, i. 12, he had said that ' it seems to come from without, and is not to be confounded with any inward emotion, any more than a dream or the sight of a painting.' But the passage is altered in the second edition.

An important question has been raised on the propriety of extending the term beyond the bounds of Scripture, as in the analogous case of Inspiration. The practice has been not uncommon: ' Innititur fides nostra revelationi Apostolis et Prophetis factæ, qui canonicos libros scripserunt, non autem revelationi, *si qua fuit aliis doctoribus facta.*'—S. Thom. Aquin., I. i. Art. viii. *fin.* 'So full, so unambiguous, is St. Paul's testimony to this revelation of God, written in " the volume of the creatures ;" and such a revelation, too, as he declares man had the intellectual eye to read, if he had but had the will to obey. But there is also a second natural revelation of God, which the Apostle will not suffer us to forget; that which is contained in the innate sense of our nature; that moral constitution of our souls,' &c.—Davison's *Remains*, p. 90. ' That supernatural notices and revealed light were communicated, more or less, to the bulk of mankind in every age is most certain and uncontestable; but whether directly by Scripture, or by other more oblique or more remote means, may often admit of a dispute.'— Waterland, *Works*, v. 15. ' I apprehend that it would be more correct to speak of the Revelation of God as consisting of four parts, or rather as made in four modes,' by creation, by miracles, by the Spirit of God, and in a written book.—Maitland, *Eruvin*, p. 2. ' Revelation, properly speaking, is an universal, not a partial gift.'—

T

Newman, *Arians*, p. 89; see below, Lecture II., *Note* 2. 'What can we really know of Him but from His own revelations of Himself; His revelations in the book of nature, in the book of the world's history, in the book of our own consciences, but, above all, in that book which contains His own utterances by His prophets, and in these last days by His Son?'—Professor H. Browne, *Messiah as foretold*, &c., p. 54. 'A Divine Revelation is knowledge bestowed on us by God in the form of human thought and speech, the Holy Spirit employing men for this end. This is what we mean when we speak of the Scriptures as a Divine Revelation; while in a larger sense, all by which God utters Himself to us in creation and providence, and the Divine constitution of things, is Revelation.'— J. M. Campbell, *Thoughts on Revelation*, p. 74. On the other hand, the Provost of Oriel has recently protested against the application of the term to 'a voice within us, prior to Revelation, or itself, as we may choose to call, or rather to miscall it, a prior Revelation.'— *Province of Private Judgment*, 1861, pp. 17, 28. So also Dr. Lee, p. 4, proposing to restrict the word *revelation* to the one sense, and to use the word *manifestation* for the other.

Note 18, *page* 24. Compare the two passages translated by Sir W. Hamilton from Kant and Jacobi; *Lectures on Metaphysics*, i. 39–41. The latter, 'Nature conceals God; man reveals God,' is also quoted by Mr. Mansel, *B.L.*, p. 343, and *Aids to Faith*, p. 28. The former has been far more widely used. 'Two things there are, which, the oftener and the more steadfastly we consider, fill the mind with an ever new, an ever rising admiration and reverence; the starry heaven above, the moral law within.' Quoted also, *Discussions*, p. 301; Young, *Province of Reason*, p. 141; Jowett, *Commentary on St. Paul*, ii. 387, 413, first ed.; Saisset, *Modern Pantheism*, ii. 146; Stanley, *Sermons in the East*, p. 75.

Note 19, *page* 26. 'In the Old Testament, as in the New, the question as regards religion is not the *reality* of the facts which are there recorded—that is a matter to be determined by historical proof—but the proper *explanation* of them. Whether the facts related in the books of Moses really happened is one thing; whether they were wrought by God, and if so, for what end, belongs to a different enquiry. So, also, when we are speaking of the facts recorded in the New Testament.'—Lyall, *Propædia Prophetica*, p. 3. 'Our revelations, we may say, were not the literary work of some sage or legislator, or put forth as a mere writing or collection of writings; but they are a series of *historical revelations*, given at different times and in different manners, and by different messengers, each for its special purpose in connection with what was then passing in the world; and yet *all having reference* to one great evangelical purpose.'—Hampden, *B. L., Preface to* 2*nd ed.,* p. xli. 'The conveyance of God's will *by means of facts* is the foundation of what we term Revealed Religion.'—Lee, p. 6. 'Much of what we learn from the sacred record is not of a spiritual nature at all; but even when that which is written is in its highest aspect purely spiritual, and what is only truly known when spiritually discerned, the spiritual is presented to us *in Divine facts*, which, *as facts*, could only become known by revelation. The Divine facts are commended to our faith by the glory of God which shines in them, and by the light which they shed on our condition as subjects of the kingdom of God; but as facts they could never have become the subjects of human knowledge, excepting by such inspiration as we ascribe to holy apostles and prophets. The great facts which our faith embraces are as the links of a Divine chain, of which some links have had a visibility here on earth, while the rest belong entirely to the invisible. But even of those links which have been visible—the life and death of the Son of God—the whole *spiritual* aspect has been invisible, and could only be known to man by revelation.'—Campbell, *Thoughts on Revelation,* p. 90. Cf. Birks, *Bible and Modern Thought,* pp. 86, 237, 340, 374, sqq.

Note 20, *page* 35. Dr. Lee has collected instances from the Fathers of the similitudes employed 'to illustrate the effect of the Divine influence upon the souls of those "holy men of old, who spake as they were moved by the Holy Ghost,"' under the two classes of musical instruments and material similitudes of any kind. *Appendix G*, pp. 503-7; cf. pp. 81-3. I annex a few from more recent writers. A HARP or LUTE (S. Justin. Mart., *Cohort. ad Gent.,* 8; *Opp.,* ii. 38, ed. Otto; S. August., *De Civit. Dei,* xvi. 2; *Opp.,* vii. 416, &c.); Hooker, *Works,* iii. 662-3: 'They neither spake nor wrote any word of their own, but uttered syllable by syllable as the Spirit put it into their mouths, no otherwise than the harp or the lute doth give a sound according to the discretion of his hands that holdeth and striketh it with skill. The difference is only this: an instrument, whether it be a pipe or harp, maketh a distinction in the times and sounds, which distinction is well perceived of the hearer, the instrument itself understanding not what is piped or harped. The prophets and holy men of God not so . . . For herein they were not like harps or lutes, but they felt, they felt the power and strength of their own words. When they spake of our peace, every corner of their hearts was filled with joy. When they prophesied of mourning, lamentations, and woes, to fall upon us, they wept in the bitterness and indignation of spirit, the arm of the Lord being mighty and strong upon them.'—(Also in Lee, pp. 22, 82.) Coleridge, *Confessions*, p. 14 : 'This is the very essence of the doctrine, that one and the same Intelligence is speaking in the unity of a Person ; which unity is no more broken by the diversity of the pipes through which it makes itself audible, than is a tune by the different instruments on which it is played by a consummate musician, equally perfect in all ;' after which he proceeds to 'enquire on what authority this doctrine rests.' An ORGAN ; Gaussen, *Théopneustie*, p. 67 : 'Avez-vous visité l'étonnant organiste qui fait couler avec tant de charme les larmes du voyageur, dans la cathédrale de Fribourg, pendant qu'il touche l'un après l'autre ses admirables claviers, et qu'il vous fait entendre tour à tour, ou la marche des guerriers sur le rivage, ou les chants de la prière sur le lac, pendant la tempête, ou les voix de l'action de grâces après qu'elle est calmée ? Tous vos sens sont ébranlés, car vous avez tout vu et tout entendu. Eh bien, c'est ainsi que l'Eternel Dieu, puissant en harmonie, a, tour à tour, appuyé le doigt de son Esprit sur les touches qu'il avait choisies pour l'heure de son dessein, et pour l'unité de son hymne céleste.' Again, p. 75 : 'Ce sont les orgues du Très-Haut, mais qui vont charmer le cœur de l'homme, et remuer sa conscience, dans les cabanes du berger, comme dans les palais ; dans les chambres hautes du pauvre, comme dans les tentes du désert.' The figure is worked out with great skill and refinement by Mr. Chretien, *Letter and Spirit*, p. 25. A PEN and PENMEN, from Ps. xlv. 2 : 'My tongue is the *pen* of a ready writer.' (Cf. S. August., *Conf.* vii. 27, *Opp.*, I. 143, E: 'venerabilem stilum Spiritus tui ;' *Enarr.* in Ps. cxliv. 17, *Opp.*, IV. 1620, F: 'chirographum Dei.') On the mechanical theory, the writer becomes 'the pen and not the penman of the Holy Spirit.'—Westcott, *Introd. to Gospels*, p. 6 ; Lee, p. 22 ; Stanley, *Jewish Ch.*, p. 433 ; Farrar, *B. L.*, p. 159. 'According to this theory, as expounded by such divines as Quenstedt and Hollaz, the prophets and apostles were mere *amanuenses* of the Holy Ghost. It was only *per catachresin* that they could be properly said to be the authors of the writings which bore their names; *utpote qui potius Dei auctoris calami fuerunt.*'—Bishop of St. David's, *Letter to Dr. R. Williams*, p. 38. On the other hand, ' if the sacred writers were not *clerks*, but, so to speak, *secretaries of state*, men entrusted with God's secrets, imbued with the mind and counsels of God, acquainted with His secret will and designs, receiving from Him, when necessary, precise verbal instructions, when this was unnecessary, speaking from the fulness of their own knowledge, but in every case (to keep up our metaphor) having to submit their despatches to the eye of the Great King, to receive His sanction and authentication, before sending them forth as documents containing their Master's pleasure; then diversities of style, and individual idiosyncrasy breaking out, is exactly what we should expect.'—Lord A. Hervey, *Inspiration of Holy Scripture*, p. 83. 'Not *copying machines*, but living men.'—Birks, *Bible and Modern Thought*, p. 283. 'No figure can more correctly represent the idea to be conveyed, as there is none more common with writers both of the Old and New Testaments, than that which teaches us to consider the prophets and apostles as *ambassadors* from God to mankind.'—Lyall, *Propædia Proph.*, p. 175.

LECTURE II.

Note 1, *page* 38. This phrase is sometimes challenged; but I think without just cause. In his *Charge* of 1857, p. 82, the Bishop of St. David's speaks of the 'original rule' of Holy Scripture 'as one superior to every other in kind as well as in degree.' Dr. Williams objects, *Earnestly Respectful Letter*, p. 30: 'Difference of degree is as of light from twilight, or full-grown manhood from childhood. Difference of kind is as of good from evil.' The Bishop rejoins by enlarging his original image. He had said: 'The fulness of the stream is the glory of the fountain; and it is because the Ganges is not lost among its native hills, but deepens and widens until it reaches the ocean, that so many pilgrimages are made to its springs.' 'I meant,' he now writes (p. 34), 'that the authority of Scripture was unique, because it is not merely *a* record of revelations, but *the* one original record of all the revelation that mankind has ever received, or has any reason to expect, concerning the objects of Christian faith and hope. I meant that it stands alone,' &c. 'If I had aimed at a more exact correspondence, I should have compared Holy Scripture to the source of a mighty stream, with the addition, that it possesses a quality distinguishing it from all other waters, and likewise a marvellous virtue, by which it assimilates all the tributaries which swell its volume to its own nature.' In Dr. Lushington's *Judgment* on Dr. Williams, June 25, 1862, p. 16, it is held that the acknowledgement of a difference in degree is not enough to satisfy the English formularies.

Dr. Lee, in like manner, had said that the inspiration of the sacred writers 'differs, not merely in degree, but absolutely in kind, from that ordinary operation of the Spirit usually called by the same name' (p. 31); and again, p. 232, *note*. For this he is taken to task by Mr. Swainson, *Authority of N. T.*, p. 60, *note*: 'How things which differ *in kind* can be compared *in degree*, I am unable to judge.' We may borrow an answer from a different branch of science, where the same denial has been often given (e. g. in *Anthrop*.

Rev., i. 117). 'Even if it were to be clearly proved, which, however, I do not say it yet is, that the differences between man's brain and that of the apes are differences entirely of quantity, there is no reason in the nature of things why so many and such weighty *differences of degree* should not amount to a *difference of kind*. Differences of degree and differences of kind are, it is true, mutually exclusive terms in the anthropomorphic language of the schools; whether they are so also in the laboratory of nature, we may very well doubt.'—Rolleston, in *Medical Times and Gazette*, March 1862, p. 262.

But in truth the matter seems sufficiently simple. The objection overlooks the fact, that inspiration can be regarded under different categories. Under one, we can mark out and compare together the different gradations of the Holy Spirit's Presence (Lecture I., *Notes* 12, 13). Under another we can deal with the highest modes of His Presence, as specifically distinct from all other forms, by the use of a differentia, in which the fulness of His influence becomes a leading feature. For purposes of comparison, we recognise the difference of degree. For purposes of contrast, we maintain that the highest form of presence combines with the gift of an objective revelation, to constitute a difference in kind.

Note 2, *page* 40. Compare Horsley's Dissertation *On the Prophecies of the Messiah dispersed among the Heathen*, p. 28, &c.; Lyall, *Propæd. Proph.*, p. 390, on the Preparation of Prophecy among the Heathen ; Mr. Gladstone's *Homer and the Homeric Age*, vol. ii.; Newman's *Arians*, p. 88, on the 'doctrine of the Alexandrian School,' which he calls '*the Divinity of Traditionary Religion*,' and more generally, such passages as the following : 'I mean those historical matters concerning the ancient state of the first world, the deluge, the sons of Noah, the Children of Israel's deliverance out of Egypt, the life and doings of Moses their captain, with such like: the certain truth whereof delivered in Holy Scripture is of the heathen which had them only by report so intermingled with fabulous vanities, that the most which remaineth in them to be seen is the show of dark and obscure steps, where some part of the truth hath gone.'—Hooker, *E. P.*, I. xiii. 2, *note*. 'Whatsoever good effects do grow out of their religion, who embrace instead of the true a false, the roots thereof are certain sparks of the light of truth intermingled with the darkness of error, because no religion can wholly and only consist of untruths.'—*Ib.*, V. i. 5. 'The pagans might be instructed in Divine things, either by reading the Scriptures, or by conversing with Jews, or by conversing with other nations that had been acquainted with Jews, or by means of public edicts of several great princes that had favoured the Jews, or lastly, *by tradition* handed down to them from Abraham, or from Noah, or from the first parents of mankind.'—Waterland, *Works*, v. 16. 'There is yet another more general way by which revealed religion, in some of the principal heads or articles of it, has been diffused through the world; I mean *tradition* delivered down from Noah, or from the first parents of the whole race, who received it immediately from God. The doctrine of one true God supreme might probably come this way, and be so diffused to all mankind. The like may be said of the doctrine of an overruling Providence, and of the immortality of the soul, and a future state of rewards and punishments. These general principles, so universally believed and taught in all ages and countries, are much better referred to *patriarchal tradition* than to any later and narrower source. I know not whether the same observation might not be as justly made of some other doctrines; as of the creation of the world, and corruption of human nature, and perhaps of several more of slighter consideration;' and possibly such rites as sacrifices, Sabbaths, and tithes, and also morality.— *Ib.*, pp. 19–22. 'The whole of the Timæus, in fact, is a *legend*, rather than a philosophical enquiry. It appeals, for the reception of its truths, to the shadows with which it veils them, and the mystic echoes of sounds heard by the listening ear from afar. In that legend, indeed, we have very considerable evidence of the pure source, from which the heathen world drew much of the sacred truth that was wrapped up and disfigured in their fables. We perceive in such a document of ancient philosophy, at once the sure and wide-spread knowledge resulting from a Scriptural Revelation, and the obscurity and fallibility of the information of Tradition.' —Hampden, *Fathers of Greek Philosophy*, p. 287. 'The most reverent regard to the inviolable sacredness of that truth with which the father of the promised seed and his descendants were peculiarly entrusted, consists well with the belief of the preservation of much original truth elsewhere.'—Mill, *Pantheistic Principles*, ii. 62. 'It would seem, then, that there is something true and divinely revealed in every religion all over the earth, overloaded as it may be, and at times even stifled by the impieties which the corrupt will and understanding of man have incorporated with it. Such are the doctrines of the power and presence of an invisible God, of His moral law and governance, of the obligation of duty and the certainty of a just judgment, and of reward and punishment being dispensed in the end to individuals; so that revelation, properly speaking, is an universal, not a partial gift; and the distinction between the state of Israelites formerly and Christians now, and that of the heathen, is, not that we can, and they cannot, attain to future blessedness, but that the Church of God ever has had, and the rest of mankind never have had, *authoritative documents* of truth, and *appointed channels* of communication with Him.'—Newman, *l. l.*, pp. 88–9. The limitations under which this view must be applied are now generally recognised. 'Few, if any, will now maintain the hypothesis of our old divines of the last century, that the stories of Iphigenia and Idomeneus are stolen from the story of Jephthah's daughter, or the labours of Hercules from the labours of Samson.'—Stanley, *Jewish Church*, p. 306. 'It seems blasphemy to consider (some) fables of the heathen world as corrupted and misinterpreted fragments of a Divine revelation once granted to the whole race of mankind.'—M. Müller, *Comparative Mythology*, p. 8 (*Oxford Essays*, 1856).

Note 3, page 41. In Waterland's Charge, *The Wisdom of the Ancients borrowed from Divine Revelation* (*Works*, v. 1–29), he gives a catena of passages in illustration of the method; tracing it through Aristobulus, Josephus, Justin Martyr, Tatian, Theophilus of Antioch, Clemens Alexandrinus, Tertullian, Minucius Felix, Origen, Lactantius, Eusebius, and Theodoret. Dr. Cæsar Morgan gives a similar set of references from Justin Martyr and Clemens Alexandrinus; *Trinity of Plato*, 91–9, ed. Holden. 'Yet this advantage, great as it really is, has not always been sufficient to satisfy the pretensions of those who have been blessed with a Divine revelation. Not contented with the bright sunshine which blazes around them, they will scarcely allow the benighted heathen the dim taper of human reason to guide their steps in their laborious travels over the dark mountains. Whatever the Apostle Paul may have said in his various expostulations with the Gentiles, and particularly in his Epistle to the Romans, there are some far wiser, in their own conceit, than seven men that can render a reason, who boldly maintain, that whatever glimmerings of light the pagans of old have been able to strike out by mere dint of labour and study, have been all either directly or circuitously derived from the sacred writings.'—*Ib.*, p. 90. On the views of Clement, see also Bishop Kaye, *Clem. Alex.*, p. 186; Mozley, *Prædest.*, 115; and on those of Eusebius, Donaldson, *Greek Lit.*, iii. 331-3.

Note 4, *page* 42. The titles of three well-known works by Mr. Blakesley (Five Sermons on *the Dispensation of Paganism*, in *Conciones Academicæ*), Dean Trench (*Christ the Desire of all Nations; or the Unconscious Prophecies of Heathendom*, being the Hulsean Lectures for 1846), and M. De Pressensé (*The Religions before Christ*, E. T., 1862). Add Mr. Maurice's *Religions of the World and their Relations to Christianity*; and a work which was unfortunate only in its title, and in the melancholy event which left it incomplete, the *Christ and other Masters* of the late Archdeacon Hardwick. A great storehouse of materials is supplied by Dr. Döllinger's *Heidenthum und Judenthum*, Regensburg, 1857 (E. T., *The Gentile and the Jew in the Courts of the Temple of Christ*, 1862). In other forms, and unhappily too often with different issues, the subject has had a strong attraction for some of the most active minds of the age; see, e.g., M. Renan's review of the great work of Creuzer and Guigniaut, in *Études d'Histoire Religieuse*, pp. 1-71, &c. Add M. Denis, *Histoire des Théories et des Idées Morales dans l'Antiquité; ouvrage couronné*, 1856.

Note 5, *page* 42. 1. 'In what sense can it be said that there is any connection between Paganism and Christianity so real as to warrant the preacher of the latter to *conciliate idolaters* by allusion to it? St. Paul evidently connects the true religion with the existing systems which he laboured to supplant in Acts xvii., and his example is a sufficient guide to missionaries now, and a full justification of the line of conduct pursued by the Alexandrians in the instances similar to it.'—Newman, *Arians*, p. 87. 'Justin's wish was to render the doctrines of Christianity *as acceptable as possible* to the Gentiles, by pointing out features of resemblance between them and the tenets of the philosophers.'—Bishop Kaye, *Justin Martyr*, p. 47. 'Earlier Christianity regarded the Gentile world more as a field of promise; and saw in it the future harvest rather than the present foe. . . . The early Church thus adopted a friendly tone toward Gentile philosophy, and acknowledged sympathies with it.'—Mozley, *Prædest.*, pp. 112-3.

2. The *Præparatio Evangelica* of Eusebius ' is the *epochal work* in regard to the new attitude assumed by Christian literature; it is the declaration of a Christian, himself learned in profane lore,

that from thenceforth the Church is as independent of heathen philosophy as it is fearless of the secular opposition of the heathen world.'—Donaldson, *Greek Lit.*, iii. 332. Compare Mr. Farrar's *B. L.*, pp. 539, 639, sqq.

The following may suffice as representative passages for the two chief stages:—

1. Ὅτε δὲ Σωκράτης λόγῳ ἀληθεῖ καὶ ἐξεταστικῶς ταῦτα εἰς φανερὸν ἐπειρᾶτο φέρειν, καὶ ἀπάγειν τῶν δαιμόνων τοὺς ἀνθρώπους, κ. τ. λ.—S. Just. Mart., *Apol.*, I. 5; *Opp.*, i. p. 11, ed. Otto. Καὶ οἱ μετὰ λόγου βιώσαντες Χριστιανοί εἰσι, κἂν ἄθεοι ἐνομίσθησαν, οἷον ἐν Ἕλλησι μὲν Σωκράτης καὶ Ἡράκλειτος καὶ οἱ ὅμοιοι αὐτοῖς, κ. τ. λ.—*Ib.*, 46; i. p. 110. Χριστῷ δέ, τῷ καὶ ὑπὸ Σωκράτους ἀπὸ μέρους γνωσθέντι, κ. τ. λ.—*Ib.*, II. 10; i. p. 194. Ἦν μὲν οὖν πρὸ τῆς τοῦ κυρίου παρουσίας εἰς δικαιοσύνην Ἕλλησιν ἀναγκαία φιλοσοφία· νυνὶ δὲ χρησίμη πρὸς θεοσέβειαν γίνεται, προπαιδεία τις οὖσα τοῖς τὴν πίστιν δι' ἀποδείξεως καρπουμένοις· ὅτι ὁ πούς σου, φησίν, οὐ μὴ προσκόψῃ, ἐπὶ τὴν πρόνοιαν τὰ καλὰ ἀναφέροντος, ἐάν τε Ἑλληνικὰ ᾖ, ἐάν τε ἡμέτερα. πάντων μὲν γὰρ αἴτιος τῶν καλῶν ὁ Θεός· ἀλλὰ τῶν μὲν, κατὰ προηγούμενον, ὡς τῆς τε διαθήκης τῆς παλαιᾶς καὶ τῆς νέας· τῶν δέ, κατ' ἐπακολούθημα, ὡς τῆς φιλοσοφίας· τάχα δὲ καὶ προηγουμένως τοῖς Ἕλλησιν ἐδόθη τότε, πρὶν ἢ τὸν Κύριον καλέσαι καὶ τοὺς Ἕλληνας· ἐπειδαγώγει γὰρ καὶ αὐτὴ τὸ Ἑλληνικόν, ὡς ὁ νόμος τοὺς Ἑβραίους, εἰς Χριστόν. προπαρασκευάζει τοίνυν ἡ φιλοσοφία, προοδοποιοῦσα τὸν ὑπὸ Χριστοῦ τελειούμενον.—S. Clem. Alex., *Strom.*, I. 5; *Opp.*, i. 331, ed. Potter. Καίτοι καὶ καθ' ἑαυτὴν ἐδικαίου ποτὲ καὶ ἡ φιλοσοφία τοὺς Ἕλληνας· οὐκ εἰς τὴν καθόλου δὲ δικαιοσύνην, εἰς ἣν εὑρίσκεται συνεργός, καθάπερ καὶ ὁ πρῶτος καὶ ὁ δεύτερος βαθμὸς τῷ εἰς τὸ ὑπερῷον ἀνιόντι, καὶ ὁ γραμματιστὴς τῷ φιλοσοφήσοντι.—*Ib.*, I. 20; i. p. 377. Τὴν δὲ φιλοσοφίαν καὶ μᾶλλον Ἕλλησιν οἷον διαθήκην οἰκείαν αὐτοῖς δεδόσθαι, ὑποβάθραν οὖσαν τῆς κατὰ Χριστὸν φιλοσοφίας.—*Ib.*, VI. 8; ii. p. 773.

2. 'Adeo quid simile philosophus et Christianus? Græciæ discipulus et cœli? famæ negotiator et vitæ? verborum et factorum operator, et rerum ædificator et destructor? amicus et inimicus erroris? veritatis interpolator et integrator et expressor, et furator ejus et custos?'—Tertull., *Apolog.*, 46; *Opp.*, i. p. 285, ed. Oehler. 'Quid ergo Athenis et Hierosolymis? quid academiæ et ecclesiæ? quid hæreticis et Christianis?'—Id., *De Præscr. Hæret.*, 7; ii. p. 10.

Note 6, page 43. 'The study of the history of the ancient

world is likewise important from another point of view. Christianity found in it, not only vigorous foes or latent sympathy, but, according to a strange law, by which the vanquished almost always end in exercising over the victors an influence, the greater because least suspected, we shall see the ancient world, at the moment that all things announced its defeat, morally regain the ground it had externally lost. Heresy was nothing but a hypocritical reaction of Paganism against Christianity.'—De Pressensé, *Religions before Christ*, p. 6. Compare Stanley, *Jewish Church*, 270, 290.

Note 7, *page* 45. 'When Joseph was brought to Pharaoh to interpret his dream, the holy patriarch and the Egyptian king speak of God in much the same language, and with the same acknowledgement of His overruling providence.'—Horsley, *Dissertation*, &c., p. 46; so before, of the Abimelechs, of the family of Nahor, &c. 'Abimelech, Ephron, Mamre, Melchizedek, all either worship the same God, or, if they worship Him under another name, are all bound together by ties of hospitality and friendship.'—Stanley, *Jewish Church*, p. 40; cf. p. 68, of Job; p. 142, of Jethro; p. 187, of Balaam; and p. 416. 'The Book of Genesis contains a record of the dispensation of natural religion, or Paganism, as well as of the patriarchal. The dreams of Pharaoh and Abimelech, as of Nebuchadnezzar afterwards, are instances of the dealings of God with those to whom He did not vouchsafe a written revelation. Or should it be said that the particular cases merely come within the range of the Divine supernatural governance which was in their neighbourhood—an assertion which requires proof—let the Book of Job be taken as a less suspicious instance of the dealings of God with the heathen. Job was a Pagan in the same sense in which the Eastern nations are Pagans in the present day. . . . If it be objected that Job lived in a less corrupted age than the times of ignorance which followed, Scripture, as if for our full satisfaction, draws back the curtain further still in the history of Balaam. There a bad man and a heathen is made the oracle of true Divine messages about doing justly and loving mercy, and walking humbly; nay, even among the altars of superstition, the Spirit of God vouchsafes to utter prophecy.'—Newman, *Arians*, pp. 90, 91.

'Other nations or persons, ordinarily, were not obliged to become Jews; and therefore Moses did not insist upon it with his father-in-law Jethro; neither did Elisha expect it of Naaman the Syrian, nor Jonas of the Ninevites, nor Daniel of Nebuchadnezzar; neither did the prophets insist upon it with the Chaldeans, Egyptians, Sidonians, Tyrians, Edomites, or Moabites, as Grotius has well observed: but though they were not obliged to become Jews, they were obliged to admit the true God, and the most substantial parts of true religion; the knowledge of which had been handed down by tradition, and was often renewed and revived by means of the Jews, who were the standing witnesses and memorials of it.'—Waterland, *Works*, v. 25. 'There is no absurdity in supposing that God might have some prophets (abroad in the heathen world) who were not of Israel. Job was undoubtedly such an one; and why might not Balaam be another?'—*Ib.*, 749. 'Whenever God brought His people into any relation with other people, He made Himself known to them. The mode of His manifestation varied; the fact remained uniform. So He made Himself known to Egypt through Joseph and Moses; to the Philistines at the capture of the ark; to the Syrians by Elisha; to Nebuchadnezzar and Belshazzar by Daniel; as again to Darius and Cyrus.'—Pusey, *Introduction to Jonah; Minor Prophets*, p. 247. Compare Mr. Gladstone, *Homer*, &c., ii. 6, 7.

That the 'Hebrew midwives' of Ex. i. 15 were Egyptian women, appointed by the king to act as midwives to the Hebrews, see Josephus, *Antiq.*, II. ix. § 2; Kalisch, *Exodus*, p. 15; Horsley, *l. l.*, p. 47.

Bishop Hampden remarks, that the verse Micah vi. 8 'may be inscribed as its motto on any authentic record of the Divine will.'— *Philos. Evidence of Christianity*, p. 26. Now we have a long series of English theologians who take that view of the dialogue in Micah which places the words in the mouth of Balaam; Butler, *Sermon* VII. p. 89; Lowth, *de S. P. Hebr.*, Præl. xviii. p. 201, ed. Lips., 1815; Horsley, *l. l.*, p. 102; Faber, *Eight Dissertations*, i. 337; Newman, *l. l.*, p. 91, and *Parochial Sermons*, iv. 28; Burgon, *Inspiration and Interpretation*, p. iii. *note*; Stanley, *Jewish Church*, p. 189, adding a confirmation of the exposition from 2 Kings iii. 27; and several others.

Note 8, *page* 48. The precise relations of Heathenism, Judaism, and Christianity are drawn out in different aspects in most of the books enumerated above, *Note* 4; and whatever is said of Judaism and Christianity can be adjusted to the Holy Scriptures, when the position of the sacred record has been accurately defined. Dr. Stanley traces out such distinctions as these; that from the days of

Abraham himself, 'the interval between the human and Divine is never confounded' (*Jewish Church*, p. 14); that the passage of the Red Sea ' was a fit opening of a history and of a character which was to be specially distinguished from that of other races by its constant and direct dependence on the Supreme Judge and Ruler of the world' (*ib.*, p. 129); that Moses received a positive revelation at Sinai, 'the very reverse of a negation or an abstraction' (p. 151); that 'the union of the qualities so often disjoined in man, so little thought of in the gods of old, "justice and mercy," "truth and love," became henceforward the formula, many times repeated, the substance of the creed of the Jewish Church' (p. 152); that 'not from want of religion, but (if one might use the expression) from excess of religion, was this void left in the Jewish mind,'—'the dimness of its conception of a future life ' (p. 154); that the prophets were distinguished, in the first place, by ' their proclamation of the Unity and of the Spirituality of the Divine nature ' (p. 446), &c.

All other distinctions, however, must be brought to their centre in the recognition of ' the one image of God in humanity, as the source of their Divine life, which is the vital principle of Christianity.'— Mill, *Pantheistic Principles*, i. 116. 'What is the reason which all sects and Churches are most likely to agree in, were they asked their reason for this veneration of the Bible ? Surely, because it contains the records of a *Life*, of the conditions which preceded it, and of the consequences which followed it; because we read there the history of Him, without whose Divine life the world was not, and without whose human life the Church was not.'—Chretien, *Letter and Spirit*, p. 41; cf. pp. 111, 114. 'The Word and the Sacraments are the characteristic of the elect people of God.'—Newman, *Arians*, p. 89. ' With the two ideas of Redemption and Salvation the entire framework of Revelation is inseparably connected. To the first man was given a hope of the redemption of his race; and beyond this the last of the prophets cannot go. The appearance of the Redeemer Himself did no more than give reality to such anticipations.'—Lee, p. 13.

Note 9, *page* 49. The doctrine of the Divine name is worked out by Dr. Moberly, *Sayings of the Great Forty Days*, p. 200, and *Law of the Love of God*, p. 98 : ' The third commandment no longer speaks of God as He is in Himself, but of the *Name* of God; of God, that is, as He can be named or spoken of in human words; of God, not as the intellect of man contemplates Him, or the faith of man holds fast the belief in Him, or the piety of man worships Him;

but as He is pleased to allow Himself and His being to be *projected*, if I may so express myself, upon the imperfect media of human and earthly things: His Name named in words, His Nature confessed in creeds, His Truth made known by inspiration to the hearts of men, and by them spoken in speech, and written down in books, His Presence attached in some manner to persons, things, and places.' Cf. p. 101. 'The name of a person is that which brings him before the mind as *all that he is*; and is often used in Scripture as a summary of the character or qualities.'—Vaughan, *on Rom.* i. 5.

The controversy, which has been recently reopened, can be traced through all the larger commentaries on the Pentateuch. Waterland's solution of the difficulty is not very satisfactory. (*Works*, i. 312.) Lightfoot closes his exposition thus: 'The name Jehovah, and the significancy of it to the utmost, did the holy Fathers know before Moses. But they saw not experience of the last signification named, namely, the faithfulness of God in His promise made to Abraham concerning His delivery of his seed from bondage, and bringing them into a land flowing with milk and honey. God gave them the promise by the name of *El Shaddai, God Omnipotent*; and they relied upon His omnipotency, because He that promised was able to perform: but they beheld it afar off, and tasted not of My performance of it. But now will I show Myself *Jehovah*, faithful to bring to pass and accomplish what I promised.'—*Works*, i. 704, ed. 1684. The word 'significancy,' at the beginning of this extract, must be qualified by what is said at the end of it. If the name was not known by personal and practical experience; if, indeed, there was a sense in which God could say, 'By My Name JEHOVAH was I *not known* to them;' its 'significancy' could not have been disclosed 'to the utmost' to the Fathers. And nearly so Pearson: 'It cannot be denied but God was known to Abraham by the true importance of the title *Adonai*, as much as by the name of *Shaddai*; as much by His dominion and sovereignty, as by His power and all-sufficiency; but by any experimental and personal sense of the fulfilling of His promises, His name *Jehovah* was not known unto him.'—*On the Creed*, Art. ii., p. 184, ed. Oxon. 1843. Compare Stanley, *Jewish Church*, p. 110. 'The assertion is not that the *word* Jehovah was not used in the patriarchal language; but that the *name* Jehovah, as a title of honour, whereby a new idea was affixed to an old word, was unknown to them.'—Warburton, *D. L.*, iv. § 6; ii. p. 300, ed. 1846.

Of what he calls 'the ordinary mode of "reconciling" these discrepancies,' as exhibited by Kurtz and Kalisch, Bishop Colenso says, that it is 'evidently an assumption made only to get over a difficulty. If Abraham made use of the name Jehovah at all, then God *was* known to him in some measure—in some sense or other—by that name, if not known so perfectly as by the Israelites in later days' (§ 299); which no one, I think, need wish to deny. The name Jehovah might have been known, and unquestionably was known, as a *denotative*, long before its complete *connotation* was revealed. That is to say, Jehovah was known 'in some measure—in some sense or other—by that name,' though the usage did not amount to what I have called the 'high and special significance,' ascribed in Scripture 'to the knowledge of the name of' Jehovah, and connected with the fulfilment of His promise.

Note 10, *page* 50. 'In the second place, I observe that this moral revelation, made by the succession of Prophets, holds an intermediate place between the Law of Moses and the Gospel itself. It is a step in progress beyond the Law, and preparatory to the Gospel.'—Davison, *On Prophecy*, p. 43. 'In the Prophets there is a more luminous, and more perfectly reasoned, rule of life and faith than in the primary Law; and therefore God's moral revelation was progressive. It is more perfect in the Prophets than in the Law; more perfect in the Gospel than in either.'—*Ib.*, p. 44; cf. p. 61. Also Dr. Stanley, *Jewish Church*, 436, 447–9. But, again, we must not draw the line so sharply, as to forget what has been before suggested on the difference between comparative and absolute exclusion; above, pp. 19, 220. So Mr. Morris urges: 'The ceremonial law was not the real object of the legislator, even from the very first: the moral law was given first in the decalogue; the ceremonial was added after, because of transgressions.'—*Essay towards the Conversion of Hindus*, p. 72. 'Revelation has all along been progressive, but not on that account self-contradictory.'—Browne, in *Aids to Faith*, p. 315, *note*.

Note 11, *page* 52. 'The true intent and scope of these *Positive* laws (and it may be of such an external promulgation of the *Moral*), seems to be nothing else but this, to secure the *Eternal* Law of Righteousness from transgression.'—John Smith's *Select Discourses*, p. 154, ed. 1673.

We may compare the account of Justice in *Eth. N.*, V. 6, which shows how the universal principles of right and wrong, to which the hearts of all mankind bear witness, receive a peculiar shape and impress, in each separate state, from the enactments which are requisite to give them efficiency. We are thus taught to distinguish between the eternal law and its temporary form; between truths which admit of no exception, and can nowhere be transgressed without sin, and statutes which are shaped by local needs and local conveniences, and possess no more than a territorial obligation. The province of equity, in conformity with this distinction, is defined to be that of recalling us, in doubtful cases, from the rule to the principle, so as to guard against the danger, which is imminent in all human arrangements, lest special wrong should be inflicted under the name and authority of Justice. For an application of this principle to the Mosaic code, and for the value of its precepts, as 'moral rules ordained by God,' I may refer to *Discourses on the Fall and its Results*, pp. 239-41. See also below, Lecture IV., Note 10.

Note 12, *page* 54. The diversity of human *characters* is recognised in most of the writers quoted above, Lecture I., *Notes* 3 and 4. With regard to human *learning* :—' There is in the world no kind of knowledge, whereby any part of truth is seen, but we justly account it precious; yea, that principal truth, in comparison whereof all other knowledge is vile, may receive from it some kind of light; whether it be that Egyptian and Chaldean wisdom mathematical, wherewith Moses and Daniel were furnished ; or that natural, moral, and civil wisdom, wherein Solomon excelled all men ; or that rational and oratorial wisdom of the Grecians, which the Apostle St. Paul brought from Tarsus ; or that Judaical, which he learned in Jerusalem, sitting at the feet of Gamaliel : to detract from the dignity thereof were to injure even God Himself, who being that light which none can approach unto, hath sent out these lights whereof we are capable, even as so many sparkles resembling the bright fountain from which they rise.'—Hooker, *E. P.*, III. viii. § 9. ' To descend to Moses the lawgiver, and God's first pen : he is adorned by the Scriptures with this addition and commendation, that he was seen in all the learning of the Egyptians. . . . So likewise in that excellent book of Job, if it be revolved with diligence, it will be found pregnant and swelling with natural philosophy. . . . So likewise in the person of Salomon the king, we see the gift or endowment of wisdom and learning, both in Salomon's petition and in God's assent thereunto, preferred before all other terrene and temporal felicity,' &c.—Bacon, *Advancement of Learning; Works*, iii. 297–8, ed. Ellis and Spedding. For Bishop Bull, see above, Lecture I., *Note* 5. On the quotations in St. Paul, cf. Bull, *l. l.*, p. 214–5; Milton, *Preface to Samson Agonistes*; Donaldson, *Greek Lit.*, iii. 316. It has been thought that the list is not exhausted by the instances ordinarily given. See Humphry on Acts xiv. 17 : ' both the language and the rhythm of this passage lead to the conjecture (which does not appear to have been proposed before), that it is a fragment from some lyric poem.' ' Very improbable,' says Dean Alford. Another suggestion, which is, however, still more improbable, will be found in Donaldson's *Christian Orthodoxy*, p. 292. See also John Gregory's Note on Jannes and Jambres, *Works*, 1684, i. 61. For a collateral enquiry of singular interest in a different field, see Dr. Neale's Essay *On Liturgical Quotations; Essays on Liturgiology*, &c., No. XV.

Note 13, *page* 55. See the details in the works of Döllinger and De Pressensé; or in Tholuck's Essay *On the Nature and Moral Influence of Heathenism*. Compare Mr. Jowett's Essays *On the Connexion of Immorality and Idolatry*, and *On the State of the Heathen World; Epistles of St. Paul*, ii. 64, 68, 1st ed. Dr. Vaughan marks the following steps in St. Paul's argument, Rom. i. 18–32 : ' 1. Knowledge abused ; 2. Ignorance and unbelief; 3. Gross corruption ; 4. Judicial hardness.'—*Comm. in loc.* Yet, ' in behalf of revelation, I should press for the *superiority* of the civilised Gentile world in art and science, poetry and eloquence, and every department of intellectual culture, together with all the wisdom of civil and political institutions derived from that source, and bright examples of patriotism, courage, and many other virtues; in a word, in all respects but one—the true religion, the possession of the oracles of God. This contrast between the inferiority of the chosen people in all secular advantages, and their pre-eminence in religious privileges, seems to me an argument which cannot be too strongly insisted on by a Christian advocate.'—Bishop of St. David's, *Letter to Dr. R. Williams*, p. 65. So from M. Renan's point of view : ' C'est la race sémitique qui a la gloire d'avoir fait la religion de l'humanité ' (*Vie de Jésus*, p. 5); yet, ' c'est beaucoup moins dans l'ordre politique que dans l'ordre religieux que s'est exercée leur influence. . . . C'est, par excellence, le peuple de Dieu et le peuple des religions, destiné à les créer et à les propager ;' but ' La race sémitique, comparée à la race indo-européenne, représente réellement une combinaison inférieure de la nature humaine.'— *Hist. des Langues Sémitiques*, i. 3, 4.

Note 14, *page* 56. The remark constantly suggests itself to students of ancient mythology, that the worshippers were often better than their gods. Compare Jowett, *l. l.*, ii. 70 (2nd ed.): 'The deities of the Homeric poems are not better than men, but rather worse; compared with heroes, they have a fainter sense of truth and justice, less certainly of moral greatness.' 'Not from religion, but from philosophy, come the higher aspirations of the human soul in Greece and Rome.'—*Ib.*, 72. 'Nothing can more clearly demonstrate that man was better than the gods he had created.'—De Pressensé, *l.l.*, p. 27; cf. pp. 78, 80, 168–9, 170. See also Mr. Cox's Introduction to his *Tales of the Gods and Heroes*: 'The contrast is very marked between the character of the people and that of their theology.'—P. 4. 'It would be difficult to discover a more marvellous combination of seemingly inexplicable contradictions; of belief in the history of gods utterly distinct from the faith which guided the practice of men; of an immoral and impure theology with a condition of society which it would be monstrous to regard as utterly and brutally depraved.'—P. 7. 'It is the character of the religions which men invent, that they begin purely and end in corruption. . . . On the contrary, in the O. T. Scriptures, it is always a growing light.'—Mr. R. P. Smith, *Messianic Interpretation of Isaiah*, p. vi.

Note 15, *page* 58. 'All superstition, all idolatry, has its root in the belief that God is made in our image, and not we in His; the most prevalent assumption of the modern as of the ancient sophist is, that man is the measure of all things; that there is nothing great or holy which is not his creation.'—Maurice, *On the Lord's Prayer*, p. 22. 'In order to show that there really is this essential distinction between that which we call revealed religion, and all the systems of belief and worship *which we can trace to a human origin*, it is necessary that we should, however briefly, examine the different modes in which the intellect has grappled with religion, and contrast them with those views respecting the personality of God and the nature of sin, which are to be found only in the religion of Jesus Christ, and in that part of the religion of Moses which the Gospel has accepted and ratified. It may be said with truth, that all false religions fall into three main classes,' namely, Polytheism, Dualism, and Pantheism.—Donaldson, *Christian*

Orthodoxy, p. 101. ' It is no matter from what point of view we commence our examination; whether, with the Theist, we admit the coexistence of the Infinite and the Finite, as distinct realities, or, with the Pantheist, deny the real existence of the Finite, or, with the Atheist, deny the real existence of the Infinite,' &c.—Mansel, *B. L.*, p. 68. Compare *Man's Conception of Eternity*, p. 10 : ' Pantheism and Anthropomorphism (using the latter term in its widest sense) are the two alternatives of religious thought; the one representing the negative, the other the positive side.' Also, *Second Letter to Professor Goldwin Smith*, p. 2 : ' From the earliest days in which Philosophy and Christianity came in contact, the aim of the Church has been to keep a just middle course between two extremes, both in themselves errors, yet both only exaggerations of truths :—the tendency to Pantheism, which perverts the true doctrine of the unity and simplicity of God, and the tendency to Anthropomorphism, which perverts the true doctrine of His personality.' So again p. 17. Compare De Pressensé, *l. l.*, p. 248 ; E. T. of Saisset, *Modern Pantheism*, ii. 203 ; M. Müller, *Comparative Mythology*, p. 48 : ' It was a mistake of the early Fathers to treat the heathen gods as demons or evil spirits, and we must take care not to commit the same error with regard to the Hindu god. Their gods have no more right to any substantive existence than Eos or Hemera —than Nyx or Apatê. They are masks without an actor, the *creations of man, not his creators* ; they are nomina, not numina ; names without being, not beings without names.'

Note 16, *page* 60. Of Bentley's eight Boyle Lectures (in *Works*, vol. iii., ed. Dyce), four are based on Acts xvii. 27, and three on Acts xiv. 15, &c. He points out the clear-sighted prudence with which, under Divine guidance, St. Paul adjusted his speech on the one occasion to the ' philosophers and that inquisitive people of Athens ;' on the other, ' to the rude and simple semi-barbarians of Lycaonia,' pp. 120–1. The one passage suggests to him arguments against Atheism, ' from the faculties of the soul,' and ' from the structure and origin of human bodies ;' the other passage suggests a confutation ' from the origin and frame of the world.' In the former series he analyses the elements of partial agreement which would extend to portions of the Apostle's hearers : the populace would admit the appeal to poets, and possibly also the Divine creation ; but would not agree with his attack on images and temples, or on the belief that the feasts of men were pleasing to the gods: the philosophers would accept his spiritual view of Deity, but would differ on almost every detail of his argument. 'The presiding idea of this portion of my work, is that which animated St. Paul in his discourse at Athens, when he found, even in that focus of Paganism, religious aspirations tending to Jesus Christ.'— De Pressensé, *l.l.*, *Preface to E. V.* 'We cannot fail to notice how the sentences of this interrupted speech are constructed to meet the cases in succession of every class of which the audience was composed. Each word in the address is adapted at once to win and to rebuke.'—Conybeare and Howson, *Life and Epistles of St. Paul*, i. 408. Compare the recent *Essays towards the Conversion of Hindus*; Morris, p. 16; Williams, pp. 1, 380, &c.

Note 17, *page* 62. Ὅτι μὲν τοίνυν εἰσὶ φύσει τινὲς οἱ μὲν ἐλεύθεροι οἱ δὲ δοῦλοι, φανερόν, οἷς καὶ συμφέρει τὸ δουλεύειν καὶ δίκαιόν ἐστι.—Ar., *Pol.*, I. 5, *fin.* 'Where the Greek saw barbarians, we see brethren.' —Müller, *Comp. Myth.*, p. 4. 'Very early in their history the Greeks explained the institution (of slavery) as grounded on the intellectual inferiority of certain races, and their consequent natural aptitude for the servile condition.'—Maine, *Ancient Law*, p. 163. On the superiority of the Hebrew law in this respect to both Greek and Roman theory and practice, see Mr. Goldwin Smith on *American Slavery*, p. 49.

Note 18, *page* 62. Τὸ γὰρ μηθὲν ἐκ μὴ ὄντος γίγνεσθαι πᾶν δ' ἐξ ὄντος, σχεδὸν ἁπάντων ἐστὶ κοινὸν δόγμα τῶν περὶ φύσεως.—Ar., *Metaph.*, K. 6; p. 1062, b. 24. With regard to Plato, on whose opinions a doubt has been raised, compare Mr. W. Mills's *Essays and Lectures*, p. 72; Professor Thompson's Note on Archer Butler's *Lectures on Ancient Philosophy*, ii. 190; Rawlinson, *Christianity and Heathenism*, Sermon I., *note* 1; Mansel, *B. L.*, Lecture III., *note* 12, p. 335. 'The later Platonists, and even the Christian Fathers, speak of Plato contradicting himself, by sometimes saying that matter was eternal, and sometimes that it was created. The Platonists went so far as to assert that Plato did not hold that matter was eternal. But the assertion was undoubtedly false.' 'Plato certainly did not believe *the world* to be eternal, though such a notion is ascribed to Aristotle. Plato held the eternity of *matter*; but he believed the arrangement and harmony of the universe to be the work of the Deity.'—Burton, *B. L.*, pp. 59, 61. More generally: 'As it was impossible for them to conceive the creation of matter, the workman, in the Stoic philosophy, was not sufficiently distinguished from the work.'

—Gibbon, *R. E.*, i. 167, ed. Smith. 'All (Gnostics) were agreed in maintaining that matter itself was not created; that it was eternal.' —Burton, *B. L.*, p. 36. 'The Egyptians held matter to be eternal, though they believed that the world was created.'—*Ib.*, p. 67. 'In the first place, as all the ancient philosophers decided that nothing can come out of nothing, I consider it certain that they all supposed matter to be eternal.'—Mosheim's Note on Cudworth, i. 301, ed. Harrison. And for details, see his Dissertation 'showing whether any heathen philosopher ever taught that the world was created by God out of nothing,' *ib.*, iii. 140.

Note 19, *page* 64. Ἔτι δὲ εἴτε νοῦς ἡ οὐσία αὐτοῦ εἴτε νόησίς ἐστι, τί νοεῖ; ἢ γὰρ αὐτὸς αὐτὸν, ἢ ἕτερόν τι· καὶ εἰ ἕτερόν τι, ἢ τὸ αὐτὸ ἀεὶ ἢ ἄλλο. πότερον οὖν διαφέρει τι ἢ οὐδὲν τὸ νοεῖν τὸ καλὸν ἢ τὸ τυχόν; ἢ καὶ ἄτοπον τὸ διανοεῖσθαι περὶ ἐνίων; δῆλον τοίνυν ὅτι τὸ θειότατον καὶ τιμιώτατον νοεῖ, καὶ οὐ μεταβάλλει, κ. τ. λ.—Ar., *Metaph.*, Λ. 9; p. 1074, b. 21. ὥστ' εἰ φευκτὸν τοῦτο (καὶ γὰρ μὴ ὁρᾷν ἔνια κρεῖττον ἢ ὁρᾷν) οὐκ ἂν εἴη τὸ ἄριστον ἡ νόησις. αὐτὸν ἄρα νοεῖ, εἴπερ ἐστὶ τὸ κράτιστον.—*Ib.*, 32. 'Ou bien, si vous voulez qu'elle s'exerce, donnez à Dieu la connaissance du monde; mais alors supprimez, avec le reste, le chapitre entier où Aristote démontre que son Dieu ne connait que lui. Et cependant ce n'est pas une affirmation, c'est une démonstration que vous supprimerez; l'affirmation aurait suffi; car si Dieu n'agit pas volontairement sur le monde, il est impossible qu'il le connaisse. Mais Aristote insiste; il démontre que la pensée de Dieu ne s'applique qu'à Dieu lui-même. Ou Dieu se pense lui-même, dit Aristote, ou il pense quelque autre objet; si quelque autre objet, c'est toujours le même, ou tantôt l'un et tantôt l'autre. Supposons qu'il change ainsi, et que sa pensée, comme la nôtre, parcoure des objets divers, Dieu tombe dans le mouvement. Voilà déjà l'univers exclu; le monde est un, sans doute, mais de cette unité qui résulte de l'harmonie entre les parties diverses; il vit d'ailleurs, il dure, et en durant, il change. Le monde a une histoire; il n'y a que Dieu, l'acte éternel et toujours le même, qui n'en ait point.'—Simon, *Études sur la Théodicée de Platon et d'Aristote*, p. 50.

The fatal defect of an impassable barrier between God and man recurs in every analysis of philosophic creeds. The Elean school 'had gone into the other extreme, by condemning the absolute Being to eternal immobility, by representing Him as an impassible intelligence holding no relations with humanity.'—De Pressensé, *Religions before*

Christ, p. 112. Even in Plato's system, 'a vast interval separates man from God.'—*Ib.*, p. 122. 'Plato, like the Gospel, says to man that his duty is to resemble God; but while Plato's god is only a sublime idea, a being of the reason, which does not enter into communication with man, the God of Christians is the living God, the most holy and the most good, the God revealed by Jesus Christ, whose name is Love.'—*Ib.*, p. 127. For Aristotle, see *ib.*, p. 134. For his immediate disciples: they had 'deliberately set aside the god of philosophy, affirming that a divinity was unnecessary to the explanation of the formation of the world.'—*Ib.*, p. 140. For the Epicureans, see *ib.*, p. 141. At a later time, Plutarch 'gave a more rigid formula to dualism, and deepened the abyss between the supreme God and creation.'—*Ib.*, p. 183. For 'the Platonic doctrine, so far as it is represented in an impure form in the early centuries:' 'its invincible dualism, separating by an impassable chasm God from the world, and mind from matter, identifying goodness with the one, evil with the other, prevented belief in a religion like Christianity, which was penetrated by the Hebrew conceptions of the universe, so alien both to dualism and pantheism.'— Farrar, *B. L.*, p. 63. For Maimonides: 'Whence did this view come? Not from Christianity. The philosophy which makes an impassable barrier between God and man was not cradled in the Gospel of reconciliation, which bridges over the chasm between God and man in the mystery of the Incarnation.'—*Christian Remembrancer*, Jan. 1863, p. 104.

Nor should we be deceived by phrases which seem to suggest a nearer view of Deity, and many of which are scattered over Aristotle's practical treatises. In a case of this kind, the exact philosophy must be held to give its interpretation to more popular language. Again, Mr. M. Müller says: 'We can hardly expect among pagans a more profound conception of the relation between God and man than the saying of Heracleitos, 'Men are mortal gods, and gods are immortal men.'—*Compar. Mythol.*, p. 8. Can we accept so good an interpretation of the phrase? Cf. Brucker, *Hist. Phil.*, i. 1222 : 'Nec aliud vult obscura sententia Heracliti, Heraclito juniori memorata: Θεοὶ ἄνθρωποι ἀθάνατοι, ἄνθρωποι θεοὶ θνητοί, ζῶντες τὸν ἐκείνων θάνατον, θνήσκοντες τὴν ἐκείνων ζωήν. Dii enim in animâ mundi comprehensi dæmonesque, quorum mundus plenus est, in eo tantum ab hominis animâ distant, quod hæc corpus subit, sicque igneâ et divinâ vi suâ quasi privatur et moritur, atque ex Deo homo fit, ubi vero homo moritur, ad Deos iterum et divinam naturam redit.' Compare Mr. Campbell, *Introd. to Theætetus*, p. xliii.: 'Indeed, as in all things else, so in man, life and death are ever working together. His body is ever absorbed into his soul, his soul is ever dying into his body; his birth into the world is the entombment of a higher life, the death of what is earthly in him is the awaking of the god.'

For the grosser form, in which the feeling of the distance of the Deity exhibited itself through the worship of men, we may turn to the hymn with which the Athenians welcomed Demetrius Poliorcetes, and which is preserved by Athenæus (Müller, *Fragmenta Histor. Græc.*, ii. 477; cf. De Pressensé, p. 137; Thirlwall, *History of Greece*, vii. 362, 382, 8vo. ed.):

"Ἄλλοι μὲν ἢ μακρὰν γὰρ ἀπέχουσιν Θεοὶ
ἢ οὐκ ἔχουσιν ὦτα,
ἢ οὐκ εἰσὶν, ἢ οὐ προσέχουσιν ἡμῖν οὐδὲ ἕν·
σὲ δὲ παρόνθ' ὁρῶμεν,
οὐ ξύλινον, οὐδὲ λίθινον, ἀλλ' ἀληθινόν.
Εὐχόμεσθα δή σοι.

Note 20, *page* 66. The five opinions summed up in this paragraph give a progressive series of the main views which man can form as to the condition of the soul after death. 1. Annihilation: the grosser heathen view, represented occasionally by the despairing language of their poets. So the Samaritans, and apparently from them the Sadducees.—Davison, *On Prophecy*, pp. 505–6; cf. Bull's *Works*, i. 35–42. The difference of tone, on this point, between Epicurus and Lucretius is admirably worked out by Professor Sellar, *Roman Poets of the Republic*, p. 296. On the notion that the book of Ecclesiasticus was written by a Sadducee, see Dean Milman, *History of the Jews*, 1863, ii. 32, *note*. 2. Absorption: the ultimate view of pantheists in every age. The mind is not now held to perish with the body, but its individuality is lost. On the view of Aristotle, see above, Lecture I., *Note* 8. In general, compare Rawlinson, *Christianity and Heathenism*, p. 32; Farrar, *B. L.*, 125, 140, 143, and their references. 3. An immortality of pure intellect: the soul immortal, and retaining its individual consciousness, but only as mind, purified by knowledge, the proper moral element being lost: the Gnostic view. See Burton, *B. L.*, p. 40, &c. 4. Immortality without resurrection: ἐπιδιαμονή without ἀνάστασις. Compare Bishop Thirlwall's vivid description of the Homeric view of a future state (*H. G.* i. 222): 'Homer views death as the separation of two distinct, though not wholly dissimilar, substances, the soul and the body. The latter has no life without the former; the former no strength without the latter . . . When the soul has made its escape through the lips or the wound, it is not dispersed in the air, but preserves the form of the living person. But the face of the earth, lighted by the sun, is no fit place for the feeble, joyless phantom. It protracts its unprofitable being in the cheerless twilight of the nether world, a shadow of its former self, and pursuing the empty image of its past occupations and enjoyments.' The hopes of the heathen might reach a higher level than this, yet without departing from the definition of the class, and without approaching to the doctrine of a future resurrection. A modification of this view would give rise to the doctrine of metempsychosis, which rests, in its exoteric form, on the fundamental distinctness of the *self* from the body. In a deeper sense, it might be brought under the second head. 5. Above all these rises the full Christian doctrine of the resurrection from the dead: above annihilation, for the life once given is never withdrawn; above absorption, for the separate individuality is never lost; above Gnosticism, for every moral faculty will find a loftier occupation in another world—an immortality of the soul, completed by the restoration of the body, of which we have both an instance and a pledge in the resurrection of our Lord.

It is clear that St. Paul was confronted at different times with upholders of all the four erroneous views: with Sadducees, Acts xxiii. 6, &c.; with Epicureans and Stoics, Acts xvii. 18; with Gnostics, 2 Tim. ii. 18, and elsewhere; and apparently with some Gentile Christians at Corinth, who had blended the errors of their old creed with the Christian faith, and were endeavouring to accept the immortality of the soul without admitting the resurrection of the body— 1 Cor. xv. On this last point, however, different opinions have been held. Burton maintains that St. Paul was there combating the *first* view; that his opponents 'denied a resurrection in any sense of the term,' and 'did not believe in any future state of the soul at all.'—*B. L.*, p. 428. Archbishop Whately thinks that they held 'some such doctrine' as the *second* view.—*Scripture Revelations of a Future State*, pp. 19, 20, 110. On the other hand, see Rückert's commentary on the passage, which has been translated as a separate tract; and compare Arnold, *Sermons chiefly on the Interpretation of*

Scripture, p. 281 : ' To be immortal was a glorious prospect ; but to rise again with a body,—not to be allowed to consider their outward body as the prison which kept in the pure spirit, and so to cast off upon it, away from their proper selves, the blame of all their evil,—this was what they could not endure.'

The fact that the apostle, in that chapter (1 Cor. xv.), is able to assume and argue on marked Christian principles with regard to our Lord's history and nature, shows that he is dealing with professing, though mistaken, Christians; and the fact that he can appeal so confidently to their own faith and hopes, as based on their personal position, shows that the errors into which they had fallen on the resurrection of the body fell short of a denial of the immortality of the soul. The argument is indeed an appeal to consistency. It rests partly on their longing for immortality, partly on their faith in Christ. The whole scope of it is to show that there is no other immortality promised to man but that which is connected with the resurrection of the body, and no certainty of the resurrection of the body but that which is rested on the resurrection of Christ.

Many detailed references on the subject will be found in the notes to Mr. Rawlinson's Second Sermon on *Christianity and Heathenism*; and for a condensed view of some recent opinions, see Mr. Mansel's *First Letter to Professor Goldwin Smith*, p. 30. Cf. *Rational Religion*, p. 66, and *Second Letter*, p. 37.

Note 21, *page* 69. There is, however, great force and beauty in the argument from imperfection to perfection, if we view it as the corroboration, not the basis, of our faith. On the Cartesian form of it, see Mosheim's note on Cudworth, iii. 41, ed. Harrison ; Hallam, *Literature of Europe*, ii. 438 ; Saisset, *Modern Pantheism, F. T.*, i. 36–38, 52 ; ii. 43, 65 ; and a review of the English Translation of that work in the *Christian Remembrancer*, Jan. 1863, p. 98, &c. ' Quia perfectiones procedentes a Deo in creaturas altiori modo sunt in Deo, oportet quod quandocunque nomen sumptum à quâcunque perfectione creaturæ Deo attribuitur, secludatur ab ejus significatione omne illud quod pertinet ad imperfectum modum, qui competit creaturæ.'—S. Thom. Aq., I. Qu. xiv. Art. i. ' Whatsoever speaketh any kind of excellency or perfection in the artificer, may be attributed unto God ; whatsoever signifieth any infirmity, or involveth any imperfection, must be excluded from the notion of Him.'— Pearson, *On the Creed*, Art. i. p. 68. Compare Bramhall, quoted by

Mr. Mansel, *Second Letter*, &c., p. 10; cf. 11, 45. 'If all true philosophy begins with the personality of man, and ends with the Personality of God, it will be seen what grand and genuine elements of Christian Theism are contained in a system which makes our personality the type of force, and applies this conception to the Personality of God, eliminating from it only that which is weak and imperfect.'—*Christian Rem.*, l. l., p. 112 (of Leibnitz).

Note 22, page 71. 'You must not suppose me to believe that the Highest of all intelligences is degraded by contact with such grovelling things as are employed in the fashioning of the world, or that His blessed calm is disturbed by anxiety about things constantly changing and being destroyed.'—Buddhist in Williams, *Christianity and Hinduism*, p. 12. For the image of the sun, see the well-known passage in Plato, *De Rep.*, vi. p. 508, with which Mr. Morris compares the Vedas, *Essay*, pp. 6, 56. The image of the sea is in S. Joann. Damasc., *De Fide Orthod.*, i. 9 : δοκεῖ μὲν οὖν κυριώτερον πάντων τῶν ἐπὶ Θεοῦ λεγομένων ὀνομάτων εἶναι ὁ ὤν, καθὼς αὐτὸς χρηματίζων τῷ Μωυσεῖ ἐπὶ τοῦ ὄρους φησίν· εἶπον τοῖς υἱοῖς Ἰσραήλ, ὁ ὢν ἀπέσταλκέ με. ὅλον γὰρ ἐν ἑαυτῷ συλλαβὼν ἔχει τὸ εἶναι, οἷόν τι πέλαγος οὐσίας ἄπειρον καὶ ἀόριστον. Cf. S. Thom. Aq., I. Qu. xiii. Art. xi.

LECTURE III.

Note 1, *page* 75. In the argument *On the Limits of Religious Thought*, which Mr. Mansel has treated with consummate ability, we must distinguish between three different terms—God as existing, God as revealed, and God as apprehended by created minds. It is allowed on all hands that the second and third of these must precisely correspond; that the revelation must be regarded as adjusted to the capacity of its recipient. But how far are we justified in assuming that the second is a sufficient index to the first? that the revelation is a direct unveiling of the Divine nature, as well as adapted to the intelligence of man? Can we possibly suppose that it is capricious and arbitrary, or must we take it for granted that it is as absolutely true and effectual as the nature of the case allows?

When Mr. Mansel spoke as follows—' ideas and images which do not represent God as He is may nevertheless represent Him as it is our duty to regard Him: *they are not in themselves true*, but we must, nevertheless, believe and act *as if* they were true' (*Man's Conception of Eternity*, p. 9); 'a conception which is *speculatively untrue* may be regulatively true' (*ib.*, p. 10); 'a regulative truth is thus designed—*not to tell us what God is*, but *how He wills that we should think of Him*' (*ib.*, and *B. L.*, 127, 143)—the rigour of the definitions which had dictated his language did not save him from the suspicion of casting doubts on the reality of the disclosures which God had made to man. But the following expressions, which occur in his two *Letters to Professor Goldwin Smith*, may serve to supply the explanation which was wanting: 'The terms Father, Ruler, Judge, Good, Wise, Just, all represent notions derived in the first instance from human relations, and applied to God, not as *exactly expressing* the perfection of His absolute nature, but as expressing the *nearest approach* to it which we are capable of receiving' (*First Letter*, p. 36); 'the word Person . . . is a mode of expressing the infinite nature of God by that which is *most nearly analogous* to it among finite things' (*Second Letter*, p. 29); 'when we speak of God as feeling anger or pity, we do not mean literally to ascribe to Him the *human* passions called by those names, yet we have *no means of expressing more exactly* the Divine perfection of which these passions are the representation' (*ib.*, p. 63). Cf. *ib.*, pp. 16, 18, 28. To doubt the reality, then, of the revelation under which God has made Himself known to His creatures, would be to place a limit on the *power* of God. But it does not follow that what forms a sure basis for our faith and love conveys to our intellects the possession of such rounded and completed knowledge as would justify a tone of argumentative confidence on any point not explicitly revealed to us.

The *Second Letter* contains a catena of passages to illustrate the mode in which the question ' has been dealt with, directly or indirectly, by the great Catholic writers of successive generations.' See also Suicer, *Thesaurus Eccles.*, under the words οἰκονομία, οἰκονομικῶς, συγκατάβασις; Glassii *Philol. Sacr.*, i. 921, ed. Dathe; Lee, *Inspiration of Holy Scripture*, pp. 63–69, 343, 411, &c.; Bishop Marsh, *Lectures on the Criticism and Interpretation of the Bible*, p. 488, ed. 1828; Bishop Kaye, *Early Church*, p. 59; *Justin Martyr*, pp. 173–4; Trench, *On the Parables*, p. 21; Waterland, *Works*, iv. 180, &c. Dean Milman observes that ' accommodation' is an ' unpopular' and ' bad word, as it appears to imply art or design, while it was merely the natural, it should seem inevitable, course of things.'—*Pref. to History of the Jews*, 1863, p. x. ' Truth is content, when it comes into the world, to wear our mantles: " Lumen supernum nunquam descendit sine indumento."'—J. Smith, *Select Discourses*, p. 165. The use of the economy is discussed at length by Dr. Newman, *Arians*, pp. 72–87.

' No doubt God's revelation of Himself through man, as also His revelation to man, is limited by what He Himself has made humanity to be; though when we think of humanity in the light of Christ, the Son of God and the Son of Man, we may question how far we are justified in speaking of limits here at all. But it is one thing to say, that, because of human limits, what God can reveal of Himself to man is to be held to be less than what God is; and it is quite another thing to say, that what God sees it good to reveal of Himself to man He cannot truly and effectually reveal through man; that the medium must more or less colour and distort the light passing through it. This consistently held makes a revelation to man and a revelation through man equally impossible. If man cannot transmit light without distorting it, then neither can he receive light without misconceiving it.' 'As we believe that God, who teaches us knowledge of Himself by the works of His hands, teaches us also by holy apostles and prophets a higher knowledge than these His material works can convey, so we also believe that in communicating that higher knowledge, He presents it to us *pure and unmixed*, as in the case of the lower knowledge He confessedly does.'—J. M. Campbell, *Thoughts on Revelation*, pp. 75–7.

I am not now concerned with the misuse of the principle of accommodation which can be traced downwards from Spinoza, *Tractatus Theologico-Polit.*, ii. 41, sqq., pp. 43–7, ed. 1846. Cf. Bauer's Glassius, iii. 29. For an account of Semler's method, more especially, see Conybeare's *B. L.*, 1824, pp. 27, 277; Pusey, *Theology of Germany*, i. 140–4; Rose, *Protestantism in Germany*, p. 74; Kahnis, *History of German Protestantism*, p. 122; Wordsworth, *On Interpretation*, pp. 11, 12 (cf. 22, 28), and in *Replies to E. and R.*, pp. 477–8, 480, 489; Farrar, *B. L.*, pp. 311–6.

Note 2, *page* 75. Mr. Mansel, in speaking of 'the image of God,' says: 'Whatever may be the exact import of that declaration, as applied to Adam in Paradise, it should not be forgotten that the same Book which tells us of man's creation in God's image, tells us also of his fall from that image.'—*First Letter*, p. 15, *note*. But man did not fall so utterly that the image was altogether destroyed. See the texts referred to at the foot of page 75. I have drawn out this distinction in a former work, *Discourses on the Fall and its Results*, Disc. iii. and iv. See especially *note* there on p. 45. Again, in the *Second Letter*, p. 61, *note*, Mr. Mansel says, of the Divine vision promised to the pure in heart (Matt. v. 8), that 'others, with more reason, maintain that this is reserved for the beatific vision hereafter.' Doubtless,—in its highest sense; but here again we need the distinction of degrees,—between comparative and absolute admission and exclusion. 'If this be the end and reward of the saints hereafter, it would seem to follow that they are *truly* made partakers of it, in *kind* and in *earnest*, now.'—Manning, *Univ. Sermons*, p. 136. Though man, in his fallen state, is both degraded and darkened, the Divine image is not wholly obliterated; the Divine vision is not absolutely withdrawn: and the relics of that image, and the glimpses of that vision, are two forms of the Divine manifestation, through which we reach forward to the knowledge of God.

Note 3, page 77. The metaphor in the text is not quite free from ambiguity; but it seems most probable that St. Paul is using the analogy, not of a window, made of half opaque material, but of a mirror with imperfectly reflecting power, which gives an incomplete picture of the objects cast upon it. (Cf. Wordsworth, *in loc.*) The figure would thus remind us of the image of God within the soul of man; a reflection which is at once imperfect, yet direct. The outline may be dim, but the image is not lost; just as a true reflection of the skies may rest by night upon the waters, though confused and shattered when the stillness is disturbed by winds which typify the wayward influence of human emotions and thoughts.

The Apostle probably referred to the passage in Numbers (xii. 8), where God contrasts the vision and dream of other prophets with the more open revelation given to Moses. They saw δι' αἰνιγμάτων· he saw στόμα κατὰ στόμα, ἐν εἴδει. Compare the earlier passage, Ex. xxxiv. 29–35, which describes how the face of Moses shone when he descended from the mountain, and how he veiled his face to hide that glory; or it may be to conceal its transitory character. To this St. Paul refers, 2 Cor. iii. 18, where κατοπτριζόμενοι appears to mean, that 'we all with open face' *reflecting* 'as in a glass the glory of the Lord,' receive and shadow back that glory; that admitting it into our spirits with the open freedom of the Gospel, we are 'changed into the same image from glory to glory, even as by the Spirit of the Lord.' (Cf. Stanley, *in loc.*, and *Sermons and Essays on the Apostolic Age*, p. 25; Moberly, *Sermon on the Transfiguration of Christians*, p. 8.) 'Dominus est exemplar, nos imagines.'—Bengel. *in loc.* The Christian thus receives the rays, and they transform him. He is transfigured as he gazes into the likeness of the glorious reality which he is contemplating, just as when we hold a mirror to the sun, it is filled with the reflection of that heavenly light.

The same figure explains St. James's contrast between 'beholding' for a moment the 'natural face in a glass,' ἐν ἐσόπτρῳ, and looking 'into the perfect law of liberty' (i. 22–5). The word παρακύψας seems to denote the attitude of one who *stoops down* to look into; as though bending to scrutinise the image of the perfect law, which is mirrored in the regenerate heart.

The parallel with Moses suggests the gradations of spiritual knowledge, to which I have made previous reference. As he was to other prophets, so shall we be to our present selves, when we rise above the conditions of humanity, and 'shall be like' Christ, 'for we shall see Him as He is' (1 John iii. 2). The vision of Moses was still imperfect; the loftiest intuition of the older covenant did not reach the level of Christian knowledge; and the knowledge of the Christian, even at its highest, falls short of the glory of the beatific vision. But the light that reaches us, however broken and fragmentary it may be, at every step flows straight from heaven.

On the degrees of access to the sight of God, see Manning, Sermon on *The Beatific Vision; University Sermons*, No. VI.; and above, *Note* 2, and Lecture I., *Notes* 12, 13.

Note 4, *page* 77. It is convenient to borrow from philosophy the Kantian term, to express what has been more vaguely called a 'mystery' in religion (Thomson, *B. L.*, p. 125; Tulloch, *Theism*, p. 370; E. T. of Saisset, *Modern Pantheism*, ii. 172, *note*; &c.); the case of 'problems insoluble theoretically, but capable of harmony when viewed on the moral side' (Farrar, *B. L.*, p. 117). Compare the word ἐναντιοφάνεια adopted by Bishop Bull; and the διαφόρως, but not ἐναντίως, of Chrysostom ; καὶ γὰρ ἕτερόν ἐστι διαφόρως εἰπεῖν, καὶ μαχομένους εἰπεῖν· *Hom.* I. in Matth.; *Opp.*, vii. p. 8, C. The subject might be illustrated at length by the history of contradiction, which is traceable in philosophy from Heraclitus to Hegel; and which is equally traceable in the history of religious thought, from the antitheses of Marcion, through the *Sic et Non* of Abélard, to the chapter in which Spinoza fixed attention on the 'discrepantes opiniones' of the prophets; *Tract. Theol.-P.*, ii. 49; p. 45.

The principle itself may be regarded as a double-edged weapon; used by error when it dwells on the apparent contradiction; used by truth when it points to the deeper harmony, in which faith sees the difficulty disappear. In this latter sense it has been a favourite instrument of recent theology; employed by Mr. Mozley to account for the Predestinarian Controversy; by Dr. Pusey and others, to remove scruples on the nature of the Eucharistic presence; by Mr. Mansel, in his exposition of the limitations of religious thought. Abundant illustrations will be found in the following Notes; but on the general subject I may refer to Archbishop King, *On Predestination*, pp. 51-62, ed. Whately; Trench, *Hulsean Lectures*, 1845, p. 118, and *On St. Augustine*, pp. 35, 61; Arnold, *Sermons*, i. 161; Davidson, ed. of Horne's *Introduction*, vol. ii. pp. 477-8; Isaac Taylor, *Restoration of Belief*, p. 279; Pusey, *The Presence of Christ in the Holy Eucharist*, p. 17; Freeman, *Principles of Divine Service*, ii. 15; Thomson, *B. L.*, pp. 124-6; Mozley, *Augustinian Doctrine of Predestination*, ch. ii., &c.; Mansel, *Man's Conception of Eternity*, pp. 14, 15; *B. L.*, pp. 8, 16, 17, 22, &c.; Wordsworth, *On Interpretation*, pp. 32, 34, 98, 100.

Note 5, *page* 79. The principle, that error generally consists in the mistake of half-truths for truths, is correlative to Leibnitz's observation, that sects are generally right in what they affirm, and wrong in what they deny. The following illustrations show the extent to which this analysis of error has been accepted:—

Αἴτιον δὲ τῆς ἐναντιολογίας, ὅτι δέον ὅλον τι θεωρῆσαι, μέρος τι τυγχάνουσι λέγοντες ἑκάτεροι· Ar., *De Gen. et Corr.*, I. 7; p. 323, b. 17. Μιᾶς τοίνυν οὔσης τῆς ἀληθείας· τὸ γὰρ ψεῦδος μυρίας ἐκτροπὰς ἔχει· καθάπερ αἱ Βάκχαι τὰ τοῦ Πενθέως διαφορήσασαι μέλη, αἱ τῆς φιλοσοφίας τῆς τε βαρβάρου τῆς τε Ἑλληνικῆς αἱρέσεις, ἑκάστη ὅπερ ἔλαχεν ὡς πᾶσαν αὐχεῖ τὴν ἀλήθειαν· S. Clem. Alex., *Strom.* I. 13; i. p. 348-9. '— si quid de scripturis ad sententiam suam excerpent, cetera nolentes intueri . . . . proprium hoc est omnium hæreticorum.' —Tertull., *Adv. Praxean*, 20; *Opp.*, ii. 679. 'J'ai trouvé que la plupart des sectes ont raison dans une bonne partie de ce qu'elles avancent, mais non pas tant en ce qu'elles nient.'— Leibnitz, *Opp.*, ed. Erdmann, p. 702; cf. Michelet, *Métaphysique d'Aristote*, p. 244. 'Each is false only as it is incomplete. They are all true in what they affirm; all erroneous in what they deny.'—Sir W. Hamilton, *Discourses*, p. 11. 'The Catholic creed is for the most part the combination of separate truths, which heretics have divided among themselves, and err in dividing.'—Newman, *Tract* 85, p. 73; *On Development*, p. 88. 'It being almost a definition of heresy, that it fastens on some one statement as if the whole truth, to the denial of all others, and as the basis of a new faith; erring rather in what it rejects, than in what it maintains.'—Id., *University Sermons*, p. 338-9; cf. *Parochial Sermons*, i. 357-8. 'Every heresy almost has been built upon some insulated statement in God's Word.'—Pusey, *Presence of Christ*, &c., p. 19. 'To mistake a part for the whole is the most common form which human error takes.'—Blakesley, *Conc. Acad.*, p. 27. 'All the ancient heresies contained a certain element of truth; but they all excluded some other truth, which was

x

necessary to complete that element of truth which they contained.'
—Wordsworth, *l. l.*, p. 32.

> 'Truth ever one,
> Not here or there, but in *the whole* hath shone.'
> *Lyr. Ap.*, xcix. 2.

'And so ye *halve* the truth.'—*Ib.*, cix. 'Locke erred only in taking *half the truth* for a *whole truth*.'—Coleridge, *Aids to Reflection*, i. 48. 'A *whole truth* instead of a *half truth*.'—Bishop Thirlwall, *Reply to Williams*, p. 27. 'The *half truth* rounding itself out with falsehoods.'—Froude, *On Job*, p. 8; cf. p. 14. 'We see in all these *half truths* of the different dividers a witness for the *whole truth*.'—Maurice, *Tracts for Priests and People*, ii. 40; cf. xiv. 74. 'One of those *half truths*, which have often the mischievous effect of entire falsehood.'—Birks, *Bible and Modern Thought*, p. 261. 'Such have been many of the capital doctrines of later theological systems; true or *half true* in themselves, but deprived of their own vitality,' &c.—Stanley, *The Bible; its Form and its Substance*, p. 96. '*Half-truths*, perhaps, but also *half-falsehoods*; for what, in science, is a *half-truth* but an error?'—I. G. St. Hilaire, in Lyell, *Antiquity of Man*, p. 475.

Note 6, *page* 81. The following are instances of the forms of expression under which the combination of half-truths in Scripture has been recognised:—

'We ought not to be surprised, when we find the Scriptures giving different and seemingly contradictory schemes of Divine things. It is manifest that several such are to be found in Holy Writ.'—King, *l. l.*, p. 51. 'It is ever the manner of that Word ... now boldly to declare its truth upon this side, and then presently to declare it as boldly and fearlessly on the other; not painfully and nicely balancing, limiting, qualifying, till the whole strength of its statements had evaporated, not caring though its truths should seem to jostle one another. Enough that they do not do so indeed. It is content to leave them to the Spirit to adjust and reconcile,' &c.—Trench, *l. l.*, p. 118. 'While each (of two seeming contradictions in Scripture) delivers a truth, each also was meant to hinder us from dwelling only upon what the other teaches us,' &c.—Arnold, *l. l.* 'Such is the well-known course of Scriptural teaching, to oppose, as it were, one evil at a time, and that with the utmost force, and often without qualification; leaving the qualification required to be sought for in other parts of Scripture directed against the opposite error.'—Id., *Sermons chiefly on the Interpretation of Scripture*, p. 360. 'It is no unusual way of teaching in Holy Scripture, to speak of that *only*, which is at the time meant to be declared or impressed upon us.' 'God inculcates, at one time, one side of Divine truth; at another, another: in order that our finite human minds may grasp, in their degree, truth after truth, and each may sink more deeply in our souls.'—Pusey, *l. l.*, pp. 17, 19. Add *Sermon on Justification*, p. 11, where he goes on to remark: 'I do not mean that uninspired man ought to use the same *fearlessness of speech* as the unerring wisdom of God.' We have 'to hold in conjunction, simply and without reserve, some *two* divinely affirmed matters or positions, either of which we should probably make no difficulty of accepting by itself, but whose *compatibility* or *possible coexistence* we are unable to perceive.'—Freeman, *l. l.* 'A contradiction requires a confession of positive error; whereas an antinomy only suggests a sense of the imperfection of our understanding, which can comprehend two opposite results, and not the mode of reconciling them.'—Archbishop of York, *l. l.* 'Such is ever the method of Scripture; to state each of two apparently conflicting principles (e. g., God's grace and man's responsibility) singly and separately, and leave conscience rather than intellect to reconcile and adjust them.'—Vaughan, *On Rom.* ix. 18; cf. *on* xii. 6. 'All revealed religion rests upon certain great principles; which the human mind can hold together in what it knows to be a true concord, whilst yet it cannot always by its intellectual processes limit, define, and reconcile what its higher gift of intuition can harmonise.'—Bishop of Oxford, *Charge*, 1860, p. 62. 'It is a characteristic of the Divine mind in Holy Scripture, to speak strongly on special points of Christian doctrine in particular places of Holy Writ, and to leave it to the reader of Scripture to supply the correlative truths from other portions of Holy Writ, which are necessary to complete the statement of the doctrine as a whole.' —Wordsworth, *l. l.*, p. 98.

Note 7, *page* 82. Such contrasted propositions must not be called *contradictories*, as though they held a distinct logical opposition to each other. This caution is implied in the quotation from the Archbishop of York's *B. L.* in the last *Note*; and compare Professor Fraser's criticism of Mr. Mozley's work in his *Essays in Philosophy*, p. 274: 'To assert that man must believe both of two "contradictory" propositions, is either to encourage absolute scepticism, or to discourage our spontaneous faith in one or other of the counter propositions. If both are intelligible propositions, every logical thinker is compelled to make his election between them, and to follow out that election into its consequences. But to offer an independent proof that, while apparently contradictory, they are really incomprehensible, opens a way for the mysterious retention of both, without offence to logic. It converts into a fact above reason what had seemed to subvert its fundamental law.' Also Mr. Mansel's *B. L.*, VII. *note* 42; p. 408.

Incommensurable propositions, here called 'incomprehensible,' can neither of them be finally reduced to the language of unqualified logical distinctness, so as to confront each other with a sharp and clear antagonism. They conform, indeed, to the laws of a loftier logic, which belongs to the highest reason, rather than the common understanding. The cry that illogical compromises are often stronger than trim logical theories, is simply a mistake, in which this truth is forgotten. The real distinction lies in the breadth and depth of those laws of the spirit, which rise above the rules of the sensational world. The former, from their very magnitude, can find no full expression in the words of man. The latter may easily be clear and orderly, because there is no reserve beneath the surface to cloud the distinctness of their lucid language.

Another evil would result from regarding such propositions as contradictories; namely, the assumption that the denial of one doctrine must needs involve the assertion of its opposite; whereas the instances in any given case may be expressed in a form so extreme as to ignore a vast range of intermediate considerations; and when so stated, neither the one nor the other would be true. Thus, in the Eucharistic controversy, those who declined to accept a particular view of Christ's presence, were alleged to teach His real absence, or to preach a dead Christ. In disputes on inspiration, the support of the special claims of Scripture is said to be an attempt to silence the Spirit in true hearts for ever. To reject one view of eternity is to identify eternity with time. To maintain the limitation of the human faculties is to deny that man possesses any real revelation from God. 'I believe,' says Dr. Williams, 'it is not sarcasm, but reason, to conclude that in a *purely dual antithesis* you hold the *opposite* of what you blame.'—*Letter to Bishop of Llandaff*, 1857, p. 70. On this principle much of the contrast between 'Modern Judaisers' and 'Rational Godliness' has been constructed.

(*Lampeter Theology*, 1856, p. 56, &c.; cf. *Letter*, as above, p. 92, *note*.) It is sufficient to answer, that in most such forms of expression the 'antithesis' is *not* a 'dual' one; and it is a groundless assumption that the rejection of one view is equivalent to the adoption of the other.

Note 8, *page* 83. 'Though the maxim, that every event must have a cause, is undoubtedly true, what kind of a truth is it? Is it a truth absolute and complete, &c., or is it a truth indistinct, incipient, and in tendency only? . . . It is a truth of the latter kind, *for this simple reason*, that *there is a contrary truth* to it.'— Mozley, *l. l.*, p. 24. Again, p. 29, as to the idea of Divine power: 'does it belong to the class of full and distinct, or of incomplete truths? Certainly to the latter, *for* there appears at once a *counter truth* to it, in the existence of moral evil,' &c. In cases of this kind, it appears to me that the difficulty is rather absolute than relative. It is not the fact of the opposition that discloses the existence of the mystery. Rather we might reason out the existence of the mystery on either side, and its recognition would then explain the fact of the opposition. Cf. Fraser, *l. l.*, p. 273.

For the rest of the paragraph, see Pascal's chapter, 'Disproportions or Inequalities in Man;' *Thoughts*, ch. iii.: 'What is man in the midst of nature? He is a nothing in comparison with infinitude; he is everything in comparison with nullity; he is a central point between nothing and everything. Their extremes being infinitely beyond his comprehension, the finality and the first principle of things are concealed from his view under an impenetrable mystery; and he is equally incapable of searching into the nonentity from which he was derived, and the infinitude into which he is absorbed.'— P. 67, ed. Pearce. Of time, viewed 'as a form or condition of our internal consciousness,' 'neither an absolute limit, whether beginning or end, nor yet an absolutely unlimited duration is conceivable.'— Mansel, *Eternity*, p. 6. 'Our mind is so constituted, that it cannot apprehend the absolute beginning or the absolute end of anything.' —Müller, *Lectures on Language*, 1861, p. 331. 'Leibnitz was never tired of proving and illustrating the principle that all in nature tends to infinity. The two abysses of which Pascal speaks—the abyss of greatness over our heads, and the abyss of littleness beneath and around us—opened out before his eyes.'—*Christian Rem.*, Jan. 1863, p. 112. So in Kant's Antinomy of Pure Reason, First Contradiction of Transcendental Ideas: '*Thesis*. The world has a beginning in time, and is also enclosed in limits as to space. *Antithesis.* The world has no beginning, and no limits in space, but is, as well in respect of time as of space, infinite.' Cf. Sir A. Grant, *On the Ethics of Aristotle*, i. 95.

Note 9, *page* 85. Many points mentioned in this and the following paragraphs are commonly discussed under the head of the *anthropomorphic* language of Scripture; e.g. the repentance ascribed to God, in Spinoza, *Tract. Theol. Pol.*, xiii. 26, p. 189. Compare Glassius, *l. l.*, i. 944; iii. 213–5; Davidson, ed. of Horne's *Introduction*, ii. 403; *Introd. to O. T.*, i. 29, 57, 159, &c.; Hengstenberg, *Genuineness of Pentateuch*, ii. 372; Kenrick, *Essay on Primæval History*, p. 43. ' There is one respect in which Strauss is himself constrained in a remarkable manner to confess, that the Hebrew religion has no mythus, viz., in its constant maintenance of the immutability of the Divine Being *in Himself*, His *aspects* only changing to the varying world—unlike in this to every heathen representation of the Divinity.'—Mill, *Pantheistic Principles*, ii. 10, *note*. In another place, ii. 50, p. 45, Spinoza treats 1 Sam. xv. 29 as a *contradiction* to Jer. xiii. 8, 10, and Joel ii. 13; whereas the counter-view of God's repentance is traceable in the same chapter of Samuel, verses 11 and 35, as has been frequently remarked; above, pp. 91, 93; Hengstenberg, *l. l.*, and *On Daniel and Balaam*, p. 425; Mansel, *B. L.*, p. 22; De Teissier, *Village Sermons*, p. 280.

On the fatal weakness of the theory which ascribes to prayer a merely subjective value, see Mansel, *B. L.*, p. 17 (and *notes*), and *Man's Conception of Eternity*, pp. 14, 15. Compare Bishop of Oxford, *Seventeen Sermons*, p. 152. I have dealt with this subject previously, in *Discourses on the Fall and its Results*, p. 259.

On the difference between the *object* of Christ's coming and its *results*, which may be connected with the larger question of the fulfilment of prophecy, see Copleston, *On Predestination*, p. 101; and Mr. R. P. Smith's *Messianic Interpretation of the Prophecies of Isaiah*, p. 295; whence it appears that the contrast which can be traced in the very words of Christ Himself and in the Gospel narrative, has been offered by Jewish objectors as a proof of contradiction between prophecies and their fulfilment; e.g. Zech. ix. 10, Mal. iv. 6. Compare Arnold's *Sermons*, i. 385 : ' How shall the truth of God's Word be reconciled with the laws of His moral government? Must He stint for our sin's sake the abundance of His mercy, or impair for His promise's sake the perfection of His justice? Surely here, too, as in other respects . . . hope and disappointment were struggling together; the promise was still of blessing, but the experience was of sin, and, therefore, not of blessing, but of judgment.' See also *ib.*, p. 102, and Stanley, *Jewish Church*, p. 465. 'Amid former promises to Israel, there had been constant warnings that the fulfilment of the promises was in great measure conditional. God's word should not fail, but it would not be found to have spoken peace to the wicked.'—H. Browne, *Messiah as Foretold and Expected*, p. 43. 'Their Lord, while His shadow brought peace upon earth, foretold that in the event, He came to send "not peace, but a sword."'—Newman, *Office and Work of Universities*, p. 158.

The Scripture antitheses on the relation between grace and man's exertions are drawn out by Hooker, *App. to E. P.*, v.; *Works*, ii. 549 : 'David, to shew that grace is needful, maketh his prayer unto God, saying, "Set Thou, O Lord, a watch before the door of my lips;" and to teach how needful our travail is to that end, he elsewhere useth exhortation, "Refrain thou thy tongue from evil, and thy lips that they speak no guile." Solomon respecting the use of our labour giveth counsel, "Keep thy heart with all the custody and care that may be." The Apostle, having an eye unto necessity of grace, prayeth, "The Lord keep your hearts and understandings in Christ Jesus."'

From the 'two cross-clauses,' Luke ix. 50, xi. 23 (above, p. 92), Bacon draws out the distinction between 'fundamental points' and 'points not fundamental ;' *Adv. of L.*, ii. ; *Works*, iii. 482 ; and *Essay of Unity in Religion, ib.*, vi. 382. On the practical perplexity, compare *Rich. II.*, Act v. Sc. 5 :

> 'For no thought is contented. The better sort,—
> As thoughts of things divine,—are intermixed
> With scruples, and do set the word itself
> Against the word :
> As thus, "Come, little ones ;" and then again,
> "It is as hard to come as for a camel
> To thread the postern of a needle's eye."'

Note 10, *page* 88. There is a doubt on the interpretation of 2 Sam. xxiv. 1, as is noted in the English margin (on which see Mr. F. Stephen's remark, *Defence of Dr. Williams*, p. 272). Compare Waterland, *Works*, iv. 271 : ' If (the objector) had been disposed to look into the original, and had known anything of the Hebrew idiom, he might have perceived that the text does not say that *God* moved David (for the word *God* is not in the text at all), but *one* moved, which comes to the same thing with, David *was moved* to say, &c., as Castalio renders.' ' Secundum Hebræos Deus non incitavit David contra populum, sed cor David incitavit ipsum,' &c.—Munster. et Clar. ' Quidam Hebræorum non malè subaudit *cor Davidis, Davidem,* q. d. David a propriâ concupiscentiâ fuit tentatus.'—Vatabl. ' Mallem personale resolvi in impersonale, *commotus seu incitatus est David,* vel si id non placet, interseri nomen *Satanæ.*'—Amam. ' Activum pro passivo, ut sæpe, id est, commotus est, nempe a diabolo.'—Grot. (All in Crit. Sacr., *ad loc.*) ' Cum tamen phrasis hæc ex se sumpta impium quid et blasphemum inferat, tribuens Deo malum, quod ab ipso alienum est, uti neque furor est ullus in Deo, vertendum videtur: *Et non cessavit irasci Dominus in populum suum, quia David malo illorum incitatus fuit ut imperaret,*' &c.—Calmet, *in loc.* See also Glassius, *Philol. Sacr.,* i. 244, 609, ed. Dathe. Mr. Barrett gives a later series of comments in his *Synopsis of Criticisms.* In some of these cases, the interpretation has been obviously governed rather by the wish to avoid a supposed difficulty, than by purely philological considerations. Dr. Stanley retains the contrast as it stands in the English version: ' The same temptation which in one book is ascribed to God, is in another ascribed to Satan.'—*Jewish Church,* p. 48, *note*; and so Lightfoot, *Works,* i. 68.

' Et tamen peccabam, Domine Deus, ordinator et creator omnium rerum naturalium, peccatorum autem tantum ordinator.'—S.August., *Conf.,* I. 16; *Opp.,* i. 75. ' Ne putemus illam tranquillitatem et ineffabile lumen Dei de se proferre unde peccata puniantur; sed ipsa peccata sic ordinare, ut quæ fuerunt delectamenta homini peccanti, sint instrumenta Domino punienti.'—Id., *Enarr. in Ps.* vii.; *Opp.,* iv. 37. ' Ista distinctio, aliud fecit et ordinavit: aliud autem non fecit, sed tamen etiam hoc ordinavit.'—*Ib.,* p. 39.

' Ὃν θέλει σκληρύνει thus becomes equivalent to, He has framed at His pleasure the moral constitution of man, according to which the rebellious sinner is at last obdurate.'—Dr. Vaughan, *on Rom.* ix. 18. ' Many other of the apparent accidents of Scripture, on what deep grounds do they rest! Thus, for example, in the history of Pharaoh's trial, that God should *ten times* be said to have hardened his heart, and he *ten times* to have hardened his own, or to have had it hardened, without any reference to other than himself ...... this exactly equal distribution of either language is surely most remarkable.'—Trench, *Hulsean Lectures*, 1845, pp. 124—5.

With the history of Balaam we may compare the answer of the oracle at Branchidæ to Aristodicus, Hdt., i. 159 : Ἀριστόδικον δὲ, οὐκ ἀπορήσαντα, πρὸς ταῦτα εἰπεῖν· Ὦ ἄναξ, αὐτὸς μὲν οὕτω τοῖσι ἱκέτῃσι βοηθέεις· Κυμαίους δὲ κελεύεις τὸν ἱκέτην ἐκδιδόναι; Τὸν δὲ αὖτις ἀμείψασθαι τοῖσδε· Ναὶ κελεύω, ἵνα γε ἀσεβήσαντες θᾶσσον ἀπόλησθε· ὡς μὴ τὸ λοιπὸν περὶ ἱκετέων ἐκδόσιος ἔλθητε ἐπὶ τὸ χρηστήριον.

Note 11, *page* 92. Compare the commentators on Eph. iii. 19 ; where the antithesis is called by Dean Alford ' a paradox ;' by Bishop Ellicott, ' an oxymoron ;' by Dr. Wordsworth, ' hyperbole.'

The principle maintained is, that Scripture anticipates all objections based on this ground, by speaking as though with an entire unconsciousness that there *is* any contradiction, even when the contrasted terms are brought into the closest union. 'How firmly the' immutability of God 'was impressed on the Israelitish mind, is testified by the *unembarrassed manner* in which repentance of a certain kind is ascribed to God.'—Hengstenberg, *Balaam*, &c., as quoted above in *Note* 9. ' Earnest men, striving for great truths, are sure to be paradoxical, and to seem to contradict themselves. Their inspiration only makes them *the more fearless* in such seeming contradictions.'—Davies, in *Tracts for Priests and People*, xi. 29. See also above, *Note* 6.

Note 12, *page* 93. Mr. Froude has spoken of the Book of Job as an extraordinary contrast to the rest of the O. T. Canon, 'smiting through and through the most deeply-seated Jewish prejudices.'—*Book of Job*, p. 3. In correction of which view, we may refer to the argument of an article in *Christian Remembrancer*, Jan. 1849, p. 196, sqq. : ' The language of Job toward the Deity is another remarkable feature of the book. This language is a startling carrying out even of that bold ground which he takes about himself; for he positively, as far as words go, accuses the Deity of injustice.' ' It is obvious at first sight that this language cannot really mean what it literally means.' 'The holy men speak as if God were hard and unjust upon them, all the while feeling the fullest and most penetrating conviction of His goodness. Indeed, just as in the case of ordinary irony, feeling expresses itself by contraries,' &c. ' All prayer may be said to partake in some measure of this irony.' 'Thus the piercing tone of prayers in the Psalms,' &c. Compare Mr. Farrar, *B. L.*, p. 7, *note*.

In like manner, on the controverted subject of the Jewish knowledge of a future state, 'we cannot but observe, upon reflection, with what religious humility the minds of holy men, under the elder dispensation, seem to have fitted themselves to that exact amount of revelation, on this subject, which they had.' 'Amid all the superior brightness of a more perfect hope, we can still allow its own peculiar beauty to the faith of the Jewish saint, believing with an obedient and resigned vagueness, and prepared in God to go he knew not and asked not whither.'—*Christian Rem.*, *l. l.*, p. 164. Compare Stanley, *Jewish Church*, p. 154, as quoted above, Lecture II. *Note* 8: and p. 471. 'The elder Hebrew Prophets were content, for the most part, with the consciousness of the Divine support in this life and through the terrors of death, but did not venture to look further.' Compare also Milman's remarks on Ecclesiasticus, *History of the Jews*, ii. 32, *note* (and above, Lecture II., *Note* 20).

Note 13, *page* 95. In this, as in so many other cases, the fact that a principle is brought out more vividly at one time than another, is constantly made the ground for the assertion, that it is absolutely excluded from the sphere where it is less conspicuously traced. See above, p. 19. The doctrine of Ezek. xviii. is distinctly recognised in the Pentateuch. 'Yet now if Thou wilt forgive their sin — ; and if not, blot me, I pray Thee, out of Thy book which Thou hast written. And the Lord said unto Moses, *Whosoever hath sinned against Me*, him will I blot out of My book.'—Ex. xxxii. 32, 33. 'The fathers shall not be put to death for the children, neither shall the children be put to death for the fathers: every man shall be put to death *for his own sin*.'—Deut. xxiv. 16; cf. 2 Kings xiv. 6; 2 Chron. xxv. 4. The subject is fully discussed in most *Introductions to the Pentateuch*. See also Spinoza, *Tract. Theol. Pol.*, ii. 49, p. 45; Waterland, *Works*, iv. 222; Warburton, *Divine Legation of Moses*, V. 5; vol. iii. p. 5, &c., ed. 1846, and the notes; Mozley, *Predestination*, p. 36; Trench, *Sermon on the Mount*, &c., pp. 41–3; 45–7; 187–8; R. P. Smith, *On Isaiah*, *Introd.*, p. xvii.

Note 14, *page* 97. See Lyall, *Propædia Prophetica*, P. III., ch. ii., especially pp. 323–4. Cf. Milman, *History of the Jews*, ii. 364. It appears that even the most advanced schools are disposed to leave us 'a chapter *possibly* in Deuteronomy foreshadowing the final fall of Jerusalem.'—*E. and R.*, p. 70.

Note 15, *page* 100. Διὰ τί οὖν, φησὶν, οὐδεὶς ἐνεκάλεσε Μωϋσεῖ ἢ ἠπείθησε κελεύοντι διὰ τὴν περιτομὴν τὸ σάββατον λύεσθαι ; δηλονότι ὡς τοῦ σαββάτου περιτομῆς οὔσης κυριωτέρας, καίτοι οὐκ ἔστι τοῦ νόμου ἡ περιτομὴ, ἀλλ' ἐκ τῶν πατέρων, ἔξωθεν ἐπεισενεχθεῖσα τῷ νόμῳ. —*Chrys. ap. Caten. G. P.*, ed. Cramer, ii. 264. 'Sententia est Hebræorum, *Circumcisio pellit Sabbatum* . . . . (Opus Christi) continetur in naturæ præceptis, quæ antiquiora sunt ipsâ circumcisione, sicut circumcisio est antiquior rigido otio Sabbati per Mosem imperato . . . Si lex ritualis cedit rituali antiquiori, quanto magis legi per naturam cordibus inscriptæ, ut quâvis occasione miseros juvemus?' —Grotius in Joann. vii. 22-3. Cf. Lightfoot, *Works*, ii. 557 ; Morris, *Prize Essay*, &c., p. 98.

St. Augustine's explanations of the position of the Law are carefully summed up by Dean Trench in the work already referred to ; pp. 67, 185, &c. The typical, and therefore temporary, character of the Law is often the sole solution offered to account for the strong language used by St. Paul ; 2 Cor. iii. 6 ; Gal. iii. 13, 19, &c. It was indeed a serious evil to mistake the shadow for the substance ; but it is not less important to establish the results of the principle, that, viewed in itself, the Law conveyed knowledge without grace. It is this which gives point to the apostolic contrast. The Law was holy; but it became an unendurable burthen (Acts xv. 10), if a rigid obedience to its dictates was regarded as the sole ground for justification. In this sense it could kill ; yet it had been obeyed, upheld, and reverenced by those who had shone forth amidst dark ages as bright examples of the power of faith. We cannot explain this sharp antagonism by proving merely that it was temporary in its obligation, unless we can show also, that throughout its course, it was equally restricted in its power. The coming of Christ might fulfil, and therefore supersede, a type : but how could it change blessings into curses ? How could it turn earlier good into present evil ? This it could not do. But what it could and did do was, to drag to the light existing evil, as the preliminary for furnishing its cure : on the one hand, by revealing and satisfying the true but forgotten scope of the promise ; on the other hand, by convicting the Jews of destroying the Law, which they professed to honour, by turning its letter against its spirit. And it is throughout this argument, as I have endeavoured to point out, that the Apostle and his Master are at one.

Note 16, *page* 101. 'To condemn works without faith is surely quite consistent with condemning faith without works. St. James says, we are justified by works, not by faith only; St. Paul implies, by faith, not by works only. St. Paul says that works are not available before faith; St. James that they are available after faith.'— Newman, *On Justification*, p. 330. Compare Neander, *Planting*, &c., p. 358, sqq., ed. Bohn; Arnold, *Sermons chiefly on the Interpretation of Scripture*, No. xxxiv. p. 358.

But in truth this contrast is only one instance of a wider characteristic, by which Scripture often speaks of *each* cause in salvation as the *sole* cause, leaving it to the enlightened conscience to ascribe to each its proper weight and province. 'Whereas faith on our part fitly answers, or is the correlative, as it is called, to grace on God's part, sacraments are but God's acts of grace, and good works are but our acts of faith; so that whether we say we are justified by faith, or by works, or by sacraments, all these but mean this one doctrine, that we are justified by grace, given through sacraments, impetrated by faith, manifested in works.'—Newman, *l. l.*, p. 348. Compare his *Parochial Sermons*, iii. 84, on 'Faith and Obedience;' and iv. 350, on 'Faith and Love.' 'Various qualities are stated as essential to salvation, one in one passage, another in another. Thus *faith* is said to save; "by *grace* ye are saved;" a man is justified by *faith*; he is justified by *grace*; he is justified by the *blood of Christ*; he is justified by *works*. In other places *love* is represented as the great justifying principle in the sight of God. One quality of the mind is connected with and implies another. Faith and love necessarily go together. Works are connected with both.'—Davidson, in *Horne*, ii. 478.

A similar principle is needed to explain many portions of the practical teaching of Scripture; e. g. :—1. 'He shall give His angels charge over thee,' Ps. xci. 11; a lesson of trust, which is not to be turned into a justification of presumption, as Christ Himself has most distinctly taught us, Matt. iv. 7.

2. 'Woe unto you that are rich!' Luke vi. 24; a lesson on God's absolute ownership, and a warning against claiming His gifts as our own, and using them for selfish ends; which is not to be turned into refusal of the duties of a 'faithful and wise steward' (Luke xii. 42), if God sees fit in any sense to set us over His household, and confide to us the management of wealth.

3. 'Turn to him the other (cheek) also,' Matt. v. 39; a lesson

of patience and humility, which is not to be turned into the sanction of injustice, in any sense that would offend against the common good, and against the laws that are needed to protect the weak against the strong.

Note 17, *page* 104. On the marvellous *unity* of Scripture, compare Trench's *Hulsean Lectures* for 1845, No. II.; Bishop Ellicott, in *Aids to Faith*, p. 442; Burgon, *Inspiration and Interpretation*, pp. cliii. 123, 234–5; Birks, *The Bible and Modern Thought*, pp. 226, 265, 377, 398, 405. 'The series of the Inspired stands out from all the generations to which they individually belonged, *one series*, by reason of the *one light* which shines from them all, and which by its unity vindicates for itself *one source*.'—Campbell, *Thoughts on Revelation*, p. 98. Not less noteworthy is the *nature* of that unity, veiled beneath such wondrous diversity. The Jews were to 'be accustomed to regard their Scriptures, not as men regard other books, but as a sort of *mine*, in which their learned men were to dig for the treasures of hidden wisdom which they contained.'—Lyall, *Prop. Proph.*, p. 301. 'Its contents are like a *vast quarry* rather than a finished building: we find the rough materials,' &c.—Stanley, *The Bible; its Form and its Substance*, p. 34. A striking passage from Burke has been repeatedly quoted lately on this subject; *National Review*, Jan. 1861, p. 159; Stephen, *Defence of Dr. Williams*, p. 60; Phillimore, *Speech* on the other side, p. 22, &c. Compare Hooker, *E. P.*, I. xiii. 3; and Trench, *On St. Augustine*, pp. 3, 5, 9, &c. 'Nimirum idem cœlestis Spiritus Isaiam et Danielem in aulâ suâ movit afflatu, Davidem et Amosum in pastorum stabulis; semper idoneos voluntatis suæ interpretes deligens, et interdum ex ore infantium perficiens laudem: aliorum utitur eloquentiâ; alios eloquentes facit.'—Lowth, *De Sacr. P. Hebr.*, p. 246, ed. Lips., 1815. Compare below, Lecture V., *Note* 20.

LECTURE IV.

Note 1, *page* 107. See, for instance, Bauer's continuation of Glassii *Phil. Sacr.*, iii. 15 : ' Sensus litteralis est unicè verus. Sensus mysticus, i. e., allegoricus et typicus, non est admittendus.' His reasons follow on p. 23. Compare Marsh's *Lectures on the Interpretation of the Bible*, Nos. x.–xii. 'If we endeavour to find an allegorical sense, either in *history* or in *prophecy*, we endeavour to find a sense with which the literal sense is wholly unconnected. The sense, therefore, will be supplied by mere imagination ; and not only will different interpreters invent different senses, but even the same interpreter may invent as many as he pleases. Indeed there have been Jewish commentators, who have boasted that they could discover seventy midrashim, or mystical meanings, in one sentence. *Some* limit, therefore, is absolutely necessary' (on which see below, *Note* 13).—*Ib.*, p. 459. (From the time of Erasmus and Luther) 'the Greek of the New Testament was interpreted like the Greek of a classic author ; the tropological and anagogical senses which had been ascribed to the Latin Vulgate disappeared ; and the names themselves ceased to occupy a place in the nomenclature of a biblical interpreter. It became a maxim among Protestants, that the words of Scripture had only *one* sense, and that they who ascribed to them *various* senses made the meaning of Scripture altogether uncertain.'—*Ib*, p. 508. Compare Maitland, *Eruvin*, p. 27.

A correction to the extreme view of the single sense is supplied by the two considerations to which I call attention in the text ; namely, the very definition of a Revelation, and the teaching of Christ and His apostles in the New Testament.

On the first of these points, compare Bacon, *Advancement of Learning*, *Works*, iii. 484, ed. Ellis and Spedding : 'The Scriptures, being given by inspiration and not by human reason, do differ from all other books in the author,' &c. And p. 487 : (the Scriptures) ' being written to the thoughts of men, and to the succession of all ages, with a foresight of all heresies, contradictions, differing estates of the Church, yea, and particularly of the elect, are not to be interpreted only according to the latitude of the proper sense of the place, and respectively towards that present occasion whereupon the words were uttered,' &c., 'but have in themselves . . . infinite springs and streams of doctrine to water the Church in every part; and therefore, as the literal sense is as it were the main stream or river, so the moral sense chiefly, and sometimes the allegorical or typical, are they whereof the Church hath most use: not that I wish men to be bold in allegories, or indulgent or light in allusions; but that I do much condemn that interpretation of the Scripture which is only after the manner as men use to interpret a profane book.' Add Selden, *Table Talk*, p. 11, ed. Singer: 'The Scripture may have more senses beside the literal; because God understands all things at once; but a man's writing has but one true sense, which is that which the author meant when he writ it.' (Cf. Warburton, *D. L.*, iii. 214.) And Butler, *Anal.*, ii. 7, p. 304: 'To say, then, that the Scriptures, and the things contained in them, can have no other or farther meaning than those persons thought or had who first recited or wrote them, is evidently saying that those persons were the original, proper, and sole authors of those books, i. e., that they are not inspired.' The argument is that of Augustine and Aquinas: 'Quia verò sensus litteralis est quem auctor intendit, *auctor autem Sacræ Scripturæ Deus est*, qui omnia simul suo intellectu comprehendit, "non est inconveniens," ut dicit Augustinus, "si etiam secundum litteralem sensum in unâ litterâ Scripturæ plures sint sensus."' —I^{ma} Qu. i. Art. x.

For the second ground, see Middleton, *Doctrine of the Greek Article*, p. 403, ed. Rose: 'else we must assert, that the multitude of applications made by Christ and His apostles are fanciful and unauthorised,' &c. And Marsh, *l. l.*, p. 455: 'In whatever case a passage of the Old Testament, which, according to its strict and literal sense, relates to some earlier event in the Jewish history, is yet applied, either by Christ or by an apostle of Christ, to what happened in their days; and moreover is so applied, as to indicate that the passage is prophetic; of such passage we must conclude, *on their authority*, that beside its plain and primary sense, it has also a remote and secondary sense. The difficulties, which no human system can remove, are in such cases removed by Divine power.' It was also a question of *fact* by which Bishop Horsley was led to change his opinion, from believing 'that every prophecy, were it rightly understood, would be found to carry a precise and single meaning;' the fact, namely, that Noah's prophecy on Japhet contained 'variety of intent and meaning,' as was proved by its repeated fulfilments.—*Sermons*, i. 344.

On the general subject of this Lecture, I may refer to Bishop Van Mildert's *Bampton Lectures*, 1814, No. VII.; Mr. Conybeare's *Bampton Lectures*, 1824, 'being an attempt to trace the history and to ascertain the limits of the secondary and spiritual interpretation of Scripture;' Dr. Neale's *Commentary on the Psalms; Dissertation III.*, ' The Mystical and Literal Interpretation of the Psalms;' *Tract for the Times*, No. 89, ' On the Mysticism attributed to the Early Fathers of the Church' (see below, *Note* 17); Mr. Isaac Williams's Commentary on *The Beginning of the Book of Genesis*, pp. 22, 37, 55, 236, &c.; Waterland, *Works*, iv. 154; Lyall, *Propæd. Proph.*, pp. 193, 245, 296, 299, 300; Fairbairn's *Typology*, Book I.; Arnold's *Two Sermons on the Interpretation of Prophecy*, &c. The topic also fills a large space in the controversy which followed the publication of *Essays and Reviews*. I am happy to find that the argument of this discourse is supported by an excellent sermon of Mr. Mansel's, which I had not seen when my own was preached: ' The Spirit a Divine Person, to be worshipped and glorified;' one of the *Oxford Lenten Sermons* for 1863.

Note 2, *page* 110. The cases of Balaam, of Jonah, and of Caiaphas, have been frequently used to prove that prophets were influenced by 'a power that would not be repressed;' e. g., by Professor H. Browne, in *Aids to Faith*, pp. 312, 316. Compare the Bishop of Oxford's *University Sermons*, p. 159 (on the other hand, see Davidson, *Introd. to O. T.*, ii. 435). On the whole subject, I may refer to John Smith's Discourse ' Of Prophecy,' *Select Disc.*, 1673, p. 161. ' Sometimes that light was more strong and vivid, sometimes more wan and obscure; which seems to be insinuated in that passage, Heb. i. 1: " God who in time past spake unto the fathers by the prophets, πολυμερῶς καὶ πολυτρόπως."'—P. 169. (Few readers will need reminding of Dr. Stanley's three sermons on *The Bible; its Form and its Substance*, and *Lectures on the Eastern Church*, p. 322.) ' He watch'd till knowledge came,' &c.; *Christian Year*, Second Sunday after Easter.

Of the ' nearer foreground of Prophecy,' many illustrations are given in Dr. Pusey's *Commentary on the Minor Prophets*, and elsewhere. Compare Dr. Stanley's account of Balaam's ' utterances,'—

'founded, like all such utterances, on the objects immediately in the range of the vision of the seer, but including within their sweep a vast prospect beyond.'—*Jewish Church*, p. 193. See, too, p. 453. Also, Mr. R. P. Smith's excellent *Introduction* to his *Messianic Interpretation of the Prophecies of Isaiah*; especially pp. vi.–viii.: 'with all this they had no conscious purpose or knowledge of the final tendencies of their works: each had his own present business, and addressed himself to the immediate wants and needs of his days.' (So of Moses, of David and Solomon, of Isaiah, of the later prophets;) 'yet, notwithstanding so great a change, no note is struck which jars with the declarations of previous prophets, nor is there a word which does not fitly belong to Him who is our Prophet, Priest, and King.'

Note 3, *page* 113. The doctrine of Typology, which has gathered to itself so large a literature, turns mainly on the question of *fact*; the proof from Scripture that this secondary intention did exist; that it extended to things as well as words; that it has received the highest sanction from the teaching of our Lord; that it reaches so closely to the frontier of the actual lessons of Scripture, as to suggest the possibility and propriety of a still wider range of analogous interpretation. The opposite tendencies may be thought to have reached their limits in the schools of Grotius and Coccejus, of which the judgment has become proverbial: 'Grotium *nusquam* in sacris literis invenire Christum, Coccejum *ubique.*' (Cf. Waterland, *Works*, iv. 163.) See Conybeare's 7th Lecture, pp. 259–67. 'No commentator ever surpassed S. Augustine in seeing Christ everywhere:

"Him first, Him last, Him midst and without end."

It has been well said that where we, after considerable study, are able to discover some distant reference to our blessed Lord, S. Augustine begins boldly: "This Psalm breathes altogether of Christ."'—Neale, *On the Psalms*, i. 77. Cf. Trench, *On St. Augustine*, pp. 54, 55.

Note 4, *page* 114. Compare Waterland, *Works*, iv. 155: 'the *words* of Scripture in such cases express such a *thing*, and that thing represents or signifies another thing. The *words*, properly, bear but one sense, and that one sense is the literal one; but the *thing* expressed by the letter is further expressive of something sublime or spiritual.' Also Van Mildert, *B. L.*, *notes*, p. 388. It does not follow, however, that we may attempt to discriminate by ascribing the *res* solely to God and the *voces* solely to man; an opinion condemned by Dr. Lee, p. 32. This is only one of the many attempts to solve the mystery of inspiration by drawing a mechanical distinction between the respective provinces of the divine and human elements.

Note 5, page 115. The instance in Hosea is discussed by Dr. Wordsworth, *On Interpretation*, pp. 79, 87, and in *Replies to E. and R.*, p. 482; Dr. M'Caul, in *Aids to Faith*, p. 118; Bishop Ellicott, *ib.*, p. 402; Dr. Neale, *On the Psalms*, i. 384. Cf. Dr. Mill, *Pantheistic Principles*, ii. 408–14. 'When Israel was brought out of Egypt, the figure took place; when Christ was called, the reality was fulfilled. The act itself, on the part of God, was prophetic. . . . The words are prophetic, because the event which they speak of was prophetic.'—Dr. Pusey, *in loc.* Dr. Stanley speaks of cases where 'a *fact* of the Mosaic history is resolved into a *truth* of the new dispensation.'—*On* 2 Cor. iii. 17. 'Is it not true that Almighty God has made even *acts and histories* to prophesy, independently of any utterance of men's mouths?'—Browne, in *Aids to Faith*, p. 312.

The allusion in Jeremiah xxxi. 15, to the lamentation which was thought to issue from the tomb of Rachel when her children were destroyed,—a reference doubtless in the first instance to some occurrences connected with the captivity,—is worked out by Dr. Mill, *l. l.*, pp. 402–8: 'The mass of Christian as well as Jewish interpreters expound this prophecy as primarily respecting the Chaldæan captivity, though involving higher and more remote events in its after development.' Dr. Stanley drops all mention of the words of Jeremiah: 'As late as the Christian era, when the infants of Bethlehem were slaughtered by Herod, it seemed to the Evangelist as though the voice of Rachel were heard weeping for her children from her neighbouring grave.'—*Jewish Church*, p. 72.

Note 6, page 116. Prophecies are 'of the nature of their Author, with whom a thousand years are but as one day; and therefore are not fulfilled punctually at once, but have *springing and germinant accomplishment* throughout many ages, though the height or fulness of them may refer to some one age.'—Bacon, *Works*, iii. 341. Compare Horsley, *Sermons*, i. 344; Arnold, *Sermons*, vol. i., *notes*, p. 396 ('so that the prophecies, as I believe, will go on continually meeting with a typical and imperfect fulfilment, till the time of the end'); 449 ('it may be that this great truth may be again partially and typically fulfilled; nay, that it may be so fulfilled many times over, the fulfilment becoming continually more' and more adequate to the prophecy, till the last and perfect fulfilment'); Wordsworth, *On Matt.*, xvi. 28, and *On Interpretation*, p. 74.

Note 7, *page* 119. The older divisions are summed up by S. Thom. Aq., I^ma Qu. i. Art. x. The foundation of all is the literal (see below, *Note* 15); and under this we may arrange what St. Augustine calls history, ætiology, and analogy, as well as parable. But the *res* being significant as well as the *voces* (see *Note* 4), there is a spiritual meaning lying beneath the literal, which may be thus divided: 1. The old law is a figure of the new law; and this is *allegory*. 2. The life of Christ recorded in the new law is the example for all Christians; and hence we derive *tropologia*, the moral sense. 3. The new law is itself a figure of eternal glory, and this is *anagoge*. The illustration of Durandus (Neale, *l. l.*, p. 380) precisely corresponds with this arrangement. The *historical* Jerusalem is 'that earthly city whither pilgrims journey,' but it is understood '*allegorically*, of the Church militant; *tropologically*, of every faithful soul; *anagogically*, of the celestial Jerusalem, which is our country.'

The question how far this scheme, in its explanation, as well as its terms, can be ascribed to Origen, is examined by Bishop Marsh, *l. l.*, p. 483. That neither of the two great divisions should be sacrificed to the other is well expressed in the quotation from St. Augustine, *De Genesi ad Lit.*, viii. 1; *Opp.*, iii. 225: 'Non ignoro de paradiso multos multa dixisse, tres tamen de hâc re quasi generales sunt sententiæ. Una eorum, qui tantummodo *corporaliter* paradisum intelligi volunt. Alia eorum, qui *spiritaliter* tantum. Tertia eorum, qui *utroque modo* paradisum accipiunt, aliàs corporaliter aliàs autem spiritaliter. Breviter ergo ut dicam, *tertiam* mihi fateor placere sententiam.' Cf. S. Thom. Aq., I^ma Qu. cii. Art. i. These early distinctions afterwards branched out into a complex system, which may be seen 'in all its grandeur' (says Dr. Maitland, *Eruvin*, p. 28) in the early editions of Glassius; or more succinctly in Waterland, *Works*, iv. 165. It is counted by Dr. Maitland among the '*impediments* to the right understanding of Scripture.'

To compare the old division with that which I have suggested: the *tropological* sense may be so expanded as, in a wider view, to answer to the symbolical; and the *allegorical* and *anagogic* are but two different stages of the typical. The older scheme leaves no place for the class which I have arranged third, unless we regard it as a subdivision of the allegorical. But if the definitions are not clearly stated, and carefully maintained, there will always be some discussion whether particular cases are to be arranged under one head or another.

The distinction drawn between *type* and *symbol*, namely, that type is a *prophetic symbol*, is now generally adopted; see, e. g., Litton's *B. L.*, p. 82; Hardwick, *Christ and other Masters*, i. 104; Macdonald, *On the Pentateuch*, ii. 452. There is more difficulty about the word *allegory*, in the ordinary usage of which ('aliud verbis, aliud sensu ostendit;' Quinctil., *Inst. Or.*, viii. 6, § 44) all hold upon a primary historical sense is lost. But Bishop Marsh points out that ἀλληγορούμενα is not rendered with precision in our authorised version: 'It is one thing to say that a history is *allegorised*; it is another thing to say that it is allegory *itself*. If we only *allegorise* an historical narrative, we do not of necessity *convert* it into allegory' (*l. l.*, p. 356). So also Bishop Van Mildert, *l. l.*, 239–40: 'some historical facts of the Old Testament appear to be *allegorised* in the new (that is, a spiritual application is given to them over and above their literal meaning), although they cannot strictly be denominated types. St. Paul, in applying the history of Sarah and Hagar to the Jewish and Christian covenants, *does not call it a type*; but only says that in giving it such an application, he had *allegorised* the history.' Again, Dr. Fairbairn (p. 18) recognises two kinds of allegory:—1. 'A narrative expressly feigned for the purpose;' 2. 'if describing *facts which really took place*, describing them only for the purpose of representing certain higher truths or principles than the narrative, in its literal aspect, whether real or fictitious, could possibly have taught.' This second sense, though less usual, corresponds more nearly to the application of St. Paul.

Note 8, *page* 120. Dr. R. Williams refers us for 'the origin of St. Paul's parable of Hagar' to Philo (*Rational Godliness*, p. 167, *note*); and Mr. Jowett calls it 'neither an argument nor an illustration, but an interpretation of the O. T. Scripture *after the manner of the age* in which St. Paul lived; that is, after the manner of the Jewish and Christian Alexandrian writers, (*in loc.*). A writer 'On Kabbalism' in the *Christian Remembrancer* for April, 1862, p. 358, *note*, says that it is 'probably an *argumentum ad hominem* of irresistible force against the Judaism of his day.' Of recent commentaries, which appear to me to give a much deeper and truer meaning, I would especially refer to that of Bishop Ellicott. On the *representative* character of Abraham and his household, see Olshausen, *in loc.*, and the passage of Calvin quoted by Dean Alford.

Note 9, *page* 124. The general law, however, that 'the elder shall serve the younger' (Gen. xxv. 23; Rom. ix. 12), has an extraordinary application through the history of the older Church. Seth was younger than Cain; Shem than Japhet (cf. Gen. x. 21; Lee, p. 532); Abraham than his brethren (see *Comm.* on Acts vii. 4); Isaac than Ishmael; Jacob than Esau; Judah than Reuben; Ephraim than Manasseh; Moses than Aaron; Samuel than the sons of Peninnah; David than Eliab, &c. Compare also, Abel younger than Cain; Joseph younger than his brethren; Solomon younger than Adonijah (1 Kings ii. 22). Gideon's family was poor in Manasseh, and he the least in his father's house (Judges vi. 15). Saul was ' a Benjamite, of the smallest of the tribes of Israel;' and his family ' the least of all the families of the tribe of Benjamin' (1 Sam. ix. 21). See Macaulay's remark on this, *H. E.*, i. 72. The Jewish history ' would rather seem to indicate that younger brothers are under the especial protection of heaven. Isaac was not the eldest son of Abraham, nor Jacob of Isaac, nor Judah of Jacob, nor David of Jesse, nor Solomon of David.' Compare Jowett *on* Rom. ix. 10; and the *Plain Commentary* on Matt. xi. 12 and Luke xv. 32.

Against what is said on the same page, 124, that the Law was ' no bondage ' to the ancient worthies, it might be objected that St. Peter calls it so; Acts xv. 10. For an answer, see Neander, *Planting*, &c., i. 117: ' By " a yoke" St. Peter certainly did not mean the outward observance of ceremonies simply as such, . . . but he meant the outward observance of the Law as far as it proceeded from its internal dominion over the conscience, so as to make justification and salvation dependent upon it.' See above, Lecture III., *Note* 15.

Note 10, *page* 129. ' The occurrence of a commandment to keep the Sabbath, in a table *generally moral*, implies that there is a *moral element* in that commandment.' . . . ' The Sabbath, as it appears in the Fourth Commandment, was a development of such moral element in a manner *suited to a particular people*, and being thus rendered *political* and ceremonial, does not, in that form, come under the precepts that are called moral.'—Hessey, *B. L.*, pp. 23–4; cf. p. 209 : ' The apostles . . . carried out the *moral part* of the Fourth Commandment, which demands a periodic devotion of time to God's service, and inculcates, by the mysterious example of the Almighty Himself, the alternation of rest with labour.' Compare above, Lecture II., *Note* 11 ; and Lecture V., p. 164. Also, Dr. Moberly, *Law of the Love of God*, p. 191: 'if God surrounded a law with temporary characteristics, such as those which invested the law of the Sabbath under the Mosaic dispensation, these same characteristics, when ceasing to form part of the law, must continue to form a *commentary* upon the law, and an *illustration of its meaning and intent.*'

In like manner, the law of circumcision, as it stood, conveyed no obligation to the Gentile; but it retained its value, as at once a record and a moral rule. It was a record of the forms through which God's older covenant had been sealed. It was a rule which embodied in the strictest shape the law of the circumcision of the heart. It ceased to be obligatory, because the time was come to which St. Paul taught that the O. T. itself had pointed, when the free admission of the Gentile would cancel the old ritual of the Jew. But what it lost in obligation it more than recovered in vitality. It rose into fresh dignity in the nobler system, when its earlier bearing was more distinctly realised; and we might almost say that it had never seemed so full of vitality, as at the very moment when it ceased to be obeyed.

Note 11, *page* 130. The difficulty is well put by Dr. Arnold, *Two Sermons on the Interpretation of Prophecy*, in *Sermons*, vol. i. pp. 367, 388. But indeed it has long claimed and received great attention; in such older works as the Βίβλος Καταλλαγῆς of Surenhusius (1713); in such recent publications as Gough's *New Testament Quotations collated with the Scriptures of the Old Testament* (1855); in the lists of Dr. Davidson, ed. of Horne's *Introduction*, ii. pp. 113-74, and Mr. Ayre, the editor of a different representative of the same volume, pp. 113-78; and in such treatises as Chapter V. in Michaelis's *Introd. to N.T.*, i. 200-46, ed. Marsh; *Appendix A.* to Mr. Westcott's *Introd.*, &c.; and Mr. Jowett's Essay ' On the Quotations from the Old Testament in the New,' *St. Paul's Epistles*, i. 353-62, 1st ed. Cf. Lee, *l. l.*, p. 334, sqq. The separate passages are also discussed, and in most cases with sufficient fulness, in the Commentaries of Ellicott, Alford, Wordsworth, and others. On the extent to which these quotations were anticipated by the Jews, and wherein the usages differ, see Lyall, *Propæd. Proph.*, pp. 184, 191, 193, &c., 301.

The position of the LXX has been thought to add considerably to the difficulty. But if it be granted that the N. T. writers were allowed to use the language which most naturally occurred to them, there is no reason for surprise when we find that, in ordinary cases, they were permitted to quote the Holy Scriptures also in the terms with which both they and their hearers were most familiar; nor is this concession in any way inconsistent with the belief, that whenever they were dealing with the inner mind of Scripture, they were guided by the Holy Spirit to unfold the deeper meaning of the words to which they appealed. Their method, I need scarcely add, is defended by the example of our Lord.

Note 12, page 131. The same watchful superintendence will account for many peculiarities of verbal expression. So Bengel of the Apostles: 'Apostoli interdum tetigere mysteria, quorum declaratio plenior postmodum per ipsos erat exitura: et iis tantisper tetigere verbis, quæ et sermoni V. T. et præsenti ipsorum, *vero*, sed *nondum pleno* sensui, et *intentioni divinæ* per eos ulterius se declaraturæ mirabiliter congruerent. Hoc loco [Act. ii. 39] Spiritus S. per Petrum ea locutus est, de gentibus cito, magno numero, citra circumcisionem adsciscendis, quæ *Petrus ipse postea non illico percepit*; et tamen cum Esaiâ congruebant; et verba etiam hæc apta sunt sensui illi, quem postea cepit. Omnia Scripturæ verba scientissimè sunt electa.' Similarly Dean Trench, *Star of the Wise Men*, p. 88, says that such analogies as Matt. ii. 15, ' ground themselves in the *intentions* of God, and are not merely traced by the ingenuity of man: we must believe that it belonged to His eternal purpose that the earlier should in manifold ways prefigure the later; and that among the other witnesses for a *Divine intention* running through the whole history of Israel, He was graciously willing that this should not be wanting.' On Gal. iii. 8, 9, Mr. Jowett comments: ' as in 1 Cor. ix. 8, 9, 10, a *providential intention* is attributed to the words of the O. T.' On the remarkable instance of Gal. iii. 16, see the notes of Grotius, Bengelius, and Ellicott. On Hebr. v. 6, &c., see Birks, *The Bible and Modern Thought*, p. 272.

Note 13, page 133. The limitation to Scripture authority is put in its most stringent form by Bishop Marsh, who rests his recognition of a secondary sense on no other ground; above, *Note* 1. ' Since *in every instance*, where a passage of the Old Testament has a secondary sense, the existence of that secondary sense depends *entirely* on the Divine authority, which has ascribed it to the passage, we must *wholly confine* the application of a secondary sense to those particular passages to which a secondary sense has been ascribed by Divine authority.'—*L. l.*, p. 457; cf. p. 374. Against this, see Fairbairn, *Typology*, i. 37–43, 2nd ed. Compare Middleton, *Doctrine of the Greek Article,* p. 407 : 'It is not for unauthorised applications that I contend; it is only for those which have been made *by Christ or His apostles.*' And Olshausen, on Gal. iv. 26 : 'Our time, therefore, as not being favoured with so intense an operation of the Spirit, cannot proceed independently in the adoption of types, but must adhere to those *expressed and sanctioned* in the Scriptures.' Dean Alford condemns Macknight's mode of stating the limitation as a 'shallow and indolent dictum.'—*On* Gal. iv. 24.

The defence of secondary applications really rests, as we have seen (above, *Note* 1), on both a principle and a fact; the principle of the Divine authorship, the fact of the interpretations given in the New Testament. Now it is not reasonable to allege, that the principle is entirely exhausted in the instances by which the fact of its use is established.

Note 14, *page* 133. See the lists of instances in Neale, *On the Psalms,* i. 379, and Ellicott, *Aids to Faith,* p. 450. Compare Mr. Medd's University Sermon, *On the Christian Meaning of the Psalms,* p. 12; Conybeare, *l. l.,* p. 314 (of Joseph and Joshua); Lyall, *Propæd. Proph.,* p. 194 (of Isaiah ix. 6), &c. But in some of these cases, the entire absence of Scriptural authority may be doubtful: e. g. on Egypt (which is urged by Bishop Ellicott), see Matt. ii. 15; Luke ix. 31; and cf. Arnold, *l. l.,* and Stanley, *Jewish Ch.,* p. 127 : on Isaac, see Heb. xi. 19, and cf. Bauer's Glass., *l. l.,* iii. 20, and Pearson, *On the Creed,* pp. 251, 297 : on Joseph, see Gen. xlix. 24, and Fairbairn, *l. l.,* 40, *note* : on Samson, see Judges, xiii. 5 ; Matt. ii. 23, and Glassius and Fairbairn as above. Dr. Fairbairn adds, of the instances of Joseph and Samson, 'Scriptural warrants of such a kind are out of date now—they can no longer be regarded as current coin.' For his 'specific principles and directions,' see *ib.,* p. 137, sqq.

Note 15, *page* 134. 'Et ita etiam nulla confusio sequitur in Sacrâ Scripturâ, cum omnes sensus fundentur super unum, scilicet litteralem, *ex quo solo potest trahi argumentum,* non autem ex iis quæ secundum allegoriam dicuntur, ut dicit Augustinus. Non tamen ex hoc aliquid deperit Sacræ Scripturæ, quia nihil sub spirituali sensu continetur fidei necessarium, quod Scriptura per litteralem sensum alicubi manifestè non tradat.'—S. Thom. Aq., I^{ma} Qu. i. Art. x. Compare Trench, *Parables,* p. 38 ; Van Mildert, *l. l.,* pp. 233, 251, 395.

On the duty of preserving intact the prior rights of the literal meaning, cf. S. Thom. Aq., I^ma Qu. cii. Art. i. : 'In omnibus autem quæ sic Scriptura tradit, est *pro fundamento* tenenda veritas historiæ, et *desuper* spirituales expositiones fabricandæ.' So constantly St. Augustine: see the reff. in Trench, pp. 52, 56, 63. 'The Scriptures have infinite mysteries, not violating at all the truth of the story or letter.'—Bacon, *Works*, iii. 297. So also p. 487 (as quoted above, *Note* 1) : 'the literal sense is, as it were, the main stream or river.' Cf. Arnold, *l. l.*, p. 397; Williams, *Beginning of the Book of Genesis*, pp. 74, 138, &c.

Note 16, *page* 134. On the rules of Tychonius and St. Augustine, see Roseumüller, *Hist. Interpr.*, iii. 407 ; and for other summaries of maxims, see Van Mildert, *l. l.*, pp. 251, 395 ; Fairbairn, *l. l.*, Book I. ch. v.; Ellicott, *Aids to Faith*, p. 445 ; Jenkins, *Scriptural Interpretation*, p. 20, &c.

Note 17, *page* 135. See Pearson, *On the Creed, notes*, p. 162, ed. Oxon., 1843; *Tract* 89, p. 17, sqq.; and Dr. Maitland's criticism, reprinted and enlarged in his *Eight Essays*, 1852, No. 1.

Note 18, *page* 135. See, for instance, Alford's Note on John ii. 19, and St. Augustine on John v. 25–9, in Trench, *On St. Aug.*, p. 81. See also S. Aug., *Enchiridion de Fide, Spe, et Caritate*, ch. lii. liii.; *Opp.*, vi. 215–6, where, commenting on Rom. vi. 2–11, he says : 'Quidquid igitur gestum est in cruce Christi, in sepulturâ, in resurrectione tertio die, in adscensione in cœlum, in sede ad dexteram Patris ; ita gestum est, ut his rebus non mysticè tantum dictis, sed etiam gestis, configuraretur vita Christiana quæ hic geritur.' Bishop Ellicott (p. 452) puts the N. T. passages as 'probably under ten,' and even of these he thinks some 'debateable.' '*Historico-prophetical* (parables) are only a few.'—Trench, *Parables*, p. 46 ; cf. p. 143. On the Good Samaritan, *ib.*, p. 318. In a more general sense, however, 'there is scarcely a fact announced but some great moral truth beams out from beneath it, and lights it up with a deeper significance.'—Birks, *l. l.*, p. 59 ; cf. p. 161 : 'the miracles of our Lord, with scarcely an exception, are parables also.' 'The narratives of the Gospel are parables as well as historics.'— Dr. Vaughan, *Sermon at St. Peter's School*, York, p. 6.

LECTURE V.

Note 1, *page* 141. The words are those of Dr. Tregelles. They have not unnaturally attracted considerable attention. See Donaldson's *Christian Orthodoxy*, p. 123; Tischendorf, *Pref.* to N. T., 1849, p. lv.; Davidson, *Facts, Statements, and Explanations*, 1857, p. 14; Bishop Ellicott, in *Aids to Faith*, p. 435; Mr. F. Stephen, *Defence of Dr. Williams*, p. 52, &c. For the next sentence, see a quotation in Dr. Lee's Preface to the second ed. of *Inspiration*, &c., p. vii. See also below, *Note* 4.

Note 2, *page* 141. The remark is constantly suggested by the history of the doctrine of inspiration since the time of the Reformers; see, e.g., Mr. Westcott, *Introd. to Study of Gospels*, p. 5; and it receives some illustration from the differences pointed out by Mr. F. Stephen, in his *Defence of Dr. Williams*, between the Fomularies of the English Church and those of other reformed Communions. For a systematic attempt to trace the pedigree of the Dictation theory, see *Christian Remembrancer* for Jan. 1863, p. 54, &c.

Note 3, *page* 142. This expression of Paley is adopted by Lyall, *Propædia Prophetica*, p. 114; Williams, *Lampeter Theology*, pp. 43, 85; Stephen, *Defence of Williams*, p. 143; Dean Milman, *History of the Jews*, new ed., Pref., p. vi.; Maurice, *Claims of the Bible and of Science*, p. 163; and it evidently colours the language of Professor Jowett, *E. and R.*, pp. 349, 350, 403. For what may be said to limit or explain it, see Mr. Birks's ed. of Paley's *Evidences*, Supplement F, p. 402.

Note 4, *page* 142. Paley goes on to urge (p. 414) that it is 'an unwarrantable as well as unsafe rule to lay down concerning the Jewish history, what was never laid down concerning any other, that either every particular of it must be true, or the whole false.' Formerly, 'any doubt about the inspiration of facts would have been a startling innovation; the whole fabric, as then constructed, would have tottered had a single stone, however small, been removed.' —Pusey, *Theology of Germany*, ii. 59. 'The supposition that a single word occurred in Scripture which was not divinely suggested and inspired was thought to overthrow the Apostle's assertion of the inspiration of all Scripture.'—*Ib.*, p. 72. '"Where am I to stop? If I pull out one brick," as a young man once said to me, "from the edifice of my faith, all falls." Well, as long as you are in this frame of mind, you are not fit to judge calmly or wisely.'— Magee, *Scepticism*, p. 22. 'All the books of the Bible must stand or fall together. . . . But remove in thought a single stone, and in thought that goodly work of lawgivers and judges, kings and prophets, evangelists and Apostles, collapses into a shapeless and unmeaning ruin.'—Burgon, *Inspiration and Interpretation*, p. 112. 'Each page of (the O. T.) is committed to the credit of the rest, and the whole book, or collection of books, is committed to the credit of each page. . . . The volume stands or falls, then, together. . . . If a verse stands, the O. T. stands.'—Eden, *ib.*, p. 268. 'It will not allow us to insist on any theory as supplying the principle of cohesion to Holy Scripture, as if the whole would break into fragments, like a Rupert's drop, were the minutest portion displaced.'—Chretien, *Letter and Spirit*, p. 75. (It is alleged that) 'if one assertion in those books be doubted, the whole cause of God and of Christ is in danger;' 'if one link is unsound, the chain breaks.'—Davies in *Tracts for Priests and People*, xi. pp. 30-2. Compare the controversy between the Bishop of Manchester and the Bishop of Natal; *Guardian* newspaper, April 1, 1863, p. 302; Colenso, *On the Pentateuch*, Preface to Part III., p. xxviii.; Maurice, *Claims of the Bible and of Science*, p. 138.

My attention has been called to a striking passage in an address on the Atonement, by one of the writers cited above, Dr. Magee, *Radley Sermons*, &c., 1861, p. 49: 'Rash speculations and unwarrantable dogmatism grow round every truth in process of time, just as suburbs grow round a fortress in long years of peace. But all such outlying buildings only endanger the citadel by giving shelter to the foe; and he is the wisest defender of the citadel of truth who, with most unsparing hand, pulls down the long suburbs of opinion which alike conceal its proportions and imperil its safety.'

Note 5, page 143. 'To make use of such an argument is, indeed, to bring the Sacred Ark itself into the battle-field, and to make belief in Christianity itself depend entirely upon the question, whether Moses wrote the Pentateuch or not.'—Colenso, Part. I., p. xxx. 'Whatever intermixture (the Bible) may show of human elements, of error, infirmity, passion, and ignorance,' &c.—*Ib.*, p. 13. 'The dark patches of human passion and error,' &c., *E. and R.*, p. 177. 'The great truth of the unity of God was there from the first; slowly as the morning broke in the heavens, like some central light, it filled and afterwards dispersed the mists of human passion in which it was itself enveloped.'—*Ib.*, p. 385. 'It may have pleased God that the vehicle of His revelation to man should not be absolutely pure, and free from the stains and inaccuracies which appear to be necessary to everything else which is in any way mixed up with human nature.'—Stephen, *Defence of Williams*, p. 21.

Note 6, *page* 143. Amongst recent definitions of inspiration in the strictest sense, besides that of Dr. Tregelles (above, *Note* 1), Mr. Burgon's, *Inspiration*, &c., p. 89, seems to have been the most commonly quoted; as by Colenso, Part I. p. 6; Part II. p. ix.; Dr. Stanley, *The Bible*, &c., p. 35, *note*; Dr. Northcote, *On the Colenso Controversy*, p. 39; and others. It is this, apparently, which a writer in the *Christian Remembrancer* for Jan. 1863, p. 243, calls 'a most extreme and entirely indefensible theory of inspiration.' Of older definitions, one of the best known is that of the *Formula Consensûs Helvetica*, 1675; Niemeyer, *Collectio Confessionum*, p. 731 (by Heidegger, *ib.*, p. lxxxi.). See, e. g., Lee, *Inspiration*, p. 417, *note*; Thirlwall, *Answer to Williams*, p. 39; Stephen, *l. l.*, pp. 124, 182; Heard, *New Wine*, &c., p. 74; Ellicott, *Pref. to Galatians*, p. viii.; Stanley, *Bible*, &c., p. v., &c. On the history of the controversy about the Hebrew vowel-points which gave rise to it, see Pusey, *Theology of Germany*, i. 141; ii. 71; Farrar, *B. L.*, p. 158, *note*; Morell, *Philosophy of Religion*, p. 188; Tholuck, *On Inspiration*, *Journal of S. L.*, July 1863, p. 361.

On the word *Dynamical*, which has been much used lately, see Morell, *Philosophy of Religion*, p. 151; Westcott, *Introduction to the Study of the Gospels*, p. 13; and especially Lee, *On Inspiration*, p. 25.

Note 7, *page* 144. See Bentley's *Remarks upon a late Discourse of Free-Thinking*, in *Works*, iii. 347–361, ed. Dyce; a passage which on that topic has since formed the storehouse of argument. See, e. g., Kennicott, *First Dissertation*, 1753, p. 563; Tregelles, *On the Printed Text of the Greek Testament*, pp. 49–57; Scrivener's *Introduction to the Criticism of the New Testament*, p. 7. Compare Dr.

Stanley, *The Bible*, &c. p. 31: 'The various readings which in the Koran were suppressed once for all by the Caliph Othman have broken out freely by thousands and thousands over the whole face of the Christian Scriptures—the stumbling-blocks here and there of faithless disciples, but the delight of Christian scholarship, the safeguards of Christian doctrine, the relics of Christian antiquity.'

Note 8, *page* 145. Compare the ὅσα ἐμνημόνευσεν of John the Presbyter in Papias, *Ap. Euseb., H. E.*, iii. 39, on which see Westcott, *Canon of N. T.*, p. 80 ; *Introd.*, &c., p. 168; and cf. Lee, pp. 27, 324, &c. For a general view of recent Literature on the Origin of the Gospels, see Lee, *Appendix O*, pp. 562–5 ; Westcott, *Introd.*, ch. iii., especially pp. 182–7 ; and compare Mr. Smith of Jordanhill, *Dissertation on the Origin and Connection of the Gospels*, 1853, and a paper by the same author in the *Journal of Sacred Literature* for April 1855, pp. 135–56.

Note 9, *page* 146. 'From one of these (Public Registers) doth Matthew fetch the latter end of his genealogy, and Luke from another the beginning of his, having then the *Civil Records* to avouch for them,' &c.—Lightfoot, *Works*, i. 416. 'It is therefore easy to guess whence Matthew and Luke,' &c., 'namely, from the genealogical scrolls at that time well enough known, and laid up in the public κειμήλια, repositories, and in the private also.'—*Ib.*, ii. 96. See Surenhusius's elaborate Dissertation, in xxxv. Theses, *De Modis explicandi Genealogias*, with the *Conciliationes de Geneal. J. C.* which follow ; Βίβλος καταλλ. pp. 89, 113. Cf. Schoettgen., *Horæ Hebr.*, i. 2; Mill, *Pantheistic Principles*, ii. 110–23. Lord A. Hervey, *On the Genealogies of our Lord*, p. 69. See especially Dr. Mill's Remarks on p. 119 : St. Matthew 'must be considered as using a liberty of abridgment well known to' his original readers, 'and only inviting, as quite sufficient for his own purpose, attention to the names he retains. Should it be said that abridgments of this nature, however justifiable in ordinary writers from the lax mode of criticism characterising their nation or age, are not to be endured in one laying claim to inspiration, we answer—1. That such a censure . . . assumes a kind of *à priori* acquaintance with what should be expected in a revelation, which we cannot either claim for ourselves or allow to be claimed by others. 2. That supposing the apparent fact to be no more than this, that the inspiration which enabled a few men of Galilee to regenerate the world, left them *under the influence of their national habits* in matters of this nature, we ought to be satisfied with that fact, without questioning the reasonableness of the dispensation. 3. That we do not, however, pronounce a thing indifferent, or done without reason, merely because we may be unable to point out the causes of it : being fully persuaded that there is nothing in revelation, as in nature, without its proper and adequate reason.'

Note 10, *page* 146. This is another instance in which Spinoza called attention to the facts on which a one-sided line of argument has more recently been based.—*Tract. Theol. Pol.*, ch. viii. p. 125, sqq. The facts, so far as they are correctly stated, must be admitted and accounted for, though we judge the inferences to be altogether erroneous. The Scripture writers ' *refer to other documents*, and in all points express themselves as sober minded and veracious writers under ordinary circumstances are known to do.'—Coleridge, *Confessions*, &c. p. 16. 'They are authors, or compilers, or arrangers; quoters of other books, stringers together of sweet songs by many hands.'—Chretien, *Letter and Spirit*, p. 64 : cf. p. 111. How much this admission really amounts to, is the point which I have endeavoured to state in the text.—For a list of the references in the Old Testament, see Dr. Lee's *Appendix D*, pp. 464-72, on *The 'Lost' Books of the Old Testament*. The instances, so far as they fall within his range, are discussed by Dr. Stanley in his *Lectures on the Jewish Church*; e. g., pp. xxxiv. 43, 185, 211, 241, 421, 431, 434, 444-5; also in 'The Songs of Israel,' an article contributed by him to *Good Words* for Febr. 1863, p. 121. (On ' The Song of the Bow,' and the Book of Jasher, see Ch. I. in the *Works* of Mr. John Gregory, 4th ed. 1684.)

Note 11, *page* 146. 'Two very considerable writers, Sir John Marsham and Dr. Spencer, . . . have not only called in question the prevailing opinion of the ancient apologists [see above, Lecture II. *Note* 3], but they have run directly counter to it, pretending that the Pagans did not borrow from the Jews, but that the Jews rather copied after the Egyptians or other Pagans in such instances as both agree in; a strange way of turning the tables, confounding history, and inverting the real order of things.'—Waterland, *Works*, v. 14. He goes on to urge that the real solution in cases of parallels between Hebrews and Pagans may rather be, that 'both had borrowed from the same common fountain of patriarchal tradition.'—*Ib.*, p. 20; see above, Lecture II. *Note* 2. See Michaelis, *Commentaries on the Laws of Moses*, Art. iii. : ' The Laws of Moses confirm, amend, or annul, a more ancient *Jus consuetudinarium.*' The point is worked out in Mr. Morris's *Essay towards the Conversion of Hindus,* pp. 23, 27, 98: 'Even supposing the whole amount of Moses' writings to have existed in tradition antecedently to their existence in writing (a supposition which I by no means contend for), still there would be room enough for inspiration to guide him in selection, juxtaposition, order, language, and many other points. But I merely assert thus much, that there existed a patriarchal tradition, from which Moses in part drew.' 'Circumcision, for instance, was of the Fathers; abstaining from the sinew which shrank, was of the Fathers; the distinction between clean and unclean animals, was of the Fathers; as were the sacrifices of certain animals, the washing of clothes before sacrifice, the anointing of things in order to consecration, the marriage of brothers' widows, the rite relating to it, and other things.' See also above, Lecture III. Note 15.

Note 12, *page* 148. Bentley put this point with his usual vigour (*Works,* iii. 360); and the Provost of Oriel has lately called attention to the concurrent testimony of Kennicott and Griesbach.—Sermon on *Liberty of Private Judgment,* 1863, p. 41. Dr. Tregelles remarks that if criticism 'takes away, on the one hand, readings which were thought to have some dogmatic value, it will give on the other quite as much.'—*Printed Text of N. T.,* p. 234. Bishop Ellicott thinks it necessary, indeed, to guard us against the opposite error, that of supposing that 'as readings affect no great points of doctrine, the subject may be left in abeyance.' 'It is indisputably a fact that but few pages of the New Testament can be turned over without our finding points of the greatest interest affected by very trivial variations of reading.'—*Aids to Faith,* p. 421. The assertion is *not* that the controversy has never turned on texts of profound doctrinal significance or historical interest, but that no debates on isolated texts have shaken doctrines which rest rather on continuous trains of argument.

Note 13, *page* 148. Pearson's remarks on Acts viii. 37, though not bearing on the critical question, illustrate what is here said on the possibility that such passages were the germs of creeds. It is in the baptismal profession that he finds 'the first occasion, rise, and original of the creed itself.'—*On the Creed,* p. 43. Cf. Bingham, *Antiq.,* X. iii. § 6. Mr. Scrivener says, 'we cannot question the spuriousness of this verse, which seems to have been received from the margin, where the formula Πιστεύω, κ.τ.λ., had been placed, *extracted from some Church Ordinal.*'—*Introd.*, p. 443. With respect to 1 John v. 7, Mr. Scrivener concludes : 'nor is there much reason to doubt the testimony of Victor Vitensis, who records that the passage was insisted on in a *confession of faith* drawn up by Eugenius, bishop of Carthage, at the end of the fifth century, and presented to the Arian Hunneric, king of the Vandals. From that time the clause became well known in other regions of the West, and was in time generally accepted throughout the Latin Church.'—*Ib.*, p. 460. He thinks that it was known to Cyprian (p. 461), to whom, indeed, or to Tertullian, its authorship has been sometimes ascribed. Compare Bentley, as quoted by Wordsworth, *in loc.*; and Porson, *Letters to Travis*, p. 400; Davidson, *Bibl. Crit.*, ii. 414.

Note 14, *page* 149. *Nil mutetur e conjecturâ.* Cf. Marsh, *Lectures*, p. 27; Scrivener, *Introd.*, p. 369; Davidson, *l.l.*, p. 371. A tempting instance to the contrary is pointed out by Lord A. Hervey in 1 Chron. iii. 22, where the obliteration of a few words, which have every appearance of a gloss intruded from the margin, is like striking off a fetter which has drawn aside and distorted the whole framework of the pedigree, and permitting it to spring back to an intelligible order.— *On the Genealogies of Our Lord*, p. 107. It is part of his argument to exclude Rhesa, in Luke iii. 27, as ' the title of Zerubbabel mistaken for ' a 'proper name.'—*Ib.*, p. 112. Kennicott quotes with approbation Walton's remark, ' that the corruptions which are found in the historical books of the Old Testament appear chiefly (and, indeed, it is natural to expect they should appear chiefly) in the several *numbers* and *proper names*.'—*First Dissertation*, p. 12. The subject of *numbers* has been brought into fresh prominence by Bishop Colenso's arguments. The remark would suggest itself to many readers of his Part I. that the discrepancies rest ' for the most part on the basis of a single fundamental number, and (are) capable, to that extent at least, of reconciliation, on the supposition of a single clerical error in a department peculiarly liable to mistake.' —Dr. Vaughan, *The Book and the Life*, p. 106 ; *contrà*, Colenso, Part II. p. 167. The question has since then received a very general discussion (e.g. *National Review*, Jan. 1863, p. 9; *North British Review*, Jan. 1863, p. 65); the most vigorous arguments to prove inaccuracy on the side of exaggeration being those of Dean Milman, *History of the Jews*, 1863, Pref. p. xxx.; and i. 189, *note*. For Laborde and Kennicott, cf. Stanley, *Jewish Church*, pp. 122,

380, 521. But Ewald and Bunsen 'accept these numbers without hesitation.' And 'A Layman' confronts the proposed reduction with the unqualified principle, '*All* mere suppositious emendations should be *rejected unhesitatingly* by every one who desires to treat the Scriptures with fairness and impartiality.'—*The Historic Character of the Pentateuch Vindicated*, p. 15, *note*. Compare, however, the note on p. 172 : 'Some of these large numbers may very probably have arisen from *errors of transcription*. There are several instances of discrepancies between the books of Chronicles, and Samuel and Kings, which have doubtless originated in this way . . . But this cannot well account for all.' What is proposed by 'suppositious emendations' but to remove apparent 'errors of transcription?' Their admissibility seems to be reduced in this later note to a question of degrees of probability ; and no one can doubt that this element must always be taken into most careful consideration.

Note 15, *page* 150. 'The usual character of human testimony is *substantial* truth under *circumstantial* variety.'—Paley, *Evidences*, Part III. ch. i. On the alleged discrepancies in the Gospels, see Dr. Lee's Eighth Lecture, pp. 384–398 ; Westcott's *Introduction to the Study of the Gospels*, p. 367 ; and the mass of materials collected in the controversy on *Essays and Reviews*, e. g., in Mr. Birks's *Bible and Modern Thought*, pp. 289–306, and by Dr. Wordsworth, Mr. Burgon, and many others.

Note 16, *page* 151. Dr. Stanley's *Lectures on the Jewish Church* are full of illustrations, many of which, however, still require further discussion : see pp. xxxviii–xl. 66, 144, 185, 345, 353, 372, 434, and the references in the next note.

Note 17, *page* 151. Lightfoot (*Works*, ii. 669) had suggested that St. Stephen was possibly referring to a transaction which could be connected with Gen. xii. 6 : 'If the word μνήματι did not lay some obstacle in the way, I should easily conceive that Stephen had his eye as intent (if not more) upon this place as upon the Cave of Macpelah,' &c. Dr. Wordsworth has worked out the same explanation in detail (*Comm. in loc.*): 'It has never been shown, nor ever can be, that Abraham did *not* purchase a plot of ground at Sichem, where Joseph and the Patriarchs were buried. Indeed (independently of St. Stephen's assertion), it is highly probable that he did.' So also Burgon, *Inspiration and Interpretation*, p. 264. Dr. Stanley seems to accept the solution, but with some misgivings. At one time he says : 'In and around Shechem arose the first national burial place, a counterpoise to the patriarchal sepulchres at Hebron. Joseph's tomb was already fixed; its reputed site is visible to this day. A tradition (*ref.* Acts vii. 15, 16) *current at the time of the Christian era* ascribed the purchase of this tomb to Abraham, and included within it,' &c.—*Jewish Church*, p. 278. So on p. 70 he gives some countenance to one of Dr. Wordsworth's arguments, by saying that the expressions used in Gen. xlviii. 22, 'rather point to incidents of the original settlement not preserved in the regular narrative.' On pp. 105-7 he gives a general recognition to the fact that St. Stephen had the command of such traditions; but, on the other hand, on p. 485, he calls it 'a singular variation,' and on p. 498, a ' perplexing addition' (so in *Sermons in the East*, pp. 143, 157); and he makes no attempt, I think, to work it into the history of Abraham at Shechem, either in *Jewish Church* p. 29, or *Sinai*, &c., p. 235. See also his note in *The Bible*, &c., p. 35.

Note 18, *page* 151. If we put together the two passages in which St. Luke records any reference to a census (Luke ii. 2; Acts v. 37), it will appear that the simplest translation of the first passage is also that which gives the most appropriate meaning: 'this enrolment was *the first which was made* when Cyrenius was Governor of Syria.' The other census is plainly that which was conducted by Quirinius some years later, viz. in A.D. 6, after the banishment of Archelaus.—Josephus, *Antiq.*, xviii. 1. Of the first there is no other record; but we are protected from the suggestion that St. Luke has erroneously transferred the later census to the earlier date, by the fact that he shows his knowledge of the later census in the Acts, while the πρώτη seems to have been inserted for the express purpose of distinguishing the one from the other. (Cf. Winer, *RWB.*, *s. v.* Quirinius; Westcott, *Introd. to Study of Gospels*, p. 370, *note*; Browne, *Ordo Sæclorum*, p. 47: 'This Census was Quirinius's *first*, not to be confounded with that which, as every one is aware, took place at a later period under the same person.' See also Euseb., *H. E.* i. 5, p. 15: ἐπὶ τῆς τότε πρώτης ἀπογραφῆς, ἡγεμονεύοντος Κυρηνίου τῆς Συρίας.)

The only question therefore is, whether we can find corroborative evidence that Quirinius held command in Syria near to the time of our Saviour's birth; i. e., in B.C. 4, as well as A.D. 6. If so, the passage ceases to be the difficulty which Strauss and many others have urged so strongly, and, like the parallel case of the title given to Sergius Paulus (Conybeare and Howson, i. 156), becomes a proof of the exactness of the sacred writer's knowledge.

Such evidence is furnished in A. W. Zumpt's enquiry into the Roman governors of Syria from Augustus to Vespasian, in his *Commentationes Epigraphicæ*, ii. 87–104, Berol. 1854. In connection with the well-known passage in Tacitus (*Ann*. iii. 48), he shows that Cilicia, when detached from Cyprus by Augustus, B.C. 22, must have been connected with some other government; that none was so likely for this purpose as Syria; and that a break occurs precisely at the necessary crisis in the Syrian list. After giving a number of converging details, he concludes: 'Quæ cum ita sint, P. Sulpicium Quirinium eo tempore, quo Homonadensium castella per Ciliciam expugnavit, certum est fuisse legatum Augusti pro prætore Syriæ.'—P. 98. The series, so far as we require it, stands as follows (p. 149):—

P. Quinctilius Varus . . . from B.C. 6
P. Sulpicius Quirinius . . ,, 4
M. Lollius . . . . . . ,, 1
C. Marcius Censorinus . . in A.D. 3
L. Volusius Saturninus . . from A.D. 4
P. Sulpicius Quirinius . . ,, 6
Q. Cæcilius Creticus Silanus ,, 11

It is true that the succession of Quirinius to Varus must fall a little later than the Nativity, because it was after the death of Herod (pp. 87, 104); but if it is brought within so near a limit, there is no difficulty in supposing that his name might be given to an 'enumeration *begun or appointed* under his predecessor Varus, and before the death of Herod,' but '*completed* after that event under Quirinius;' which is the form in which Zumpt's conclusion is accepted by Mr. Merivale.—*H. R. E.*, iv. 457, *note*.

For the older discussions, see Lardner, *Credibility of the Gospel History*, Part I., B. II. i.; *Works*, i. 248–329; Greswell, *Dissertations on the Harmony, Diss*. XIV. i. 466–549; Davidson, in Horne's *Introd*., ii. 554.

A different series is represented by Mr. Browne, *Ordo Sæclorum*, pp. 40–9, and Patritius, *De Evangeliis*, Lib. III. Diss. xviii. But the two inscriptions cited by those writers are set aside by Zumpt, the one as 'fraus turpis,' p. 107; the other as relating to Saturninus, p. 125. Zumpt's own arguments are summed up by Davidson, *l. l.*, p. 1059; Dr. Wordsworth, *in loc.*; Dean Alford, in Smith's *Dictionary of the Bible*, s. v.; and Lee, *Inspiration*, &c., pp. 578–81.

There is also a pamphlet by Johannes von Gumpach on the subject, published early in the present year, but making no reference to Zumpt's enquiries.

Note 19, *page* 152. 'The third thing which Ezra did about the Holy Scriptures in his edition of them was, he added in several places throughout the books of this edition what appeared necessary for the illustrating, connecting, or completing of them; wherein he was assisted by the same Spirit by which they were at first wrote: of this sort we may reckon the last chapter of Deuteronomy,' &c. 'And such also may we reckon the several interpolations which occur in many places of the Holy Scriptures; for that there are such interpolations is undeniable,' &c.—Prideaux, *Old and New Testament Connected*, i. 382, ed. 1851. Again, 'he changed the old names of several places that were grown obsolete, putting instead of them the new names,' &c.—*Ib.*, p. 384. Compare Shuckford, *Sacred and Profane History Connected*, ii. 317, ed. 1848; and especially Dean Milman, *History of the Jews*, 1863, i. 134, *note*. For illustrations of the 'two opposite theories' which I have mentioned, we may turn, on the one hand, to the *National Review*, No. XXXII., p. 362, &c., which bases a far more advanced commentary on the vivid picture drawn by Dr. Stanley, *Jewish Church*, p. 415; and on the other hand, to the *Christian Remembrancer*, No. CXX., 490-7: 'It is worth while . . . to expose the fallacy contained in the view, that later writers, who added to the text of inspired documents, could never have ventured so to tamper with them if they had believed them inspired. We ask, why not? Supposing a later writer had believed himself to be inspired *for this special work*,' &c. 'Everybody knows that the number of such passages as these is very great, both in the Pentateuch and the Book of Joshua. *Such passages were undoubtedly inserted by a later hand.*'

Note 20, *page* 153. See, for instance, Spinoza, *Tract. Theol. Pol.*, ii. 19, p. 36: 'Stylus deinde prophetiæ pro eloquentiâ cujusque prophetæ variabat. Prophetiæ enim Ezechielis et Amosis non sunt, ut illæ Esaiæ et Nachumi eleganti, sed rudiore stylo scriptæ,' &c. In this case, too, we might accept the fact without the inference; but in this particular instance the statement itself, though it dates from a much earlier period, has been recently modified. With regard to Amos, for example, Dr. Pusey (*Introd. to Amos*, p. 151) and Dr. Davidson (*Introd to O. T.*, iii. 257) agree to qualify the judgment of St. Jerome by quoting the criticism of

Bishop Lowth, *De Sacr. P. Hebr.*, p. 245, ed. Lips. 1815: 'evolvat modo scripta ejus æquus judex, de re non de homine quæsiturus; censebit, credo, potius pastorem nostrum μηδὲν ὑστερηκέναι τῶν ὑπερλίαν προφητῶν, ut sensuum elatione et magnificentiâ spiritus prope summis parem, ita etiam dictionis splendore et compositionis elegantiâ vix quoquam inferiorem.'

Note 21, *page* 153. See Dean Lyall's application to Holy Scripture of Paley's argument from 'Prospective Contrivances' (*Nat. Theol.*, ch. xiv.), in his *Propædia Prophetica*; especially Part II. Ch. v. p. 199: 'Prophecies not understood before Christ.' Compare Mr. R. P. Smith's *Messianic Interpretation of Isaiah*, p. 21: 'When God, therefore, gave (Ahaz) a sign, it was a *veiled sign*, which not till centuries afterwards would be clearly understood.' See also above, Lecture IV. *Note* 12.

Note 22, *page* 154. See Spinoza, *Tract. Theol. Pol.*, viii. p. 125, sqq.: 'in quo ostenditur Pentateuchon, et libros Josuæ, Judicum, Rut, Samuelis, et Regum non esse autographa. Deinde inquiritur, an corum omnium scriptores plures fuerint, an unus tantum, et quinam.' From this point it is a mere question of degree till we reach the large collections of difficulties in the works of Dr. Davidson and Bishop Colenso. For an intermediate stage, see Graves's replies to Le Clerc's series.—*Lectures on the Pentateuch*, pp. 439–52. See also above, *Note* 19.

Note 23, *page* 157. We have seen above (Lecture III.) that no exegetical error is more common than to build a whole theory on one expression, or to urge the literal sense of an isolated text against the general drift of other passages. Bishop Colenso has been unfortunately successful in transferring this method to the sphere of history. Arguing from the words 'this night,' in Ex. xii. 12, he persists, in the face of both context and philology, in denying that the Israelites had received a longer and more sufficient warning: *Pentateuch*, &c., § 65: compare the *Answers* of a Layman, p. 70; Dr. M'Caul, p. 62; Mr. Greswell, p. 89; Mr. Birks, p. 82; and, in reply, the Bishop's rejoinder to Dr. M'Caul, § 19. Arguing from the words 'which came into Egypt,' Gen. xlvi. 8, &c., he maintains an interpretation of the list of families which is equally at variance with probability and fact. It is at variance with probability, because his account is far less likely than either the opinion that the narrative was regulated by 'the sacred number seventy' (Birks, p. 22), or the opinion that it gives the eponymous heads of families, arranged, as among so many ancient peoples, on a peculiar national theory of number; it being comparatively indifferent whether they were sons or grandsons of Jacob, and whether they actually travelled with him on his journey to Egypt, or were born in Egypt before the final adjustment of the *gentes* was completed (Rogers, p. 13). And it is at variance with fact, because the same expression is confessedly used, in the general summary of verse 27, to include the two Egypt-born sons of Joseph,—'inaccurately,' the Bishop in this instance tells us, pp. 22, 27; because the plainest interpretation of the narrative would lead us to believe that two of the four sons of Reuben, verse 9, were also born in Egypt (Rogers, p. 7); and because the list of ten sons assigned to Benjamin, verse 21, is found to include two grandsons, who certainly could not have been born in Canaan (Numb. xxvi. 38–40; Rogers, p. 10). Though opinions will continue to differ on some of these details, they embody a sufficient amount of certainty to corroborate the hypothesis that Hezron and Hamul were born in Egypt, and were *substituted* as heads of families for their uncles, Er and Onan, who died in Canaan (Birks, pp. 12, 22); nor have the Bishop's arguments done more than expose the weakness of some careless and indefensible explanations, for which the truth cannot be made to suffer. Another instance of the same kind is the Bishop's interpretation of 'the fourth generation,' in correction of which see the careful analysis of Mr. Birks, p. 62. Other cases, where he refuses to admit the most reasonable suggestions, are his positions that all who were summoned to hear the voice of Moses or of Joshua attended; that all the laws came into immediate operation in the desert; and that even the most servile duties fell to the lot of the highest dignitaries. In the Preface to his Third Part, p. ix., *note,* an elaborate historical argument in a Layman's *Vindication of the Historic Character of the Pentateuch*, p. 16, sqq., to prove that the patriarchs must have been attended by a large following (as in Gen. xiv. 14; xxx. 43, &c.), is 'disposed of' as merely '*assuming* that Jacob went down to Egypt with a thousand or more followers.' In some of the above instances, Bishop Colenso substitutes assumption for argument; in this case he disparages argument by calling it assumption.

Note 24, *page* 157. 'Tamdiu non est contra fidem, donec veritate certissimâ refellatur. Quod si factum fuerit, non hoc habebat divina Scriptura, sed hoc senserat humana ignorantia.'—St. August., *De Gen. ad Lit.,* i. 38; *Opp.,* iii. 129. 'Aliud est quid potissimum scriptor senscrit non dignoscere, aliud autem a regulâ pietatis errare.'—*Ib.*, 41; p. 132. 'Brevitur dicendum est de figurâ cœli hoc scisse auctores nostros, quod veritas habet; sed Spiritum Dei, qui per ipsos loquebatur, noluisse ista docere homines nulli saluti profutura.'—*Ib.*, ii. 20; p. 138. Compare Whewell, *History of Scientific Ideas*, ii. p. 308; Pratt, *Scripture and Science not at Variance*, pp. 14, 17, *notes.*

Note 25, *page* 158. '"After all," says Buckland, "it should be recollected that the question is not respecting the correctness of the Mosaic narrative, but of our interpretation of it," a proposition which can hardly be sufficiently reprobated. Such a doctrine, carried out unreservedly, *strikes at the root of critical morality.*'—Goodwin, in *E. & R.*, p. 231. We are here on the track of an older controversy. 'A rule on this subject, propounded by some of the most enlightened dignitaries of the Roman Catholic Church, on the occasion of the great Copernican controversy begun by Galileo, seems well worthy of our attention. The following was the opinion given by Cardinal Bellarmine at the time: "When a *demonstration* shall be found to establish the earth's motion, it will be proper to interpret the Sacred Scriptures otherwise than they have hitherto been interpreted in those passages where mention is made of the stability of the earth and movement of the heavens." This appears to be a judicious and reasonable maxim for such cases in general.'—Whewell, *l. l.*, p. 306. The position as thus stated was assailed by Mr. Kenrick on much the same grounds as by Mr. Goodwin (*Essay on Primæval History*, 1846, p. xvii.). The objectors in both cases appear to miss the senso in which the word 'interpretation' is used. The question is not what the actual words of Scripture signify, but whether their literal meaning conforms to a temporary or permanent conception of science. So long as science proves nothing to the contrary, we take the words literally. If the literal sense is found to rest on a scientific belief which has now passed away, we simply transfer the passage to another class, and explain it as language appropriate to the writer, whose words it was no part of the Divine plan to modify, so as to meet the future disclosures of scientific doctrines which were then undiscovered and unknown.

Note 26, *page* 158. For the word 'phenomenal,' see Trench, *Star of the Wise Men*, p. 57, *note*. For the word 'optical,' see Hitchcock, *Religion of Geology*, p. 32, &c. (quoting Rosenmüller); Hugh Miller, *Testimony of the Rocks*, pp. 134, 166-7, 169, &c.;

Davidson, in Horne, ii. 372, and *Introd. to O. T.*, i. 158; Birks, *The Bible and Modern Thought*, &c., p. 317, sqq. 'According to the appearance,' Keil, *On Joshua*, pp. 257–8; Pratt, *Scripture and Science not at Variance*, p. 8; Challis, *Creation in Plan and in Progress*, p. 6; Huxtable, *Sacred Record of Creation Vindicated and Explained*, p. 25, *note*. But 'it is a great mistake to conceive that the language of common life, adopted also in Scripture, is the expression of simple falsehood, and not of a most important *variety of scientific truth*.'—Birks, *l. l.*, p. 312. The above writers differ in some cases on the degree in which this solution of the difficulty is applicable.

Note 27, *page* 160. The proof of this assertion must be sought for by an analysis of any hostile, but reasonably fair, summary of the geological difficulty. See, for instance, Kalisch, *Genesis*, pp. 43–52; Colenso, *Pentateuch*, &c., p. 172; Davidson, *Introd. to O. T.*, i. 151–164, &c.

Note 28, *page* 161. 'In the delineation of the future state, given in the closing part of the Apocalypse, and given, too, at considerable length, we are all aware that it does not, strictly speaking, furnish any historical statement of the outward conditions of our state as it will then be, but that it simply images forth certain spiritual characteristics of that future state; giving, in short, merely religious truth, and not information about physical facts.'—Huxtable, *l. l.*, p. 73. 'The account in the first chapter of Genesis having reference to facts out of the pale of human experience, clearly comes under the same category as prophecy. It equally claims to be Divine revelation; to be a communication from the Spirit of the Creator Himself.'—Challis, *l. l.*, p. 3.

Note 29, *page* 162. See the table in Kalisch, *Genesis*, p. 63; and compare Dr. Rorison, in *Replies to E. & R.*, p. 284.

Note 30, *page* 163. Moreover, 'A prophetic vision which reveals *past events* is without example or analogy in the whole range of the Biblical records.'—Kalisch, *l. l.*, p. 47, where this theory is examined more at length.

Note 31, *page* 163. See Professor Challis's *Creation in Plan and in Progress*, 1861.

Note 32, *page* 163. For the one opinion, see Mr. Huxtable's *Sacred Record of Creation*; for the other, Dr. Rorison's Essay, *The Creative Week*, in *Replies to Essays and Reviews*.

Note 33, *page* 166. See Hugh Miller's *Old Red Sandstone*,

p. 136, &c.; and *Testimony of the Rocks*, Lectures V. and VI.; 'Geology in its bearings on the two Theologies.' Also Huxtable, *l. l.*, p. 57, sqq. But the recent controversy on the antiquity of man is an additional lesson, had one been needed, to teach us the danger of grasping precipitately at gains which have scarcely yet become our own. Compare Hardwick's *Christ and other Masters*, i. 47; a page which could hardly have been written now.

LECTURE VI.

Note 1, *page* 172. For the double sense of leaven, as used in Scripture, see Trench, *On the Parables*, p. 113; Stier, *Words of the Lord Jesus*, ii. 254, E. T.: 'With this expansion of the small seed in the field of the world the tares of corruption will mingle all the more powerfully (like a leaven), but the good seed will notwithstanding choke the thorns; the mustard-seed will gain the victory; what is heavenly will also mingle itself with every mixture; in a word, will show itself as *a subduing anti-leaven*.'

'Humanity before Jesus Christ may be divided into two categories; one, a privileged minority, placed under the immediate direction of God. This was the Jewish theocracy. Later on, we shall show how this privilege was in reality in the interest of the whole race.'— De Pressensé, *Religions before Christ*, p. 15; cf. pp. 189, 202, 204, 258; and Mr. Goldwin Smith, *Rational Religion*, &c., p. 57.

'We must consider what was the object of God's dealings with man recorded in the Bible. If it was to put human society at once in a state of perfection, without further effort, political, social, or intellectual, on the part of man, the inference is irresistible that every institution enjoined in the Bible is part of a perfect scheme, and that every institution mentioned in the Bible without condemnation will be lawful to the end of time. But if the object was to implant in man's heart a principle, viz. the love of God and man, which should move him to work (God also working in him) for the improvement of his own state and that of his fellows, and for the transforming of his and their life into the image of their Maker; in this case it will by no means follow that any social institution recognised in Scripture for the time being, or mentioned by it without condemnation, is for ever good or lawful in the sight of God.'—Mr. Goldwin Smith, *Does the Bible sanction American Slavery?* pp. 2, 3. 'The religious system of the Jews was primitive, and therefore gross, compared with Christian worship. It was spiritual compared with the religious system of the most refined and cultivated heathen nations.'—

Ib., p. 23. 'If we look at the Mosaic dispensation in itself, we may regard it as peculiarly ceremonial; but if we compare it with any other dispensation except the Christian, we shall probably find that, instead of being peculiarly ceremonial, it is peculiarly moral.'— *Ib.*, p. 57.

Note 2, *page* 175. See also above, pp. 99, 100. On the laws of slaves and children, and some other points of the same kind, compare Mr. Goldwin Smith, *l. l.*, pp. 12, 37, 50, 54; and *Rational Religion*, &c., p. 51; a Layman's *Pentateuch Vindicated*, pp. 202, 205, *note*; Stanley, *Jewish Church*, p. 170 (usages 'assumed and tolerated,' but 'restrained'); Milman, *History of the Jews*, i. 168 ('of all the ancient lawgivers, Moses alone endeavoured to mitigate' the evils of slavery); 171 ('Moses, while he maintained the dignity and salutary control, limited the abuse of the parental authority').

Note 3, *page* 175. Most of the difficulties which are usually urged are detailed and discussed in the *Introductions to the Pentateuch* of Hengstenberg, Macdonald, and others, and will be found under their respective places in the recent works of Dr. Davidson, Dr. Stanley, and Dean Milman. Some points which are generally connected with them are discussed above in Lecture III.: e.g. the repentance ascribed to God, pp. 84, 91; the hardening of Pharaoh's heart, p. 88; and the visiting of the sins of the fathers on the children, p. 96. On the special difficulty of the apparent commendation of falsehood in such cases as the midwives of the Hebrews and Rahab, see the notes to Grotius, *De Jure B. et P.*, iii. c. i. 16; S. Thom. Aquin., II^{da} II^{dae} Qu. cx. Art. iii.; and Whewell, *Lectures on Moral Philosophy*, ii. 78, 1862; 'Christian morality; St. Augustine on Lying.' On the Destruction of the Canaanites, see a sermon by Dr. Mill, *University Sermons*, 1845, No. vii. p. 117. On the general question, compare Mr. Mansel's *B. L.*, pp. 42, 243–4, and the controversy to which those passages gave rise.

To a great extent, in truth, the argument falls under the erroneous belief, against which Art. vii. is directed, that the Old Testament is contrary to the New. Hence such works as the *Christianity without Judaism*, of the late Professor Powell. On the other side, I may refer to Mr. Macleane's *Unity of God's Moral Law as Revealed in the O. and N. Testaments*, 1847; and Mr. Perowne's *Essential Coherence of the O. and N. Testaments*, 1858.

Note 4, *page* 176. 'There are some particular precepts in Scripture, given to particular persons, requiring actions which would be immoral and vicious were it not for such precepts. But it is easy to see that all these are of such a kind as that the precept *changes the whole nature of the case and of the action*, and both constitutes and shows that not to be unjust or immoral which, prior to the precept, must have appeared and really have been so; which may well be, *since none of these precepts are contrary to immutable morality.*'—Butler, *Anal.*, ii. 3, p. 220. This last qualification supplies the precise protection which I plead for against supposing that God could utter a command for the purpose of turning wrong into right. Butler expressly excludes actions that are wrong in themselves, and expressly confines his argument to acts of a judicial character, by means of which the command of God deprives the unworthy possessor of either property or life.

Compare S. August., *Contra Mendacium*, 34, *Opp.*, vi. 469 : ' Et ubi ponimus voluntatem ac potestatem Dei ? ' or, as Dr. Whewell states it, *l. l.*, p. 86 : ' God's Providence can bring about its purposes without being aided by the false utterances of men.' Almost the very phrase of a recent writer of fiction : ' God's omnipotence did not need our sin.'

Note 5, *page* 176. On 'the imperfect standard allowed and even approved under the old dispensation, as contrasted with the perfect law of love in the new,' Dr. Stanley cites the judgment of St. Chrysostom ;—*Sermons and Essays on the Apostolical Age*, p. 41 ; also in *Jewish Church*, p. 250. Similarly Dr. Whewell quotes from St. Augustine, *l. l.*, p. 83 : ' That these women were " *according to their degree* approved and rewarded of God." Their act was better than a lie of malice, but it was not absolutely good.' The hypothesis is put more antagonistically by Dr. Davidson, *Introd to O. T.*, i. 474 : ' The morality of the Old Testament was *progressive, incomplete, imperfect* : it was simply the reflection of the purest existing morality. To say that it was a *standard* morality for all time, or even for the time of its manifestation, is to mistake its character,' &c.

Note 6, *page* 181. The principle is traced on from Joshua and Judges to the Psalms and Ezra, and thence to the New Testament, in Dr. Newman's sermon, ' Jewish zeal a pattern to Christians,' *Parochial Sermons*, iii. 197, sqq. On its counterpoise ' Sobriety,' see *Lyra Ap.*, lxv.-ix.

Note 7, *page* 182. For the use which has been made of the death of Sisera, see Coleridge, *Confessions*, &c., pp. 34, 44, 54 ; Mr. F. W. Newman's *Phases of Faith*, p. 69, 3rd ed. ; Davidson, *l. l.*, p. 475.

The subject is discussed, with various results, in almost every treatise bearing on these questions. Compare Waterland, *Works*, iv. 254; Arnold, *Sermons chiefly on the Interpretation of Scripture*, No. viii., p. 76; R. Williams, *Rational Godliness*, Sermon vii., p. 89; Burgon, *Inspiration and Interpretation*, p. 223, sqq.; Stanley, *Jewish Church*, n. 329, sqq.

Note 8, page 182. 'The solemn religious commencement, the picturesque description of the state of the country, the mustering of the troops from all quarters, the sudden transition to the most contemptuous sarcasm against the tribes that stood aloof; the life, fire, and energy of the battle; the bitter pathos of the close—lyric poetry has nothing in any language which can surpass the boldness and animation of this striking production.'—Milman, *l. l.*, i. 246. 'The song of Deborah is a very old specimen of Hebrew poetry, which may challenge comparison in sublimity and beauty with the lyrics of any other language.'—Davidson, *l. l.*, i. 471. 'The song of Deborah bears in itself the marks of antiquity, and may have been written soon after the time of the prophetess herself.'—*Ib.*, p. 465. We may fairly set this opinion against Bishop Colenso's attempt to bring down the poem to a later date. *Pentateuch*, §§ 447–452; *Answer to Dr. M'Caul*, p. 14. See also Dr. Donaldson, *Jashar*, pp. 269, 289. For the antiquity of the oldest uninspired compositions, see Max Müller on the Veda, *Ancient Sanskrit Literature*, p. 65; 'the most ancient literary work of the Aryan race, a work more ancient than the Zendavesta and Homer;' the published form of the Vedic hymns the same 'in which they existed at least 800 years before the Christian era.'

Note 9, page 183. On the days of the Judges, compare Stanley, *Jewish Church*, pp. 305, 308, 328, 337; on Jephthah, p. 358; on Samson, pp. 364, &c. In these and in many similar cases throughout these Notes mere reference must not be taken to imply any further agreement than may be inferred from the argument of the Lectures.

Note 10, page 184. Compare Dr. Newman's sermon above referred to, and Milman, *l. l.*, i. 187 : 'How wonderfully the event verified the prediction of the inspired legislator, how invariably apostasy led to adversity, repentance and reformation to prosperity, will abundantly appear during the course of the following history.'

Note 11, page 185. For the geographical and other details, it is sufficient to refer to Dr. Stanley's *Sinai and Palestine*, p. 339; *Jewish Church*, pp. 316, sqq.

Note 12, *page* 187. Dr. Milman still follows the older version: 'For the noise of plundering archers by the wells of water, now they meet and sing aloud Jehovah's righteous acts.'—i. 248. So also Dr. Williams, *l. l.*, p. 95 : 'The places of drawing water were beset by the bow of the oppressor;' and p. 105 : 'Like the archers of Canaan by the watering-places of Israel.' But Dr. Stanley : 'From amidst the shouting of the dividers of spoils, between the water-troughs, there let them rehearse,' &c., p. 334 ; and Dr. Davidson : 'For the rejoicing of those who divide the spoil between the draw-wells, there they celebrate,' &c., p. 473. Dr. Donaldson, again, on a different hypothesis : 'meditaminor, ob jubila lignatorum inter aquarum diluvia.'—*Jashar*, p. 238; cf. pp. 276–80.

Note 13, *page* 189. The point is put with earnest force by Dr. Arnold, *l. l.*, p. 33, Sermon on the *Wars of the Israelites* : 'It is better that the wicked should be destroyed a hundred times over, yea, destroyed with everlasting destruction, than that they should tempt those who are as yet innocent to join their company. And if we are inclined to think that God dealt hardly with the people of Canaan in commanding them to be so utterly destroyed, let us but think what might have been our fate, and the fate of every other nation under heaven at this hour, had the sword of the Israelites done its work more sparingly. . . . The Israelites' sword, in its bloodiest executions, wrought a work of mercy for all the countries of the earth to the very end of the world.' So also Stanley, *l. l.*, p. 253. See too Lord A. Hervey, *Inspiration of Holy Scripture*, p. 68, who discusses, in the following pages, the killing of Eglon and Sisera, and the question of Deborah's inspiration.

Note 14, *page* 192. Compare Dr. Pusey's Sermon on the *Day of Judgment*, 1839 : 'As He unfolds the fuller measures of His goodness in our redemption, He accompanies them with more awful notices of His wrath ; He disclosed not to us everlasting joys, without warning us of everlasting fire.'

Note 15, *page* 193. ' It is a remarkable circumstance which has been often observed, that if we look to some of the most eminent saints of Scripture, we shall find their recorded errors to have occurred in those parts of their duty in which each had had most trial, and generally showed obedience most perfect. *Faithful* Abraham through want of faith denied his wife. Moses, the *meekest* of men, was excluded from the land of promise for a passionate word. The *wisdom* of Solomon was seduced to bow down to idols.

Barnabas, again, the *son of consolation*, had a sharp contention with St. Paul.'—Newman, *Parochial Sermons*, i. 53–4. Compare *Lyra Ap.*, xx. But I have pointed out that the history appears to prove the existence of the double strain of temper through all portions of the legislator's life. Dr. Stanley says, however, that 'no modern word seems exactly to correspond to that which our translators have rendered "the meekest of men," but which rather expresses "enduring," "afflicted," "heedless of self."'—*Jewish Church*, p. 199.

Note 16, *page* 193. Compare Arnold, *Sermons chiefly on the Interpretation of Scripture*, pp. 396–9; Stanley, *Apostolic Age*, pp. 246, 258, 278–80; Westcott, *Introd. to Study of N. T.*, pp. 234, 281. So of Christ Himself, Newman, *l. l.*, iii. 200 : 'There was an occasion when our Lord is expressly said to have taken upon Him the zeal which consumed David,' &c. 'Such is the pattern afforded us by our Lord; to which add the example of the angels which surround Him. Surely in Him is mingled "goodness and severity;" such, therefore, are all holy creatures, loving and severe.'

LECTURE VII.

Note 1, *page* 200. See this remarked in Dr. Stanley's *Apostolic Age*, pp. 381-2 (partly repeated in *Comment.* on Corinth., i. p. 46): 'It is by catching a glimpse, however partial, of those wild dissensions which raged around and beneath the Apostolic writings, that we can best appreciate the sublime unity and repose of those writings themselves.' Compare p. 298, of St. James: 'It was not, we may believe, without an object that the Divine Providence, which so carefully excluded from the sacred volume those harsher or more temporary peculiarities on which the Palestine Jews dwelt with exclusive pleasure, has admitted into it the great Epistle, where the same general character, indeed, appears before us, but refined and purified from the earthly admixture by which the merely human record of him is marred.' And of St. Peter, Neander, *Planting*, &c., i. 372, *note*; defending 'the old distinction for securing the idea of inspiration between *vitium conversationis* and *error doctrinæ*.'

Note 2, *page* 200. 'Every one has a distinct conception of St. Peter. . . . Quick in action even to rashness, and bold in word even to presumption, he is yet the founder of the outward Church.' '—Eager to realise to the full a blessing of which he only half perceived the import, and unable to wait in calm assurance on the will of his Master. This impatient energy, which seems to be ever striving after the issues of things, made him give expression in many cases to the thoughts which others cherished, perhaps vaguely.' 'He cannot rest in uncertainty where knowledge might prove the guide to deeds.' 'We feel at once that the walking on the waters and the failing faith are a true figure of his following Christ to the place of judgment and then denying Him. Then follows the swift and complete reaction.'—Westcott, *Introd.*, &c., pp. 277-280. 'Peter, over-hasty, as was so often the case.'—Trench, *Miracles*, p. 377. 'By the natural constitution of his mind, he was disposed to surrender himself at the moment entirely to the impression which seized him ... but he was easily misled by a rash self-confidence to say more, and to venture more, than he could accomplish.'—Neander, *Planting*, &c., i. 368, ed. Bohn: cf. pp. 66, *note*; 72, &c. 'Boldness and timidity, first boldness, then timidity, were the characteristics of his nature.'—Jowett, *Comment.* on Gal. ii. 11. Compare p. 343 (first ed.): 'He who is the first, and even the ablest to speak, may be often deficient in firmness of will or grasp of mind.' Also Stanley, *Apostolic Age*, pp. 82, 95 ('whose characteristic it was, that, with his thoughts ever bounded by time, his spirit was ever open to the first dawn of things eternal'), 104 ('who took the first critical step in advance?' 'the characters of simple unhesitating zeal, which act instead of reflecting, which venture instead of calculating, which cannot or will not see the difficulties with which the first struggle of an untried reformation is of necessity accompanied'), &c.

The reverent analysis of the human characteristics of the Scripture saints is a work of deep interest and constant profit; but only so long as we recollect that their mission contributed a very different element, in the message of pure revelation which was entrusted to their keeping, and which was received and handed on through the presence and light of a special inspiration.

Note 3, page 202. Compare Neander, *Life of Christ*, p. 281, ed. Bohn; Moberly, *Sayings of the Great Forty Days*, pp. 14, 39–42; Stanley, *l. l.*, p. 92; Ellicott, *Historical Lectures*, &c., pp. 202, 218, 220. On the steps by which the early Church disengaged itself from Judaism, cf. Trench, *St. Augustine*, pp. 61, 71; Neander, *Planting*, &c., p. 29; Baumgarten, *Apostolic History*, i. 176, Clark. On the effect of the Fall of Jerusalem in completing the transition, see Lyall, *Propæd. Proph.*, pp. 316, sqq.

With the reference on p. 203 to Mark vii. 31, we must compare Matt. xvi. 13, Mark viii. 27; our Lord's retirement to Cæsarea Philippi, on which see Dr. Stanley's remarks, *Apostolic Age*, p. 112, and *Sinai*, &c., pp. 399, 419. 'Césarée de Philippe, sa pointe la plus avancée dans le monde des Gentils.'—Renan, *Vie de Jésus*, p. 28.

Note 4, page 204. 'It is most probable that, in Peter's mind, when he used this expression (Acts ii. 39), there floated an indistinct allusion to believers from other nations, though it did not appear of sufficient importance for him to give it a greater prominence in his address, as it was his conviction that the converts to Christianity from heathenism must first become Jews.'—Neander, *Planting*, &c.,

p. 20. Compare Bengelius, *in loc.*, as quoted above, Lecture IV., note 12.

Note 5, *page* 207. Each step of this history has been the subject of discussion. Without entering into further details of reference, I must leave the historical views adopted in this and other parts of the Lecture to suggest their own evidence, by the degree in which they seem to harmonise the probabilities of the case with the statements of Scripture. It might, indeed, be objected that, though the leaving Titus uncircumcised may be properly described as 'one immediate result' of the Council (Conybeare and Howson, i. 234), yet St. Paul's consent to circumcise Timothy appears to fall later than the rebuke to Peter (*ib.*, 239, 286), which could not, therefore, have rested on the ground which I have suggested. But that consent would be merely (as in Acts xxi. 26, and 1 Cor. ix. 20) the temporary concession of a question which had been raised, but not decided; while St. Peter might have taken alarm at the very fact of its being mooted, and have withdrawn on that ground from an intercourse which he had previously and rightly sanctioned.

That it is not easy to adjust the narrative without such an explanation, the tone of the following comments will suffice to prove :—

1. On Acts x. 'That such fresh revelations should have been necessary may appear strange,' &c.; 'but the effect of Pentecost was not suddenly to dispel all ignorance and wavering.'—Humphry, *in loc.* ' It appears surprising that the Apostle Peter,' &c.; but ' it must not be overlooked that St. Peter was by no means uncertain about the entrance of the Gentiles into the Church considered in itself, but only about the point whether they could be admitted without being circumcised, and taking upon themselves the obligation of the law.'—Olshausen, *in loc.*

2. On St. Peter at Antioch, Gal. ii. 11. 'The conduct of Peter is not easy to understand,' &c.—Jowett, *in loc.* And again, the passage is important ' as pourtraying the state of indecision in which all, except St. Paul, even including Barnabas, were in reference to the observance of the Jewish law.' 'Peter in their society began to vacillate. In weak compliance with their prejudices,' &c., ' we find him contradicting his own principles, and, "through fear of those who were of the circumcision," giving all the sanction of his example to the introduction of *caste* into the Church of Christ.'—Conybeare and Howson, i. 239. (It appears to me that the language of verse 16,

&c., proves the social question named in verse 12 to have been merely the symbol of a deeper difference.) Compare Neander, *Planting*, &c., i. pp. 67 (and *note*), 211 ; and *Additions and Corrections*, ii. 81, sqq.; and more generally, on the modes of reconciling Acts xv. with Gal. ii., cf. Conybeare and Howson, i. 244, sqq., and Ebrard, *Gospel History*, p. 502, Clark.

Mr. Westcott gives the following as the 'steps by which the distinction of Jew and Gentile was removed in the Christian Church:' '1. The admission of Gentiles, Acts x., xi.; 2. The freedom of Gentile converts from the ceremonial law, Acts xv.; 3. The indifference of the ceremonial law *for Jewish converts*, Gal. ii. 14-16, Acts xxi. 20-26 ; 4. The incompatibility of Judaism with Christianity. The first three—that is, the essential—principles are recognised in Scripture ; the last, which introduces no new element, is evolved in the history of the Church.'—*Canon of N. T.*, p. 73, *note*. Mr. Greg calls the council at Jerusalem and the dispute at Antioch 'the same transaction;' and very naturally infers that, in that case, there must be 'some mistake on the historian's part.'—*Creed of Christendom*, 1863, p. 164. But he annexes two footnotes which utterly destroy his text: first, 'The same *or a similar one*;' next, 'unless, as has been suggested, Peter afterwards, overpowered by the unanimity of the Judaisers, flinched from his principles, and so incurred Paul's indignation.'

Note 6, *page* 208. Compare Stanley, *Apostolic Age*, p. 90; and for the Epistles, pp. 100-1. His first Epistle 'may well be taken as the pledge of the last work of St. Peter, in crushing absolutely and for ever this fatal schism, which would have divided the two great Fathers of our faith—him who gave it its first outward form, and him who proclaimed its deep inward spirit.' For a similar remark on the second Epistle, see Conybeare and Howson, i. 242. A brief summary of the relation between the speeches and epistles, and of the respective characteristics of St. Peter, St. Stephen, St. Luke, and St. Paul, is given in Ebrard's *Gospel History*, pp. 499-500. On the extent to which 'St. Peter's First Epistle derives special interest from his personal history,' see Dr. Wordsworth's *Introduction* to it.

Note 7, *page* 213. For the interpretation of 2 Cor. v. 16, which is here examined, see Professor Jowett's *Introduction to the First Epistle to the Thessalonians*, pp. 7, sqq.

No rejoinder to what I have urged could be based on any proposal to correct the chronology. Mr. Jowett says that 'the series (of letters) begins with the Epistles to the Thessalonians, *identified with the second apostolical journey* by the mention of Timothy and the sojourn of the Apostle at Athens, after a previous stay at Thessalonica.'—i. 281, 2nd ed. In the same volume he tells us, that 'more than half the Apostle's ministry had already elapsed ere he set his hand to this the first of his extant writings.' 'It is a fragment, *the earliest we possess*, of the Apostle's life and the history of the Church.'—i. 6. Now it is surely a most important addition to these statements, and a correction of the inferences founded upon them, to note that by the side of the Thessalonian Epistles we have the discourse at Athens, which gives the most mature view of the position of the Gentiles; and that some time before the date of those Epistles, we have the discourses at the Pisidian Antioch and at Lystra; the former embodying the most complete conception of the doctrine of justification, and the relation which existed between the law and the gospel.

Note 8, *page* 214. 'The words lead us to infer that something of this kind had once been his own state of mind, not only in the time before his conversion (which he would have condemned more strongly), but since. If so, it is (like Phil. iii. 13–15) a remarkable confession of former weakness or error, and of conscious progress in religious knowledge.'—Stanley, *on* 2 Cor. v. 16; cf. p. 295, first ed. See another interpretation in Mr. Bright's *Notes on XVIII. Sermons of St. Leo*, p. 131. Compare Neander, *Planting*, &c., i. 82, *note*, and pp. 93, 526–9; and from a different quarter, Mackay, *Tübingen School*, &c., 1863, p. 239, *note*.

Note 9, *page* 217. 'Here in this first sermon which St. Paul is recorded to have preached in a Jewish synagogue, we have the germ of his two Epistles to the Galatians and Romans—an internal evidence of genuineness and veracity.'—Wordsworth, *on* Acts, xiii. 36. 'His concluding words, as St. Luke relates them, might stand as a summary, representing in outline the early chapters of the Epistle to the Romans.'—Conybeare and Howson, i. 188. It is to the passage, Acts xiii. 39, that Mr. Davison makes his appeal, for 'the general doctrine of St. Paul, when he explains to the *Israelite* the difference between the Legal and the Evangelical systems,' adding in a note: 'This single sentence, therefore, is decisive of the nature of the Mosaic dispensation.'—*On Sacrifice: Remains*, pp. 74–5.

Note 10, *page* 217. Dr. Wordsworth proceeds, in the passage cited in the last Note : ' It is observable also that St. Paul's address appears to be formed on the same model as St. Stephen's—another proof of its influence on him and of the truth of the history.' So also Conybeare and Howson, i. 190, *note*. ' In short, Stephen was the forerunner of the great Paul.'—Neander, *Planting*, &c., i. 50, 52, 97. ' In many particulars St. Stephen was the forerunner of St. Paul.'—Conybeare and Howson, i. 73, sqq.; Stanley, *Apostolic Age*, p. 61; *Jewish Church*, p. 29; Trench, *St. Augustine*, p. 114; Humphry, *Boyle Lectures for* 1858, p. 12.

Note 11, *page* 218. ' We have seen elsewhere (chap. iii. 1-8; v. 12-21; vii. 7-11) that in many passages the Apostle wavers between the opposite sides of a question, before he arrives at a final and permanent conclusion. The argument in such passages may be described as a sort of struggle in his own thoughts, an alternation of natural feelings, a momentary conflict of emotions. The stream of discourse flows onward in two channels, occasionally mingling or contending with each other, which meet at the last.' ' Nowhere does the logical control over language, that is, the power of aptly disposing sentences so as to exhibit them in their precise relation to each other, so fail the Apostle as at the conclusion of the tenth chapter. We see his meaning, but his emotions prevent him from expressing it.'—Jowett, *on* Rom. ix.-xi.; *l. l.*, ii. 269, 271. Compare Mr. Mozley's *Letter to Dr. Stanley on Subscription to the Articles*, p. 15. The principle of interpretation which I have suggested is illustrated by Bishop Ellicott's remark on Rom. viii. 20, 21, *Destiny of the Creature*, p. 3 : ' No text has suffered more from the arbitrary limitation of the terms in which it is expressed; and in no case will it be found more advisable to give boldly to every term the most comprehensive meaning the context will warrant, and to every clause its fullest and most extended significance.'

The language of Professor Jowett is not in this case framed on Dr. Arnold's model : ' In " St. Paul " there is not only all Christian truth, but it is free from the mixture of human foolishness and error. In his Epistles all is equal; all is grave and sober, and wise and true; all is fitted to be an authority and a rule.' ' He who amidst the goodness and the sense of the Fathers is grieved from time to time at those marks of human infirmity which make it clear that they are no staff to lean upon, may turn with greater thankfulness to the Epistles of St. Paul and of the other apostles, and may there find that which the human heart so eagerly craves for—an authority which it may trust without reserve.'—*Sermons chiefly on the Interpretation of Scripture*, pp. 269–70.

Note 12, *page* 219. The highest sense of law, within the moral and spiritual sphere, is that in which God 'is a law both to Himself and to all other things besides.'—Hooker, *E. P.*, I. ii. § 3. The purest reflection of that law may be conceived to guide the movements of unfallen spirits; but the introduction of evil introduces that element of severity which causes law, in its ordinary sense, to be adjusted to the vicious rather than the virtuous ($\nu\acute{o}\mu o\varsigma\ \delta$', $\dot{\epsilon}\nu\ o\tilde{\iota}\varsigma\ \dot{\alpha}\delta\iota\kappa\acute{\iota}\alpha$.—Ar. *Eth. N.*, V. vi. § 4; 1 Tim. i. 9). It is according to this, which in the text I call the 'third sense,' that 'by the word Law' St. Paul 'means "any rule of life which restrains our natural inclinations, and which we obey *through fear and with an effort.*"'—Arnold, *Sermons*, i. 139. 'Laws do not only *teach* what is good, but they *enjoin* it, they have in them *a certain constraining force.*'—Hooker, *l.l.*, I. x. § 7. And at this point we meet with two contrasted statements: on the one hand, that there is no need of law where there is no risk of transgression (1 Tim., as above); on the other, that there is no possibility of transgression where there is no law (Rom. iv. 15; v. 13; vii. 13; 1 Cor. xv. 56). To reconcile them we observe that, in this sense, law as well as sin implies a state of evil; a race which is not only imperfect by creation, but deteriorated by actual transgression. And on this basis we may arrange the order of conceptions thus: 1. There is *potential* sin—evil which is not yet developed or made active. Where this is not present as the groundwork, there is no room for law, as above defined, any more than there is room for sin. 2. For the prevention or removal of this evil, it is necessary to bring in the restraints of law, which in itself, however, conveys only knowledge, but not grace (cf. above, Lecture III., *Note* 15, and *Discourses on the Fall and its Results*, pp. 227–8). Here we reach the first of the above contrasted statements—that there is no need of law where there is no risk of transgression. 3. This law may be either obeyed or disobeyed. If obeyed, it leads to a recovery, in which law conveys the knowledge while grace effects the cure; if disobeyed, the grace is rejected, and the law becomes 'the savour of death unto death.' In this calamity, we trace the operation of the second of the two contrasted statements, when law becomes 'the strength of sin.' What was given as a *guide* now remains only as a *witness* (cf. Blakesley, *Conc. Ac.*, p. 175); in which character law points the condemnation, which leads through disobedience to death. We may divide it according to the three stages of the law of conscience, the Old Testament, and the Gospel; and in each of these we may confront it with the uniformity of evil, which constitutes 'the law of sin and death.' By this method, therefore, we reach the same four ultimate meanings, which I have pointed out in the usage of St. Paul.

Note 13, *page* 220. 'The *granite* mountains, on whose hard blocks were written the Ten Commandments of the Mosaic Law.'—Stanley, *Sinai and Palestine*, p. 11.

LECTURE VIII.

Note 1, *page* 232. 'Speciatim in sermonibus et actionibus Christi elucet ejusmodi Decorum, quod ab evangelistis tam bene expressum argumento est, illos a Spiritu S. actos scripsisse ; neque enim id humani ingenii quamlibet excellentissimi fuisset . . . In rebus summè humilibus tamen Filius Dei cavet juri majestatis suæ.'— Bengel., *in* Matt. iii. 15. 'In omni humiliatione Christi, per decoram quandam protestationem cautum est gloriæ ejus divinæ. Hoc loco, per præconium angeli ; in circumcisione, per nomen Jesu ; in purificatione, per testimonium Simeonis ; in baptismo, per exceptionem Baptistæ ; in passione, modis longè plurimis.'—Id., *in* Luc. ii. 9. 'Cum decoro divino pulcrè congruit, quod præsente vitæ duce nemo unquam legitur mortuus.'—Id., *in* Joann. xi. 15.

Recent publications on the Life and Opinions of Mr. E. Irving have recalled to prominent notice the errors on our Saviour's human nature into which he was betrayed, and another phase of which was represented in some unhappy speculations of the late Dr. Donaldson. Compare the strong remonstrances of Dr. Mill, *Five Sermons on our Lord's Temptation*, pp. 37, 53, 152 ; and Bishop Ellicott, *Historical Lectures*, &c., p. 111. Also see Mr. Mozley, *Augustinian Doctrine of Predestination*, p. 97. A firm grasp on the doctrine of Christ's Divine Personality will save us from embarrassment in connexion with the collateral error of His alleged human ignorance, as it has been still more recently maintained. I am thankful to be exempted by the date of the controversy (which falls later than the delivery of these Lectures) from entering here upon the painful subject of M. Renan's *Vie de Jésus*.

Note 2, *page* 233. Compare the answer given by Bishop Ellicott to the question whether any inaccuracies are really to be found in Scripture : 'As, in the case of the Incarnate Word, we fully recognise in the Lord's humanity all essentially human limitations and weaknesses, the hunger, the thirst, and the weariness on the side of the body', and the gradual development on the side of the human mind

(Luke ii. 40)—in a word, all that belongs to the essential and original characteristics of the pure form of the nature He vouchsafed to assume, but plainly deny the existence therein of the faintest trace of sin, or of moral or mental imperfection,—even so in the case of the written Word, viewed on its purely human side, *and in its reference to matters previously admitted to have no bearing on Divine Truth*, we may admit therein the existence of such incompleteness, such limitations, and such imperfections as belong even to the highest forms of purely truthful *human* testimony, but consistently deny the existence of mistaken views, perversion, misrepresentation, and any form whatever of consciously committed error or inaccuracy.'—*Aids to Faith*, pp. 417-8. The same course of reasoning is suggested by others of the writers cited above, Lecture I., *Note* 4.

When it is wished to prove by such catenæ as those of Dr. Davidson and Mr. Stephen, that high authorities in the English Church have gone beyond this position, by teaching, either that the inspiration of Holy Scripture was only partial, or that it is accompanied by an acknowledged fringe of definite error, we must submit the passages cited to a critical examination, and exclude all those which fail, for any of the following reasons, to support either of the above propositions. We must exclude, then :—

1. Those passages which merely teach that the *revelation* is partial; or which allege, that no *revelation* was required for matters which fell under the personal knowledge of the inspired writers; above, pp. 25, 146, and *Notes*. If the word *inspiration* is occasionally used in this connexion, it is simply because the exact difference between inspiration and revelation (above, Lecture I., *Note* 5) has not been always present to the minds of the writers. The context will generally show that what they really mean to limit is not the inspiration, but the revelation of Scripture. See, e. g., Tillotson, as referred to in Lecture I., *Note* 5 ; Warburton, in Stephen, p. 142 ('it would be putting the Holy Spirit *on an unnecessary employment*'); Watson, *Ib.*, p. 146 ; Tomline, *Ib.*, p. 149 (they 'did not upon every occasion stand in need of *supernatural communication*'); Whately, *Ib.*, p. 156, &c. Some of the passages here cited might be alleged also under the following head, viz :—

2. Those which distinctly recognise the presence of collateral information, the use of common sense in ordinary matters, the employment of current scientific terms, and other indications that the human element was complete ; admissions which, as I have urged

(Lecture V., and above, pp. 231, 234), amount to neither an exclusion of the inspiration nor an acknowledgment of error. To this head belongs the use of optical or phænomenal language; above, p. 158 and *Note*. Passages of this kind, I repeat, simply carry out the full recognition of the human element. They do not involve any necessary limitation of what is strictly called inspiration—the special presence of the Holy Spirit, which raised those human agents to a loftier power.

3. Those which merely coincide with Butler's warning, above, pp. 155, 233 (cf. Stephen, p. 138 ; and Dr. Mill, cited in Lecture V., *Note* 9), against all attempts to impose a deductive theory of inspiration, and against the disposition to complain if others think that the facts will not support the position which such reasoners had no right to assume.

4. Those which merely warn us against staking too much on difficult or questionable positions; as Paley, above, pp. 141–2.

5. Those which insist on the argument which has been worked out by several recent writers, on the large share which must be ascribed to our own ignorance of details, as an explanation of countless Scripture difficulties. Compare Heber, in Stephen, p. 154. This position must of course be used with judgment : for it is obviously inadmissible to argue, as some have done, that we may *expect discrepancies*, because a more minute acquaintance with the facts would cause discrepancies to disappear. What is meant can only be that this consideration might lead us to expect the *appearance*, but not the *reality*, of discrepancies.

6. Those which cannot be used without an alteration of the language of the writer quoted, by arguing across from assertions to negations, or from admissions to exclusions. Compare Lecture III., *Note* 7. We find a remarkable instance in the use which Mr. Stephen repeatedly makes of Hooker's words (*E. P.*, I. xiv. § 3,&c.), that ' the several books of Scripture having had each some several occasion and particular purpose which caused them to be written, the contents thereof are *according to the exigence of that special end* whereunto they are intended.' ' The substance of his view is this : Scripture is perfect *for the end for which it is designed* ;' and therefore, it is argued, *for that end only*.—Stephen, pp. 96–7, 128, 131–4–7, 146–9, 151, 161, 173. For the real rigour of Hooker's opinion, see the extract above in Lecture I., *Note* 20 ; and cf. Burgon, *Inspiration and Interpretation*, pp. 77, 115 ; Phillimore,

NOTES TO LECTURE VIII. 363

Speech, &c., pp. 92–96; M'Caul, *Testimonies*, &c., pp. 100–8, 'The word of God in itself is *absolute, exact, and perfect.*'—*E. P.* III. viii. § 4, &c.

Note 3, *page* 234. Particular attention has been lately called to this point by Dean Milman, *History of the Jews*, *Pref.*, p. xxix.; and i. 65, 98, 120, 122.

Note 4, *page* 234. See above, Lecture V., *Note* 14.

Note 5, *page* 235. See above, Lecture V., *Notes* 24, 25, and 26.

Note 6, *page* 240. Compare Van Mildert, *B. L.*, p. 139; and the summary of opinions in the *Commentaries* of Ellicott and Alford, *in loc.*

Note 7, *page* 241. *E. and R.*, p. 377. See Bishop Marsh also, *l.l.*, pp. 321, 466, 508; and above, Lecture IV., *Note* 1; Coleridge, *Confessions*, &c., p. 24 (those 'who take up the Bible as they do other books, and apply to it the same rules of interpretation'); Davidson, ed. of Horne's *Introduction*, ii. 207 ('the Bible is to be explained on the same principles as other books;' 'yet we cannot go all the length of those who insist on the fact *absolutely* and *unqualifiedly*'). See also above, quotation from Bacon in Lecture IV., *Note* 1, &c. And for Dr. Arnold's feeling on this subject, compare Mr. B. Price's letter in Stanley's *Life of Arnold*, p. 167, ed. 1846.

Note 8, *page* 244. 'A doctrine which is based on *one* text of Scripture will generally be found to rest on *no* text at all.'—Wordsworth, *Lectures on the Apocalypse*, p. 33. In one of Mr. P. Freeman's papers on the Eucharistic Controversy, he asks: 'Is it not the case that most of such errors in doctrine as the Irvingite, Mr. Maurice's as to eternal punishment, the Arian, all rest on single texts (Eph. iv. 11; John xvii. 3; xiv. 28)?' See above, Lecture III., *Note* 5; Lecture V., *Note* 23. On the other hand, compare Mr. Jowett's Essay 'On the Imputation of the Sin of Adam;' *St. Paul's Epistles*, ii. 162, first ed., 'How slender is the foundation,' &c.; 'two passages in St. Paul at most, and these of uncertain interpretation. The little cloud, no bigger than a man's hand, has covered the heavens.' Also *E. and R.*, p. 358. It is felt in such cases that an important step has been gained against doctrines which really lie beneath vast portions of Scripture, if they can be forced back within the confines of a single text. The fact that the method admits of a right application as well as a wrong one, makes it all the more necessary that any alleged instances should be carefully tested.

Note 9, *page* 246. On this point I would refer especially to the valuable work of Wilson, *An Illustration of the Method of Explaining the N. T.*, &c., chapters ii., iii., &c. Compare Lyall, *Propæd. Proph.*, p. 247; H. Browne, *Messiah as foretold and expected*, p. 77; Trench, *On the Parables*, p. 11, *note*. But the details of the argument are most elaborately examined in Mr. Wilson's treatise.

ALBEMARLE STREET,
October, 1863.

MR. MURRAY'S
FORTHCOMING WORKS.

THE COMPLETION
OF
The Dictionary of the Bible;
ITS ANTIQUITIES, BIOGRAPHY, GEOGRAPHY, AND NATURAL HISTORY.

BY THE FOLLOWING WRITERS:—

ARCHBISHOP OF YORK.
BISHOP OF CALCUTTA.
BISHOP OF KILLALOE.
BISHOP OF GLOUCESTER AND BRISTOL.
REV. LORD ARTHUR HERVEY.
DEAN OF CANTERBURY.
BAILEY, REV. HENRY, B.D.
BARRY, REV. ALFRED, M.A.
BEVAN, REV. WILLIAM L., M.A.
BLAKESLEY, CANON, B.D.
BROWN, REV. T. E., M.A.
BROWNE, ARCHDEACON.
BROWNE, PROFESSOR HAROLD, B.D.
BULLOCK, REV. W. T., M.A.
CLARKE, REV. SAMUEL, M.A.
COOK, REV. F. C., M.A.
DAVIES, REV. LLEWELYN, M.A.
DEUTSCH, EMANUEL.
DRAKE, REV. WILLIAM, M.A.
EDDRUP, REV. E. P., M.A.
FARRAR, REV. F. W., M.A.
FERGUSSON, JAMES, F.R.S.
FFOULKES, EDMUND S., M.A.
GARDEN, REV. FRANCIS.
GOTCH, REV. F. W., LL.D.
GROVE, GEORGE.
HAWKINS, REV. EARNEST, B.D.
HAYMAN, REV. HENRY, M.A.
HESSEY, REV. DR.
HOOKER, JOSEPH D., F.R.S.
HORNBY, REV. J. J.

HOUGHTON, REV. W., M.A.
HOWSON, REV. DR.
HUXTABLE, REV. EDGAR, M.A.
JONES, REV. W. BASIL, M.A.
LAYARD, A. H., M.P.
LEATHES, REV. STANLEY, M.A.
LIGHTFOOT, PROFESSOR, M.A.
MARKS, PROFESSOR D. W.
MEYRICK, REV. FREDERICK, M.A.
ORGER, REV. E. R., M.A.
ORMEROD, ARCHDEACON.
PEROWNE, REV. J. J. S., B.D.
PEROWNE, REV. THOS. T., B.D.
PHILLOTT, REV. H. W., M.A.
PLUMPTRE, PROFESSOR E. H., M.A.
POOLE, E. STANLEY, M.R.A.S.
POOLE, R. STUART, M.R.S.L.
PORTER, REV. J. L., M.A.
PRITCHARD, REV. CHAS., M.A.
RAWLINSON, PROFESSOR, M.A.
ROSE, REV. H. J., B.D.
SELWYN, PROFESSOR, D.D.
STANLEY, CANON, D.D.
THRUPP, REV. J. F., M.A.
TREGELLES, S. P., LL.D.
TRISTRAM, REV. H. B., M.A.
TWISLETON, HON. EDW., M.A.
VENABLES, REV. EDMUND, M.A.
WESTCOTT, REV. B. F., M.A.
WORDSWORTH, REV. DR.
WRIGHT, WILLIAM A., M.A.

EDITED BY WM. SMITH, LL.D.
Editor of the Dictionaries of Greek and Roman Antiquities, Geography, Biography, &c.

Vols. II. and III. (completing the Work.) With Woodcuts. Medium 8vo.

In consequence of the great importance of many of the subjects contained in the later letters of the alphabet, it has been found necessary to extend the work to three volumes instead of comprising it in two, as originally intended. It is believed that this extension will add greatly to the value and usefulness of the work. It has also enabled the Editor to give, at the end of the Third Volume, an Appendix to Volume I., containing many important articles on Natural History, as well as some subjects omitted in the First Volume, such as "Antichrist," "Baptism," and "Church."

Selections from the Poetical Works

OF

RICHARD MONCKTON MILNES (LORD HOUGHTON).

Fcap. 8vo.

The Financial Statements of 1853–60–63,

WITH SPEECHES ON TAX-BILLS, 1861, AND CHARITIES, 1863.

BY THE RIGHT HON. W. E. GLADSTONE,

Chancellor of the Exchequer, and M.P. for the University of Oxford.

8vo.

History of Charles the Bold, Duke of Burgundy.

BY JOHN FOSTER KIRK.

Portrait. 2 Vols. 8vo.

The career of Charles the Bold has usually been regarded as merely a romantic episode in European history. As such it forms the framework of two of Scott's most brilliant fictions,—Quentin Durward and Anne of Geierstein. That great writer has exhibited its salient features, if not with strict fidelity, yet with a vigorous touch and in vivid colours that seemed to forbid any attempt of a weaker hand to produce the same effects by a more literal treatment of the subject. Even on the Continent it has never been presented with fulness and in detail, except in M. de Barante's elegant *rifacimento* of the French Chroniclers of the 15th century. That it was, however, a subject deserving closer research and an ampler delineation has been apparent to those scholars in Belgium, France, Germany, and Switzerland, who, during the last twenty years have found in its separate portions a fresh and fruitful field for their investigations. Some correspondence in reference to the matter passed between the late Mr. Prescott and the distinguished Belgian archivist, M. Gachard, who expressed a wish that the American historian might be induced to employ his pen on so attractive a theme. Availing himself of his well-known facilities for procuring the necessary materials, Mr. Prescott formed a collection, but only that he might, with his accustomed generosity, place it at the disposition of the friend who had first conceived the idea, and who had long shared with him in those studies from which the world has derived no ordinary advantage. The result is a work of which two volumes are now offered to the public, and which a third volume in course of preparation will complete. It is an attempt to bring together and to embody in a symmetrical narrative all that the contemporary chroniclers and memoir-writers, the extant letters and other documentary evidence, and the critical discussions of the present day, could contribute for the just appreciation of a remarkable epoch, grand historical figures and an eventful story. An entirely new light is thrown on some of the most important events in Charles's career, his position as the "Napoleon of the Middle Ages" is fully indicated, and the influence is traced both of his ambition and of his fall upon the destinies of the principal European states.

The Metallurgy of Iron and Steel.

BY JOHN PERCY, M.D., F.R.S.

With numerous Illustrations, drawn to Scale. 8vo.

The New Testament,
ILLUSTRATED AND ANNOTATED;
WITH
A PLAIN EXPLANATORY COMMENT FOR PRIVATE AND FAMILY READING.
FORMING THE FIRST PORTION OF
THE HAND BIBLE.
EDITED BY THE REV. F. C. COOK, M.A.,
Preacher at Lincoln's Inn; and
REV. W. BASIL JONES, M.A.,
Examining Chaplain to the Archbishop of York.
ACCOMPANIED BY FAITHFUL VIEWS OF BIBLE SCENES FROM SKETCHES AND PHOTOGRAPHS.
Two clearly printed and portable volumes, crown 8vo.

The Notes to the HAND BIBLE are not didactic or hortative, like those of Henry and many more; but are designed to explain the text—to correct wrong readings, to illustrate prophecy, and to remove difficulties—so briefly as not to withdraw the attention unnecessarily from the text.

Life and Times of Sir Joshua Reynolds;
WITH NOTICES OF HOGARTH, WILSON, GAINSBOROUGH, AND OTHERS.
BY THE LATE C. R. LESLIE, R.A.,
Author of "The Memoirs of Constable," and "Handbook for Young Painters."
EDITED, WITH ADDITIONS, BY TOM TAYLOR.
With Portraits. 2 Vols. 8vo.

The Rock-Cut Temples of India,
ILLUSTRATED BY 75 PHOTOGRAPHS TAKEN ON THE SPOT.
BY MAJOR GILL.
DESCRIBED BY JAMES FERGUSSON, F.R.S.,
Author of "Handbook of Architecture."
Medium 8vo.

The Diary of Mary, Countess Cowper,
WIFE OF LORD CHANCELLOR COWPER,
AND LADY OF THE BEDCHAMBER TO CAROLINE, PRINCESS OF WALES, AFTERWARDS QUEEN OF GEORGE I.
From the Original MS. in the possession of the family.
Portrait. 8vo.

Life of General Sir William Napier,
AUTHOR OF "HISTORY OF THE PENINSULAR WAR," &c., &c.
EDITED BY H. A. BRUCE, M.P.
With Portraits. 2 Vols. Crown 8vo.

A New History of Painting in Italy,

FROM THE 2ND TO THE 16TH CENTURY.

Derived from Original Researches and inspection of the Works of Art in Italy.

By J. A. CROWE, AND SIGNOR CAVALCASELLE,

Authors of "A History of Early Flemish Art."

With Illustrations. Vols. I. & II. 8vo.

The Bampton Lectures for 1863.

THE RELATION BETWEEN THE DIVINE AND HUMAN ELEMENTS IN HOLY SCRIPTURE.

By REV. J. HANNAH, D.C.L.,

Warden of Trinity College, Glenalmond; late Fellow of Linc. Coll., Oxford.

8vo.

Sermons Preached at Lincoln's Inn,

AND ON SPECIAL OCCASIONS.

By REV. F. C. COOK, M.A.,

Chaplain in Ordinary to the Queen, one of H.M. Inspectors of Schools, Examining Chaplain to the Bishop of Lincoln, and Preacher to the Hon. Society of Lincoln's Inn.

8vo.

Narrative of Travels and Discoveries in the Kingdoms of Siam, Cambojia, and Lao.

By HENRI MOUHOT, F.R.G.S.

With Map and Illustrations. 8vo.

A New Life of Cicero.

By WILLIAM FORSYTH, M.A., Q.C.,

Author of "Hortensius," "History of Trial by Jury," &c.; late Fellow of Trinity Coll., Cambridge.

With Illustrations. Post 8vo.

The object of this work is to exhibit Cicero not merely as a Statesman and an Orator, but as he was at home in the relations of private life, as a Husband, a Father, a Brother, and a Friend. His letters are full of interesting details, which enable us to form a vivid idea of how the old Romans lived two thousand years ago, and the biography embraces not only a history of events, as momentous as any in the annals of the world, but a large amount of anecdote and gossip which amused the generation that witnessed the downfall of the Republic.

The Works of Alexander Pope,

WITH A NEW LIFE, INTRODUCTIONS, AND NOTES.

By REV. WHITWELL ELWIN.

Vols. I. to III. With Portraits. 8vo.

History of Christianity,
FROM THE BIRTH OF CHRIST TO THE ABOLITION OF PAGANISM IN THE ROMAN EMPIRE.

By HENRY HART MILMAN, D.D.,
Dean of St. Paul's.

A New and Revised Edition. 3 vols. 8vo.

Industrial Biography:
IRON WORKERS—AND TOOL MAKERS.

By SAMUEL SMILES.

Post 8vo.

History of Babylon, Media, and Persia;
BEING THE CONTINUATION OF THE FIVE GREAT MONARCHIES OF THE ANCIENT EASTERN WORLD.

By REV. GEORGE RAWLINSON, M.A.,
Camden Professor of Ancient History at the University of Oxford.

With numerous Illustrations from Ancient Monuments. 2 Vols. 8vo.

Hymns in Prose, for Children.
By MRS. BARBAULD.

Illustrated with 112 Original Designs by BARNES, WIMPERIS, COLEMAN, and KENNEDY.

Small 4to.

Laws of Nature, the Foundation of Morals.
By DAVID ROWLAND,
Author of "A Manual of the English Constitution."

Post 8vo.

The Music of the Most Ancient Nations;
PARTICULARLY OF THE ASSYRIANS, EGYPTIANS, AND HEBREWS;

WITH SPECIAL REFERENCE TO DISCOVERIES IN WESTERN ASIA AND EGYPT.

By CARL ENGEL.

With numerous Illustrations. 8vo.

Principles of Surgery.
By JAMES SYME, F.R.S.E.,
Professor of Clinical Surgery in the University o Edinburgh

5th Edition, revised. 8vo.

A History of Latin Christianity,
INCLUDING THAT OF THE POPES TO THE PONTIFICATE OF NICHOLAS V.

By HENRY HART MILMAN, D.D.,
Dean of St. Paul's.

Third and Revised Edition. 8vo.

Elements of Geology;
OR, THE ANCIENT CHANGES OF THE EARTH AND ITS INHABITANTS.

By SIR CHARLES LYELL, F.R.S.

A new and revised Edition. With considerable Additions.

With numerous Woodcuts. 8vo.

Handbook to the Western Cathedrals;
BRISTOL, GLOUCESTER, HEREFORD, WORCESTER, AND LICHFIELD.

By RICHARD J. KING, B.A.

With Illustrations. Post 8vo.

A New English-Latin Dictionary,
COMPILED FROM ORIGINAL SOURCES.

By WILLIAM SMITH, LL.D.,
Editor of the "Latin-English Dictionary," "Classical Dictionaries," &c.

8vo and 12mo.

Student's Manual of English Literature.
BY THE LATE T. B. SHAW.

A New Edition, carefully revised, and partly re-written by the Author.
EDITED WITH NOTES AND ILLUSTRATIONS BY WM. SMITH, LL.D.

Post 8vo. 7s. 6d.

Murray's Handbook for Paris.
A GUIDE FOR VISITORS TO THAT METROPOLIS AND ITS ENVIRONS.

With Clue Map and Plans. Small 8vo.

Murray's Handbook for Ireland,
FROM ORIGINAL SURVEY AND JOURNEYS IN THAT COUNTRY.

With a first-rate Travelling Map. Post 8vo.

The Book of Common Prayer,

ILLUSTRATED WITH ORNAMENTAL BORDERS, INITIAL LETTERS, AND WOODCUTS.

The Embellishments of the present edition consist of Ornamental Borders, Scrolls, Foliage, Head-pieces and Vignettes, and many hundred Initial Letters, together with the following Historical Engravings, to illustrate the Gospels, from the works of RAPHAEL and the early Masters of the Italian School, with some few derived from modern German Masters.

CHRIST'S ENTRY INTO JERUSALEM	ANG. DA FIESOLE.
ST. JOHN IN THE WILDERNESS	OVERBECK.
CHRISTMAS DAY—THE NATIVITY	RAPHAEL.
STONING OF ST. STEPHEN	RAPHAEL.
ST. JOHN EVANGELIST	RAPHAEL.
FLIGHT INTO EGYPT	ANG. DA FIESOLE.
ADORATION OF THE MAGI	RAPHAEL.
INFANT JESUS IN THE TEMPLE	OVERBECK.
CHRIST HEALING THE BLIND	POUSSIN.
MARY MAGDALEN	RAPHAEL.
JUDAS RECEIVING THE MONEY	ANG. DA FIESOLE.
THE LAST SUPPER	RAPHAEL.
CHRIST BEFORE PILATE	OVERBECK.
GOOD FRIDAY—THE CRUCIFIXION	RAPHAEL.
" " CHRIST BEARING THE CROSS	RAPHAEL.
THE ENTOMBMENT	RAPHAEL.
EASTER DAY—THE RESURRECTION	RAPHAEL.
THE GOOD SHEPHERD	OVERBECK.
DAY OF PENTECOST	RAPHAEL.
THE ASCENSION	RAPHAEL.
MIRACULOUS DRAUGHT OF FISHES	RAPHAEL.
THE WIDOW'S SON OF NAIN	OVERBECK.
TRIBUTE MONEY	NAEKE.
THE RAISING OF JAIRUS' DAUGHTER	OVERBECK.
ST. ANDREW	RAPHAEL.
ST. THOMAS'S INCREDULITY	RAPHAEL.
ST. PAUL	RAPHAEL.
CONVERSION OF ST. PAUL	RAPHAEL.
PRESENTATION IN THE TEMPLE	FRA BARTOLOMEO.
ANNUNCIATION OF THE VIRGIN	RAPHAEL.
ST. MARK	FRA BARTOLOMEO.
ST. PETER	RAPHAEL.
ST. BARTHOLOMEW	RAPHAEL.
ST. MATTHEW	RAPHAEL.
ST. MICHAEL	RAPHAEL.
ST. LUKE	OVERBECK.
ST. SIMON AND ST. JUDE	RAPHAEL.

FURNISHED WITH NOTES EXPLAINING THE ORDER AND HISTORY OF THE OFFICES.

By REV. THOMAS JAMES, M.A.,

Honorary Canon of Peterborough, Rural Dean and Vicar of Sibbertoft and Theddingworth.

A New Edition. One Volume. Medium 8vo.

Student's Manual of Ancient Geography.

By REV. W. L. BEVAN, M.A.,
Vicar of Hay, Brecknockshire.

EDITED BY WM. SMITH, LL.D.

A New and Cheaper Edition. With 250 Woodcuts. Post 8vo. 7s. 6d.

A new and cheaper edition of this work, which has been introduced into Eton and other public schools, will be published in November, uniform with the "Student's Hume," "Liddell's Rome," and other works of the same series.

ALBEMARLE STREET,
October, 1863.

MR. MURRAY'S
LIST OF NEW WORKS.

THE NATURALIST ON THE RIVER AMAZONS,
WITH ADVENTURES AND STUDIES OF NATURAL HISTORY DURING ELEVEN YEARS OF TRAVEL.

BY H. W. BATES.

With Map and 40 Illustrations. 2 Vols. Post 8vo. 28s.

"We have never seen a more graceful record of strange, out of the world experiences, or a more luminous art in the exposition of scientific details. We assume that the book will be most prized by the present school of naturalists for its generalisations on species, sex, climatal influences, &c., and we have heard especial stress laid on its illustrations of the general adaptation of so many animal and vegetable forms to the conditions of a purely arboreal life; but we rest content with the power of description of detached phenomena to assign the book a high *status* in a purely literary sense as well. It imparts the fascination which the great river and great forest exercised on the writer himself, and makes the reader his absorbed companion to the end.

"The merit of the illustrations throughout the book is one of its greatest charms, due principally to that gifted pencil which is confessedly such a great advantage enjoyed by the naturalists of our own day, as compared with the illustrations provided for their predecessors. But the skill with which the narrative itself is framed, if it does not render it independent of such assistance, itself leaves the effect of a series of pictures on the reader's memory."—*Times,* Sept. 24, 1863.

ADDRESSES DELIVERED TO HIS CLERGY,
AT HIS VISITATION, 1863; TO WHICH IS ADDED, A SERMON PREACHED ON WHIT-SUNDAY.

BY HENRY LORD BISHOP OF EXETER.

8vo. 1s.

LIFE OF GENERAL SIR HOWARD DOUGLAS,
BART., G.C.B., &c.

FROM HIS NOTES, CONVERSATIONS, AND CORRESPONDENCE.

BY S. W. FULLOM.

With Portrait. 8vo. 15s.

THE HISTORY OF THE JEWS,

FROM THE EARLIEST PERIOD, CONTINUED TO MODERN TIMES.

BY HENRY HART MILMAN, D.D.,
Dean of St. Paul's.

Third Edition, revised, and enlarged. With a New Preface.

3 Vols. 8vo. 36s.

LISPINGS FROM LOW LATITUDES;

AN ILLUSTRATED JOURNAL OF A TOUR IN EGYPT.

By THE HON. IMPULSIA GUSHINGTON.

EDITED BY LORD DUFFERIN.

With 24 Large Plates. 4to. 21s.

THE WARS OF THE 18TH & 19TH CENTURIES,
1700—1815.

INCLUDING THE BATTLE OF WATERLOO.

BY LIEUT.-GEN. THE HON. SIR EDWARD CUST, D.C.L.

Maps. 9 Vols. Fcap. 8vo. 5s. each.

"The great merit of General Cust's 'Annals' are the accuracy and impartiality with which they are written. The spirit of the partisan is entirely absent from his pages, he renders to all the merit which he believes to be their due, neither forbearing to praise his foe, nor shrinking if the need exist from visiting censure on his friend. Unlike M. Thiers, who in his military histories has only one object in view, to exalt his nation at the expense of all others, Sir Edward Cust never loses an opportunity of commending a masterly movement, a gallant action, or a deed of personal daring, though the subject of his commendation be the enemy; while on the other hand he freely expresses his opinion where he perceives an error committed by even the greatest of his countrymen."—*Examiner*.

JAPAN AND CHINA.

A NARRATIVE OF JOURNEYS TO YEDO AND PEKIN;

WITH NOTICES OF THE NATURAL PRODUCTIONS, AGRICULTURE, HORTICULTURE, TRADE, AND OTHER THINGS MET WITH BY THE WAY.

BY ROBERT FORTUNE

Author of "Three Visits to China.

With Map and Illustrations. 8vo. 16s.

MISCELLANIES.

COLLECTED AND EDITED BY EARL STANHOPE.

Second Edition. With some Supplementary Letters. Post 8vo. 5s. 6d.

₊ The Supplementary Letters may be obtained separately.

HISTORY OF THE RACES OF THE OLD WORLD.

DESIGNED AS A MANUAL OF ETHNOLOGY.

BY CHARLES L. BRACE.

Post 8vo. 9s.

REMAINS OF ARTHUR HENRY HALLAM.

WITH PREFACE AND MEMOIR.

Third Edition. With Portrait. Fcap. 8vo. 7s. 6d.

AIDS TO FAITH.

A SERIES OF THEOLOGICAL ESSAYS BY THE FOLLOWING WRITERS:

Rev. Canon Harold Browne.	Rev. Dr. McCaul.
Rev. F. C. Cook, M.A.	Rev. Professor Mansel.
Bishop of Gloucester and Bristol.	Rev. Professor Rawlinson.
Bishop of Killaloe.	The Archbishop of York.

EDITED BY THE ARCHBISHOP OF YORK.

8vo. 9s.

THE BAMPTON LECTURES FOR 1862.

A CRITICAL HISTORY OF FREE THOUGHT IN REFERENCE TO THE CHRISTIAN RELIGION.

BY REV. ADAM STOREY FARRAR, M.A.,

Michel Fellow of Queen's Coll., Oxford.

8vo. 16s.

PALERMO AND NAPLES IN 1859—61.

WITH NOTICES OF VICTOR EMMANUEL, FRANCIS II., AND GARIBALDI.

BY ADMIRAL SIR RODNEY MUNDY, R.N., K.C.B.

With Frontispiece. Post 8vo. 12s.

LIFE OF GEN. SIR ROBERT WILSON.

FROM AUTOBIOGRAPHICAL MEMOIRS, JOURNALS, NARRATIVES, CORRESPONDENCE, &c.

Containing an Account of his Birth, Parentage, Early Life, Entrance into Army, Various Campaigns, Diplomatic Services, &c., down to the Peace of Tilsit.

Edited by his Nephew and Son-in-Law,

REV. HERBERT RANDOLPH, M.A.

Portrait. 2 Vols. 8vo. 26s.

RECOLLECTIONS OF TARTAR STEPPES AND THEIR INHABITANTS.

CHIEFLY EXTRACTED FROM LETTERS ADDRESSED TO FRIENDS.

BY MRS. ATKINSON.

With Illustrations. Post 8vo. 12s.

THE GREAT RIVER OF CHINA:

A NARRATIVE OF AN EXPEDITION SENT TO EXPLORE THE UPPER WATERS OF THE YANG-TSZE.

BY CAPTAIN T. W. BLAKISTON, R.A.

With Maps and Illustrations. 8vo. 18s.

THE MESSIAH.

A NARRATIVE OF THE LIFE, TRAVELS, DEATH, RESURRECTION, AND ASCENSION OF OUR LORD.

BY A LAYMAN,
Author of the "Life of Bishop Ken."

With Map. 8vo. 18s.

BRITISH COLUMBIA AND VANCOUVER'S ISLAND.

THEIR FORESTS, RIVERS, COASTS, GOLD FIELDS, AND RESOURCES FOR COLONISATION.

FROM PERSONAL OBSERVATION DURING A FOUR YEARS' RESIDENCE.

BY COMMANDER MAYNE, R.N.

With Map and Illustrations. 8vo. 16s.

THE GRAND REMONSTRANCE, 1641;

WITH AN ESSAY ON ENGLISH FREEDOM UNDER PLANTAGENET AND TUDOR SOVEREIGNS.

BY JOHN FORSTER,

Author of "Arrest of the Five Members by Charles I."; "Biographical Essays," &c.

Second Edition, revised. Post 8vo. 12s.

TRAVELS IN PERU AND INDIA.

FOR THE PURPOSE OF COLLECTING CINCHONA PLANTS AND INTRODUCING THE CULTURE OF BARK INTO INDIA.

BY CLEMENTS R. MARKHAM.

With Map and Illustrations. 8vo. 16s.

LIVES OF THE STEPHENSONS.

FORMING A THIRD VOLUME OF "LIVES OF BRITISH ENGINEERS."

BY SAMUEL SMILES.

With Portraits and Illustrations. 8vo. 21s.

VISITS TO THE RUINED CITIES OF ANCIENT NUMIDIA AND CARTHAGINIA.

WITH NOTICES OF ARAB LIFE.

BY NATHAN DAVIS, F.R.G.S.

With Map and Illustrations. 8vo. 14s.

POETICAL WORKS OF GONGORA.

TRANSLATED, WITH AN HISTORICAL AND CRITICAL ESSAY ON THE TIMES OF PHILIP III. AND IV. OF SPAIN.

BY ARCHDEACON CHURTON.

With Portrait. 2 Vols. Small 8vo. 15s.

THE STORY OF LORD BACON'S LIFE.

BY W. HEPWORTH DIXON.

With Portrait and Vignette. Post 18vo. 7s. 6d.

LECTURES ON THE JEWISH CHURCH.
FIRST PART—ABRAHAM TO SAMUEL.

BY REV. A. P. STANLEY, D.D.,
Regius Professor of Ecclesiastical History, and Canon of Christchurch, Oxford.

Second Edition. With Plans. 8vo. 16s.

THE TAEPING REBELLION;
ITS RISE AND PROGRESS, FROM DOCUMENTS AND INFORMATION COLLECTED IN CHINA.

BY COMMANDER LINDESAY BRINE, R.N.

With Plans. Post 8vo. 10s. 6d.

SECULARIA;
OR, SURVEYS ON THE MAIN STREAM OF HISTORY.

CONTAINING

1. Ancient and Modern Revolutions.
2. Revivalists.
3. The Mediæval Castle.
4. The Mediæval Borough.
5. The Coming of the Armada.
6. Alternative of 1640-41—Old or New England?
7. The New England Theocracy.
8. Preparatives of the American Revolt.
9. The Revolution of 1688 and its Historian. [Worship.
10. The Hohenzollern Stage of Hero-
11. Absolutism in Extremis.
12. Revolutions in Progress and Prospect.

BY SAMUEL LUCAS, M.A.

8vo. 12s.

MEMOIR OF BISHOP BLOMFIELD, D.D.,
WITH SELECTIONS FROM HIS CORRESPONDENCE.

BY REV. ALFRED BLOMFIELD, M.A.,
Incumbent of St. Philip's, Stepney.

With Portrait. 2 Vols. Post 8vo. 18s.

WILD WALES.
ITS PEOPLE,—LANGUAGE,—AND SCENERY.

BY GEORGE BORROW,
Author of "The Bible in Spain," "The Gipsies in Spain," &c.

3 Vols. Post 8vo. 30s.

THE ANTIQUITY OF MAN, FROM GEOLOGICAL EVIDENCES;

WITH REMARKS ON THEORIES OF THE ORIGIN OF SPECIES BY VARIATION.

BY SIR CHARLES LYELL, F.R.S.,

Author of "Principles of Geology," "Elements of Geology," &c., &c.

Second Edition. With Illustrations. 8vo. 14s.

TRANSACTIONS OF THE ETHNOLOGICAL SOCIETY OF LONDON.

NEW SERIES. Vol. II.

CONTENTS:

CONNEXION BETWEEN ETHNOLOGY AND PHYSICAL GEOGRAPHY. By JOHN CRAWFURD.
WILD TRIBES OF THE NORTH-WEST COAST OF BORNEO. By the BISHOP OF LABUAN.
OSTEOLOGY AND DENTITION OF THE ABORIGINES OF THE ANDAMAN ISLANDS. By PROF. OWEN.
ETHNO-CLIMATOLOGY. By JAMES HUNT.
NUMERALS AS EVIDENCE OF THE PROGRESS OF CIVILIZATION. By JOHN CRAWFURD.
IDOL HUMAN HEAD OF THE JIVARO INDIANS OF ECUADOR. By WILLIAM BOLLAERT.
SHELL-MOUNDS OF PROVINCE WELLESLEY, IN THE MALAY PENINSULA. By G. W. EARL.
HUMAN CRANIA AND BONES, preserved in a Crypt at Hythe. By ROBERT KNOX, M.D.
ANCIENT INDIAN TOMBS OF CHIRIQUI IN VERAGUAS. By WILLIAM BOLLAERT.
STONE CELTS FROM CHIRIQUI. By C. C. BLAKE.
ANTIQUITY OF MAN FROM THE EVIDENCE OF LANGUAGE. By JOHN CRAWFURD.
COMMIXTURE OF THE RACES OF MAN AS AFFECTING THE PROGRESS OF CIVILIZATION. By JOHN CRAWFURD.
DIFFERENCES IN WEIGHT AND STATURE OF EUROPEANS AND SOME NATIVES OF INDIA. By JOHN SHORTT.
BUDDHISM. By G. M. TAGORE.
CRANIAL CHARACTERS OF THE PERUVIAN RACES OF MEN. By C. C. BLAKE.
WILD TRIBES OF THE NORTH-WEST COAST OF BORNEO. By SPENCER ST. JOHN.
THE TRIBES OF NORTHERN KURDISTAN. By WILLIAM SPOTTISWOODE.
ON COLOUR AS A TEST OF THE RACES OF MAN. By JOHN CRAWFURD.
ETHNOLOGY OF EGYPT. By R. S. POOLE.
HUMAN REMAINS FOUND IN THE SHELL-MOUNDS. By PROFESSOR HUXLEY.
HUMAN REMAINS FROM MUSKHAM, IN THE VALLEY OF THE TRENT, &c. By S. J. MACKIE.
WILD TRIBES OF THE VEDDAHS OF CEYLON. By JOHN BAILEY.
SIERRA LEONE AND ITS INHABITANTS. By ROBERT CLARKE.
HUMAN REMAINS FOUND AT WROXETER. By THOMAS WRIGHT.
FORMATION AND INSTITUTION OF THE CASTE SYSTEM — THE ARYAN POLITY. By G. M. TAGORE.
RELATION OF DOMESTICATED ANIMALS TO CIVILIZATION. By JOHN CRAWFURD.

8vo. 12s.

PERSONALITIES OF THE FOREST OF DEAN;

BEING A RELATION OF ITS SUCCESSIVE OFFICIALS, GENTRY, AND COMMONALTY,

Drawn from numerous sources, but chiefly from unpublished data and local information.

BY REV. H. G. NICHOLLS, M.A.,

Perpetual Curate of Holy Trinity, Dean Forest, &c.

Post 8vo. 3s. 6d.

Uniform with Nicholls's "Historical Account of the Forest of Dean."

LECTURES ON JURISPRUDENCE.

A CONTINUATION OF THE "PROVINCE OF JURISPRUDENCE DETERMINED."

BY THE LATE JOHN AUSTIN.

Now first published. 2 Vols. 8vo. 24s.

JURISPRUDENCE.

BY CHARLES SPENCER MARCH PHILLIPPS.

8vo. 12s.

THE KNAPSACK BYRON.

A Complete Edition of the Poetical Works of Lord Byron, printed for the convenience of travellers in a small but clear type.

Portrait and Index. Post 8vo. 6s.

DR. WM. SMITH'S IMPROVED GRAMMARS.

1. **THE STUDENT'S GREEK GRAMMAR.**

   FOR THE USE OF COLLEGES AND THE UPPER FORMS IN SCHOOLS.

   BY PROFESSOR CURTIUS.

   Post 8vo. 7s. 6d.

2. **THE STUDENT'S LATIN GRAMMAR.**

   FOR THE USE OF COLLEGES AND THE UPPER FORMS IN SCHOOLS.

   BY WILLIAM SMITH, LL.D.

   Post 8vo. 7s. 6d.

3. **CURTIUS'S SMALLER GREEK GRAMMAR.**

   ABRIDGED FROM THE LARGER WORK,

   FOR THE USE OF THE MIDDLE AND LOWER FORMS.

   12mo. 3s. 6d.

4. **DR. WM. SMITH'S SMALLER LATIN GRAMMAR.**

   ABRIDGED FROM THE LARGER WORK,

   FOR THE USE OF THE MIDDLE AND LOWER FORMS.

   12mo. 3s. 6d.

H.R.H. THE PRINCE CONSORT'S PRINCIPAL SPEECHES AND ADDRESSES.

WITH AN INTRODUCTION, GIVING SOME OUTLINES OF HIS CHARACTER.

With Portrait. 8vo. 10s. 6d.

SERMONS IN THE EAST,

PREACHED BEFORE H.R.H. THE PRINCE OF WALES DURING HIS TOUR.

WITH NOTICES OF SOME OF THE LOCALITIES VISITED.

BY REV. A. P. STANLEY, D.D.,
Deputy-Clerk of the Closet and Honorary Chaplain to the Prince of Wales.

Third Edition. 8vo. 9s.

DISCOURSES ON THE WORD OF GOD AND THE GROUND OF FAITH.

BY ARCHIBALD CAMPBELL TAIT, D.D.,
Lord Bishop of London.

8vo. 2s. 6d.

LIFE OF THE RIGHT HON. WILLIAM PITT.

WITH EXTRACTS FROM HIS MS. PAPERS.

BY EARL STANHOPE,
Author of the "History of England from the Peace of Utrecht."

Second Edition, revised. With Portraits. 4 Vols. Post 8vo. 42s.

HISTORY OF THE MODERN STYLES OF ARCHITECTURE.

BY JAMES FERGUSSON, F.R.S., F.R.A.S.

With 312 Illustrations. 8vo. 31s. 6d.

Uniform with Fergusson's "Handbook of Architecture."

www.ingramcontent.com/pod-product-compliance
Lightning Source LLC
Chambersburg PA
CBHW030426300426
44112CB00009B/865